DISTRACTED SUBJECTS

DISTRACTED SUBJECTS

*Madness and Gender
in Shakespeare and
Early Modern Culture*

C AROL T HOMAS N EELY

C ORNELL U NIVERSITY P RESS
Ithaca and London

First published 2004 by Cornell University Press
First printing, Cornell Paperbacks, 2004

Design by Scott Levine

Printed in the United States of America

Library of Congress Cataloging-in-Publication Data

Neely, Carol Thomas, 1939–
    Distracted subjects : madness and gender in Shakespeare and early modern culture / Carol Thomas Neely.
        p. cm.
Includes bibliographical references and index.
    ISBN 0-8014-4205-2 (cloth : acid-free paper) — ISBN 0-8014-8924-5 (pbk. : acid-free paper)
    1. Shakespeare, William, 1564–1616—Characters—Mentally ill. 2. Shakespeare, William, 1564–1616—Knowledge—Psychology. 3. Mental illness—England—History—16th century. 4. Mental illness—England—History—17th century. 5. Literature and mental illness—England. 6. Psychoanalysis and literature—England. 7. Mental illness in literature. 8. Mentally ill in literature. 9. Sex role in literature. I. Title.
    PR2992.M3N44   2004
    822.3'3—dc22
                                                    2003024991

Cornell University Press strives to use environmentally responsible suppliers and materials to the fullest extent possible in the publishing of its books. Such materials include vegetable-based, low-VOC inks and acid-free papers that are recycled, totally chlorine-free, or partly composed of nonwood fibers. For further information, visit our website at www.cornellpress.cornell.edu.

Cloth printing   10 9 8 7 6 5 4 3 2 1
Paperback printing   10 9 8 7 6 5 4 3 2 1

To my students

CONTENTS

Illustrations

ACKNOWLEDGMENTS

More people than I can possibly acknowledge here have contributed to this book during its long gestation: students and colleagues at Illinois State University, the University of Illinois at Urbana-Champaign, and the University of Michigan's Institute for the Humanities; organizers of and participants in Shakespeare Association of America seminars; colleagues and friends everywhere. Its errors are due entirely to my own distraction.

I am grateful for many kinds of support to Illinois State University, which first allowed me to air the project at its Annual Humanities Lecture and whose Outstanding University Researcher Award funded books; to the Humanities Institute at the University of Michigan and its wonderful director, James Winn, its incomparable staff, Mary Price, Eliza Woodford, and Linnea Pearlman, and the other fellows and faculty there for energizing dialogue; and to the University of Illinois for the Sabbatical, Research Board, and Center for Advanced Study leaves that steadily advanced the project. My participation in several interdisciplinary venues enriched the book immeasurably, and I thank all those involved in the New Languages for the Stage conference at the University of Kansas (1988); the Renaissance Society of America's conference plenary session on Renaissance psychology (1990); the University of Miami's Interdisciplinary Symposium on Madness (1992); the British Society for the History of Medicine Annual Meeting (1994); and the workshops at meetings of the Society for the Study of Early Modern Women that I co-organized: "Women and Madness" with Michael MacDonald and Jane Kromm in 1990, and "Lovesick/Ragesick" with Judith Kegan Gardiner and Linda Pollock in 1994. Audience responses at Dartmouth College, the University of Wisconsin-Milwaukee, Illinois State University, the University of Pittsburgh, Colorado State University, the University of Illinois at Urbana-Champaign, Duke University, the Folger Shakespeare Library, and the Clemson and Oregon Shakespeare Festivals always posed salient questions that spurred the book's development.

Many students and colleagues have likewise contributed to this book. Graduate research assistants Alan Walworth, Amy Smith, and Chuck Conaway found materials I didn't even know I needed. I learned from students whose scholarship overlapped with mine—William Gulstead, Alan Walworth, and Yvette Koepke-Nelson—and Ann Christiansen and Barb Sebek cheered me on. Elin Diamond, Gayle Greene, Coppelia Kahn, Marianne Novy, and Mimi Sprengnether continue to provide feminist inspiration and sustaining friendship, and Linda Gregerson, Stephen Mullaney, and Carol Dickerman made my Michigan semester a perfect blend of work and play. Many thanks to the gang at Ashland—Alan Armstrong, Carol McNair, Bob DeVoe, Emily Hexter, and Vince Wixon—who rejuvenate me each summer. I am grateful to Natalie Zemon Davis, who, with her customary generosity and acuteness, made suggestions that helped me redefine the project.

My wonderful Illinois colleagues have debated ideas, suggested readings, and commented astutely on my work, making this a much better book; warm thanks to Amanda Anderson, Clare Crowston, Jan Hinely, David Kay, Joan Klein, Ania Loomba, Sonya Michel, Dana Rabin, Michael Shapiro, Paula Treichler, Joe Valente, and Dick Wheeler. Cary Nelson provided much-needed advice and assistance with the illustrations, as did Zachary Lesser with the cover design, and the Research Board helped fund them. Chapter 1 benefited from the expert comments of Suzanne Gossett, as chapter 4 did from those of Valerie Traub. I am indebted to Jonathan Andrews and Patricia Allderidge, historians who generously shared with me their knowledge of Bedlam and aided my own neophyte attempts at archival research. Most of all I am grateful to Michael MacDonald: for his book, which catalyzed mine; for his loan of transcripts of Richard Napier's notes; and for his knowledge, collaboration, and support.

At a late stage, Lori Newcomb and Meredith Skura provided brilliant, incisive readings of the whole manuscript, helping me to see its shape and its value. Two Cornell University Press readers, Mary Beth Rose and Gail Kern Paster, were the best I could have hoped for; stringent and generous in equal measure. I am especially grateful to Gail for two rapid and discerning readings when there were many other demands on her time. Marsha Clinard, friend and editor par excellence, meticulously uncovered errors in successive drafts; her own skill as a stylist and expertise as a psychiatric social worker made her an ideal reader. Carol Severins and Sharon Decker kept me and the graduate office functioning, leaving time for the book. Bernie Kendler at Cornell is an editor to die for; his persistent support for the project was equaled only by his urgent demands that it be improved. Thanks are due to Karen Hwa, Kay Scheuer, and Scott Levine, who expertly saw the manuscript through the press, to Kay Banning for her index, and to Charlie Boast and Sara Luttfring for reading page proofs.

I am forever grateful to my family for keeping me sane. My sister, Lynn, and my niece, Christine, and nephew, Tom, kept insisting that I could do it (as my parents did early in the project). My children, Sophia, Mark, and Juliet, and my grandchildren, Craig and Ella, are still teaching me how to "chill"—along with much else. Finally my thanks to the many students I have taught—and who have taught me. I dedicate this book to them.

I am grateful for permission to reprint previously published work. An early version of chapter 2 appeared as "'Documents in Madness': Reading Madness and Gender in Shakespeare's Tragedies and Early Modern Culture" in *Shakespeare Quarterly* 42, no. 3 (1991): 315–338. It is copyrighted by the Folger Shakespeare Library and is reprinted with permission of The Johns Hopkins University Press. A short version of chapter 4 appeared as "Lovesickness, Gender, and Subjectivity: *Twelfth Night* and *As You Like It*" in *A Feminist Companion to Shakespeare,* edited by Dympna Callaghan and published in 2000 by Blackwell Publishing, which has given its permission to reprint.

BIBLIOGRAPHICAL NOTE

All Shakespeare plays are cited from Sylvan Barnet, ed., *The Complete Signet Classic Shakespeare* (New York: Harcourt Brace Jovanovich, 1972) with the exception of *The Comedy of Errors*, which is cited from the Arden edition, ed. R. A. Foakes (London: Methuen, 1962).

Mr. S., *Gammer Gurton's Needle*, is cited from Charles W. Whitworth, ed., *Three Sixteenth-Century Comedies*, New Mermaids series (New York: Norton, 1984).

Thomas Kyd, *The Spanish Tragedy*, is cited from J. R. Mulryne, ed., 2d ed., New Mermaids series (New York: Norton, 1989).

Thomas Middleton and William Rowley, *The Changeling*, is cited from Joost Daalder, ed., 2d ed., New Mermaids series (New York: Norton, 1990).

All other Renaissance dramas are cited from the editions listed in the Works Cited.

I regularly cite the multivolume edition of Robert Burton's *The Anatomy of Melancholy*, edited by Thomas C. Faulkner, Nicolas K. Kiessling, and Rhonda L. Blair, 3 vols. (Oxford: Clarendon, 1989–94). When quoting, I first indicate the partition, section, membrane, and subsection numbers, followed by the volume and page numbers from this edition, to make the material easy to find in other editions of the work.

I quote from Michael MacDonald's transcriptions of Richard Napier's casenotes and cite their location in the manuscripts of Elias Ashmole in the Bodleian Library, Oxford.

I quote from Patricia Allderidge's transcripts of citations to Bethlehem Hospital in the Court of Aldermen Repertories, and from the courtbooks of Bridewell and Bethlehem citing their date and folio number. These are available in the Guildhall Library, London, and at the Bethlehem Library and Museum, Bethlehem Hospital, Kent.

I cite *The History of Bethlem* by Jonathan Andrews, Asa Briggs, Roy Porter, Penny Tucker, and Keir Waddington (London: Routledge, 1997) parenthetically as *HB*.

DISTRACTED SUBJECTS

INTRODUCTION

Divisions in the Discourses of Distraction

Seventeen years ago, during a class discussion of *King Lear,* a student asked me what the Renaissance thought about madness, and I said I would find out. This book is the result. In the long process of reflecting on the question and formulating answers to it, all of my original assumptions about madness and its representations have proved groundless. Madness is not a distinctively female malady in the early modern period. Indeed "madness" is not a unified or especially validated term during the Renaissance; it is only one (not particularly common) word among the many that denote mental distress. Melancholy, which *is* a widely used term, is likewise diffuse. It is not only a fashionable intellectual condition for gentlemen and tragic heroes but also a pathology of the uterus—or a tool for rethinking the human. Renaissance humoral medicine, which theorizes melancholy, is not ridiculous or static, mere matter for arcane footnotes. It is a supple conceptual framework that generates powerful diagnoses and practices—and promotes change. Although a few severely distracted persons did end up in Bedlam, this small hospital for the mad has only the most tenuous links with the Bedlamites that are represented on the Jacobean stage. The hospital does not confine madpersons cruelly or indiscriminately; but stage madhouses make spectacles of them as the hospital is imagined to do. Although Renaissance conceptions, representations, and treatments of madness seem at first impossibly distant and alien, our own debates about the condition often recapitulate or grow out of those earlier ones. I no longer believe that the Renaissance is obsessed with madness. But our own era may be. Or perhaps it is just me.

For some time I have been asking, only in part facetiously, whether madness had a Renaissance. This book shows how it did. Between 1576, the opening of the first public theater in London, and 1632, the year that Bethlehem Hospital's administrative status was consolidated (after a long struggle for control by the Crown and the City of London), early moderns drew on the traditional humoral discourses of Galen and Aristotle to rethink the parameters of the human by reimagining madness. Although historians have claimed that the theories and practice of madness, like those of humoral medicine, were essentially static until the end of the seventeenth century and although they, with literary historians, have postulated a unified discourse of madness on and off stage, this period manifests heterogeneity, regendering, and widespread change in the discourses of distraction.[1] Distracted subjects became a newly urgent focus of representation, theorization, and treatment across a wide range of cultural documents and practices: doctors' case notes, medical and witchcraft treatises and their case histories, parish and city records of confinement, and, especially, stage representations. As a result of this interest, divisions in the discourses of distraction emerged. Supernatural rituals were adapted for secular and social ends. New languages for the mad were invented on stage. Conditions such as lovesickness took on changed gender associations. New subcategories such as women's melancholy were theorized. The practices of confinement were reinvented in the theater. The discourses of madness flourished because they were useful in reconceptual-izing the boundaries between natural and supernatural, masculinity and femininity, body and mind, feigned and actual distraction. Though these changes are heterogeneous, the primary impact of cultural debates that discredited possession, exorcism, and witchcraft was to encourage the secularization and medicalization of distracted subjects, separating them off from the supernatural and theological. But these discourses did not yet dehumanize distracted persons, as the concept of "insanity" later would do. Thus the re-naissance of madness was a process of secularization, recategorization, and, in effect, humanization in early modern England. The gendered boundaries of the secular human subject were being redefined through their dislocations and excesses. The early modern period's new articulation of the human participates in the centuries-long, still unfinished process that Ian Hacking calls "the secularization of the soul" (*Rewriting* 5), and we have inherited this subject and these discourses.

I use the terms "distracted" and "distraction" in my title and text to historicize and animate my topic. The term signifies how early modern subjects felt when mad; it calls up early modern attitudes toward madness as a temporary derailing; and it emphasizes that there are multiple signifiers for conditions of mental disturbance. Today the word "distraction" signifies a mild temporary diversion of consciousness. But in the early modern period, "distract" was a common symptom of and name for extreme cases of mental dis-

---

[1] In *Mental Disorder in Earlier England: Exploratory Studies,* Basil Clarke's overview of madness from Roman Britain to the seventeenth century, the focus on medical theory and reit-erated themes leads to his claim that there was in this period "no integrated development, no boundary to the middle ages," and no new formulations of madness until after the scientific rev-olution (207). Michael MacDonald, in *Mystical Bedlam: Madness, Anxiety, and Healing in Sev-enteenth-Century England,* agrees that "the perception and management of mental disorders did not change fundamentally before 1660" (3). Roy Porter in *Mind-Forg'd Manacles* traces changes in configurations of madness from the Restoration to the Regency but finds the period before that "curiously ill-researched as a whole," excepting Michael MacDonald's book. H. C. Erik Midelfort's *History of Madness in Sixteenth-Century Germany* examines a wide range of specific theories and attitudes toward madness, some of which show change in the period.

order. The widely used term meant "Deranged in mind; crazy, mad, insane" (*OED* 4), as indicated in the dictionary's citations of a 1481 legacy "for seke and distract people" and a 1581 quotation, "To rave and act distract or furious." The term emphasizes that sufferers of mental distress were viewed as divided, diverted, disassembled—as beside themselves—*temporarily.* Like the many other overlapping adjectives that label disordered states— "lovesick," "troubled-in-mind," "idle-headed," "melancholic," "lunatic," "frenzied," "mad"—"distract" (or "distraught" or "distrait") is an adjective denoting not permanent attributes, but temporary behaviors (Porter, *Mind-Forg'd* 22–23). Thomas More exemplifies the period's view when he says of one who recovered from distraction that he "gathered hys remembraunce to hym and beganne to come agayne to hym selfe" (9:118). The distract may be "restored to perfect memory" (Court of Aldermen Rep. 18, fol. 24, 4 June 1573) when their "wits stand in their right place" (Dekker, *Honest Whore Part I* 5.2.430), and they can once more follow their business. The term "distraction" also signals my thesis—that new divisions emerge when mental disorders change their epistemological profile and their cultural place. In this period, the cultural discourses that narrate and stage disorder themselves divide and produce reclassifications, revised diagnoses, changing gender associations, and new remedies. The Renaissance most often used "distraction" as a near synonym for extreme madness. I use it, sporadically, as a general term encompassing all forms of mental distress in order to defamiliarize the condition and to express the inner experiences of sufferers as they perceived themselves and were perceived by others.

The, to us, more familiar terms "madness" and "melancholy" are in the period used diffusely and imprecisely. Both terms exist on a continuum and signify conditions either figurative or literal and ranging from mild to severe. Their unstable meanings (like those of "distraction") signal the "low epistemological profile" (Foucault, "Truth and Power" 29) of psychiatry and the fact that mental disorder is "theoretically indeterminate" (Scull 8). The fluidity of its conceptual categories contributes to the heterogeneousness of madness discourse and to its capacity for rapid change. "Madness," for us, is the more extreme, the more inclusive, the more literary, and less explicitly medical term; hence it is the term I use most often. Although "madness" is in existence as an old English word from 1000 A.D., it is not yet the dominant term for mental disorder in the early modern period. As its *OED* citations and proverbial uses suggest, it is often figurative and can include almost any excessive expression of emotion: anger, especially, but also lust, jealousy, folly, stupidity.[2] "Madness" can also name extreme forms of mental distress.

[2] *OED* definitions (with citations in the sixteenth and seventeenth century) include out of one's mind, foolish, stupid, carried away by enthusiasm or desire, rage, uncontrolled by reason. Proverbs in Tilly's *Dictionary of Proverbs* include: Too much learning makes a man mad. He that will have all dies of madness. Anger is short madness. Melancholy is the pathway to madness. Mirth without measure is madness. Great wits to madness sure are near allied.

In Dr. Richard Napier's medical consultations in Great Linford in Buckinghamshire between 1598 and 1634, as Michael MacDonald's cross tabulations of symptoms reveal, it is an exact synonym for "lunatic," a near synonym for "distract," and associated with the symptoms "light-headed," "frantic," "raging," and "violent" (MacDonald, *Mystical* 121–132 and tables 117, 124).

While "madness" and "distraction" denote excessive and often violent activity and behavior visible to others, "melancholy," in contrast, denotes torpor, passivity, and the inner emotions of fear and sorrow. It can be a less severe condition, and its milder, often female, form is called "mopishness" in Napier's consultations (MacDonald, *Mystical* 150–164 and table 161). As most readers know, the condition is theorized as rooted in the black bile (or melancholy), one of the four humors that together constitute the body. It circulates along with blood, choler (or yellow bile), and phlegm and, when in balance with them, produces health. However, if excessive, black bile creates the affective symptom melancholy, or, in cases of permanent imbalance, a melancholy temperament. And as the proverb "melancholy is the pathway to madness" indicates, and as we will see, the depressive condition can breed more severe disorders. Because the term refers to a material fluid, an emotional state, and a temperament, it acquires a host of meanings beyond its medical ones, ranging from depression to brilliance, and generates productive thinking about the constituents of the human. For Robert Burton, in *The Anatomy of Melancholy* (1621–1638), "melancholy" becomes the umbrella term for all disorders involving the mind. As his frontispiece manifests (fig. 1), the term includes many subdivisions: religious melancholy, lovesickness, mania, and hypocondriacus (or windy melancholy, the standard bile-caused depression). I analyze my sources' now contracting, now expanding, now subdividing uses of these overlapping terms. I deliberately avoid the term "insane," which the *OED* shows did not appear until the eighteenth century. When it does, it signals a newly emergent conception of mental disorder, now characterized as an incurable and dehumanizing pathology that is the opposite of health and marks the end limit of my exploration of madness. In contrast, distraction, madness, melancholy, and lovesickness are excesses of the human, and temporary curable disruptions of health.[3]

New conceptions of madness and of the human were encouraged and welcomed by the particularly fertile "ecological niche" (Hacking, *Mad* 80–87) that England, and especially London, offered from 1576 to 1632, the period of my study, as a result of multiple intersecting institutions and cultural practices. Public theaters opened in London, staged madness regularly until 1623, and not long after were closed down. In England witchcraft accusa-

---

[3] *OED*. "Insane, from the Latin root in-sanus not sound, not healthy, not curable." There are a few scattered early *OED* citations to forms of insane (insanable, insanation, and insane itself—this last with only one citation before 1721), but it is not in widespread use until the eighteenth century—where it most often appears in legal and medical contexts.

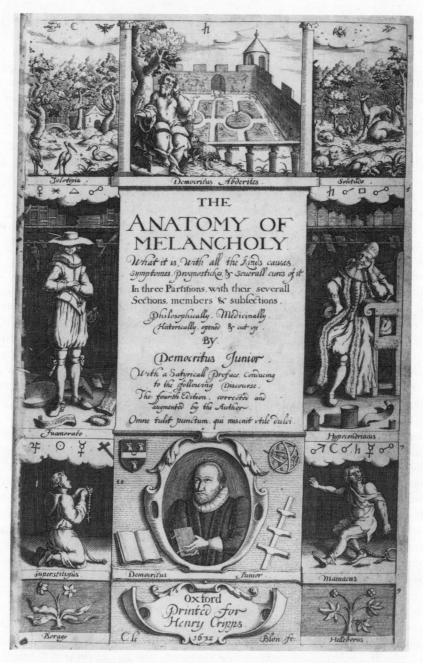

FIG. 1. Title page, Robert Burton, *The Anatomy of Melancholy*, 1632. Courtesy of the University of Illinois at Urbana-Champaign Library.

tions, trials, and prosecutions increased, peaked (in the 1580s and 1590s), and later declined as did possessions and exorcisms and the infamous career of exorcist John Darrell, which flourished from 1586 to 1598. In these years, licensed physicians grew more numerous and medical texts increasingly circulated in the vernacular (Slack). Dr. Richard Napier, whose case notes record the experience of distracted subjects, practiced medicine in Great Linford from 1597 until his death in 1634. Bethlem Hospital, nominally controlled by the City of London after 1574 (*HB* 62), was the object of struggles among City, Crown, and petitioners until its administrative status was regularized in 1632 with the dismissal of its corrupt keeper, Helkiah Crooke. Readings of madness were produced at and circulated through all these local sites, changing as they did so, and gender ideologies helped constitute and were in turn shaped by the new configurations of madness that emerged.

The ecological niche promoted change by cross-fertilization. As, in these years, medicalized diagnoses of madness became more widely available, the just opened popular stage, which thrived commercially on representations of behavioral excess and cultural contention, seized on and disseminated traditional models of supernaturally inflected tragic madness side by side with new ones of medicalized female lovesickness and farcical maddening and confinement. These newly available secular representations of distracted behavior circulating in medical and dramatic discourse proved conceptually and strategically useful across a wide range of cultural spaces. The Anglican church hierarchy used them to reinterpret possession as illness so as to discredit the charismatic exorcisms performed by its Catholic and Puritan rivals. Local and state authorities used, for example, medical diagnoses of Mary Glover's fits to discredit witchcraft accusations, which subsequently declined. Prescriptive writers as well as playwrights took up novel female maladies to defend or attack new conceptions of sexual desire and debate its place in companionate marriage. Hospitals, prisons, and workhouses, the emergent institutions of newly consolidating nation states, drew on diagnoses of madness as they sought prestige and funds to exercise their increased capacity to succor and to confine subjects. Each cultural location planted new strains of madness, and they spread. The stage, medical discourse, local authorities, and institutions all contributed to the gradual replacement of supernatural explanations of distracted subjects with medical ones. Since most of those accused of witchcraft or found bewitched or possessed were women (as were the majority of those visiting doctors), women's afflictions, whether or not they were in reality more common or more intense, were disproportionately the object of cultural diagnosis and reinterpretation. As a result, some medicalized mental disorders began to be recategorized to include women and others were newly associated with women—a process I term the regendering of madness. This gradual regendering was both a cause and an effect of madness's democratization in the period. By the end of the seventeenth century, as a result of these changes, there were the first (partial and gradual) hints of the dehumanization of the mad. This potential for their seg-regation and silencing famously theorized by Foucault is first anticipated in England not in historical institutions, but in stage representations of Bed-lamites at the beginning of the seventeenth century.

Across these many locations where conceptions of madness show contra-diction and change, this book analyzes a process similar to what Stephen Greenblatt in *Shakespearean Negotiations* calls the "circulation of social en-ergy." Although Greenblatt most often postulates an essentially one-way process—whereby drama "appropriates," "purchases," or "symbolically acquires" and encodes material from culture (6–13)—I explore fluid and re-ciprocal exchanges among multiple cultural locations, each influenced and altered by gender as a category of analysis. Medical and political texts are not subordinated as background for dramatic texts. But neither are dramatic texts disempowered as passive recipients of externally derived ideological and cultural formations. Dramatic texts are players in culture, history, and ideology. They participate with many other documents in circulating inno-vative representations and precipitating change: new categories of disease and varying attitudes toward the distracted. Drama's history—its develop-ment, rivalries, generic experiments, and innovative representations—is cen-tral to the story I narrate and the changes I trace. Such changes are, of course, heterogeneous, only sporadically visible, uneven and gradual, and not nec-essarily progressive—or regressive. They do not advance in tidy chronolog-ical order, and neither does this book.

I think of this book as formalist as well as historicist—because it exam-ines how the formal properties of all texts contribute to historical change. If one accepts the commonplace formulations of the "textuality of history" and the "historicity of texts" (Montrose, *Purpose* 5), it follows that all texts must be read not just closely, but formally, with attention to their structure, metaphors, and inherited conventions that articulate the debates they en-capsulate, the stories they circulate, the contradictions they wrestle with, and the imperfect resolutions they propose (see essays in Rasmussen). In this book, each text is given weight, resonance, and nuance and their different ideological agendas, rhetorical strategies, and cultural effects are taken into account. Forms, whether aesthetic forms such as theater, genres such as com-edy, or verbal figures such as metaphor exist and change in history and can, like ideology, be residual, dominant, or emergent. Since dramatic texts rep-resent the mad and their therapies more extensively and fully than do other extant texts and since they have the widest audience, they receive the fullest readings. Shakespeare's plays provide the most numerous, extensive, and richest representations of distracted subjects. Therefore his plays are at the center of this work. Although my history is, necessarily, discursive, I try to provide what sense I can of the material culture in which cases of madness unfold: the shape of therapeutic regimens, the ingredients of cordials, the "tumultuous events" of the consulting room (Sawyer 205), the geography of

early modern London, and many visual representations of distracted subjects.

It is important to insist that the precise path by which new ideas circulate
cannot be perfectly mapped; nor is the direction of influence always dis-
cernible. In order to respect such fluid exchanges, I seek for each chapter the
structure that best represents its particular source of innovation and direction of cultural flow. This methodological innovation is true to the heterogeneous interactions of my material.[4] Chapters 1 and 2 analyze how the
innovative representations of madness and the new language invented for it
on the stage introduce distinctions that influence cultural debates about gender, the supernatural, and the subject. Chapters 3 and 4 explore how revisions in the medical tradition generate new disease categories and new
conceptions of erotic desire, which are picked up by drama and circulated.
The final two chapters show that institutions of confinement and the stage,
in their separate struggles for recognition and success, develop divergent uses
of and attitudes toward the confinement of the distracted, one compassionate, the other farcical, one dominant and humanizing, the other emergent
and dehumanizing.

My eclectic, interdisciplinary history of madness learns from but also
challenges some claims made by scholars of early modern madness in many
disciplines and of several theoretical persuasions.[5] Unlike social historians
of madness and of Bethlem (Basil Clarke, Michael MacDonald, and
Jonathan Andrews) who assume that medical theory and practice remain static from the late Middle Ages to the Restoration, I trace gradual shifts in the
history of medicine between 1576 and 1632. Unlike literary and art historians of melancholy and madness (coauthors Raymond Klibanski, Erwin
Panofsky and Fritz Saxl; Robert Reed; Lawrence Babb; and, more recently,
Duncan Salkeld), who construct a unified picture of these conditions that is
derived from culture or ideology and reflected in art, I postulate disunified
discourses of distraction and heterogeneous interactions between dramatic
texts and other texts. Unlike psychoanalytic critics (Juliana Schiesari and
Lynn Enterline), who analyze the function of sexual difference in psychological constructions of melancholia and mourning, I locate psychic formations and sexual difference solidly within the context of historical, social, and
material practices. Unlike feminist critics (Elaine Showalter, Gail Kern Paster,
and Laurinda Dixon), who analyze (almost) exclusively women's madness

---

[4] Other books that treat madness in dramatic and social contexts such as Reed's *Bedlam on
the Jacobean Stage* and Salkeld's *Madness and Drama in the Age of Shakespeare* posit uniform
and unidirectional influence from the cultural into the dramatic texts. Similarly, but with more
nuance, John Twyning, in *London Dispossessed,* suggests that "as the leitmotiv of *The Honest
Whore, part I,* madness symbolized the stress of metropolitan life" (11).

[5] See my review article "Did Madness Have a Renaissance?" and my review of Winfried
Schleiner's *Melancholy, Genius, and Utopia in the Renaissance* for additional discussion of
works on madness.

or female bodies, I treat gender as a constituent category of analysis that shapes the complementary construction of male and female disorders.

Michel Foucault's *Madness and Civilization* (1976) is the first, and remains the most powerfully influential, skeptical history of madness. His theoretical argument continues to generate debate and new work, and its traces permeate every corner of madness studies.[6] In place of his bold sketch of Renaissance and Enlightenment madness, I offer a detailed series of genre paintings of distraction in England between 1576 and 1632. My discussion challenges his conventional periodization, his claims for epistemic rather than gradual historical change, his de facto segregation of literary from medical texts, and his elision of gender difference. In Foucault's history of madness, the Renaissance is briefly evoked as backdrop, as a flourishing of heroically expressive madness that makes possible the claim of a mid-seventeenth-century epistemic break when madness is decisively separated from reason and truth and silenced, and the mad are confined and dehumanized. The Renaissance he conjures up is unitary—without change, without cultural exchange, and without gender difference. In the first paragraph of the English translation of *Madness and Civilization,* Foucault powerfully imagines the empty leper houses that symbolize the exclusion he claims will subsequently be the lot of the mad: "From the fourteenth century to the seventeenth century they would wait, soliciting with strange incantations a new incarnation of the disease, another grimace of terror, renewed rites of purification and exclusion" (3). Like those houses, Foucault's Renaissance is "outside of time" (31), expectantly stranded between the "end of the Middle Ages" (3) and the beginning of "the Great Confinement" which is his primary focus. It reiterates the tragic, religious, unsilenced madness of the Middle Ages. This static moment is represented by a collage of fragments from a handful of masterpieces: Brandt's and Bosch's *Ships of Fools,* Erasmus's *Praise of Folly,* Brueghel's *Dulle Griet,* Cervantes' *Don Quixote,* Shakespeare's tragedies. (In contrast, the period after the Great Confinement is represented almost entirely by medical and institutional texts.) His selection and deployment of disparate sources allows Foucault to postulate his epistemic break in the history of madness.[7] It is Foucault's powerful notion of a static unified medieval/renaissance madness, rooted in elite art, followed

[6] One obvious indication of continuing influence is the volume *Rewriting the History of Madness: Studies in Foucault's "Histoire de la folie,"* edited by Arthur Still and Irving Velody, and its annotated bibliography of material on *Madness and Civilization.*

[7] In the parts of the original *Folie et deraison: Histoire de la folie à l'âge classique* (1961) omitted from the English translation, venereal disease (associated with moral judgment but soon medicalized and treated) provides a kind of transition from leprosy to madness (17–18), and the blurred images representing the Renaissance take clearer shape as an opposition between "une experience cosmique" and "une experience critique de la folie" (37) modulating into the suppression of tragic madness and a newly reciprocal relation ("ce movement de reference reciproque") between reason and madness (41). See Colin Gordon, "Histoire de la folie," and H. C. Erik Midelfort, "Madness" (261 n 14), for discussions of the French version. I am indebted to my daughter, Sophia Neely, for her careful translations of Foucault's manic prose.

by a sudden absolute break, not his oft-noted smaller historical errors, that I most wish to dislodge.[8] My book however, concurs with his that, by the eighteenth century, attitudes to the mad were shifting. In chapters 5 and 6, I examine seventeenth-century stage representations that anticipate the later and more dehumanizing confinement practices that Foucault exposes. My examination of madness's secularization, subdivisions, and regendering from 1576 to 1632 maps an alternative—and messier—route to the changes that would gain ground with the Enlightenment.

These and other works on madness with their differing methodologies, objects of study, and agendas have contributed to the multifaceted story I tell. The unanswered questions raised by Foucault's *Madness and Civilization,* considered in tandem with those that emerge in Elaine Showalter's *Female Malady: Women, Madness, and English Culture, 1830–1980* (1987), opened up the conceptual space within which my historically situated study of newly gendered conditions took shape.[9] These works encouraged me to seek the madwomen Foucault overlooks, to analyze change in the period he skips over, and to ask when madness began to be a gender-differentiated, although not a female, malady. Two books by literary critics on early modern madness, Robert Reed's historical *Bedlam on the Jacobean Stage* (1952) and Duncan Salkeld's cultural materialist *Madness and Drama in the Age of Shakespeare* (1993), which see the stage as reproducing institutions or ideology, have led me to seek a model of more flexible interaction. Social histories of early medicine afforded me the fruits of their archival research, laying out a richly particularized landscape of the early modern period to compare with that which Showalter delineates at the turn of the nineteenth century. Michael MacDonald's *Mystical Bedlam: Madness, Anxiety, and Healing in Seventeenth-Century England* (1981), through its wonderful analysis of Richard Napier's diagnostics, its keen attention to gender difference, and its careful situating of Napier's practice within the broader culture, has provided my best evidence for how doctors, sufferers, and their relatives described, felt about, and sought to manage mental disorders. In contrast to

[8] Leper houses were not places of complete exclusion and denigration and were never filled by the mad. There is no historical evidence of the existence of the ships of fools that symbolize for Foucault the liminality and inclusion of the mad. Nor did the indiscriminate confinement of the mad begin in the seventeenth century, as Midelfort shows in "Madness." Midelfort's sharp critique of Foucault's claims about unsilenced madness and of his history of confinement is developed further in "Reading" and in *A History of Madness in Sixteenth-Century Germany.* These criticisms are unfounded, Colin Gordon claims, if the original French version, twice the length of the translation, is consulted. These and other essays in *Rewriting the History of Madness,* edited by Still and Velody, continue the debate over the insights and flaws of Foucault's influential study.

[9] Showalter, like Foucault, has been criticized for failing to historicize carefully enough (especially by neglecting earlier periods), for declining to challenge conventional periodization, for insufficient distinctions between different modalities of representation, and for segregating madwomen from madmen. See Nancy Tomes, "Historical" 154–155; Tomes, "Feminist" 364–366; Mark Micale and Roy Porter, *Discovering* 75–77.

this study of an individual practice, the painstaking archival work of Jonathan Andrews, Patricia Allderidge, and the authors of *The History of Bethlem* (1997) has allowed me to understand the small but important place of Bethlem Hospital and enabled me to discard long-standing assumptions about its protocols and its relation to drama.

If the work of social historians has brought me closest to the voices of the mad and their caretakers, two complementary literary histories have influenced my analysis of how gender divisions help institute changes within the discursive discourse of melancholy. Winfried Schleiner, in *Melancholy, Genius, and Utopia in the Renaissance* (1991), reads treatises on melancholy closely for their contradictions and shifts and uncovers a skeptical European countertradition in the sixteenth and seventeenth centuries that, intersecting with religious, political, and social discourses, discredits and pathologizes accredited male melancholy by associating it with imagination, prophecy, divination, and religious enthusiasm. In contrast, Juliana Schiesari, in *The Gendering of Melancholia: Feminism, Psychoanalysis, and the Symbolics of Loss in Renaissance Literature* (1992), undertakes an ahistorical Lacanian feminist deconstruction of melancholy, moving back from Freud and Kristeva to Tasso, Burton, and Shakespeare to argue that the heroic tradition of male melancholy is always erected over and against representations of discredited female mourning. Although neither book makes dramatic texts primary, taken together they fuel my arguments about the gender implications of historical and theoretical shifts in the discourse of madness. The current work most closely and usefully in dialogue with my own is that of Ken Jackson; his essays examine stage representations of the mad in the context of debates after the Reformation about the form, function, and effects of charity.

The two books that have been my most important theoretical and methodological models address distant historical periods and specific disorders and focus primarily on medical discourse. Both understand mental disorders, as do I, as dynamic and shape-shifting catalysts embedded in historical and cultural change.[10] Mary Frances Wack's *Lovesickness in the Middle Ages: The Viaticum and Its Commentaries* (1990) traces minute shifts in medical treatises on lovesickness in the twelfth and thirteenth centuries to decode the gendered social relations and cultural contexts of the disease "from their inscription in the medical accounts of lovesickness" (149). Her analysis provides an earlier benchmark by which to measure Renaissance regendering of the condition. Ian Hacking's work explores most fully how and why new categories of mental disorder develop at particular historical moments. Hacking's powerful formulation of an "ecological niche within which mental

[10] Mark Micale's *Approaching Hysteria* and his two earlier review essays likewise advocate a method for "theorizing disease historiography" that acknowledges changes in definition and nosology, in theory, practice, and patient suffering, and emphasizes connections between medical diagnosis and wider cultural conditions (108–149), as discussed in chap. 3 below.

illnesses thrive" (1) is central to his *Mad Travelers: Reflections on the Reality of Transient Mental Illnesses* (1998) and implicit in his earlier *Rewriting the Soul: Multiple Personality and the Sciences of Memory* (1995).[11] Like Hacking, I analyze the cultural and historical conditions under which categories of mental illness arise and are consolidated. Like Hacking, I explore "the dynamics of the relation between people who are known about, the knowledge about them, and the knowers" (*Rewriting* 6).

Here at the opening of this book it is useful to provide a broad historical context for early modern distraction by highlighting three foundational moments in the long history of melancholy from Aristotle and Galen through to Freud. First, this section situates the period 1576–1632 within a long historical perspective. Second, this discussion models how medical theory, by drawing on tradition, instigates change and relocates the subject. Third, the major texts treated here introduce ideas that will be important throughout. I analyze closely the continuities, discontinuities, and changes in subject formation visible in: *Problem XXX, 1* (fourth century B.C. and long attributed to Aristotle), Timothy Bright's *Treatise of Melancholie* (1586 and supplemented by moments in Spenser's *Faerie Queene* and Descartes's *Meditations*), and Sigmund Freud's "Mourning and Melancholia" (1917). Through this analysis, I demonstrate how the discourse of melancholy acts like a sourdough starter, a leaven which, by passing on the contradictory residue of older traditions, catalyzes new theories of the subject.[12] As Julia Kristeva comments in her own revision of the discourse in *Black Sun,* "melancholia does assert itself in times of crisis; it is spoken of, establishes its archeology, generates its representations and its knowledge" (8). Because the term "melancholy" designates a material bodily humor, an emotional or psychological affect, and a characteristic individual temperament, it is an especially supple conceptual tool for thinking about the human. In these texts we watch it used to reconfigure the connections and boundaries we need to talk about ourselves at all—the relations, for example, between supernatural and natural, soul, mind, and body, pathological and normal.

Each text can precipitate changed conceptions of the melancholy subject because it straddles two different explanatory systems, one material, one nonmaterial, and seeks to adjudicate their claims. These efforts produce struggle, contradiction, and both a new configuration of the systems and a gradual relocation of the suffering melancholic. Within and across these

---

[11] I was fortunate to attend a lecture by Ian Hacking on the material from *Mad Travelers* at the University of Illinois in March 1997 and especially benefited from the extended exchanges that followed and were subsequently incorporated into the book.

[12] In *Saturn and Melancholy,* Klibansky, Panofsky, and Saxl use a similar metaphor to describe the continuing influence of the discourse: "It is understandable that the special problem of melancholy should have furnished as it were, the leaven for the further development of humoralism" (14).

three texts, material explanations gain ground from nonmaterial ones, the pathological is reconceived as the normal, and women eventually replace men as exemplary subjects. Although Bright's treatise is less influential than the other two, it is (along with parallel moments in Spenser and Descartes) symptomatic of the role played by early modern discourses of distraction in the long-term project of secularizing the soul and relocating the boundaries of the normative subject.[13]

The pseudo-Aristotle *Problem XXX, 1* sets the question, "Why is it that all those who have become eminent in philosophy or politics or poetry or the arts are clearly melancholiacs, and some of them to such an extent as to be affected by diseases caused by the black bile?" (Klibansky, Panofsky, and Saxl 18). It attempts to adjudicate between the Platonic tradition's positive interpretation of the bile-caused "eminence" of poetic ecstasy or heroic frenzy and the Hippocratic medical tradition's negative interpretation of the "disease" caused by excess of "black bile." The *Problem* gradually subordinates the disease interpretation and privileges the cultural temperament through three deft moves that cleverly manipulate the bile's amazing variability of quantity, temperature, and adjustability. Each of the three stages of the argument increasingly accentuates the positive effects of the bile and downplays the negative ones. The first section (18–22) balances the two potentialities: bile is both a disease that causes temporary bodily symptoms (for example tumescence, black skin, firm flesh, sores, or epilepsy) *and* an aspect of one's habitual or "natural" constitution or character. Melancholy, because it varies in amount and mixture from one individual to another and from one moment to the next, causes negative and positive emotional excesses, making one reckless or cowardly, grandiloquent or suicidal, brilliant or stupid. Only "particularly unhealthy humors" (22) are responsible for the most noxious effects, including the despondency and self-destruction central to melancholy and painfully exemplified by suicides like Bellerophon, who Homer tells us wandered "alone" "eating his own heart out" (19).

With a "return to our original subject" (22), the treatise turns its attention to a second aspect of bile's variability: it is sometimes hotter, sometimes colder. When the bile is not too hot or too cold or too much or too little, but just right, the melancholy constitution creates its own "superior" norms and disease symptoms virtually disappear. In the first section, melancholics are poised between illness and heroic achievement (like Bellerophon or Ajax), but in this (especially influential) section, melancholics are made superior poets or prophets *by* their bile-filled constitution: "Maracus, the Syracusan, was actually a better poet when he was out of his mind" (24). They are "elated and brilliant or erotic or easily moved to anger and desire, while

[13] *Problem XXX, 1* generated many centuries of commentary and philosophical development all the way into the seventeenth century (Klibansky, Panofsky, and Saxl 67–123; Schleiner 9–108), and Freud's "Mourning and Melancholia" continues to stimulate commentary and revision almost a century after it appeared.

some become more loquacious. Many too are subject to fits of exaltation and ecstasy because this heat is located near the seat of the intellect; and this is how Sibyls and soothsayers arise and all that are divinely inspired, when they become such not by illness but by natural temperament" (24). In this second move (23–26), melancholy is said to produce character types who are not "abnormal" but rather "outstanding" (26).

The third section explores a third variable of the bile—its alterability in respect to altered contingent "circumstances" (27), for example age, sex, wine. All can deprive one of heat, leading to depression or even suicide. But the variability that makes bile dangerous also makes it wonderfully adaptable: "It is possible for this variable mixture to be well tempered and well adjusted in a certain respect—that is to say to be now in a warmer and then again in a colder condition, or vice versa, just as required, owing to its tendency to extremes" (29). The *Problem* concludes that "therefore all melancholy persons are out of the ordinary, not owing to illness, but from their natural constitution" (29). The original question implied that melancholy is and creates disease and that all superior persons are diseased melancholiacs. But by the discussion's end, all melancholiacs are superior. The human subject is expanded as behaviors once attributed to the supernatural actions of gods and mythological heroes or to "divine inspiration" can now be accounted for within the material body's "natural nexus of cause and effect" (40). Melancholy is now construed not as a specific disease but as a constitution shared by many superior subjects and as a valued cultural asset. From this reinterpretation emerges the long-influential tradition that Winfried Schleiner calls "genial melancholy," familiar from literary scholarship. Since women appear in the *Problem* only once, as sibyls, melancholy, for now, is for men only.

The pathological aspects of melancholy that are subordinated in *Problem XXX, 1* grow once more dominant in the ensuing Christian era when the disease of the black bile continues to be elaborated in eastern and western medicine. Because Christianity devalued individual achievement and associated melancholy with *acedia* (the sin of despair growing from loss of faith), the negative aspects of the disease regained precedence, and melancholy was increasingly devalued as lack of faith in the dominant Christian religious tradition.[14] During the Renaissance and Reformation, melancholy emerged again into cultural debate; humanists such as Melanchthon and Ficino renewed the *Problem*'s claim for its cultural bile-caused superiority, whereas Protestant reformers, following Luther, associated melancholy with susceptibility to the temptations of the devil.[15]

---

[14] Klibansky, Panofsky, and Saxl discuss complex developments in medicine, scholastic philosophy, and literature in the Middle Ages (67–123). Schleiner's book traces the devaluing of melancholy in spiritual and secular traditions throughout Europe in the sixteenth and seventeenth centuries.

[15] On Luther and Melanchthon, see Schleiner 56–98. On neoplatonists like Ficino and Tasso, see Klibansky, Panofsky, and Saxl 254–274, Schiesari 112–141, and Enterline 85–145.

Faced thus with competing material and spiritual explanations for melancholy, Timothy Bright's *Treatise of Melancholie* (1586), unlike the Aristotelian *Problem XXX, 1,* does not choose between them, but seeks to give both Galenic medicine and Protestant theology their due. Because his treatise is designed as a practical aid to help his friend M and others who suffer from melancholy, it strives to distinguish between natural melancholy and spiritual doubt and advocate the appropriate cures for each: "the phisicke cure" for the "strange effects" of melancholy "in our minds and bodies" and "spirituall consolation for such as have thereto adjoyned an afflicted conscience" (title page).[16] But in the course of Bright's struggle to fix a boundary between the incorruptible soul and the medicalized body, material explanations gain ground from theological ones, and the melancholy temperament becomes almost as universal as human fallenness.

There are several reasons for this expansion of the material self. First, the sheer mass and complexity of Bright's discussions of the workings of the black bile and of possible cures for melancholy occupy almost all of the work's forty-one chapters and overwhelm the more contained discussion of spiritual despair and consolation, which is confined mostly to one monstrously long chapter (misnumbered XXX but actually XXXVI). Second, Bright fails in his strenuous efforts to differentiate the spiritual from the physiological—in general and "in the same person" (193)—and to map distinct causes and cures for the two kinds of despair. An afflicted conscience, he claims, generates fear and sorrow *with* cause (i.e., the requisite acknowledgment of sin), whereas the melancholy humor produces the same emotions *without* cause—as delusions (188). In sinfulness, the body and senses are healthy; in melancholy, they are obstructed and disordered (188). The afflicted conscience derives from the mind's apprehension of sin; melancholy derives from the mind's obstruction by humors. The spiritual condition can be cured only by the "anker" of Scripture and by faith in God; the bodily one can be alleviated by bleeding, purging, and pleasant surroundings (200).

But the afflicted body and soul cannot be kept distinct because they are inseparable, united in a "true love knot" (35) or "handfasted" (37) as a husband and wife are through marriage. Hence each influences the other's disease. Because the black bile (as in Aristotle) generates excessive thought, it incites doubt; hence Satan cannily makes use of melancholic fears to tempt men to fall (192). The afflicted conscience is "so beset with infinite feares and

---

[16] The work has ambitious goals, including the nationalistic one of benefiting Englishmen by writing in his "mother tong" (Epistle Dedicatorie); it also furthers Bright's personal and professional agendas. In 1580, a year after he received his M.D. from Cambridge University, he had published *A Treatise wherein is deduced the Sufficiency of English Medicine.* In spite of the degree and publication, because he was not a member of the London College of Physicians, that body reprimanded him for practicing in London and objected to his appointment, in 1584, as attending physician at St. Bartholomew Hospital—which was terminated in 1591 for neglect of duties (Pelling and Webster 180 n 41). He subsequently became an Anglican priest. His treatise provides credentials in both of his professions and also serves to advance "English Medicine."

distrust, that it easilie wasteth the pure spirit, congeleth the lively bloud, and striketh our nature in such sort, that it soone becommeth melancholicke, vile and base, and turneth reason into foolishnesse, and disgraceth the beautie of the countenance, and transformeth the stoutest Nabucadnezar in the world into a brute beast" (195). In turn this spiritually caused bodily corruption exacerbates "the terrour of the afflicted minde" (196). Finally the effects of natural melancholy impede the work of spiritual consolation, which is the only cure for the afflicted conscience. Natural melancholy and spiritual despair render each other incurable.

One effect then of the treatise is to create a material self as full, as dark, and as tragic as the sinful soul constructed through the imagery of Christian theology.[17] Bright's treatise provides a system potentially separable from religion that can explain and cure human misery. While sin is the more universal of the two conditions he analyzes, natural melancholy now describes a potential present in everyone that can account both for individual peculiarity and widespread feelings of inadequacy—apart from morality or theology. The Aristotelian *Problem,* by reshaping the pathological into the superior, shifted the ground of normality. Bright's *Treatise,* within a Christian dispensation, extends the domain of the material and implicitly begins the work of refiguring spiritual fallenness as a ubiquitous curable bodily disease. Because the treatise is addressed to a male friend and because both kinds of melancholy are always attributed to men, the condition continues to be almost exclusively associated with them, as the all-male figures of melancholy we have seen in Burton's frontispiece to the *Anatomy of Melancholy* make visible (fig. 1). However, a women's subset of the disease, which we will watch grow more prominent, is acknowledged in the special phlebotomy instructions given for melancholy that is caused by uterine congestion (171–172).

Two other early modern texts, one literary, one philosophical, both draw on medical concepts and emphasize the centrality of melancholy to subject formation and the heterogeneousness of the discourse as it brings together medicine, literature, and philosophy. The concept makes brief but crucial appearances at well-known moments in Edmund Spenser's *Faerie Queene,* book 2 (first published in 1590), and in the first of René Descartes's *Medi-*

---

[17] Hence the discourse of melancholy proves portable and is picked up by early modern tragedy. The loose "parallels" frequently adduced between Bright's *Treatise* and Shakespeare's *Hamlet* do not necessarily reveal the influence of Bright on Shakespeare but likely manifest shared cultural images for representing human distress and self-division, which easily cross the porous border between the material and spiritual domains. Whereas in Bright it is the body and the senses that are "stained with the obscure and dark spots of melancholy" (196), in *Hamlet,* "dark and grained spots" afflict Gertrude's guilty "soul" (3.4.90–92; 4.5.17–20). The images Bright employs to describe how the afflicted conscience wastes the body (195, quoted above) are used by Hamlet to describe a world turned empty. Harold Jenkins, the Arden editor of *Hamlet,* discusses some of these parallels in his introduction and longer notes (106–108, 468, 470, 484).

tations on First Philosophy (1641), works that appear conveniently at either end of the ecological niche my book explores. Both moments have the effect, already seen in Bright, of extending the boundaries of the secular subject and shrinking (or putting in abeyance) the domain of the spiritual or supernatural. Both locate the potential for melancholy more thoroughly in the head/mind with the effect of exaggerating the mind's separation from the body and its own divisions. In each, excessive melancholy generates delusions about the world and self that both make possible and trouble knowledge.

In *The Faerie Queene,* book 2, at the conclusion of Arthur and Guyon's journey through the ideally regulated body/castle of Alma, Phantastes, the first of the three sages chambered within the crowning tower/head, is characterized as melancholic. Together the three sages allegorize the operations of the intellect: the third remembers the past; the second processes present sense impressions; the first, Phantastes, imagines/foresees the future. Only he generates knowledge; the other two merely receive or remember it. His intellectual power is symbolized and accounted for by his melancholy-marked body and temperament. Phantastes is:

> Of swarth complexion, and of crabbed hew,
> That him full of melancholy did shew;
> Bent hollow beetle browes, sharpe staring eyes,
> That mad or foolish seemed: one by his vew
> Mote deeme him borne with ill disposed skyes,
> When oblique *Saturne* sate in the house of agonyes.
>
> (2.ix.52)

Like the superior melancholics in the Aristotelian tradition, melancholy produces "sharpe foresight," "working wit," and the ability to predict the future (2.ix.49). But the description of the figure and of the products of his imagination betrays growing early modern ambivalence about melancholy's effects, which may be artistic triumphs, lies, or demonic delusions. Phantastes seems "mad or foolish" and his chamber swarms with "idle fantasies": "Infernall Hags, *Centaurs,* Feendes, *Hippodames,* / Apes, Lions, Aegles, Owles, fooles, lovers, children, Dames" (50) and, more troublingly, with "Devices, dreams, opinions unsound, / Shewes, visions, sooth-sayes, and prophesies: / And all that fained is, as leasings, tales, and lies" (51). Since the head/intellect's function is to teach Alma, the soul/mistress, "how to governe well" (2.ix.48), melancholy's delusions have the potential to disrupt or disassemble the temperate interactions of intellect, body, and the soul. But Phantastes' crucial place in the head implies that neither mind nor body can function without the creative power that melancholy gives to the intellect.[18]

---

[18] Harry Berger (85–88), reading Phantastes and Maleger as contrasted threats to Temperance in book 2, argues that Phantastes is a milder, classical version of the mortality and original sin embodied by the nearly indestructible Maleger, the book's central threat. Hence Guyon,

Later, in the seventeenth century, Descartes, in a famous passage at the beginning of his *Meditations,* makes use of an example going back to Galen to initiate his influential new project of universal doubt. Descartes calls up images of deluded melancholics, crazed by bile, to postulate a freelance subject, cut off not just from the divine and the world, but from his/her own body and hence from all certainty. Descartes seeks to convince himself and his readers to doubt that which "plainly cannot be doubted," his sensation of his own body: "such as that I am now here, that I am sitting by the fire, that I am clothed in a winter robe, that I am holding this piece of paper with the hands, and similar things" (*Meditations* 89). So he selects from among the standard examples of deluded melancholics those which contrast with and potentially undermine his certainty. What if he is one of those "insane people, whose brains the stubborn vapor of black bile so weakens that they might constantly assert that they are kings when they are very poor, or that they are clothed in purple when they are nude, or that they have an earthenware head, or that they are—as wholes—pumpkins or made of glass" (89). His robe, his authorship, his hand may be similar delusions.[19] But these images introduce more division and doubt within the subject than Descartes can overcome. He abandons these melancholics and abruptly shifts ground in a new paragraph that opens with an exclamation, "*Praeclare sane*"— which means, "clearly," "sanely," or, in Cottingham's translation, "A brilliant piece of reasoning!" (*Descartes* 77). Descartes turns away from the darkness of bile toward light and reason by substituting for madmen dreamers who believe they are by the fire clothed although they are in bed nude.[20]

---

representing the classical virtue of temperance, is not threatened by Phantastes, but is incapable of recognizing or overcoming Maleger without the help of Arthur. But Spenser perhaps here represents, much as Bright does, two separate but parallel threats to all Christian subjects' health, one bodily, one spiritual.

[19] Renaissance thought often appropriates and revises these exempli to forward different agendas. Bright, for example, uses them to differentiate between melancholy and the afflicted conscience: "In this [conscience] the body standeth oft times in firme state of health, perfect in complexion, and perfect in shape, & al symmetrie of his partes, the humors in quantitie and quality not exceeding nor wanting their naturall proportion. In the other [natural melancholy], the complexion is depraved, obstructions hinder the free course of spirits & humors, the blood is over grosse, thick & impure, & nature so disordered, that diverse melancholicke persons have judged themselves some earthie pitchers, othersome cockes, other some to have wanted their heades &c, as if they had bin transported by the evill quality of the humor into straunge natures" (188–189). Chapter 3 will explore how such case histories are used to produce a new subset of women's melancholy.

[20] Although Descartes does not explain the shift, dreamers suit his purposes better. As Derrida argues, the experience of dreaming is more common than delusional melancholia and therefore is more useful to the readers that Descartes hopes will imitate his process of doubt. (His preface to the reader addresses only "those people who will be able and willing to meditate seriously with me" *Meditations* 75.) Additionally, the "*insani*" are, in his Latin text, *a-mens*— away from their minds, and if he identifies with them, he will be *de-mens,* likewise away from his mind and incapacitated for further meditation (88): "But these people are without minds, nor would I myself seem less demented if I were to transfer something as an example from them to me" (89). Moreover, distinctions between dreams and melancholic delusions are not as sharp for early moderns as they are today. In early modern texts, both are seen as comparable effects of the bile-infected imagination. Both are alike products of Phantastes in *The Faerie Queene*

The potential division and delusion that bile-infected fantasies pose to the integration of mind, body, and soul are put behind him, and the threat of a freelance subject is temporarily laid to rest when Descartes reintroduces the existence of God. But his moment of melancholy-instigated doubt reverberates down through the history of philosophy to the present.

Although in his *Meditations* Descartes quickly moves beyond his madmen, his doubt, and the mind/body split, contemporary theorists of the subject return to this passage to reappropriate the discourse of melancholy for their own projects of radical skepticism, emphasizing the continuing influence of the discourse. Foucault and Derrida debate its implications to advance their own theories of a contradictory and disunified subject.[21] Foucault, in the original edition of *Madness and Civilization,* claims that Descartes's turn away from the *insani* inaugurates the rupture that excludes and silences madness, discursively and institutionally, through the operations of power/knowledge. Derrida disagrees, claiming instead that Descartes's example assimilates the mad into the discourse of reason. He uses the passage to charge Foucault with reinscribing an untenable idealist metaphysics by postulating an originary unity of reason and madness and to defend his central deconstructive claim that reason, like all other binaries, includes (yet represses) its opposite, madness. There is no need to adjudicate this debate but only to emphasize how melancholy discourse continues to generate "new knowledge" and new debates about the appropriate place of the material and the nonmaterial in the construction of the subject.

Earlier, in 1915, Sigmund Freud wrote "Mourning and Melancholia" (published 1917), the last of his series of foundational metapsychology essays: "Narcissism," "Instincts and Their Vicissitudes," "Repression," and "The Unconscious." As his use of the Latin term for melancholy suggests, Freud incorporates and revises in his account the Galenic bodily pathology, the superiority of intellect, and the afflicted conscience long associated with the condition, relocating these and reversing the gender configurations of melancholy. The divisions of the subject are now resituated from the soul and body to the ego that "debases itself and rages against itself" (257).

Freud, like Aristotle and Bright, analyzes the operations of melancholy by

---

passage. And Burton's *Anatomy of Melancholy* cites indiscriminately numerous victims of vapor-troubled phantasy, including sleepers who have nightmares, women who conceive monsters they have imagined, and those who believe the "absurd apparitions, as that they are Kings, Lords, cocks, bears, appes, owls, that they are heavy, light, transparent, great and little, senseless and dead" (1.2.3.2; 1:250–255, esp. 252).

[21] Foucault's discussion occurs at the beginning of chap. 2, pp. 56–59 in the original 1961 Paris edition, *Folie et deraison: Histoire de la folie à l'âge classique* (and is omitted in Howard's translation). Derrida disagrees in "Cogito and the History of Madness." Foucault's response to Derrida's criticism, "My Body, This Paper, This Fire," is included as an appendix to the second (1972) Paris edition of *Histoire de la folie.* While Foucault does not successfully defend himself against Derrida's allegations, his brilliant close reading of the Descartes passage better reveals its operations and subtleties than does Derrida's briefer appropriation. See Geoff Bennington's introduction to his translation of "My Body" in the *Oxford Literary Review* for a summary of the debate.

a "correlation" (243) with its nonpathological twin—no longer artistic genius or Christian guilt, but "normal mourning" (255, 256). Like both predecessors, Freud strives to establish causal distinctions between two conditions that seem to have identical emotional causes and affects. Both mourning and melancholia involve a refusal to let go of a lost object. This refusal absorbs energy and results in "painful dejection, cessation of interest in the outside world, loss of the capacity to love, inhibition of all activity" (244). But mourning, Freud argues, has a discernable cause in a real loss—of a loved one or an abstraction (243), whereas melancholia's cause is unknown or unclear; neither observer nor melancholic is sure who or what has been lost (245). He adds, in a second distinction: "In mourning it is the world which has become poor and empty; in melancholia it is the ego itself" (246). This is because, Freud speculates, in mourning, the decathecting of "memories and expectations in which the libido is bound to the object" is gradually achieved, but in melancholia, the process is blocked. The object has been taken up within the ego where it is ambivalently clung to and attacked. Hence, whereas in mourning the "loss in regard to the object" can be healed, in melancholia the "loss in regard to the ego" cannot (247). But the fragile boundary between the pathological and normal states erodes as it has in earlier treatises. Both in this essay and in subsequent writings, Freud "discovers" the cause of melancholia, and so eliminates its key difference from mourning. The precipitating events are similar, and the "ambivalence" that attaches to lost love objects impoverishes self and world. The only difference, by the end of the essay, is a highly provisional and unconfirmed hypothesis that mania succeeds melancholia but not mourning (253) and that "regression of libido into the ego" (258) is the dynamic of melancholia and not of mourning.

As Freud strives to understand and articulate the psychic process "dynamically, topographically, and economically,"[22] in the absence of "empirical material" (250), his graphic representations of melancholia draw on and transform the traditional metaphors and dynamics of the condition. Blackness, long melancholy's key feature, is incorporated and redeployed in a powerful image that represents the painful identification with the object: "Thus the shadow of the object fell upon the ego" (249). As melancholy was traditionally caused by the paradoxical diffusion and congestion of the black melancholy humor, in Freud the libido (as fluid and mysterious as the black bile) is "bound" (255, 258) and "blocked" (257). Freud likewise reanimates and transforms the tradition's conception of melancholy as a state of paradoxical intensity and inhibition in his powerful representation of melancholia as an open incurable wound: "The complex of melancholia behaves like an open wound drawing into itself cathectic energies—from all directions . . . emptying the ego until it is totally impoverished" (253).[23] With this

---

[22] From a letter to Karl Abraham, quoted in Schiesari 34 n 3.

[23] Earlier, in the draft essay "Melancholia" in the Fliess papers, Freud understands the psy-

extraordinary image, Freud unites the intensity of Aristotle's artists, the torpor of Bright's friend M, and the voracious self-consumption of Bellerophon or those who have lost God's grace. He turns inside out the tradition he inherits; now the psyche wounds itself as well as body and soul.

This dramatic inversion of the dynamics of melancholy leads to two others. For Aristotle melancholiacs were a superior minority; for Bright they were a curable majority. However, in "The Ego and the Id" (1923), Freud derives from his analysis of melancholy an account of the formation of the normal psyche. Mourning and melancholy are now the same, and the hypothesized cause of "the painful disorder of melancholia"—the "setting up of the object inside the ego"—is discovered to be "common" and "typical," to be a "substitution" that "has a great share in determining the form taken by the ego" (28). The critical agency (now called the superego or ego ideal) is operative not only in melancholia but also throughout psychic development, as it "rages against the ego with merciless violence" (54). Joining, in effect, the pathological disease of black bile that haunts the exemplary melancholiacs of the Aristotelian *Problem* to the state of anxiety and guilt that characterizes human fallenness for Bright, Freud theorizes an incurable psychic malady at the heart of every normal human being.

In Freud's most dramatic revision of the inherited discourse of melancholy, ordinary women, excluded by Aristotle, Bright, Spenser, and Descartes, serve as his case histories and his exemplars of the normal subject.[24] In "Mourning and Melancholia," the commonplace case of a betrothed girl who has been jilted illustrates not mourning but "a loss of a more ideal kind" (later explained as introjection) that will become central to the dynamics of melancholia and ego formation (245). Next, the inappropriate self-abasement of the "good capable, conscientious woman" illustrates the work in melancholy of the "critical agency" (later to become the superego) (247). Finally, the woman who, in accusing herself, is really accusing her husband of

---

chic condition through its connections and correlations with sexual anesthesia (frigidity and inhibition): "*melancholia consists in mourning over loss of libido*" (SE 1:201). The "*in-drawing (as it were) in the psychical sphere*" closely parallels the ceasing or indrawing of somatic excitement, and the healthy discharge that cures melancholy and anesthesia seems virtually indistinguishable from ejaculation (SE 1:201, 205). Freud's early writings further suggest that, unlike wounds to the surface of the body that discharge damaged matter and promote healing, this wound is an "*internal haemorrhage.*" "In melancholia the hole is in the psychical sphere," paralleling the operations of neurasthenia in which there is "excitation running out, as it were, through a hole" which is "pumped empty" (SE 1:205, 206).

24 Juliana Schiesari, whose analysis of Freud's gendering of melancholia has been widely accepted, usefully identifies traces of the tradition of genial melancholy in his writings, but fails to realize how radically he revises that tradition. Her study overestimates the role of Hamlet in Freud's text. She identifies mourning with women and claims, inaccurately, that Freud trivializes this process, forgetting that it becomes synonymous with melancholia. However, Schiesari usefully enumerates Freud's repeated attempts to separate melancholic (narcissistic) identification from hysterical identification and his repeated attributions of depression, but not melancholy, to women—from Frau Emma (SE 1:118–119) through to "Analysis Terminable and Interminable" (SE 23:252), where penis envy is said to cause depression in women (Schiesari 55–57 and esp. 57 n 19).

impotence, allows Freud to formulate the ambivalence that attaches to the identification (248). When, later, melancholia is theorized as normal ego development, women in love again best exemplify the process: "In women who have had many experiences in love there seems to be no difficulty in finding vestiges of their object-cathexes in the traits of their character" ("Ego and Id" 29).

As ordinary women become exemplars of normal psychic development, Hamlet (and the Galenic and Christian paradigms of melancholy and guilt he stands for) is pushed to the margins of text and theory. The single off-handed reference to him in "Mourning and Melancholia" is triply distanced from the central argument. It is within a digression puzzling out the causes of the melancholic's heightened self-criticism. It is an answer to a rhetorical (and Aristotelian) question: "we only wonder why a man has to be ill before he can be accessible to a truth of this kind." It occurs (parenthetically) within a reassertion of the claim that excessive self-vilification is an illness: "For there can be no doubt that if anyone holds and expresses to others an opinion of himself such as this (an opinion that Hamlet held both of himself and of everyone else) he is ill." More oddly, the footnote quotation cites not Hamlet's famously melancholic self-loathing, but his misanthropic put-down of Polonius: "use every man after his desert, and who shall scape whipping?" [2.2] (246). With this shadow appearance of Hamlet's sardonic wit, Freud ambivalently gestures toward and subordinates the long-standing tradition of accredited male melancholy, in effect wiping the slate clean for his subsequent rewriting of melancholy as central to normal development.

Freud does not, however, abandon the generic man as his subject, nor does women's privileged access to melancholy undo their asymmetrical position in the whole of Freud's theory with its positing of a "normal development" for girls that inverts the stages and oedipal dynamics of boys. Contemporary feminist theory hence seizes on melancholy discourse to critique or to revise Freud, continuing its role in reformulating the subject. Luce Irigaray, in *Speculum of the Other Woman* (1974, trans. 1985), appropriates melancholia to deconstruct Freud's asymmetrical theory of sexual difference. In a section titled "A Very Black Sexuality," she characteristically parallels and contrasts (or "crosschecks" 66) Freud's account of the girl child's discovery of castration with the symptoms of melancholia. Julia Kristeva's *Black Sun: Depression and Melancholia* (1987, trans. 1989), as her title signals, returns to an Aristotelian metaphorics of heat, blackness, and artistic exemplarity, comparing melancholy with depression (mourning) to promote the parallel cathartic cures of psychoanalysis (for women) and artistic representation (for men). For Judith Butler, from *Gender Trouble* to her most recent work, melancholy is a crucial tool in her critique of Freud and in the development of her own theory of performative citational subjects. These feminist rereadings of melancholy continue the discourse's work of making and breaking boundaries, exposing the fault lines of the self, and exploring the patholog-ical to map the normally turbulent human subject and its gendered place in the social and symbolic order. The "elegiac" ego (Sprengnether 229), founded in loss, attacked by the id and the superego, and mourning its forever un-attainable desires, is catalyzed by our current philosophical and cultural conflicts just as the Aristotelian melancholic genius or the conscience-stricken and bile-contaminated M were by theirs. This analysis of selected moments in the history of melancholy reveals how medical discourse ap-propriates older constructions of disease at particular historical moments to make possible new maps of the subject's divisions, changed formations of distracted and normal subjects, and new gender configurations.

In the six chapters that follow, I examine closely changes in the discourse of madness occurring at disparate, intersecting cultural locations between 1576 and 1632, with particular but not exclusive focus on Shakespeare's plays. Chapter 1, "Initiating Madness Onstage: *Gammer Gurton's Needle* and *The Spanish Tragedy*," shows how madness is imbricated in the origins of both university and public drama where its representation helps initiate two popular theatrical genres: farcical domestic comedy and revenge tragedy. Diccon the Bedlam, the beggar/presenter and inciter of the action in Mr. S.'s *Gammer Gurton's Needle* (ca. 1550s at Cambridge University), uses his role as a Bedlam to mock ritual and sow anger and status disruptions. Successors like Poor Tom, Trouble-all, Bedlamites, and maddened men who are victims of mock exorcisms extend his farcical challenges to normative or-der. The representation of Hieronimo's mad grief and rage in *The Spanish Tragedy* (performed ca. 1587–1592) proves yet more influential as it grows increasingly prominent, first in additions to the text and then through the numerous allusions, redactions, and appropriations that circulate through the seventeenth century. In time, his madness is imitated and elaborated in characterizations of some Shakespearean tragic protagonists. These comic and tragic representations of the mad help to initiate genres, popularize the-ater, and stimulate later renditions of gendered madness, heroic and farcical.

Chapter 2, "Reading the Language of Distraction: *Hamlet, Macbeth, King Lear*," shows how Shakespeare's tragedies, imitating Hieronimo's success, invent a new language for the mad, a stylistically italicized and culturally in-flected speech peculiar to distracted characters. Through this language and representation, the plays instruct audiences in diagnosing psychic disorder and distinguishing it from supernatural invasion, spiritual sin, and fraud, an enterprise simultaneously undertaken in cultural treatises such as Bright's *Treatise of Melancholie* (as we have seen) and Samuel Harsnett's *Declaration of Egregious Popish Impostures* (1603), and by Dr. Napier. Shakespeare's tragedies likewise represent distinctions between Hamlet's melancholy and feigned madness and Ophelia's distraction and suicide; between the witches' spells and Lady Macbeth's sleep-walking, diagnosed by a doctor; between

Edgar's feigned demonic possession and Lear's natural madness. These plays' theatrical innovations thus contribute to secularization and gender distinctions in mental disorders.

Chapter 3, "Diagnosing Women's Melancholy: Case Histories and the Jailer's Daughter's Cure in *The Two Noble Kinsmen*," focuses on how cultural pressures lead polemic texts to revise the Galenic tradition of deluded melancholics and create a new subdivision, female melancholy. This condition is theorized in case histories of women sufferers in André Du Laurens's *Of melancholike diseases* (1599), Edward Jorden's *Briefe Discourse of a Disease called the Suffocation of the Mother* (1603), and Reginald Scot's *Discoverie of Witchcraft* (1584), and later is picked up and circulated in Shakespeare and Fletcher's *Two Noble Kinsmen* (1613). The treatises reconceptualize supernatural visitations as natural disease by arguing, innovatively, that witches, the bewitched, and the possessed (all predominantly women) are deluded melancholics. Emergent female melancholy, like the suffocation of the mother (uterine infirmity caused by humoral disease), becomes associated with women's congested reproductive organs and wandering wombs so women grow deluded by desire. The new remedies prescribed for women conflate theatrical cures for deluded melancholics with marriage cures for the suffocation of the mother, and coital cures for the lovesick, creating irresistible opportunities for stage representation and new models of female subjectivity.

Chapter 4, "Destabilizing Lovesickness, Gender, and Sexuality: *Twelfth Night* and *As You Like It*," argues that lovesickness, like women's melancholy a disease of mind and genitals, undergoes a parallel regendering and hence reconceptualization through revisions of the disease's exemplars and etiologies. As it does so, and as the culture seeks cures, gender and sexuality are detached. Heterogeneous objects of desire, homo- and heteroerotic desires, and unstable gender identities are licensed and allowed representation, especially for women. This process is equally visible in the new resolutions to old medical debates in André Du Laurens's chapter on lovesickness (trans. 1599) and in Jacques Ferrand's *Treatise on Lovesickness* (1623); in the fluid gender identifications and desires of cross-dressed women such as Rosalind in *As You Like It* and Viola in *Twelfth Night*; and in the comically sympathetic treatment of lovesick maidens in Jan Steen's *Doctor's Visit* paintings. Desire deserves satisfaction by any means necessary.

When the sufferers of melancholy, lovesickness, or madness cannot be cured or controlled by therapy or marriage, they become candidates for some form of restraint. Chapter 5, "Confining Madmen and Transgressing Boundaries: *The Comedy of Errors, The Merry Wives of Windsor,* and *Twelfth Night*," analyzes the disparate intentions and effects that characterize domestic confinement in play texts and period records. In Shakespeare's three comedies, the brief scenes of confinement of sexually and socially aggressive men who commodify women—the two Antipholuses, Falstaff, and Malvolio—enhance unfestive farce and license others' romantic release. Blatantly faked exorcisms comically appropriate supernatural rituals for social ends, thus discrediting possession and exorcism, but empowering women and servants. But if in drama confinement is a farce by which women scapegoat men, in contemporary parish records men and women were equally candidates for compassionate restraint that was negotiated by family, local authorities, and professionals to provide "relief and maintaynence," to cure the distressed.

Chapter 6, "Rethinking Confinement in Early Modern England: The Place of Bedlam in History and Drama," examines five plays featuring groups of Bedlamites and uses institutional histories to rethink the divergent cultural and theatrical functions of Bedlam—in London and on stage. As City, Court, and patrons struggled for control of the newly secularized institution, Bethlem's size, purpose, admissions procedures, and treatment assumptions remained relatively unchanging throughout the period I study.[25] Confinement in Bethlem Hospital, like restraint in the family, was temporary, therapeutic, and without visible gender bias. But the new representations of Bedlamites in a handful of Jacobean plays—Dekker and Middleton's *Honest Whore Part I* (1604), Dekker and Webster's *Northward Ho* (1607), Webster's *Duchess of Malfi* (acted before 1614), Fletcher's *Pilgrim* (1621), and Middleton and Rowley's *Changeling* (acted 1623)—tell a different story. They present satiric caricatures of madpersons who perform in metatheatrical scenes for the amusement of onstage and offstage spectators in ways that deflect the attacks of the stage's enemies. These representations, by segregating and dehumanizing madpersons and making spectacles of them, anticipate and may help to produce the gradual isolating and denigrating of the mad and their emergence as spectacles for amusement, which was likely first encouraged after Bethlem Hospital was enlarged in 1676.

At the conclusion of each chapter, the perspective widens out from the particular ecological niche, England between 1576 and 1632, just as it did in my mini-history of melancholy above. I glance beyond the specific period, geography, and dramatic and medical texts studied to trace later reception, developments, or visual illustrations that reveal ongoing ramifications of the emergent changes I analyze. Then, in a brief epilogue (which can be read before or after the rest of the book), I remind readers of how the debates over madness that occupied early modern subjects are recapitulated in our own time and how the changes we watch emerging between 1576 and 1632 continue to influence us. Some conceptions, such as women's lovesickness, have been consolidated; some, such as the movement toward institutionalization of the mad, have been reversed; some, such as treatment of deluded melan-

---

[25] The *History of Bethlem,* which covers the period from 1247 to the present, suggests this in both organization and contents. Part 1 deals with 1237–1633. The introduction to part 2, covering 1633–1783, suggests some changes before the move to Moorfields in 1676 but places most changes after this move (*HB* 145–155, esp. 147).

cholics, we continue to struggle with. Through this study of heterogeneousness, change, and gender representation as they circulate through a range of texts in the ecological niche offered by early modern culture, I hope, like Ian Hacking, to "get a glimpse of how our fellow men and women break up, in a time and at a place" (*Mad* 5).

CHAPTER I

INITIATING MADNESS ONSTAGE

Gammer Gurton's Needle and *The Spanish Tragedy*

Hieronymo's mad againe
T. S. ELIOT, *The Wasteland*

Just before and during the period I focus on, madness emerged as central to theme, plot, and character in two founding plays of popular English theatrical genres. Mr. S.'s *Gammer Gurton's Needle,* one of the first English domestic comedies, was performed in the 1550s at Christ's College, Cambridge, and published in 1576. Thomas Kyd's *Spanish Tragedy,* probably the inaugurating English revenge tragedy, was first performed on the public stage in the 1580s.[1] Each play introduces innovative representations of madness. These representations enable the plays' transformation of their Latin models (Terence, Plautus, Seneca) into English drama. They drive the plots and spark the plays' popularity and influence, showing why drama thrives on innovation. As we will see, successors of Diccon the Bedlam, Hieronimo, and Isabella will proliferate in the drama throughout the period. Feigning or errant madmen will be maddened or madden others, appropriate supernatural rituals to practical ends, and expose and disrupt social hierarchies. In tragedy, mad protagonists and madwomen, whose distract conditions are triggered by loss, grief, and rage, will represent inner turmoil with new verbal strategies and in culturally inflected ways.

---

[1] On unsettled questions of dating and authorship of *Gammer Gurton's Needle* see Whitworth's introduction ix–xvii. On the equally uncertain dating of *The Spanish Tragedy,* see Boas xxvii–xxx (1585–1587), Edwards, *Spanish* xxi–xxvii (who proposes 1582–1592), and Freeman 70–79 (who proposes 1584–1599).

Dramatic Innovation: *Gammer Gurton's Needle*

In *Gammer Gurton's Needle,* Diccon the Bedlam, the beggar/presenter/
protagonist, is central to the play's plot, farce, and resolution although his
role and its connection to his name has rarely been the focus of scholarship.[2]
His centrality is evident for, in spite of his low status, he is the character listed
first in the Dramatis Personae, his actions catalyze the play's conflicts, and it
may originally have borne his name. (An entry in the Stationers' Register in
1562–1563 licenses Thomas Colwell, the eventual publisher in 1576, to
publish a play titled *Dyccon of Bedlam.*) Diccon's association with Bedlam,
emphasized in the early title, in the Dramatis Personae, and in the Prologue,
marks him as a sort of Abraham man, one who, as Thomas Harmen says in
A Caveat of Warening for Common Cursetors Vulgarely called Vagabonds
(1566), "faine themselves to have beene mad, and have bene kept either in
Bethelem or in some other prison a good time, and not one amongst twenty
that ever came in prison for any such cause" (47). By revising the trickster
figure of Latin drama into a Bedlam who plays into current cultural debates
about vagabondage, the play creates a new type. Diccon's name and its associations emphasize his Englishness and denominate him as a disruptive
outside figure with no fixed social place, a type that contemporary legisla-
tion and City institutions strove, without success, to control.[3] And disrupt
he does.

Diccon's characterization as "the Bedlam" does not signify that he has
been in Bedlam or that he himself is mad; indeed he is in control of the play.
It is a metonymy for his capacity to trigger excess, folly, and loss of control

[2] J. W. Robinson, however, interprets Diccon's role as central, reading him as a wise fool who
exposes rather than exacerbates the village squabbles and hence contributes to the play's humanist moral that casts down the proud and teaches Christian humility. Douglas Duncan, interpreting the play instead as a Saturnalian parody of Latin comic form, humanist education,
and the pretensions of its learned audience, reads Diccon, somewhat as I do, as a licensed outsider figure who inverts hierarchies (186).

[3] Harman 47, quoted in Carroll 191. In his study of the discourse of poverty, *Fat King and
Lean Beggar,* William Carroll discusses the cultural stereotype of the fraudulent Bedlam beggar,
Poor Tom, or Abraham man, and the role of Bridewell and Bethlem Hospital in incarcerating
the poor, vagabonds, and madmen (102–108). Although Bedlam was tiny, released its recovered patients into custody, and did not license them to beg, this stereotype persisted. The period
1550–1576, which encompasses the play's probable performance, early licensing, and eventual
printing, was one of considerable negotiation about the appropriate responsibility for and control of the poor, debates that may have indirectly influenced the characterization of Diccon. For
example, although the Poor Laws of 1547 (under Edward) and 1572 (under Elizabeth) ordained
especially harsh punishments for vagabonds, including the gallows for repeated offenses, those
of 1550, 1553, and 1563 experimented with others less harsh, for example branding by ear-
piercing (A. L. Beier, *Masterless Men* chap. 2; Carroll, *Fat King*). The founding of Bridewell, the
first English workhouse, in 1553 by a coalition of humanists, Anglican preachers, and City magistrates is a new strategy for managing poverty, vagabondage, crime, and begging (Beier, "Foucault *Redux*?" 40–45). Similarly the control of Bedlam and its responsibility for the distracted
poor were, after 1547 when its management was given to the City of London by Henry VIII, a
part of this larger negotiation that drew attention to beggars, vagabonds, and the sick.

in others and disrupt the social order—which he does freely because, as a vagabond, beggar, thief, and trouble-maker outside of social hierarchies, he has no allegiances or rules.[4] In his role of Bedlam, a revision of the trickster role in Latin plays, he plants "madness" in others or ascribes it to them. By exacerbating rivalries and fears, he overturns all the controlling social hierarchies of the town: household, class status, age, gender, heterosexuality, religion, and law. It is not just the loss of the needle, but Diccon's manipulation of this that opens up "holes" in the community and in individuals. His exposure and "punishment" in the last act only appear to restore order in the community; he eludes reform or containment just as does the potential for madness in everyday life that he stands for.[5]

Diccon instigates such madness by bringing to the surface the rivalry, anger, and fear that underlie the village community's fragile status hierarchies. He elicits rage from Gammer Gurton and Dame Chat by his fabrications that the needle was stolen by Chat and that she in turn has accused Gurton of cock-stealing; then he ascribes madness to them (2.4.6). They end up enacting this by bashing heads and flinging insults that reveal how each's authority can be dangerously threatened by bodily and economic vulnerability. Dame Chat's insults most often attack Gammer Gurton for being old (and poor?) as her title, "Gammer," implies she is. She is called "old witch," "old gib," "hog," "bag," and inventively, "Thou scald, thou bald, thou rotten, thou glutton." Gammer Gurton retaliates against the younger and apparently higher-status Dame Chat by calling her every variation on "whore." Chat is called "ramp," "rig," "callet," "bitch," and, finally, "Thou slut, thou cut, thou rakes, thou jakes" (3.3.17–26).[6] The proverbial "short madness" which Diccon elicits undermines their authority to control servants and gain respect in the community. This spreads chaos further.

Diccon likewise manipulates Gurton's boy Hodge's unhappiness with the hard work (1.4.25–27), bad food (2.1.11–30), torn breeches (1.2.1–16), and lack of sexual satisfaction that are his servant's lot with a mock oath and

---

[4] His behavior does have some faint symbolic associations with the sort of behavior by which madness was recognized in the early modern period, behavior that, as Michael MacDonald shows, "repudiated one's place in the family, destroyed the symbols of social and economic status, and disregarded the conventions of deference and demeanor" (*Mystical* 126). Diccon wanders, steals, incites violence, and attacks social hierarchies and authorities.

[5] Alternatively, Gail Kern Paster and Wendy Wall interpret the ownership and loss of the needle as the cause and signifier of reversals of gender and sexual roles in the play and read its recovery as implying the restoration of normative roles. Paster understands the needle as a kind of phallus, a "floating signifier" (*Body* 118), whose loss symbolizes the loss of male heterosexual authority and bodily control that are symbolically restored by its recovery (119). Wall analyzes a wider set of reversals of gendered domestic relations in which the needle, "a female economic dildo" (11), signifies the productive role played by the domesticity of female-headed households in the construction of the sex-gender system, Englishness, and vernacular drama.

[6] Other characters' insults to the women show a similar pattern. Chat is called "quean" by Diccon (2.4.23), by Gammer (2.4.41), and by Rat (5.2.18). But Gammer is also occasionally dubbed whore, as are Tib and Gib, and Chat is sometimes called old in the blizzard of name-calling that fills the play.

mock conjuration that make him eventually "like a madman" (4.3.24). Diccon subordinates and maddens Hodge by making him swear allegiance on
his breeches instead of on the Bible (2.1.69–76): "I, Hodge, breechless, /
Swear to Diccon, rechless, / By the cross that I shall kiss, / . . . To work that
his pleasure is" (2.1.71–76). Subsequently he enforces Hodge's participation
in a mock conjuring of the devil into the circle. Hodge, in his terror that the
devil will seize him, opens his body to contamination in another way: his
"arse-strings bursten" and he "bewrays the hall" and runs away (2.1.105–
112). This scene anticipates later exploitation of supernatural rituals by the
mad or to madden, enactments that gradually drain these rituals of credibility and power but also, as here, open them to use by those at the bottom of
social hierarchies. Chapter 5 will analyze this process in Shakespeare's farcical comedies. As a result of Diccon's parody rituals, Hodge becomes Diccon's servant and his tool in the plot: "Chill be thy bondman, Diccon, ich
swear by sun and moon" (2.1.59). His sodomitical breech-kissing and cat-
raking show the extent of the incontinence and misrecognition Diccon can
conjure. Hodge's fear and humiliation lead him to pass on Diccon's lies to
Gurton, Chat, and Rat, setting them up for humiliation and madness.

Doctor Rat, the Curate, prides himself on his superior class and religious
status and patronizes Diccon and the rest of the community; however, he betrays his pastoral responsibility by spending his time drinking and eating (like
Diccon).[7] In payment he suffers at Diccon's instigation an ignominious punishment, which is social, physical, and implicitly sexual and which maddens
him—both enrages him and gets him labeled mad. Diccon calls him by the
familiar "man," and the ironically contemptuous "Sir John" (4.4.29–38),
and tricks him into disrobing to crawl into the "hole" in the back of Chat's
house, where he gets his head beaten in by her. When he tries to bring charges,
he is further humiliated because no one believes him: "Think you I am so
mad" (5.2.17). Even after he admits trickery, Diccon continues his insolent
attribution of madness to destroy Rat's gender, class, and professional status:

> Hath not such an old fool wit to save his ears!
> He showeth himself herein, ye see, so very a cox,
> The cat was not so madly allured by the fox
> To run into the snares was set for him, doubtless,
> For he leapt in for mice, and this Sir John for madness!
>   (5.2.227–231)

By displacing the madness that his name implies onto others, Diccon undoes
all the social hierarchies of the town; in their place he substitutes lies, inverted rituals, and head-bashing.

---

[7] Duncan, "*Gammer Gurton's Needle*" 187, notes that Rat "alone addresses Diccon in the
contemptuous second person singular." At 4.4.3–4 Rat calls Diccon, familiarly, "fellow" and
Chat "Mother," and Diccon replies to him, probably ironically, as "sir."

Although the revelation of Diccon's trickery allows the members of the community to displace their anger and rivalry onto him momentarily and to reconcile temporarily with each other (5.2.202–207), nothing in the play's ending suggests that order has been permanently resecured or that Diccon or the everyday madness he catalyzes can be contained for long. Even after Diccon's lies are exposed, he never restrains his insolence or is penitent. In fact Master Bailey, the magistrate, is his "friend" (5.2.267) and takes his part, appreciatively relishing his "sport" (5.2.196–201) and seconding his satire of Rat and Hodge.[8] He pretends the Bedlam has confessed and is penitent when he has not and is not (5.2.255). Refusing Dr. Rat's demand that Diccon be punished by whipping or the gallows, he orders instead a sham penance and a mock ritual that resanctions Diccon's Bedlam role. Diccon's "recompense" merely reauthorizes his beggar status, as he is to continue to beg; the villagers' "satisfaction" is to give him what he asks for (5.2.268–269) and his punishment is to take ale from the well-off Rat and Chat without paying for it (5.2.273, 276, 279), and to not mistake Hodge for a "fine gentleman" (285). The oath he is made to swear on Hodge's breech, unlike the one Hodge swore earlier on Diccon's breeches, maintains the beggar's superiority to Hodge and the rest. Diccon's prescribed breeches-oath, supposedly a penance, is an aggressive slap on Hodge's buttocks that drives the needle into them, thereby sodomizing his dupe and ironically fulfilling Hodge's promise "to help her to her needle again if it do lie in thee" (5.2.281). Again his butt, Hodge, is declared "mad" (295). Diccon retains his privileges and even improves his status at the conclusion, when he is invited inside to drink with the rest.

Diccon's "bedlam" status is a metonymy for madness that is not outside but inside the normative social categories of gender, class, sexuality, locale, and profession. Hence his ability to undo or reverse them. He stands for and incites all those forces that threaten precariously constructed boundaries and hierarchies: rage, jealousy, insolence, blows, hunger, dirt, shit, holes, assholes, sex, animals, the devil, the phallus itself that, like the needle, is "worthless, nonunique, and too tiny to find" (Paster, *Body* 117) amidst the debris of everyday life. Finding it seems beside the point since its double, Diccon, a diminutive free-floating Dick, is the more important catalyst to madness and remains at large to wreak havoc. At the play's end, he continues to apply carnivalesque reversals: "As proud comes behind, they say, as any goes before" (5.2.329; see Duncan 186).

Diccon's Epilogue, delivered to an audience of Cambridge students and their masters, both confirms their insularity and calls for their identification with that which is excluded from academic life.[9] By claiming to leave his au-

---

[8] Bailey's connivance with Diccon renders his name ironic since it should stand for the criminal justice meted out by "baileys" or "municipal magistrates" (*OED*) at the main criminal court, nicknamed Old Bailey for the street it was built on in 1550.

[9] Wall's essay explores the discursive links between housewifery, national and sexual identities, and the advent of English comedy. She elaborates on the play's debates about education

dience "behind" (as he turns to exit?) and "all alone" (331), he keeps alive
the play's scatological punning and reminds its academic audience that they
(like the actor who plays the role) are part of a circumscribed, celibate, all-
male, Latin-speaking, intellectual community, one supposedly segregated
from women, households, domesticity, the vernacular, sexuality, and all the
sorts of madness that fill the play. But by asking the audience to join in a
plaudite "for Gammer Gurton's needle's sake" (333), Diccon metatheatrically joins their high Latin to the play's low matter, identifies himself with
the academic author by echoing his Prologue, and asks the audience to affirm all that their rational, educational world excludes. As a "bedlam," a
counterfeit beggar madman, Diccon crosses boundaries, breaks rules, undermines status roles, and makes everyone he encounters eat shit.

While there is no evidence that *Gammer Gurton's Needle* was acted on
the public stage, it became "remarkably well-known" (Whitworth xx)
through its original performance, its subsequent publication, and perhaps its
word-of-mouth reputation. Early allusions and imitations such as those in
Ulpian Fulwell's *Like Will to Like* (1568) and Francis Merbury's *Marriage
between Wit and Wisdom* (1579) imitate its names, its low comedy, trickster
figure, and proverbial wit (Robinson 59, 68–71). Later it is used to satiric
purpose in the 1580s (in the Marprelate controversy) in an attack on John
Bridges, Dean of Salisbury (Boas 80–88; Whitworth xxvi–xxvii), and in
Histriomastix (1599) where "*Mother Gurton's Needle*, a tragedy" is found
in the repertory of the banished Sir Oliver Owlet's men. It is even reissued in
1661 after the Restoration. The influence of the Diccon figure is more
broadly felt in a host of trickster, mad, or maddened characters in later
drama. Outsiders/travelers like Antipholus and Dromio of Syracuse in *Comedy of Errors*, Feste in *Twelfth Night*, Falstaff in *The Merry Wives of Windsor*, Trouble-All in *Bartholomew Fair*, Alinda in *The Pilgrim*, and of course
Poor Tom in *King Lear* similarly feign or ascribe madness or have it ascribed;
they trigger confusion and provide distraction that exposes or conceals other
status disruptions which, as in *Gammer Gurton's Needle*, are never "recti-
fied" (Wall 10).

Dramatic Innovation: *The Spanish Tragedy*

Just as *Gammer Gurton's Needle* anglicized Latin comedy, so *The Spanish Tragedy* translates Senecan tragedy to please English audiences. The play
initiates a hugely popular and powerfully influential early modern genre, revenge tragedy. Its elements permeate every aspect of Tudor and Stuart drama:

---

and the nature of academic communities, and on the ways in which *Gammer Gurton's Needle*
blurs the distinctions between public and private, Latin and the vernacular, and male and female that university education sought to uphold.

spectacular revenge; political and social corruption engendered by a Machiavel and resisted by the protagonist; a racy love plot centering on a noblewoman who refuses to know her place; the dramatic use of Petrarchan motifs; intertwined family, class, and national conflict; the matter of Spain; a trend-setting play within the play; newly heuristic soliloquies.[10] But none is so important to its legacy as the madness of the protagonist, Hieronimo. This motif is central to characterization, to the revenge plot, and to the staying power of the play. In the first extant edition (Q1, ca. 1592), this madness is only briefly represented in a couple of scenes, which blend classical motifs with early modern vocabulary of distraction. However, in the fourth extant edition (Q4, 1602), the protagonist's madness is developed further in five (inappropriately named) "additions"; these 325 new lines are not add-ons but significant textual revisions that, by transforming Hieronimo's madness, make a new play.

The successful innovativeness of this representation is evident in the fact that Hieronimo and his madness eventually become synonymous with the play. From the first, "Hieronimo" is the name Henslowe uses in his *Diary* notations; in the frontispiece to the 1615 edition, the new subtitle, "Hieronimo's Mad Againe," is almost as prominent as the original title; and it is what Pepys calls the play when he reports seeing it in 1668.[11] Allusions to and appropriations of Hieronimo's madness that proliferate through the culture up to the closing of the theaters increasingly identify it with the towering passion and self-representation that the revisions emphasize. By tracing the development of Hieronimo's madness and its cultural reception, we can watch how the popular stage, by remaking its classical heritage for English consumption and by updating its own former hits, pioneers and disseminates a model of human madness which is not that of gods, legendary heroes, sibyls, or artists. Instead it newly endows a middling-sort character with the heightened intensity and articulate self-representation of Aristotelian melan-

[10] Although the play uses motifs from Senecan tragedy, it has no specific known source. Andrew Cairncross, like many other editors of the play, claims Kyd as "a seminal force in Elizabethan drama" and "the father of the revenge play, if not of English tragedy" (xii). The play was, however, anonymous throughout the seventeenth century. Wolfgang Clemen, *English Tragedy before Shakespeare*, provides a useful analysis of the psychological and dramatic properties of the soliloquies, noting their innovative incorporation of stage business, props, gestures, and psychological changes of direction (107–111).

[11] Philip Henslowe's entries from February 23, 1592 to October 1597 always call the play "Ieronymo" (or "Ioronymo" or, once, "Iereneymo"), whereas its counterpart or forepiece is called, on its 1605 title page, *The First Part of Hieronimo* and in Henslowe sometimes "comodey of done oracio," sometimes "spanes comodye doone oracoe," and once "comodey of Ieronymo." Boas reproduces Henslowe's entries on xl and cites Charles Cotton in the prologue to his 1675 poem "The Scoffer Scoffed," who claims, "And of all plays *Hieronimo*'s the best." Pepys writes on February 24, 1668, "Their play was a bad one, called 'Jeronimo is Mad Again,' a tragedy. Here was some good company by us who did make mighty sport at the folly of their acting, which I could not neither refrain from sometimes, though I was sorry for it" (Samuel Pepys, *Diary*, quoted by Freeman 131). "Hieronimo, both parts," is attributed to Shakespeare in Edward Archer's 1656 *Catalogue of all the Plaies* (Ingleby 2:59).

cholics along with psychological development that draws audience identification and sympathy.

In quarto 1 of *The Spanish Tragedy* (quartos 2 and 3 are identical except
that they correct old misprints and add new ones), Hieronimo's distraction
following the murder of his son, Horatio, by Lorenzo and Alonzo is present
but rudimentary. It is named by others, displayed through bizarre behaviors
usually signaled in stage directions, and confined to act 3, scenes 11, 12, and
13. His condition is seen to grow out of grief at his son's death, rage at the
murderers, and the frustration of his hope for justice. He is first diagnosed
by the second Portuguese as "passing lunatic, / Or imperfection of his age
doth make him dote" (3.11.32–33). In the next scene, Lorenzo calculatedly
claims Hieronimo is "Distract, and in a manner lunatic" (3.12.89) to deflect
his accusations, and the King proffers a somewhat milder diagnosis of "outrage," "fury," and "melancholy" to justify firing him (3.12.79, 80, 99). Each
of Hieronimo's increasingly bizarre behaviors fantasizes entrance into the
classical underworld, which is dramatized in the frame narrative in which
Andreas, the murdered ghost, watches over the action of the play with Revenge, who promises him his due. In act 3, scene 11, with the identity of his
son's murderers and hence his impotence confirmed, he responds to Portuguese who come seeking Lorenzo by acting out his inability to "find" this
murderer anywhere: he *goeth in at one door and comes out at another*
(stage direction following l. 8). He then provides directions to hell, where he
imagines Lorenzo suffering deserved punishment:

> There, in a brazen cauldron, fixed by Jove
> In his fell wrath upon a sulphur flame,
> Yourselves shall find Lorenzo bathing him
> In boiling lead and blood of innocents.
>   (3.11.26–29)

By scene 12, Hieronimo enters *with a poniard in one hand, and a rope
in the other* and contemplates using the weapons that killed his son to em-
bark on his own journey to hell, where he hopes to find justice—but again
his way is lost: "Turn down this path, thou shalt be with him straight; / Or
this . . . This way or that way?" (3.12.8–10, 14–16). When further attempts
to seek justice from the King are rebuffed at court, "*He diggeth with his dagger,*" seeking Horatio in the underworld (stage direction following 3.12.70).
The final outburst in scene 13 grows from his desire to provide satisfaction
to his double, Bazulto, who solicits from Hieronimo justice for the murder
of *his* son. Unable to provide it, Hieronimo acts out frantically and futilely
the revenge that eludes him by "shivering the limbs" of the petitions for justice with his teeth as he would "rent and tear" the murderers (3.13.122–
123). After this, the behaviors stop. These isolated outbursts lay the groundwork for representing tragic madness onstage; they are diagnosed by on-

lookers; they express the emotion and enhance the theatrical power of the protagonist; they elicit audience sympathy.

The revised text adds new verbal expressiveness and psychological development to the portrait. The "additions" to *The Spanish Tragedy,* as they are customarily called, were added to the play text somehow and sometime between the publication of the undated (already "newly corrected") quarto 1, printed by Edward Allde for Edward White, and the publication in 1602 of quarto 4, printed by William White for Thomas Pavier. The latter's title page emphatically announces its "newness." It is "Newly corrected, amended, and enlarged with new additions of the Painters part and others as it hath of late been divers times acted." These "new additions" are five separate sections of text, which total about 325 lines and are deftly dovetailed into the original so as to make perfect sense to readers or spectators. Chunks 1 and 3 are additions; 2, 5, and probably 4 are substitutions for sections of the original, as Pavier's "corrected, amended" suggests. Whether these are by Kyd, by Ben Jonson or another playwright, or developed collaboratively by one or more of the companies who performed it, they were clearly designed to renovate the play, and they indeed proved to be actor-friendly, crowd-pleasing, and sympathy-inducing.[12] This revised text is the basis for all subsequent seventeenth-century editions (except 1610–1611) and, presumably, performances. But most twentieth-century editors take the quarto 1 as their copytext and relegate the "additions" to an appendix, where they languish unread and ignored by critics.[13]

[12] All the questions about these additions—who wrote them? when? why? how were they added to the text?—remain unanswered. Most think it unlikely that the "additions" Henslowe records paying Ben Jonson for in September 1601 and June 1602 (generously and on spec) are those found in Pavier's text. (The style is not Jonsonian, publication follows hard upon payment, and a parody of one appears already in 1599 in Marston's *Antonio and Mellida*). Andrew Cairncross speculates they may be material by Kyd himself, first cut and later restored to the text (xxii). Arthur Freeman proposes, suggestively, that "the additions surviving through Pavier's printing of 1602 represent revisions at different times and possibly by different companies of the acting text, but are not those commissioned by Henslowe from Ben Jonson" (130). For discussions, see Freeman 117–118, 125–131; Edwards lxii–lxv; Cairncross 21–24; and Mulryne xxxiii–xxxiv. Although Edwards (lxiv) and Mulryne (xxxi) call these "replacements" and Cairncross calls them "duplications" (xxii), their editions do not excise the first quarto accordingly. I quote from J. R. Mulryne's New Mermaids edition of the play.

[13] Although there is agreement that the additions were added to "help rescue the play from seeming out of date" (Bevington 14; and see Edwards lxiii), there has been little exploration of how they did so, and no standard modern edition takes the "new-furbished play" (Edwards lxiv), the 1602 quarto, as copytext. (The current emphasis on the collaborative authorship and the validity of multiple play texts should encourage this step.) Instead, editors base editions on the first quarto and discredit the additions by segregating them in an appendix (Edwards, Mulryne, Bevington) or inserting them into the original set apart by italics or separate line numbers (Boas, Cairncross). They are most fully integrated into the text in Russell Fraser and Normal Rabkin's collection, *Drama of the English Renaissance I: The Tudor Period.* This editorial policy has critical fallout. Mulryne's introduction does not mention madness, Bevington alludes to it once, as feigned, and Edwards downplays it. Criticism such as that of Frank Whigham, James Siemon, Eugene D. Hill, and Carla Mazzio follows suit.

But the revisions change the play by "enlarging" the madness of Hieronimo and altering its function. Whereas in quarto 1, Hieronimo's condition was defined by others, and termed "mad" only once when Hieronimo sarcastically mimics Lorenzo's taunt (4.4.120), in the 1604 text the protagonist repeatedly names his own condition by the terms "mad" or "madness," which occur ten times, making the state central (Crawford 247). By first introducing madness in act 2, scene 5, just after the discovery of Horatio's murder and reprising it in the last scene, the additions trace Hieronimo's psychological development as he vacillates between grief, rage, and embittered helplessness. With his condition named and acknowledged by the protagonist, extended scenes of madness provide the glue that transforms isolated behavioral episodes into psychologically coherent character development; they drive the plot by accounting for Hieronimo's original delay and validating his subsequent decision to take revenge.

The revisions accomplish this by documenting Hieronimo's painful vacillation between delusional denial and acceptance of Horatio's death and his gradual tortured movement from sardonic paralysis to acknowledgment, expressive grieving, and, hence, to plotting revenge—from, in Freud's terms, melancholia to mourning. The first addition, extending the scene of discovery of Horatio's body in act 2, scene 5, dramatizes Hieronimo's retreat from his immediate drive to revenge ("For in revenge my heart would find relief" 2.5.41) into denials that Horatio is dead. He claims that Horatio, "so generally beloved" and so recently "frolic and merry," "cannot be short-lived," and he defensively attributes his apparent death to "strange dreams," delusions, "great persuasions," and the "like" garments the corpse wears (first addition 10, 2, 13, 19, 31, 30). When his wife, Isabella, and a servant counter these defenses, Hieronimo returns to the reality of his loss in the addition's stark monosyllabic last line: "How strangely had I lost my way to grief" (54). The second ten-line addition (which replaces a two-line speech in act 3, scene 2, lines 65–66) develops denial into an aggressively sardonic repudiation of Lorenzo through an ironic trivialization of the death as "a toy," an "idle thing," "The murder of a son, or so; / A thing of nothing, my lord" (second addition 3, 5, 10–11).

In the third addition, following the first line of act 3, scene 11, Hieronimo's bitterness ripens into cynical satire, a more desperate disavowal of loss. In the first half of a long monologue, he argues that sons are nothing to make a father "run mad," as they are merely "A thing begot / Within a pair of minutes, thereabout: / A lump bred up in darkness, and doth serve / To ballace [i.e., ballast] these light creatures we call women." Children pout, cry, must be cared for, and end up "unsquared, unbevelled," and ungrateful (third addition 10, 4–7, 22). But in the second half of the speech, Hieronimo rebuts his own cynicism by naming and mourning Horatio's lost virtues. He was loving, magnanimous, honorable: "He was my comfort, and his mother's joy, / The very arm that did hold up our house: / Our hopes were stored up in him" (31–33). This acknowledged grief leads on to fantasies of revenge as the brief image of hell's punishments at the end of the addition merges into the earlier quoted visions of the underworld that conclude the original scene.

The longest and most important addition is the fourth (inserted between 3.12 and 3.13 and often called 3.12A), which exacerbates the father's conflict between fantastic denial and acceptance and dramatizes how grief and madness are purged through identification and self-representation. At first, Hieronimo seeks poignantly in the garden for a Horatio he still imagines alive. But jolted by Isabella's forthright reference to Horatio's death, he displaces his consequent rage onto the tree that "grew a gallows, and did bear our son. / It bore thy fruit and mine: O wicked, wicked plant" (3.12A.70–71). The entrance of Bazardo the painter, who has also lost a son (a replacement for Bazulto, the justice-seeker with the lost son in the first quarto), allows Hieronimo to recover his lost son and let him go. First he acknowledges their shared madness and grief: "How dost take it? Art thou not sometimes mad? Is there no tricks that comes before thine eyes?" (fourth addition 108–109). Then he reconnects with the vitality of his child by lovingly describing the portrait he wishes painted of the living family's shared affection: Isabella with a "speaking look," he with his hand leaning on Horatio's head (120–122).

Having re-membered his son, Hieronimo can mourn. He acknowledges his death by reseeing the moment of the murder (and its effect on him) so Bazardo can paint it: a murdered boy, a murderer, and a valiant father who could not save him: "bring me forth in my shirt, and my gown under mine arm, with my torch in my hand, and my sword reared up thus: and with these words: '*What noise is this? Who calls Hieronimo?*'" (136–139). He retrospectively refigures the condition the death created: "bring me forth, bring me through alley and alley, still with a distracted countenance going along, and let my hair heave up my night-cap. . . . And then at last, sir, starting, behold a man hanging. . . . And looking upon him by the advantage of my torch, find it to be my son Horatio" (142–151). This done, identifying with Priam of Troy, he fully embraces his grief and rage: "Make me curse, make me rave, make me cry, make me mad" (152, 154–155). These successive self-portraits represent his progression from love to loss to madness to mourning. This catharsis leads Hieronimo first to act out his rage by beating the painter, and then to his considered decision to take revenge in his immediately following soliloquy, which begins "*Vindicta mihi!*" in act 3, scene 13. He acts on this resolve directly, first forging a canny reconciliation with the murderers in 3.14 and then organizing the fatal play within the play in the first scene of act 4.[14] Thus the added advertised painter's scene models

---

[14] There is no comparable progression in the first quarto. There, the *vindicta mihi* soliloquy precedes Hieronimo's encounter with the justice-seeker, Bazulto, whom he mistakes for his son, then sees as the "lively image of his grief" (3.13.162). But he does not confront his loss through self-representation as in the substituted painter scene.

the modalities of identification and the uses of representation for self-expression and subversive ends that the play will circulate to and elicit from its successors and audiences.

Hieronimo's recovery from distraction leads to new resolve and renewed satiric attacks on the court, expressed in the "willful playfulness" and "echoing obsequiousness" (Siemon 569) with which he manipulates them, most famously apparent in his punning and "menacing promise of accommodation" to Lorenzo and Balthazar: "Why then I'll fit you" (4.1.70). Although the court's corruption is exposed in Hieronimo's sarcastic taunts and his calls for justice, much of the play's social satire is outside the context of his madness.[15] However, the final addition/substitution (which extends 22 of the lines of the last scene to 46 but includes 11 lines of the original) allows Hieronimo additional exalting against corruption as he maliciously lacerates the Viceroy and Castile with the fact of their own murdered sons and heirs. While he is not clearly presented as mad here, he is (briefly) more out of control than in the original version and harps on his obsessive theme, the murder of his son, by killing the King of Portugal's son: "'Twas I that killed him; look you, this same hand, / 'Twas it that stabbed his heart; do ye see, this hand? / For one Horatio, if you ever knew him . . ." (fifth addition 37–39). His final line before he bites off his tongue is given new power by the revised couplet in which it is embedded and which continues his habit of self-conscious self-representation: "Now to express the rupture of my part, / First take my tongue, and afterwards my heart" (47–48). In these dying lines, Hieronimo sums up the rupture of all of his "parts": father, husband, Knight Marshall, the Bashaw in "Soliman and Perseda," as well as the self-rupture that madness has created.

Isabella's madness, identical in the two texts, is sharply contrasted to her husband's. Unlike Hieronimo's, it has an abrupt onset and rapidly leads to suicide. It is represented as a bodily ailment that she turns against her own maternal body. Its two manifestations, isolated from the main action of the play, frame the climax of Hieronimo's madness and contrast with his recovery from it (as Ophelia's movement into madness will be concomitant with Hamlet's recovery from it). In the first, Isabella, who hitherto has tried to

---

[15] C. L. Barber's reading precisely unpacks the pun's three layers: "It says, covertly, 'I'll give you what you deserve', along with the surface, 'I'll give you what you need', and a further suggestion, 'I am joining in the games you play'" (*Creating* 146). Barber, Siemon, and Whigham all address from different angles the multiple social tensions that are explosively released in the play. Barber explores how their lack of resolution leads to the uncontained "theatrical aggression" of the play's (for him) unsatisfactory ending. Siemon probes the relation of this aggression to the contradictory class positions of both Hieronimo, the Knight Marshall, and of Kyd, the scrivener's son. Whigham reads closely the "seizures of the will" by Bel-Imperia, Pedringano, and Hieronimo, which seek to dissolve gender, class, and political hierarchies and "mark the text as very strongly dissident" (26). Although some of the "resistant subjectivity" of the play (Siemon 581) is outside of the context of Hieronimo's madness, that helps account for and validate it.

reason with Hieronimo, now enters, ill, longing for an herb to purge her eye and head, but laments: "No, there's no medicine left for my disease, / Nor any physic to recure the dead" (3.8.4–5). A bare stage direction tells us *She runs lunatic* (stage direction following l. 5), and she now, like Hieronimo earlier, imagines Horatio and fantasizes revenge in nonsense lines to her attendant maid: "Why, did I not give you gowns and goodly things, / Bought you a whistle and a whipstalk too, / To be revenged on their villainies?" (10–12). We do not see her again (except for a brief appearance in the fourth addition) until act 4, scene 2 when, impotent and ignorant of Hieronimo's plan for revenge, she attacks the site of Horatio's birth and death. She hacks down the tree on which Horatio was hanged and, still unsatisfied, stabs herself: "And as I curse this tree from further fruit, / So shall my womb be cursed for his sake; / And with this weapon will I wound the breast, / *(She stabs herself)* The hapless breast that gave Horatio suck" (35–37). Unable either to represent the moment of the murder itself or to distance herself from her feelings by "painting" them as her husband has done, Isabella completes by suicide the trip to the underworld that Hieronimo had earlier contemplated, mutilating herself as Horatio was mutilated on the spot of his death. Hieronimo and Bel-Imperia later stab themselves in more aggressively calculated gestures.

Although traditional associations of madness persist, many characteristics of later representations of madness are initiated, especially in the revised text. Hieronimo and Isabella contemplate their own distraction. Madness begins to be not only articulated through delusional associations with classical gods and the underworld but represented as inward, secular, self-generated. The representation of interiority grants the mad male protagonist psychological development and emotional self-representation. Hieronimo's powerfully expressed grief and his use of theatrical means to gain revenge connect him to the intensity and prescience of Aristotelian melancholics, but draw also on unquenchable grief delineated by Bright, whose treatise was published about when the play was likely first performed. Isabella's madness, in its rootedness in the body, detachment from the plot, and concluding suicide, introduces gender associations in the representation of madness that would be influential. The sympathy of many onstage characters for the mad attracts audience support and identification with the hero, which makes palatable, even desirable, his resistance to authority and his brutal revenge. Some later uses of the motif are, however, not yet in evidence in *The Spanish Tragedy*. Although the additions are metrically "very rough" (Edwards, lxiii) and Hieronimo's distracted dialogue with the painter is virtually in prose (which will become the standard form for mad speech), his verbal madness has few distinctive semantic or stylistic markers. And while he seeks justice from the heavens and vengeance from hell, Hieronimo is not shown to be invaded by the supernatural, or to be possessed or bewitched. There is likewise no hint in the original text of the feigned madness that later plays include and interrogate.[16]

It is difficult to speculate on what cultural changes, outside the history of drama, might have influenced these revisions since the dates when the play was originally staged and published (in the nonextant first edition) and the dates when the additions were first added or first staged are uncertain. What is certain is that, from the first, Hieronimo's madness was central to the play's popularity and influence and that the revised text capitalized on the motif's repute and succeeded in outdoing the imitations the play had already spawned. *The Spanish Tragedy* was likely written and first performed sometime between 1582 and 1592 (a performance is recorded by Henslowe on March 14, 1592, and the play is entered in the Stationers' Register later in the same year—and subsequently withdrawn). Most commentators assume a date of composition between 1585 and 1587.[17] Whenever it first appeared, its popularity was immediate. Following hard upon the first two undated editions, others appeared in 1594, 1599, 1602 (with additions), 1603, 1610–1611, 1615 (with new subtitle and woodcut), 1618, 1623, and 1633.[18] The play was probably first staged between 1587 and 1590. Its first recorded performances were in 1592–1593 by Lord Strange's Men; it was revived by the Admiral's company in 1597; it was probably performed by the Chamberlain's company and Children of the Chapel as well before 1604 (Freeman 120–125; Knutson, "Influence" 269–270), supporting the claim of the 1602 edition that it "hath of late been divers times acted." It may have been performed at as many as eight London theaters as well as on tour in England and abroad (Hattaway 103–104; Boas xcix–ciii). A comic forepiece or prequel, "spanes comodye donne oracoe" or "I Hieronimo," was repeatedly performed in conjunction with *The Spanish Tragedy* during the 1597 revival and was printed in a corrupt quarto in 1605.[19] The play's success was astounding.

The widespread popularity of the play in the 1590s is fueled by and fuels the developing motif of madness, as the many successor plays and the revisions show. The fame of the madness motif encouraged its intertextual dilation within and across plays and companies according to what Roslyn Knutson identifies as the "principle of duplication" that drives the repertory

[16] Critics who claim otherwise offer no evidence or arguments for such feigning. See especially Bevington, who says that Hieronimo, to test the accusations of the dropped letter, "assumes a guise of madness to throw off his enemies" (11); and Siemon, who implies feigning when he suggests that "under license of 'madness,'" Hieronimo mocks others (570). Bowers denies assumed madness (72), as do Hallett and Hallett (148–149).

[17] For speculation about the dates of composition, production, and the first two quartos, one not extant, one undated, see Edwards xxi–xxvii, Cairncross xxx–xxxiii, and Mulryne xiii–xix.

[18] For discussion of editions up to 1602, see Edwards xxvii–xliii; for those after 1602, see 1925 Malone Society reprint edition of 1602, ed. W. W. Greg in consultation with F. S. Boas.

[19] This text, possibly an incomplete memorial reconstruction, is in Cairncross.

system.[20] Just as today rival studios peddle look-alike blockbuster movies and hopeful sequels, competitive early modern repertory companies imitated each other's most popular features: *The Spanish Tragedy,* then *Ur-Hamlet.* They mounted prequels or sequels: *The Spanish Tragedy* and *The Spanish Comedy.* They revived, sometimes refurbished, plays made newly appealing by the popularity of their successors: *Hamlet* and the "new" *Spanish Tragedy.* Competition and collaboration generate the circulation of madness in the drama of the 1590s from *The Spanish Tragedy* through the *Ur-Hamlet,* Greene's *Orlando Furioso* (1592, 1594), Shakespeare's *Titus Andronicus* (1594), *Tasso's Melancholy* (1594) and its revised version in 1602 by Dekker, and Marston's *Antonio's Revenge* (1601), a sequel to *Antonio and Mellida* (1599).[21] This extensive intertextual tradition likely provides the impetus for the revised representations of madness that quarto 4 of *The Spanish Tragedy* offers.

The influence of the play stretches far beyond this specific impact on the shape and substance of early modern tragedy into a host of imitations, allusions, and parodies that emerge even before the first quarto and continue through the closing of the theaters and beyond.[22] These increasingly cite Hieronimo. Most early allusions echo or parody the dazzling rhetoric of Andreas's prologue, Balthazar's and Lorenzo's petrarchanism, Horatio's murder, and Hieronimo's discovery of the body, especially his line, "What outcries pluck me from my naked bed" (2.5.1) and his expression of grief in his "O eyes, no eyes" speech at 3.2.1 (Freeman 133). Along with his grief, Hieronimo's canny self-concealment from the King is marked in endless reiterations of his "go by, go by" (3.12.31).

[20] Roslyn Knutson, "Influence of the Repertory System on the Revival and Revision of *The Spanish Tragedy* and *Dr. Faustus,*" demonstrates how additions to these two plays "exaggerated features of the old plays that had originally made them popular" (274) and shows that companies revised and revived plays that could compete in their content with those mounted by rival companies, were appropriate for the available actors, and would fill generic needs, especially for tragedy, the genre in shortest supply. She claims that *The Spanish Tragedy* was revised for revival (in her view in 1597, in mine in 1602) to make Hieronimo's madness more sentimental, sardonic, and bloodthirsty so the play could compete with its successor revenge tragedies, *Titus Andronicus* and *The Jew of Malta* (270–271). Her discussion in "The Repertory" is likewise useful.

[21] See Harold Jenkins for the unconventional claim that the *Ur-Hamlet,* probably by Kyd, precedes and makes possible *The Spanish Tragedy.* Dates, authorship, and direction of influence of the two plays remain the object of speculation. Gurr (*Shakespearean Stage* 104–105) discusses the texts of *Orlando Furioso* and their circulation among acting companies. For discussion of the now lost *Tasso's Melancholy* see C. P. Brand 206. *Antonio's Revenge* imitates or is imitated by *Hamlet:* see Jenkins 7–13; G. K. Hunter, ed., *Antonio's Revenge* xviii–xxi; and Smith, Pizer, and Kaufman 483–488, 493–498. The difficulty of determining direction of influence among these plays richly supports Knutson's claim that the "principle of duplication" drives the repertory system.

[22] *The Spanish Tragedy*'s echoes, imitations, allusions, and parodies are cataloged and discussed by Boas (lxxxiii–ciii) and Freeman (131–137). Mulryne, "Nationality" (88) says that Claude Dundrap, "'La Tragédie Espagnole' face à la Critique Elisabéthaine et Jacobéenne," in *Dramaturgie et Société,* ed. Jean Jacquot (Paris, 1968), 2:628–630, traces 111 allusions; I have not examined them all.

As allusions proliferate and become more elaborate, imitation and parody center increasingly on the powerful effect on audiences of Hieronimo's madness and grief. In *The Poetaster* (1601), Jonson ridicules *The Spanish Tragedy*'s vengeful ghost (Boas xc), and in turn he is mocked in Dekker's *Satiriomastix* (1602) where Horace, the character who represents Jonson, "took'st mad Ieronimoes part" and "ranst mad for the death of Horatio" (quoted in Boas lxxxiv). Likewise in the satirical *Parnassus Trilogy* (1598–1603), the character Studioso parodies Kyd's rhetoric and, when auditioning for the stage for Burbage, he is asked to imitate Burbage's delivery of Hieronimo's part (Boas xciii). Later in an elegy on his death, Burbage's performance of Hieronimo exemplifies his power to move audiences with vividly lifelike renditions of maddened tragic passion: "No more young Hamlett, ould Heironymoe. / Kind Leer, the greved Moore, and more beside, / That liued in him, haue now for ever dyde. . . . so liuely, that spectators, and the rest / Of his sad crew, whilst he but seem'd to bleed, / Amazed, thought euen then he dyed in deed" (Nungezer 74).[23] Thomas May's *Heir* (1620) reiterates the sympathy-inducing emotionality of the part when a player personating Hieronimo is said, "for false / And acted passion" to have "drawn true tears / From the spectators" (Freeman 135). Through its cultural dissemination, whether satirical or serious, the play becomes increasingly identified with Hieronimo's mad passion.

The 1616 edition registers and accelerates this ongoing process by adding to its title page a new subtitle, *Hieronimo is mad againe,* and a new woodcut representing Hieronimo's discovery of Horatio's body.[24] This woodcut (fig. 2) dramatizes the murder scene as Hieronimo describes it for the painter in the fourth addition. At the center is a heroically defiant Hieronimo with sword drawn, torch high, feet firmly planted, with Horatio hanging to the left and a haughty Bel-Imperia to the right who shouts "murder, helpe, Hieronimo" and defiantly pulls away from Lorenzo's grasp. The murderer is villainized by his black mask and squeezed outside the frame. Even before this edition, the ballad "The Spanishe Tragedie," which had at least seven editions between 1599 and 1638, circulated widely the grief and madness of its speaker, Hieronimo, who retells the plot accurately in the ballad's 96 lines and narrates his gestures of madness.[25]

[23] Burbage died March 13, 1619 (1618 old style). The elegy exists in 86- and 112-line versions and is ascribed to Jo Ffletcher. For short version, see Nungezer 72–76.

[24] There is little discussion of the meaning of this subtitle, of the reason for its late inclusion, or of why Hieronimo is described in it as mad *again.* Cairncross implies that it provides evidence that *The Spanish Tragedy* is part two of the work he calls, in the reprint in his edition, *The First Part of Hieronimo* (xiv). "Againe" might also refer to the episodic nature of Hieronimo's madness, which comes and goes in the play—more markedly so in the additions. It might also allude self-referentially to the play's many editions, additions, revivals, and cultural circulations, in which madness indeed appears again and again. Whatever the reason for it, the late-appended subtitle cements the identification of the play with the hero and his madness.

[25] The extant copy (reprinted in Boas 343–347) is undated, but it includes the woodcut.

The Spanish Tragedy:

Or,

HIERONIMO is mad againe.

Containing the lamentable end of *Don Horatio*,
and *Belimperia*; With the pittifull Death
of HIERONIMO.

Newly Corrected, Amended, and Enlarged with new
Additions, as it hath of late been diuers
times Acted.

LONDON,
Printed by *Augustine Mathewes*, and are to bee sold by
Iohn Grismand, at his Shop in Pauls Alley, at the Signe
of the Gunne. 1 6 2 3.

FIG. 2. Title page, Thomas Kyd, *The Spanish Tragedy,* 1623. Courtesy of the
University of Illinois at Urbana-Champaign Library.

The growing potential for transgressive identification with Hieronimo's madness and the self-representation that this enables is manifest in the attacks on such identification in Richard Braithwait's *English Gentlewoman* (1631, 1641) and in William Prynne's *Histriomastix* (1633). Braithwait, in a series of anecdotes of women who seek too much liberty, condemns "a Gentlewoman of our owne Nation, who so fairly bestowed the expence of her best houres upon the Stage, as being surprized by sicknesse, even unto death, she became so deafe to such as admonished her of her end, as she clozed her *dying scene* with a vehement calling on *Hieronimo*" (Braithwait, 1631 53). Instead of dying a good death by calling on Christ for forgiveness, she desires a theatrical exit. William Prynne in *Histriomastix,* elaborates this cautionary anecdote on the dangers of pleasurable play-going to suit his own antitheatrical agenda. He claims that Braithwait was present and heard the woman ignore the minister who had been sent for and instead "cryed out *Hieronimo, Hieronimo;* O let me see *Hieronimo* acted (calling out for a Play, in stead of crying unto God for mercy)" (Prynne, 1633, fol. 556). Here the woman, corrupted by representation, wants to die heretically, viewing Hieronimo instead of turning her eyes heavenward and submitting her sins to God's mercy. Braithwait's own subsequent revision of the anecdote completes the woman's delusional identification with Hieronimo. She now does not just call on him or want to see him acted, but becomes him. Braithwait represents her as appropriating Hieronimo's words to imitate his refusal of comfort when she identifies her doctor with Horatio and refuses his remedies: "Thankes good Horatio, take it for thy paines" (Braithwait, 1641 299, and see Shapiro 108–109). The play has by now come to represent cross-gendered possibilities for identifications with madness that are heretical. Madness is now not only segregated from sin and guilt as in Bright's treatise but is represented as subversive of religious belief. Centuries later, T. S. Eliot, like Braithwait's gentlewoman, lets Hieronimo ventriloquize his own loss of faith when he appropriates "Why then Ile fit you. Hieronymo's mad againe" as two final "fragments" shored against ruin in the last lines of *The Wasteland* (1922).

If early modern women can use performative identification with Hieronimo to resist submission to the dominant ideology, so perhaps, hints one fi-

---

Either it is later than 1615, or the woodcut originated with the ballad (Boas xcvii). The fact that, apart from the title, this ballad does not name the location of its events suggests the decreasing importance of the matter of Spain in the seventeenth century. Perhaps the madness, already popular, was enlarged partly to compensate for the increasing outdatedness of the politics. Hieronimo's first masque displaying England triumphing over Spain and Portugal, and the destruction, at the conclusion, of the dynastic marriage unifying Spain and Portugal and of their royal lineage would surely have fed the especially virulent hispanophobia of the 1580s. Roland Broude, Hill, Mulryne, "Nationality," and Mazzio all discuss how anti-Spanish sentiment in the play supports English nation-building. However, none of the ballad's allusions register the Spanish matter, which likely lost its immediacy after James's alliance with Spain in 1604 and its decline as an imperial power by the 1640s.

nal reworking, can those of lower status. In Thomas Rawlins's *The Rebellion* (1640), in act 5, scene 1, a group of tailors decide to perform the play (and part) of "Jeronimo," whom they describe as "a mad rascall to stab himselfe" (I2r). Imitating Bottom's desire to play all the parts in the Pyramus and Thisbe play in *Midsummer Night's Dream,* the symbolically named character Virmine volunteers to play the ghost, Hieronimo, the king, Horatio, and Balthazar. He not only calls up the plot and characters of the now over-fifty-year-old play but quotes all the favorite lines including "who calls Hieronimo from his naked bed," and "pass by" (I2r–I2v). The tailors' play is aborted because most of its potential spectators are killed when King Philip of Spain suppresses a rebellion by Machivill, his courtier, and Raymond, a Moor. Although the play explicitly celebrates the restoration of order and the confounding of traitors, its dates—performed from 1629 to 1639 and published in 1640, two years before the outbreak of the Civil War—suggest it could have been read as a primer for rebellion by spectators so inclined. Might not the extended allusion to Hieronimo's mad grief, however comically rendered, recall his destruction of the monarchical line? Might not this doubly allusive insert be read as conjuring up a play within a play that, like the Pyramus and Thisbe play or Hieronimo's, could have provided a variant ending to the main tale—one in which the King was killed? However unlikely, it nonetheless remains the case that the motif of tragic madness initiated in *The Spanish Tragedy,* enlarged in the additions, and circulated widely throughout the culture, created a powerful secular model of tragic madness that would be subsequently developed for many different ends.

In these two initiating plays of the early modern theater, dramatic texts, by reviving and revising motifs from Latin drama and resituating them for English audiences, circulate new representations of feigned and heroic madness that will be broadly influential. Like the constructions of melancholy examined in Bright, Spenser, and Descartes, they represent madness that is secular, disrupts body and mind, allows self-representation, and offers challenges to subjects' unity and to normative social order.

CHAPTER 2

READING THE LANGUAGE
OF DISTRACTION

Hamlet, Macbeth, King Lear

Lord, we know what we are, but know not what we may be.
Hamlet

As we have seen in the last chapter, the huge popularity of Hieronimo's madness in Kyd's *Spanish Tragedy* spawns many imitations throughout the 1580s and 1590s and into the seventeenth century. In the same period, cultural debates over witchcraft, possession, and exorcism heat up and produce new cultural demands to read madness in order to distinguish it from conditions that look just like it: bewitchment, possession, or feigning. These theatrical and broader cultural imperatives come together in three tragedies produced in the first six years of the seventeenth century: *Hamlet, Macbeth,* and *King Lear.* These tragedies develop further the representations of distraction in Kyd and his successors by inventing a new language through which madness can be voiced. Taking advantage of this innovation, the plays proliferate, in rapid succession, contrasted representations that address current cultural needs. The new language and these new representations produce increased emotional intensity and psychological development, gender-differentiations, and theatrical spectacle. Through a series of contrasts, the plays display the sorts of distinctions between men and women, body and mind, natural and supernatural, distraction and feigned madness that were being demanded at other cultural sites. By doing so, they resituate ailments that are potentially seen as supernaturally instigated within the parameters of the human world and seek human remedies. As Diccon did in *Gammer Gurton's Needle,* characters appropriate supernatural rituals for secular ends, especially Edgar in his role as Poor Tom. Although the importance of madness in the period's drama has long been acknowledged and although critics such as Lawrence Babb, Robert Reed, Bridget Lyons, and Lillian Feder have traced the individual significance of its occurrences and its humoral grounding, there have been few attempts to understand its linguistic coding, its development in the drama, or its cultural function in shaping attitudes toward madness and toward the human.

Documents in Madness

In the Middle Ages, and also in Greek and Latin drama, for different reasons, madness was often seen as a point of intersection between the human, the divine, and the demonic. It was viewed as a God-inflicted condition—as possession, sin, punishment, and sometimes disease, which confirmed the inseparability of the human and transcendent (Neaman 45–55; Doob chap. 1; MacDonald, *Mystical* 3–4). In the early modern period and especially in the decades before and after the beginning of the seventeenth century, several cultural debates in process (over the prerogatives of medicine, the validity of witchcraft accusations, the control of possession and exorcism) have the effect of requiring and welcoming the separation of human madness from the similar-appearing conditions caused by sin and guilt, demonic and divine possession, bewitchment, or fraud. By making such distinctions, these debates gradually map out the normal, "natural," and self-contained secular human subject—one that of course exists within a divinely ordered and devil-threatened cosmos but is not entirely shaped by supernatural forces.

Several pressing issues and contests create the "ecological niches" in which madness requires examination. Medical, religious, and legal authorities enter into these debates as some well-known examples can begin to show us. Three doctors, Richard Napier, Timothy Bright, and Edward Jorden, display the complexities of diagnosis and the different emphases that were possible. Richard Napier, doctor, minister, and astrologer, from 1597 to 1634 treated about sixty thousand patients in Great Linford in northern Buckinghamshire, taking notes on each consultation. Two thousand and thirty four of these patients (from all social classes) consulted him for disorders of mind.[1] Patients frequently believed that such disorders were caused by witchcraft. Since symptoms attributed to bewitchment—having visions, feeling haunted, suicidal, out of control or suffering fits, swoonings, or tremblings (Sawyer 333–336)—could have natural origins, Napier had to assess the circumstances of each case to determine the cause and prescribe appropriate remedies. He offered all sorts—magical, medical, astrological, and spiritual. To some distracted patients he gave advice, to most he prescribed purges, cordials, and blood-letting; for a few he gave astrological amulets,

---

[1] These cases are analyzed in the invaluable epidemiology of mental disorder constructed by Michael MacDonald in *Mystical Bedlam*. Ronald Sawyer's unpublished dissertation, "Patients, Healers, and Disease in the Southeast Midlands, 1597–1634," studies Napier's general practice and pays particular attention to cases where bewitchment is suggested.

recited prayers, or even performed exorcisms. He was cautious about crediting patients' claims of bewitchment. Hence he sought all-purpose or combination remedies (bleeding *and* prayer *and* an astrological amulet) which would work whatever the cause. He wrote a memorandum, for example, on how to cure "anyone who is mopish or distempered in brain or else [harmed by] any witcheries, sorcery, or inchantment. . . . First let them blood . . . then say, 'Lord, I beseech Thee, let the corruption of Satan come out of this man or woman or child that doth so trouble or vex her or him, that he or she cannot serve Thee as it may please Thee to call them . . . into Thy heavenly kingdom.'" His astrological amulets were "good against all spirits, fairies, witcheries, sorceries . . . That [*sic*] be lunatic . . . or out of their wits" or "good for many infirmities . . . against all evil spirits, fairies, witcheries, possessed, frantic, lunatic."[2] Clearly he did not trust himself to distinguish sharply among the causes of mental distraction and was comfortable assuming multiple causes.

As we saw in the introduction, Timothy Bright, also a doctor and subsequently a parson, in his somewhat earlier *Treatise of Melancholie* (1586), is confident of his ability to recognize and theorize the fine distinctions between the spiritual and the psycho-physiological causes for melancholy. He even believes he can teach laypersons to tell the difference between spiritual and bodily conditions and treat each. But in that treatise, as in Napier's practice, distinctions between the two similar conditions tend to collapse with the effect of privileging the natural causes of melancholy, which doctors and laypersons can treat, over spiritual versions, which they can't. Yet another doctor, Edward Jorden, went still further than Bright in reinterpreting, as disorders of mind and body, behaviors that others attributed to supernatural forces. Jorden's treatise, *A briefe discourse of a Disease Called the Suffocation of the Mother* (1603), is composed to decisively distinguish bewitchment from the distraction caused by the uterine disease, suffocation of the mother or wandering womb. Like Bright's and Napier's, his purpose is partly to legitimate the expertise of the licensed physicians he addresses who he claims, with more confidence than Napier feels, are "best able to discerne what is naturall, what is not naturall, what praeternaturall and what supernaturall" (fol. C1r). More important, he justifies his earlier testimony (in the trial of Elizabeth Jackson, accused of bewitching Mary Glover) that the victim's symptoms were natural in origin, the result not of possession caused by bewitchment, but of the suffocation of the mother. But not everyone agreed; doctors testified on the other side about the source of Glover's fits, and Jackson was found guilty. Had the cause been natural, she would have been acquitted, as over half of accused witches were (Thomas 451–452). However,

---

[2] Quoted in MacDonald, *Mystical* 213, and see 171–231 on Napier's healing strategies. See also Sawyer 315–344 on witchcraft and healing in Napier's practice and 548–555, his appendix on "Bewitchment Cases" for a list.

Elizabeth Jackson was released after a short sentence, and the possessions that had been so frequent in the last decade of the sixteenth century declined in England after this case.[3]

Substituting a diagnosis of mental distress for one of bewitchment was also a strategy used by those skeptical about witchcraft, as in Reginald Scot's ironically titled and cogently argued *Discoverie of Witchcraft* (1584). A justice of the peace, Scot denies the supernatural powers of witches themselves and the credibility of their confessions by attributing both to the effects of melancholy. This carefully crafted diagnosis has the effect of medicalizing witches' behavior and producing categories of menarcheal and menopausal melancholy that will be examined more fully in the next chapter. Witchcraft had earlier been treated as a secular crime when its disposition was consigned to civil courts by a 1542 statute. By the early seventeenth century, both church and state are increasingly reluctant to countenance witchcraft accusations, so alternative diagnoses are welcome. As is well known, Samuel Harsnett (an ambitious chaplain to Richard Bancroft, the bishop of London) joins the established church's coordinated campaign against Catholic and Puritan exorcists with the publication of his *Declaration of Egregious Popish Impostures* (1603), which attacks illegal Catholic exorcism rituals, exposing both possession and exorcism as feigned and theatrical. Jorden's *Discourse* likewise aims to expose "impostures" (Epistle Dedicatorie, fol. A3) who fake the fits of the possessed just as Scot discredits confessions as either naively melancholic or fraudulent. Witchcraft prosecutions continue to take place in England until 1680, but with less and less frequency as these treatises, in conjunction with medical practice and stage representations, medicalize the behavior of witches, the bewitched, and the possessed.

The public stage assists the culture in making such distinctions and finding alternative explanations by showing them what madness looks like and contrasting it to similar conditions. By representing both madness and the process of reading madness, plays teach audiences how to identify and respond to it. Onstage and off, madness is diagnosed by observers—first laypersons and then, in some cases, specialists. The period's audiences participate with onstage watchers in distinguishing madness from sanity and from its look-alikes: loss of grace, bewitchment, possession, or fraud. Madness is represented as a state of dislocation—separated in part from the self who performs and the spectators who watch—but not as a supernatural invasion. For theater to reach its audiences, it must be readable. For this the stage develops a new form of speech, peculiar to the mad, and cues for how to read it. In doing so it makes itself popular and useful.

Madness in these three tragedies is dramatized through a peculiar lan-

---

[3] For discussion of the political climate and the debate over exorcism that produced Jorden's and Harsnett's pamphlets in 1603, see Thomas 482–486; Greenblatt 94–128; MacDonald, *Witchcraft*, "Introduction"; and Walker, "Introduction" and 43–73, 75–84 on English cases of possession.

guage more often than through physiological symptoms, stereotyped behaviors, or iconographic conventions although these are present. This characteristic speech is something and "nothing"; both coherent and incoherent, it is located in characters and dislocated from them. Unlike that of Hieronimo or Isabella in *The Spanish Tragedy,* this speech is characterized by fragmentation, repetition, and most importantly by what I will call "cultural quotation"; it might also be called, following Luce Irigaray and Nancy K. Miller, "bracketing" or "italicization."[4] The mad are "beside themselves"; they are, like Ophelia, "divided from [themselves and their] fair judgment" (*Hamlet* 4.5.86) so their discourse is not entirely their own. But the voices that speak through them are not (except occasionally in the case of Edgar's parody of possession), supernatural voices, but gendered human ones—cultural remnants. The prose that is used for this mad speech (although it includes embedded songs and rhymes) implies disorderly shape, associates madness with popular tradition, and contributes to its colloquial, "quoted" character.[5] These quoted voices and fragments, however, have connections with (or can be interpreted to connect with) the characters' pre-mad history and their psychological afflictions—as well as with larger themes of the plays and of the culture. The alienated speech is a flexible instrument that allows psychological intensity and development, thematic emphasis, cultural resonance, and social critique. It represents the fractures of disordered subjectivity while connecting to large cultural voices and issues.[6] It also invites variety, increasing its stageworthiness and cultural usefulness. By the unfolding of different types of distraction, distinctions between female distraction and feigned madness and melancholy are represented in *Hamlet,* those between witchcraft and natural alienation in *Macbeth,* and those between feigned demonic possession, natural madness, and guilt-caused despair in *King Lear.*

Distraction, Feigning, and Melancholy: *Hamlet*

Onstage characters mediate this pregnant, mad discourse, explicitly teaching audiences how to translate it into the discourse of reason. Hence characters' madness is always interpreted for the audience when it first ap-

[4] Miller extends Irigaray's analysis of women's special relation to the mimetic, defining italics as a modality of intensity, intonation, and emphasis that characterizes women's writing (334).

[5] A. C. Bradley (336–337) notes that Shakespeare invariably uses prose to represent abnormal states of mind like madness or Lady Macbeth's somnambulism. I am indebted to Lars Engle for bringing this discussion to my attention.

[6] One of Foucault's central claims is that language constitutes madness: "*Language is the first and last structure of madness*" (*Madness* 100) and that this "*delirious discourse*" (99) is the inverse of reason. But the mad language constructed in these plays is always in dialogue with reason: because it incorporates the words of others; because it fragments but does not excise coherent claims; and because others are in dialogue with it, and collect and interpret it through the lens of reason.

pears.[7] This is made explicit by the anonymous Gentleman in *Hamlet* who prepares the onstage and offstage audiences for the entrance of Ophelia and solicits their sympathy by announcing: "She is importunate, indeed distract. Her mood will needs be pitied" (4.5.2–3).

> [She] . . . speaks things in doubt
> That carry but half sense. Her speech is nothing,
> Yet the unshapèd use of it doth move
> The hearers to collection; they yawn at it,
> And botch the words up fit to their own thoughts,
> Which, as her winks and nods and gestures yield them,
> Indeed would make one think there might be thought,
> Though nothing sure, yet much unhappily.
>
> (4.5.6–13)

The speech here described is painful, unshaped un-sense that can be "botched" up or "collected" into shape by an audience's readings. Ophelia's alienated discourse invites a psychological, thematic, and gendered interpretation. Although it partly adapts spiritual formula to a secular, psychological context, there is no doubt that her madness is natural.

Ophelia's madness is represented almost entirely through fragmentary, communal, and thematically coherent quoted discourse. Unlike Isabella and Hieronimo, she does not seek or hallucinate journeys to heaven or hell. The rituals she articulates and enacts are mainly earthbound. She recites proverbs, formulas, tales, and songs that ritualize passages of transformation and loss—lost love, lost chastity, and death. These transitions are alluded to in social formulas of greeting and leave-taking: "Well, God dild you!" "Good night, ladies, good night"; in religious formulas of grace and benediction: "God be at your table!" "God 'a' mercy on his soul! / And of all Christian souls, I pray God" (4.5.42, 73, 44, 198–199); in allusions to folk legends or tales of daughters' metamorphic changes in status: tales of the "owl [who] was a baker's daughter" (4.5.42–43), and of the "false steward that stole his master's daughter" (4.5.173).

Her songs likewise enact truncated rites of passage. Love and its loss are embodied in the song of the "true love," imagined with a cockle hat, staff, and sandals, icons of his pilgrimage. She sings of a Valentine's Day loss of virginity when a maid crosses a threshold both literal and psychological:

---

[7] Most mad characters are introduced with commentary that explicitly cues audiences to the mad state and invites sympathy. Isabella's maid tells her not to "affright" herself and says of her mistress that "these humors do torment my soul" (*Spanish Tragedy* 3.8.7, 13), and early in the first addition, Isabella comments of Hieronimo, "Ay me, he raves" (8). Similar introductions are found in the conversation between Lady Macbeth's waiting woman and the doctor (5.1.1–20) and in Edgar's commentary as he disguises himself as Poor Tom in *Lear* (2.3.1–21).

Then up he rose and donned his clothes
And dupped the chamber door,
Let in the maid, that out a maid
Never departed more.

. . . .

Young men will do't if they come to't,
By Cock, they are to blame."

(4.5.52–55, 61–62)

This deflowering (whether imagined or experienced) preempts and precludes a marriage ritual. Other songs mourn a death and represent the concrete markers of a spare funeral ritual—a flaxen poll, a bier, a stone, but no priest. This speech enables Ophelia to mourn her father's death, enact his funeral, encounter his dead body, and find consolation for her loss: "He is gone, he is gone, / And we cast away moan" (4.5.196–197). Into this central loss and its rituals, Ophelia's other losses or imagined losses—of lover, of virginity, of "fair judgement"—are absorbed. Her distribution of flowers to the court is an extension of her "quoted" discourse, an enacted ritual of dispersal, symbolizing lost love, deflowering, and death. A secularized cultural ritual of maturation and mourning is enacted through Ophelia's alienated speech.[8]

Ophelia's madness, as the play presents it, begins to be gender-specific in ways Isabella anticipates and that later stage representations of Ophelia will exaggerate by associating her with the condition of female hysterics (Showalter, "Representing"). Her agitation, verbal shifts of direction, her "winks and nods and gestures" (4.5.11) suggest the spasms of the mother and show that madness is exhibited by the body as well as in speech: gesture and speech, equally convulsive, blend together: "[she] beats her heart, / Spurns enviously at straws" (4.5.5–6). The context of her disease, like that which will (much later) be termed hysteria, is sexual frustration, social helplessness, and enforced control over women's bodies. The content of her speech reflects this context. The chastity that her brother and father commanded her to guard is characterized as lost. Laertes' anguished response to Ophelia as a "document in madness"—"Thought and affliction, passion, hell itself, / She turns to favor and to prettiness" (4.5.187–188)—shows how the reading of madness's self-representation can aestheticize the condition, ignoring its social critique and its dislocated aspects. Likewise Gertrude narrates Ophelia's

---

[8] Joan Klein reads Ophelia's madness closely and attends to its cultural lore. But whereas she sees Ophelia's role as providential, as a minister to Hamlet, in fact, Ophelia's scant religious references are split off from any theological context. Much attention has been devoted to determining who the referents of her songs are, especially the "true love," and to which characters they are addressed. But it may not be possible to identify a single referent or audience given the quoted cultural resonance of her speech. In her madness, she does enact a ritual of mourning, the work that Schiesari argues has been culturally allotted to women. See Seng 131–156 for a summary of commentary on Ophelia.

death as beautiful, natural, and eroticized. Ophelia's characterization, developing that of Isabella, represents women's madness as gender-inflected in the context of bodily illness, lost love, and family. The representation of Ophelia's madness is innovative, then, in several ways. Her speech, as her introduction by the Gentleman emphasizes, is the main symptom of her distraction—which is never associated with specific humoral disorders or supernatural afflictions. The addition of her role and language adds novelty to the source stories in which there is no precedent for Ophelia's madness (Jenkins 98). Her role likewise adds variety to a tradition of madness most often represented in grieving fathers like Hieronimo and Titus or feigning mad revengers like Antonio and Hamlet. But there is social grounding for it as well. It is noteworthy that in Napier's practice, women consulted him for all causes more often than did men (ratio of 78 men to 100 women, similar to the ratio of visits to physicians today); they consulted him more for mental disorders than men (ratio of 58.2 men to 100 women, similar to that in England today); and they reported suffering almost twice as much stress as men (ratio of 52.3 men to 100 women, MacDonald, *Mystical* 35–39).[9] Most of Napier's female and male patients alike suffered mental stress and depression from some of the same causes that drive Ophelia to break down: courtships (23.6%), marital problems (17.6%), bereavements (17.5%) (MacDonald, *Mystical* 75).[10] Although grief over bereavement, as registered in Napier's practice, rarely results in the extreme of distracted behavior enacted by Ophelia, the losses of father and lover she vividly narrates would have been shared by many in the audience.

Perhaps the most important aspect of her role is the contrast with Hamlet that it introduces. Ophelia in her mad scenes serves as a double for Hamlet during his absence from Denmark and from the play.[11] His madness is in every way contrasted with hers, in part, probably, to emphasize the differ-

[9] The reasons why women are overrepresented in Napier's practice, especially in consultations for mental distress, are as complex and difficult to analyze as why women visit doctors more than men do today and report more depression. Then as now it may result from their vulnerability to diseases of the reproductive system, which encourages more visits to doctors, the extra stress that family life in patriarchy puts on women, their gender-role socialization, or the construction of diseases (MacDonald, *Mystical* 35–40, and Tomes, "Historical" 145–146). For a discussion of the gender distribution of psychiatric illnesses in twentieth-century London, see Shepherd et al. 164–166; for American statistics, see essays cited in note 29.

[10] Analysis of the casebooks of John Hall, Shakespeare's son-in-law and a successful doctor who practiced at the same time as Napier (1600–1635) in nearby Warwickshire, shows that his patients presented similar symptoms of mental disorder in similar ratios. In his published cases (included in Harriet Joseph's book), Hall treated 70 men and 109 women: 13 of the men (or 7%) and 39 of the women (or 22%) showed signs of emotional disorder as analyzed by Howells and Osborn. These figures are based on only a small sample of Hall's cases, which were published to disseminate his recipes for purges, not to explicate his patients' symptoms. "Emotional disorder" is more broadly defined by Howells and Osborn than by MacDonald.

[11] Klein analyzes Ophelia as Hamlet's surrogate and Lyons (11–12) claims she mirrors aspects of Hamlet's melancholy. I see her rather as a "dark double," in Gilbert and Gubar's sense (360), who acts out what is repressed in Hamlet.

ence between feigned and actual madness, melancholy, and distraction. Significantly, the one time Hamlet's state is most "like madness," that is, like Ophelia's speech, is after the encounter with his father's ghost, when Hamlet must abruptly reenter the human, secular world of his friends. The "wild and whirling words" (1.5.133) that he utters to effect this transition are quoted truisms and social formulas for parting that are incoherently deployed:

> And so, without more circumstance at all,
> I hold it fit that we shake hands and part:
> You, as your business and desire shall point you,
> For every man hath business and desire
> Such as it is, and for my own poor part,
> Look you, I'll go pray.
>
> (1.5.127–132)

After this moment of dislocation Hamlet announces a plan to feign madness, "put an antic disposition on," and is able to "go in together" with his friends, reuniting with the world of human fellowship (1.5.172, 186). When he assumes his "antic disposition," as in his dialogue with Polonius, his speech, although witty, savage, and characterized by non-sequiturs and bizarre references, almost never has the "quoted," fragmentary, ritualized quality of Ophelia's. He uses proverbs and puns that not only the audience but even Polonius, who (absurdly) believes him mad for love, can understand as calculated jibes: "Let her not walk i' th' sun. Conception is a blessing, but as your daughter may conceive, friend, look to't" (2.2.184–186). We are also specifically told by Hamlet himself and by Claudius that he is not mad: "Nor what he spake, though it lacked form a little, / Was not like madness" (3.1.164–165).

The stylistic distinction between Hamlet's feigned madness and Ophelia's actual madness is emphasized by other distinctions. When he is not feigning and especially in his soliloquies, Hamlet is presented as fashionably introspective and melancholy whereas Ophelia, distract, acts out the madness he only plays with. As with Aristotelian melancholics and those in Bright's treatise, the circumstances of his father's death, his mother's remarriage, Claudius's usurpation of the throne, and his father's commandment make him feel the world empty and himself impotent—especially in his opening soliloquy: "O that this too too sullied flesh would melt, / Thaw, and resolve itself into a dew. . . . How weary, stale, flat, and unprofitable / Seem to me all the uses of this world!" (1.2.129–134). He also wonders, conventionally, if perhaps "Out of my weakness and my melancholy, / As he [the devil] is very potent with such spirits, / Abuses me to damn me" (2.2.608–610) and uses this as a reason (or perhaps rationalization) for mistrusting the ghost. His feigning, which most often takes the form of satiric attack, is viewed as politically dangerous (which it is). Ophelia must be watched, contained within the family, within the castle; Hamlet must be expelled to England to be murdered. By acting out the madness Hamlet feigns and the suicide that he theorizes, the representation of Ophelia absorbs pathological excesses that threaten Hamlet but never overwhelm him, and enables his reappearance as a more sensible and self-assured hero. Ophelia's madness emerges just when Hamlet departs for England (and, in Quarto 1, just after his most vigorous commitment to revenge: "O, from this time forth, / My thoughts be bloody, or be nothing worth!" 4.4.65–66). His restored identity is validated—symbolically as well as literally—over Ophelia's grave: "This is I, / Hamlet the Dane" (5.1.257–258). In the last act he is increasingly detached from family and sexuality and apparently freed from melancholy and passivity. Hence he grows capable of philosophical detachment and, finally, revenge, proving himself worthy of a spiritual epitaph and a soldier's funeral.

This contrast between Ophelia's mad suicide and Hamlet's contemplated one represents in drama another subtle distinction that turned on being able to diagnose madness. This is the distinction between calculated suicide, a religious sin and a civil crime (*felo-de-se*), and insane self-destruction (*non compos mentis*). If the act was judged self-murder, the deceased's property was seized by the state and Christian burial was not encouraged. Madness, however, rendered suicide innocent and permitted conventional inheritance and Christian burial. The secularization of suicide and that of madness reinforced each other.[12] The play enacts these distinctions complexly and does not clearly choose sides about when suicide is forgivable. Whereas Hamlet's calm contemplation of suicide would render the act on his part a crime and a sin (as he recognizes with his reference to the "canon 'gainst self-slaughter" 1.2.132), Ophelia's suicide is depicted by Gertrude as accidental ("an envious sliver broke" 4.7.173). She is "as one incapable of her own distress" (4.7.178): hence the act can be construed as involuntary, an effect of madness. In England during this period, drowning was the most common type of female suicide and, since it was also a common accident, was the cause of death that made distinctions between accident and volition most difficult (MacDonald, "Ophelia's" 311, and "Inner" 566–567).

The play keeps both explanations in suspension, in effect requiring spectators to decide how the death should be judged. Gertrude's representation of Ophelia's death neither condemns it on religious grounds nor explicitly condones it on medical/legal grounds. Instead she narrates it without interpretation, as a beautiful, "natural," ritual of passage and purification, the mad body's inevitable return to nature:

---

12 Some form of Christian burial might be possible, even in cases of suicide, as we see in the play. See MacDonald, "Ophelia's" 314–315. For discussions of suicide, and mental disorder, see MacDonald, *Mystical* 132–138; "Inner" 566–567; "Secularization" 52–70; and *Sleepless*.

> Her clothes spread wide,
> And mermaidlike awhile they bore her up,
> Which time she chanted snatches of old lauds,
> As one incapable of her own distress,
> Or like a creature native and indued
> Unto that element.
>
> (4.7.175–180)[13]

Later the issue of Ophelia's death is reopened when the lower-status grave-digger and priest skeptically challenge the "crowner's" warrant and suggest that only aristocratic prerogative permits Ophelia the Christian burial usually denied suicides since "she drowned herself wittingly" (5.1.12–13). The introduction of the role of Ophelia and the language that represents her madness invites the audience to examine the differences between female distraction and male melancholy, madness and feigned madness, and voluntary and involuntary suicide.

Witchcraft, Guilt, and Sleepwalking: *Macbeth*

Macbeth was likely first performed in 1606, some five years after the first performances of *Hamlet*. Through the representation of Lady Macbeth's somnambulism and the presence of witches, the play introduces a new kind of female distraction and a new context for reading it. The division between Lady Macbeth's powerful will in the early acts of the play and her alienated loss of it in the sleepwalking scenes, her connections with and dissociation from the witches, and their bifurcated representation all construct—and blur—another set of distinctions turning, in part, on reading madness: those between supernatural and natural agency, diabolic and human malevolence.

In *Macbeth*, Lady Macbeth's suicide is introduced only speculatively, after the fact, when Malcolm's final speech wraps up her story as one who: "as 'tis thought, by self and violent hands took off her life" (5.8.70–71), and raises none of the questions Ophelia's does. But it occurs following a diagnosed state of alienation represented through quoted discourse with similarities to Ophelia's. The alienation of Lady Macbeth in sleepwalking is, like Ophelia's, represented by means of quoted speech, read by representatives of the community, and associated with symbolic purification, and culminates in suicide. Her breakdown is feminized and guilt-ridden in contrast with Macbeth's excessive, enraged, bloody ambition ("Some say he's mad" 5.2.13).

Lady Macbeth's sleepwalking, like Ophelia's madness, occurs after an absence from the stage. It is presented as a sharp break with earlier appearances

---

[13] Immersion is conventionally both a sign of madness and a cure for it. See Foucault, *Madness* 166–172, and Clarke, 229–230.

in which she has mostly been in control of herself and events, and is introduced by an onstage observer. When sleepwalking, Lady Macbeth quotes
proverbial commonplaces ("Hell is murky" 5.1.38) and chilling pseudo-
nursery rhymes ("The Thane of Fife had a wife. Where is she now?" 5.1.44–
45), as well her own earlier words (or perhaps thoughts) and Macbeth's. She
refers to Duncan's murder, Banquo's ghost, and the death of Lady Macduff
all in the mode of advice and comfort to Macbeth ("No more o' that, my
lord, no more o' that!" 5.1.46). She narrates Macbeth's bloody acts, talks directly to him although he is not present, and acts out her own complicity in
her ritual of "washing" her hands to remove the smell and sight of the blood
that taints them. This "quotation" has the effect of distancing this alienated
discourse from its speaker and inviting a reading. But it is less communal and
thematic, more personal and psychological than Ophelia's. The doctor explicitly reads Lady Macbeth's state as religious despair that is the result of
guilt—in Bright's terms, caused by a sense of sin rather than natural melancholy: "More needs she the divine than the physician" (5.1.77). But in Bright,
as in Burton, perturbations in one part flow elsewhere. Burton attributes
night-walking to the diseased imagination, but he traces all the ways in which
the imagination, the body, the mind, and the soul can infect one another: "A
most frequent and ordinary cause of Melancholy . . . , this thunder and light-
ning of perturbation [of mind], which causeth such violent and speedy alterations in this our Microcosme, and many times subverts the good estate
and temperature of it. For as the Body works upon the minde, by his bad humours, troubling the Spirits, sending grosse fumes into the Braine; and so *per
consequens* disturbing the Soule, and all the faculties of it, . . . with feare,
sorrow, &c. which are ordinary symptoms of this Disease: so on the other
side, the minde most effectually workes upon the Body, producing by his passions and perturbations, miraculous alterations; as Melancholy, despaire,
cruell diseases, and sometimes death it selfe" (Burton 1.2.2.7; 1:246–247,
and see 247–250). Hence the doctor's confident distinction between diseases
requiring divines and those requiring doctors may be too simple.

The parallels and contrasts between the witches and Lady Macbeth that
the play sets out require audiences to interrogate the sources of the malevolence let loose in the play. She and the witches are indirectly identified with
each other by their departures from prescribed female subordination, by
their parallel role as catalysts to Macbeth's actions, and by the structure and
symbolism of the play (Stallybrass 189–209). They function as cultural
scapegoats for the unnaturalness, disorder, and violence that unfold. But the
play also contrasts Lady Macbeth and the witches in ways that sharpen disjunctions between the natural and the supernatural. The witches' supernatural ambiguity is contrasted with the "natural" ambiguity of Lady Macbeth's
sleepwalking scene. In their early appearances, they are described as ambiguously male or female, as on the earth but not of it; they speak equivo-
cally (but not madly). Lady Macbeth, when sleepwalking, is in a state that

combines "the benefit of sleep" with "the effects of watching!" (5.1.11–12); "Her eyes are open . . . but their sense are shut" (5.1.26–27). The witches are dramatized in connection with some of the conventional accouterments of witchcraft belief: familiars, submission to Hecate, spells, potions, fortune-telling, and successful conjuring. But Lady Macbeth's attempted (and un-successful) invocation is to spirits that seem more natural than supernatural: they "tend on mortal thoughts" and "wait on nature's mischief" (1.5.41, 50). She does not ask directly for help to harm others as witches typically do, but only for a perversion of her own emotions and bodily functions: "fill me, from the crown to the toe, top-full / Of direst cruelty! Make thick my blood" (1.5.42–43). In contrast, the witches plot to cause the kinds of harm to others conventionally associated with witches' *maleficium*: interference with livestock, weather, male sexuality.

The witches are then ambiguously associated with and dissociated from Lady Macbeth.[14] Their own representation is likewise bifurcated. They themselves seem ambiguously "natural" and supernatural. They are repre-sented partly as the disgruntled outcasts of Scot's *Discoverie*, partly as the agents of harmful activities like those charged in English witch-trials, and partly as devil-possessed like the witches described by continental witch-mongers in Sprenger and Kramer's *Malleus Maleficarum*. In the opening scenes, they seem to invite Scot's psychological interpretation (statistically supported by Alan Macfarlane's social, structural analysis); they are frus-trated, melancholic women who, on the margins of society, get back at those who have disregarded them by muttering curses and plotting revenges—"I'll do, I'll do, and I'll do" (1.3.10)—and hence attract blame and punishment. However, they do have familiars and seem capable of preternatural travels, so are not represented merely as social misfits. In their later appearances (3.5 and 4.1), although their agency is diminished, the witches are endowed with all the theatrical paraphernalia of demonic possession from continental witchlore. They serve Hecate (in what may be a later addition, perhaps to enhance a popular feature of the play), use illusion to influence Macbeth, and mix a "charm" made from the noxious parts of animals (and humans).[15]

[14] The dramatized relationship between the witches and Lady Macbeth is more ambiguous and unstable than that proposed by Janet Adelman (*Suffocating* 130–147). Their relationship is not a literal or symbolic "alliance" (134, 136), and neither the witches nor Lady Macbeth are unstintingly malevolent and powerful. In fact the witches wish Macbeth to fail while Lady Mac-beth wishes him to succeed, and their relation to the supernatural is represented while hers is only sought. Furthermore, both the witches and Lady Macbeth lose what power they have by the end of the play, though Adelman never discusses the implications of Lady Macbeth's som-nambulism and suicide. Whatever power each has exists only contingently through Macbeth.

[15] Thomas (chap. 14) discusses how continental views of witchcraft, conceived as a heresy marked especially by a pact with the devil, were only gradually filtered into England, where witchcraft was more often defined as harmful activities. The fact that the witches are also called "weïrd women" (3.1.2) and compared with "elves and fairies" (4.1.42) emphasizes their shift-ing (and shifty) representations. If Hecate and the songs from Middleton's *Witch* were later in-terpolations at odds with the earlier portrayal, this supports my claim that the representations

Macbeth "conjures" them by their "profess[ed]" supernatural powers (4.1. 50–61).

The effect of these representations of an alienated Lady Macbeth and divided witches, ambiguously connected with each other, is to create a continuum of malevolence in the play that blurs the boundaries between natural and supernatural agency, between witchcraft of English or continental sorts, between guilt and illness. This continuum has made it tempting to put to the play the questions the period (through witchcraft prosecutions and through reading madness) was wrestling with—who is to blame for Duncan's murder, Macbeth's fall, Scotland's decline? Who or what is the source of harm and evil? The questions produce no simple answers. The continuum of malevolence blurs the question of agency in the play as it blurs the question of the ontological status of "witches." It reproduces the period's "hovering" between contradictory belief systems and conflicting attributions of causality and agency: melancholy or the devil, madwomen or witches, castrating wives or ambitious tyrants.

Distraction, Possession, and Healing: *King Lear*

King Lear, which was likely first staged in 1605, a bit earlier than *Macbeth,* represents another contrasting pair of distracted characters in Lear and Edgar. But in this play supernatural explanations are completely abandoned since Lear suffers from natural madness and the supernatural possession that Edgar assumes in his role of Poor Tom is explicitly feigned. The play further represents, as the other two tragedies do not, two remedies for distraction— one physiological, administered by a doctor, and one psychological, administered by a layperson, which is a secular appropriation of exorcism ritual, used to cast out despair, but drained of supernatural connections. Hence *King Lear* extends conventions for representing and assessing distraction and so contributes further to the secularization, psychologizing, and medicalization of madness and its remedies.

Edgar's feigned possession, like Ophelia's madness and Lady Macbeth's sleepwalking, is carefully introduced, represented through dislocated quotation, and it has psychological, thematic, and cultural resonance. Edgar, victimized by his bastard brother, Edmund, assumes the speech of Poor Tom the Bedlam beggar and feigns demonic possession as a role—as a disguise.[16] In

---

of witches shape contested notions of them in the period. For arguments that 3.5 and 4.1.39– 43 and 125–132 are interpolations, see Muir, *Macbeth* xxxii–xxxv. That the witches are more powerful when presented more naturalistically early in the play may be connected to the weakening of beliefs in witchcraft in England in the beginning of the seventeenth century.

[16] Edgar's use of madness as disguise is a striking new variation on the motif seen in *Antonio's Revenge* and *Hamlet* and associates him with the trickster Diccon the Bedlam and, like him, with feigning lower-class con men who pretended to have been in Bedlam.

his explicit assumption of the role, he imbues the beggars he imitates with the stereotypical marks of possession: strange voices, numbness, and curses:

> The country gives me proof and precedent
> Of Bedlam beggars, who, with roaring voices,
> Strike in their numbed and mortified bare arms
> Pins, wooden pricks, nails, sprigs of rosemary;
> And with this horrible object from low farms.
>
> . . . .
>
> Sometimes with lunatic bans, sometime with prayers,
> Enforce their charity.
>
> (2.3.13–20)[17]

Tom's mad speech is a pastiche of quoted fragments, but his discourse incorporates differently inflected cultural voices from those uttered by Ophelia or Lady Macbeth. His speech embeds song fragments—"Through the sharp hawthorn blows the cold wind"—bits of romance—"But mice and rats, and such small deer, / Have been Tom's food for seven long year"—formulaic commandments and proverbial sayings—"obey thy parents; keep thy word's justice," "Keep thy foot out of brothels, thy hand out of plackets"— and even perhaps an indirect citation of Hieronimo in *The Spanish Tragedy* relayed through the Induction of *The Taming of the Shrew*: "Go to thy cold bed, and warm thee" (3.4.45–46, 136–137, 79–80, 95–96, 46–47).

These quotations transmit through Edgar a theological discourse of sin and punishment in which Poor Tom is an emblematic fallen Christian, a "servingman, proud in heart and mind; that . . . served the lust of my mistress' heart, and did the act of darkness with her," "hog in sloth, fox in stealth, wolf in greediness, dog in madness" (3.4.84–87, 92–93). Embodying the seven deadly sins, especially those of pride and lust, he acts out guilt and the punishment of demonic possession, signified by bodily humiliation and torment by fiends named by the demonics whose cases Samuel Harsnett ridicules. He is led by the "foul fiend" "through fire and through flame, through ford and whirlpool, o'er bog and quagmire," and "eats the swimming frog, the toad, the todpole, the wall-newt and the water" (3.4.51–52, 127–128). He also suffers torments from fiends within: "The foul fiend bites my back" (3.6.17), "Hoppedance cries in Tom's belly for two white herring" (3.6.30–31), and the devil-instigated temptation of suicide.

Quotation is, in effect, tripled in Tom's mimicry of possession. Disinherited Edgar speaks in the voice of Poor Tom, the Bedlam beggar, who is possessed by devils who are quotations from Harsnett's melodramatic exposure

---

[17] MacDonald (*Witchcraft* xxxv) summarizes the standard signs of diabolical possession: "They included extraordinary strength, convulsions and violent motions, knowledge of facts and languages the victim could not naturally have learned, speaking in strange voices, vomiting foreign objects such as nails or pins, insensitivity to pain and revulsion at sacred things."

of the drama of bewitchment and exorcism.[18] Hence Edgar's quoted religious discourse of possession, sin, and punishment is italicized, rendered doubly theatrical: both because the discourse is feigned and because it is constructed through quotation of Harsnett, who himself narrates possession as theatrical role-playing instigated by the suggestion and rehearsal of the exorcists. Because a "documented fraud" (Greenblatt 175) is appropriated for Poor Tom, the spuriousness of Edgar's madness is emphasized, possession and divine retribution are mocked through mimicry, and the church's attempt to outlaw exorcism is furthered. At the same time the surviving belief in possession, perhaps especially prevalent among middle and lower ranks, is represented on stage. While Greenblatt (119) sees spiritual rituals as *"emptied out"* in *King Lear,* in fact, through this invented mad discourse, sacred meaning is resituated: grief, guilt, anger, and punishment are understood within human psychological parameters, and supernatural rituals are adapted for therapeutic purposes.

Supernatural explanations are discredited but replaced by natural ones, for the mad discourse functions variously. It provides continuity with Edgar's earlier parts by permitting him, as Tom, both to conceal and to express his sense of victimization by and anger at Edmund as well as his suppressed desire for self-punishment and revenge.[19] The disguise and speech function thematically by allowing the disinherited Edgar to identify with the middling or lower sorts and, by taking on their speech and experiences, to participate with the Fool and naked Lear in the reversals of class and status that pervade the play. He registers harassment not only by demons but also by men: Poor Tom is "whipped from tithing to tithing, and stocked, punished, and imprisoned" (3.4.132–133). His role also functions dramatically to trigger, mark, and counterpoint the specific moment of Lear's own break with sanity, which occurs decisively at his emotionally apt but logically groundless identification with Poor Tom at 3.4.62: "What, has his daughters brought him to this pass?"[20] Like Diccon, but for very different reasons, Edgar as Poor Tom has notable effects on those he comes in contact with, eliciting pity from Kent, identification from Gloucester, camaraderie from the Fool.

Most notably, Edgar as Poor Tom twice adapts the ritual of exorcism

[18] See Greenblatt, and Muir, "Samuel," who finds over fifty separate fragments from Harsnett's *Declaration* embedded in the play, the largest number of them connected with the role of Poor Tom.

[19] Adelman (*Twentieth* 8–21) has a fine discussion of how the role of Poor Tom turns blame inward and preserves Edgar. In contrast, Carroll (*Fat King* 436) argues that the disguise is a source of pain and suffering for Edgar as well as a release from them.

[20] Lillian Feder (132) and Paul Jorgensen (80) concur. Lear's breakdown via his identification with Edgar is emphasized by his four times repeated claim that Tom's daughters are to blame for his state: "Didst thou give all to thy daughters?" "What, has his daughters brought him to this pass?" "Now . . . plagues . . . light on thy daughters!" "Nothing could have subdued nature / To such a lowness but his unkind daughters" (3.4.48, 62, 66–67, 69–70). Theatrically, this iteration of loss and projection of it onto Poor Tom marks Lear's crossing of the boundary into madness.

(whereby possessing demons are miraculously driven out as in figs. 3 and 4) to comfort Lear and Gloucester. This ritual is ingeniously combined with a traditionally recommended medical remedy for delusion, a strategy that Burton and others record and which Foucault calls "continuing the delirious discourse" (*Madness* 154). The delusions of the mad are complied with and extended through theatrical representation in order to undo them. Doctors and friends fraudulently extend the delusions of the mad to manipulate them toward a cure, a motif that will be revisited in chapter 3. The most frequently cited exemplar of this is a story of a melancholic man who, believing himself dead, refused to eat. Friends costumed themselves as dead men and consumed a banquet in front of him to demonstrate that the dead eat; he then ate too and recovered. A more bizarre example is that of a man who refused to urinate, believing that if he did, he would drown the world; friends set fire to the house next door and prevailed on him to put it out lest the town burn. He "pissed, emptied his bladder of all that was in it, and was himselfe by that means preserved" (Du Laurens 103).[21] When Lear, following the mock trial (in Quarto 1), imagines himself barked at by dogs, Edgar pretends to drive them away by means of a song in which he impersonates a dog, shaking his head as if to attack them: "Tom will make him weep and wail; / For, with throwing thus my head, / Dogs leaped the hatch, and all are fled" (3.6.70–72). Later he more elaborately "trifle[s]" with his father's "despair" to "cure" it, engineering Gloucester's mock suicide and the mock exorcism of his demons to save his father from actual suicide. In his elaborately staged scenario, he also exorcises his own demon-riven persona. After telling Gloucester that he has been preserved miraculously by the gods in his fall, he denounces and casts off the figure he was: "As I stood here below, methought his eyes / Were two full moons; he had a thousand noses, / . . . . It was some fiend" (4.6.69–72). In these feigned performances of exorcism, the rituals of the supernatural are appropriated and secularized, and used by humans to reverse human fear and sorrow. In this way, while discrediting possession, they gain new uses and new power.[22]

In stark contrast to Edgar's feigned delirium of sin, guilt, and divine punishment, Lear's madness is staged as entirely bodily and "natural," though, like Edgar's, added to the source story, as Ken Jackson's essay on the play remarks (225). Lear's condition is rooted in obvious physical and psychological causes: his exposure to the cold and storm in old age, his mistaken banishment of Cordelia, his other daughters' betrayals, and, climactically,

---

[21] Clarke (222–223, 226) discusses such ingenious cures, dubbing them "part of the folklore tradition of the profession" (222). As we have seen in my introduction, Bright, Burton, and Descartes make use of these cases, as does Jorden. The next chapter will explore additional appropriations of them.

[22] Winfried Schleiner discusses revisions of these cases including Luther's (66–68) and emphasizes the kind intentions and effects of Edgar's therapy for Gloucester in the context of the tradition of such cures (274–286).

his encounter with Poor Tom. His alienation is rendered on a continuum with his normalcy, from which it gradually emerges. He is metaphorically described by Kent as "mad" in the first scene, and Lear marks the developing signs of breakdown in his mind, senses, and heart. He asks if "his notion weakens, or his discernings / Are lethargied"; he begs, "Keep me in temper; I would not be mad!"; he cries "O, how this mother swells up toward my heart!" He tries to contain rupture: "*Hysterica passio,* down, thou climbing sorrow," but refuses the outlet of weeping: "but this heart / Shall break into a hundred thousand flaws / Or ere I'll weep" (1.4.229–230; 1.5.46; 2.4.56; 2.4.282–283). As Lear loses his kingdom, his soldiers, his children, his house, his robes, he gradually loses control, describing how this feels by attributing it to the multiple sites that could, by interacting with one another, cause madness. But once he is beside himself and seeks out Poor Tom as his philosopher (3.4.152), his madness grows self-authorizing, aggressive, and satiric and he remains obsessed with wrongs done him.[23] He is subsequently restored to sanity by conventional remedies, conventionally applied by a doctor—herbal medicine, sleep, clean garments, and music. (At least in Quarto 1, the man to whom Cordelia turns for remedies in 4.4, who suggests "simples operative," and who takes charge of Lear in 5.1 is always identified as "Doctor" in his speech prefixes and entrances; in Folio the character is always called "Gentleman.")

The construction of Lear's mad discourse, like that of Ophelia and Poor Tom, involves fragmentation, formula, depersonalization, the intersection by communal voices, and secularized ritual. Like Ophelia, he uses tags of social formulas incongruously—"We'll go to supper i' th' morning," "Give the word," "Pull off my boots: harder, harder: so" (3.6.83; 4.6.92, 173)—to reestablish his shattered world. But more often, rather than being transected by quoted voices, Lear envisages hallucinatory cultural dramas in which he is both narrator and participant. Whereas Poor Tom acts out victimization and guilt by presenting himself as poor and persecuted, Lear defends himself against guilt by acting as persecutor: "cry / These dreadful summoners grace" (3.2.58–59). Whereas Hieronimo looks to hell or heaven for justice or revenge, mad Lear seeks justice on earth but finds it corrupted. His hallucinations of the rituals of secular trial and judgment mount a searing social critique, exposing the fraudulence of secular justice just as Edgar's feigned possession implicitly exposes demonic punishment as fraud. In the

---

[23] Coppelia Kahn argues that Lear's madness results from his rage at maternal deprivation and his suppression of the "mother," his maternal side, and that through madness he comes to accept his own vulnerability. Adelman (*Suffocating* 112–114) extends Kahn's argument by analyzing the suffocating maternal sexual monstrousness of the storm that engulfs him. But Lear's madness is not feminizing. His identification with the storm and subsequent break with normal speech forestall tears and powerlessness and restore his authority through expressions of rage and fantasies of judgment. His new acceptance of vulnerability after recovering is likewise deeply compromised, as Adelman (121–125) shows, by his unchanged need to love Cordelia "all" without consideration of her needs.

enacted mock trial on the heath (in Quarto), Lear plays the judge who "arraigns" (3.6.20) his absent daughters, Goneril and Regan, for their crimes against him while Edgar, Kent, and the Fool serve as jury. But the ritual trial, like rituals in Ophelia's songs, is aborted, and the judge, humiliated, is barked at by dogs (3.6.61–62).[24]

During Lear's encounter with Gloucester on the heath, his identification with the persecutor and his demonizing of women's sexuality continue to protect him from a sustained realization that he is not "ague-proof" (4.6.105).[25] He fantasizes scenarios of justice undone by the corruption of women's "riotous appetite" (123) and the complicity of the judge. In his first fantasy, Lear, as judge, will "pardon that man's life" because all are guilty of copulation centered in the "sulphurous pit" of female sexuality, the domain to which the fiend is metaphorically confined in Lear's discourse (4.6.109–129). Whereas Edgar's feigned supernatural madness locates lust in himself, Lear's natural madness displaces it onto women and their judges. In Lear's second fantasy, following a series of reversals, the punisher and the punished become indistinguishable: the constable who whips the whore "hotly lusts to use her in that kind / For which thou whip'st her" (4.6.162–163). These fantasies expose Lear's habit of persecuting others to conceal his own guilt and also provide a critique of a class-determined system of justice. Social status and the costumes that the period prescribed to mark it control guilt, judgment, and punishment: "Through tattered clothes small vices do appear; / Robes and furred gowns hide all. Plate sin with gold, / And the strong lance of justice hurtless breaks; / Arm it in rags, a pygmy's straw does pierce it" (4.6.164–167). Justice, like demonic possession, is theatrical, a matter of costumes, and hence fraudulent. But, in Lear's fantasies, it is not sought futilely from heaven or hell but only on earth.[26]

---

[24] Although there are numerous much-analyzed differences between the Quarto and Folio text of *King Lear,* likely due to the kind of revisions represented by the additions of *The Spanish Tragedy,* the only major difference that bears on Lear's madness or Edgar's role as Poor Tom is the presence of the mock trial of Goneril and Regan in Quarto 1 (3.6.17–55 in Signet), but not in Folio. There is also a (perhaps compensatory) extension of Lear's hallucinations of justice undone in act 4, scene 6 of Folio that is lacking in Quarto (lines 165–170 in Signet). Jackson ("I Know Not") reads the scene as a contrast to the scene of comic Bedlamites in Dekker's *Honest Whore I* and part of a larger aim in Quarto to distinguish Lear's authentic madness from the feigned madness and inappropriate theatricality of Bedlam beggars and residents, eliciting pity to take sides in current debates about appropriate means of charity. "Doctor" in Quarto 1 seems more likely to be a revision of the bland "Gentleman" in Folio than vice versa—which tells against the usual assumption that Folio is a revision of Quarto. If Quarto is a later revision, it might suggest that doctors are increasingly viewed as appropriate authorities to provide remedies for mental disorder—or, if earlier, it might support Ken Jackson's thesis of connections to early seventeenth-century debates on poverty.

[25] A long and influential tradition of *King Lear* criticism, represented by, for example, Heilman (chap. 6), Jorgensen (78–82), and Mack (*King*), interprets Lear's madness as a means to illumination and self-knowledge. But the dislocation of the state and the way it extends Lear's need for command, judgment, and sympathy qualify any such knowledge. During the meeting with Gloucester, however, Lear does express, briefly, a sense of vulnerability and fault.

[26] Several influential analyses of *King Lear* oddly pass over Lear's madness without notice, even when it seems germane to their arguments. Stanley Cavell's influential essay "The Avoid-

In this way, the impertinent madness of Lear (like that of Edgar and Ophelia, and, earlier, Hieronimo) serves to provide moments of social critique somewhat detached from the characters, including the satiric "disenchantment" of conservative values and hierarchies that Robert Weimann analyzes. Lear hallucinates the corruption of justice, and Edgar as Poor Tom exposes the harassment of the poor and claims: "The Prince of Darkness is a gentleman" (3.4.141). Ophelia's madness functions similarly to disenchant domestic values: she "marks" the falsehood of love, the emptiness of religious formula, the betrayal of men. Ophelia, like Lear and Hamlet, speaks impertinently, proverbially, bawdily, disturbingly. She too is both actor and character, partly an object of the audience's gaze, partly a spokesperson for their contempt for Claudius and his court.[27] Ophelia, as much as (or perhaps even more than) Lear, "disrupts the authority of order, degree, and decorum" (Weimann, "Bifold" 417). But neither madness nor the critique it enables is seen as dangerous. Although Hamlet and Lear do have a "plot of death" contrived against them (*King Lear* 3.6.88), this is not specifically because they are mad but because of the threat they pose as past or potential kings and inspirers of rebellion.[28]

Playwrights and Madness

Shakespeare, drawn to madness perhaps because of its proven popularity, invented for it a new italicized language and reiterated and developed its representations through three tragedies in the first six years of the seven-

ance of Love" bypasses the long period when Lear is, as he puts it, "stranded in madness" (77). Stephen Greenblatt's important historicist chapter "King Lear and the Exorcists" cannily reinterprets Edgar's feigned madness but occludes Lear's actual madness (94–128). Jonathan Dollimore, in *Radical Tragedy,* implicitly denies radical theatrical or social implications to Lear's madness by dismissing it as "demented mumbling interspersed with brief insight" (193).

[27] Weimann (*Shakespeare* 120–135, 215–220) uses the range and scope of Hamlet's and Lear's mad speech to exemplify the flexible alternation possible in Renaissance popular theater between the dialogue of naturalistic character staged from the illusionistic *locus* position and the nonrealistic monologue staged from the nonillusionistic *platea* position, which draws on popular tradition, induces audience identification, and permits social critique. This flexibility also reveals "the twofold function of *mimesis* ('enchantment' and 'disenchantment'), which we have seen to be so fundamental a part of popular drama" (132). In "Bifold," Weimann again uses the "impertinent" language of Hamlet and Lear to define the "bifold authority" generated by the Elizabethan theater (410, 416), but never notices that Ophelia serves the same function. Weimann's analysis uncovers the blend of individualized psychology, italicized cultural critique, and connections to the spectators that characterize mad speech.

[28] Duncan Salkeld in *Madness and Drama in the Age of Shakespeare* and Karin S. Coddin in her essays on *Hamlet* and *Macbeth* claim that madness functions in these tragedies as a rupture in subjectivity that threatens power and reveals contradictions in ideology. Coddin identifies it as "the faltering of ideological prescriptions designed to define, order, and constrain subjectivity" ("'Suche Strange Desygns'" 61) and Salkeld as, in Shakespeare's tragedies, the undoing of reason and power. These readings broadly characterize any sort of rupture as madness and collapse madness into a deconstruction of representation, subjectivity, and ideology. They link disordered subjectivity with treason without examining closely either the broad historical contexts or the individual tenor of its several dramatic enactments.

teenth century. Through variety and contrast, the theater established distinctions that helped redefine the human as a secular subject, cut off from the supernatural and incomprehensibly unstable and permeable, containing in itself a volatile mix of body, mind, emotions, and soul, of warring and turbulent elements: "For seeing we are not maisters of our owne affections, wee are like battered Citties without walles, or shippes tossed in the Sea, exposed to all manner of assaults and daungers, even to the overthrow of our owne bodies" (Jorden G3v). C. L. Barber has suggested that the Elizabethan theater is a place apart, a space where the sacred is reconstituted in the human (*Whole* 20ff.). In the discourse of madness, this reconstitution is especially visible. The characters' madness does not make them nonhuman or inhuman, but, however disruptive, might be said to represent them as excessively human. It enlarges their expressiveness and emotional range, allowing for intense articulations of rage, betrayal, guilt, and, above all, loss—of the sort summed up in Lear's poignant response to his first glimpse of naked, cold Edgar: "Didst thou give all to thy daughters? And art thou come to this?" (3.4.48–49). It allows for psychological development (most clearly in the extended portrayals of Lear and Edgar) and abrupt breaks in continuity (as in the roles of Ophelia and Lady Macbeth). It gives to the theater the opportunity to perform resonant and theatrical rituals such as Ophelia's flower distribution, Lear's mock trial, and Edgar's mock exorcism as well as to include italicized social critique and still evade censorship. These and later dramatic representations of human madness begin to circulate especially gender-marked maladies before these markings are visible in other documents.[29] Gender distinctions may develop earlier in the theater than in the visual arts or in Napier's practice because of the need for variations on the popular motif or because the stage's reliance on adult actors to play men and boy actors to self-consciously perform femininity may have encouraged gender stereotyping in dramatic characters. These three plays are still, in the twenty-first century, considered Shakespeare's "major" tragedies and remain among the most performed and studied of the plays of the bard and of the period. They

[29] Although more women come to Napier with symptoms of mental distress, identification of women or men with certain sorts of madness is less apparent than in the drama, and there is little difference in the percentages or even the numbers of men and women identified as suffering extreme forms of mental disturbance. Patients who report severe symptoms (designated by terms such as mad, lunatic, manic, distract, raging, furious, frantic) are rare. There are more cases for women in almost every category (because there are so many more women in the sample), but the percentages are virtually identical. For example, of the 2,039 patients, 34 of the men (or 5%) and 54 of the women (or 4%) are designated "mad"; 25 of men (3%) and 21 of the women (2%) as "lunatic." There is 1 man with "mania" and 7 men and 3 women with "frenzy" (MacDonald, *Mystical* 243–245). Likewise, recent findings by medical historians and sociologists show that while today women see doctors more for depression, anxiety, insomnia, and other imprecisely identified disorders, they do not suffer from extreme pathological states like schizophrenia more often than do men and, contrary to earlier claims, are not more likely than men to be institutionalized for mental disorders. See Tomes, "Historical" 146–147 and her numerous sources, especially Goldman and Ravid 31–55; and Belle and Goldman 21, 30.

still profoundly shape conceptions of Shakespeare, of tragedy, and of human nature.

All these circulating images open up questions about human possibility, thus participating in larger cultural changes to which we are heirs. By discrediting supernatural explanations and rituals, these plays bring madness into the realm of the human. By representing diagnosis onstage, they encourage it in audiences. They also circulate attitudes toward the mad that are shared in other cultural documents. The speech and emotions of the mad are paid close attention to (Lear calls Edgar his "philosopher"). The mad are cared for with compassion and provided with remedies that, whether medical or ingenious, seek to coax them back to their "business," back into the rituals of everyday life. These attitudes are characteristic of and also help shape most early modern documents that treat distracted persons. Even where the mad or maddened are represented in comedy and romance, their recovery is sought and, as we will see, achieved by increasingly ingenious healing practices.

Although these Shakespeare plays represent madness to heal or purge it, and although the gender distinctions they initiate can still prove oppressive to women, performed madness continues not just to elicit attention and compassion but to be potentially transgressive through unsettling productions, adaptations, or indecorous interventions by actors that highlight the social critique in these three plays. Hamlet's feigned madness and Lear's natural madness can be performed and read as political criticism (for example, as in Grigori Kozintsev's 1970 film of *King Lear* or in the Studio Theater of Moscow's 1989 production of *Hamlet*). Ophelia's madness can be politicized by an actress who might represent the mad female body now as an eroticized and aestheticized object of desire and repulsion and now as an agent of uncontrollable voice, desire, pain, and rage (as in performances by Helena Bonham Carter in Zefferelli's *Hamlet,* by Kate Winslet in Kenneth Branaugh's *Hamlet,* or by Ange Magnetic's 1989 adaptation, "Ophelie Song," an "opera minimal" derived from Ophelia's songs).[30]

The complexities of reading the discourse of madness in a range of cultural documents suggest the varied ways in which dramatic texts intersect with others to imagine new structures of human subjectivity. While plays are historical documents among others, they do not exist in quite the same register with all the rest. The theater is not simply seamlessly embedded in the dominant ideology and it does not, in any straightforward way, simply reflect, contain, or subvert the cultural milieus in which it is embedded. It is in certain ways, dislocated from them, encouraging a reading. But finding the

[30] The Studio Theater of Moscow performed *Hamlet* at the University of Illinois, Urbana-Champaign, February 12, 1989. "Ophelie Song" was a co-production by Ange Magnetic and Mon Oncle d'Amerique, collaborated on by French director Antoine Campo and American choreographer Clara Gibson Maxwell, and produced in 1989 in Paris, in New York, and at the Edinburgh Fringe Festival.

right metaphor for the relationship is difficult. Perhaps, in the context of this chapter, it is appropriate to note that the playwright, like the mad, expresses inner conflicts, quotes cultural voices, speaks through disguises, enacts emotions visually and verbally, performs for diverse audiences, and is protected from harm because play texts are illusions. These play texts, moreover, like other "documents in madness," both do and do not belong to the authors who generate them. They are read, performed, and used by others as they like.

CHAPTER 3

Diagnosing Women's Melancholy

Case Histories and the Jailer's Daughter's Cure in *The Two Noble Kinsmen*

But where am I? Into what subject have I rushed? What have I to doe with
Nunnes, Maids, Virgins, Widowes?
ROBERT BURTON, *Anatomy of Melancholy*

In the last chapter we watched how the drama, by inventing a new language to represent distraction and varying its representations, sharpened the distinctions between natural and supernatural and male and female madness, and shaped cultural debates. In this chapter, we will look at how, in the same period, dynamic interactions between women sufferers and creative doctors result in the invention of a new subcategory, women's melancholy. This innovative amalgamation of the formerly distinct conditions of the suffocation of the mother, genital congestion, and melancholy newly locates the cause of women's perturbations of mind in disordered female wombs and genitals. These changes in medical theory grow out of the urgent scrutiny of women's distraction in the light of pressing needs to reassess supernaturally caused ailments as natural diseases. In time the new condition shows up on the stage.

This chapter will trace the constitution of women's melancholy in current case histories that are appended to diverse texts. To diagnose these fascinating "late" (i.e., recent) cases of distracted women, revision of the handed-down exempla of deluded melancholics is undertaken. Such revision makes possible the deft insertion of a new subdivision into traditional theories of melancholy. Visible first in medical and witchcraft treatises, the reiterated tale of delusion is eventually elaborated and circulated widely in the case history of the Jailer's Daughter in Shakespeare and Fletcher's *Two Noble Kinsmen*. In medical practice, the powerful illness narratives of women patients and the ingenuity of doctors and relatives promote changes in the theory of melancholy that, to make room for women, develop a new etiology and new therapies. The disease, a distant precursor of what would much later be called hysteria, emerges, becomes widespread, and enters the early modern equivalent of DSM, the American Psychiatric Association's *Diagnostic and Statistical Manual* when in 1628 Robert Burton appends a new subsection, "Symptomes of Maides, Nunnes, and Widowes Melancholy," to the third edition of *The Anatomy of Melancholy.*[1]

We can identify with particular clarity the "ecological niche" that becomes available and allows a newly articulated diagnosis of women's melancholy to emerge and generate theories and dramatic representations. Each of Ian Hacking's four "principal vectors" (*Mad* 81), whose intersection creates the appropriate conditions for culturing new diseases, are present in England in this period: a slot in existing medical taxonomy; cultural polarities that elicit it; observability; and the release offered to sufferers.[2] Melancholy is a capacious disease with a flexible taxonomy that, as Burton's encyclopedic and expanding work shows, can easily absorb new subdivisions. Two cultural polarities exist that encourage the formulation of women's melancholy. The first polarity is between the continuing belief in the reality of possession, exorcism, and witchcraft and the growing skepticism about these. The second is between patriarchal prescriptions that subordinate wives to husbands and denigrate or subdue their sexuality, and an emerging view of marriage as a promoter of friendship and sexual satisfaction for husband and wife. Observability of women's disorders was increasingly possible and important because as suspected witches or possessed they demanded attention, because the medical profession was gaining prestige, practitioners were increasing in numbers, women were the majority of patients, vernacular medical treatises circulated widely, and the stage spread images of women's conditions. Finally as my discussion in this chapter and the next shows, the diagnosis of women's melancholy (and also lovesickness) acknowledged and provided for satis-

---

[1] (1.3.2.4.) My book as a whole and this chapter in particular provide the contextualized, historicized examination of emergent women's melancholy that Mark Micale calls for in the first of his two important review essays and in his subsequent book, *Approaching Hysteria.* I engage with six of the ten recommendations he proposes for interpreting the disease ("Future" 41–84; *Approaching* 108–149). I look at the shifts in terminology and nosography for madness, the mother, melancholy, lovesickness, and distraction in early modern England, emphasizing their lack of "definitional clarity" (Micale, "Future Perspective" 41; *Approaching* 108). In this chapter I examine a small group of "patients" (Micale 47; 116) and emphasize how the patient/doctor relation is central to healing rituals and how patient behavior influences practice and theory (Micale 53, 70; 120, 139). Throughout, I seek the "rapprochement of internalist and externalist methodologies," the examination of medicine within wider cultural contexts (including literature) that Micale calls for (Micale 61; 129).

[2] Hacking, in *Mad Travelers* (81–87), discusses the four vectors that made possible in the late nineteenth century "hysterical fugue," a disease of working-class men who wandered far from home and suffered episodes of amnesia or dissociative fugue. It fit into existing medical taxonomy but complicated it. It existed in the cultural polarity between romantic tourism and criminal vagrancy, offering, in effect, travel for working-class men. Hence it provided them with release from the strictures of their lives. Observability was newly possible because by the end of the nineteenth century, travelers, and especially draft-age men, needed papers and were under potential surveillance as they wandered.

faction of their desire, serving as an antidote to prescriptive discourses that sought to harness it.

Early Modern Medical Practice

A brief look at the conditions of early modern medical practice manifests how it encourages patient initiative, innovative diagnoses, and revisionary interpretations of case histories—especially when the illness in question is a disorder of mind. Humoral theory survived as long as it did as an explanatory system due to its "seductive coherence" and "experiential suppleness" (Schoenfeldt 3). The body of humoral theory was transmitted from the fourth century B.C. Hippocratic treatises to Galen's works in the second century A.D., through Arabic medicine in the Middle Ages, and then into Italy during the twelfth-century medical renaissance. Subsequently it was rediscovered and widely edited and translated into Latin and then into vernacular treatises throughout Europe. Throughout its long journey, the theory underwent continual revision and grew more and more heterogeneous and contradictory.[3] In the period of this study, two influences from outside of humoralism also began to have an impact on the discourse. The first was the growing importance of dissection and the new knowledge of anatomy it produced. The second was the Paracelsian medicine that theorized external rather than internal sources of disease now localized in organs instead of generalized in humors, and cured by chemical preparations. Neither of these new developments seemed to have much immediate impact on theories or therapies for mental disturbance—since the condition was not (usually) thought visible through dissection, believed to be centered in a single organ, or transmitted from outside the body.[4] Neither one influenced the reconceptualizations of distraction that emerge within humoral theory under the pressure of medical practice and catalyze new uses of old case histories.

In the texts I examine, the human being is still conceived as a unified package of body, mind, fantasy, and soul. Emotional and mental affects are caused by and registered in the body. This body is traversed by canals (veins, arteries, spirits) which circulate the four humors (black bile or melancholy,

[3] Between 1500 and 1600, over 590 editions of Galen were published in Europe (Wear, "Medicine" 253).

[4] Paracelsian theory did lead to the development of new chemical prescriptions that were used eclectically along with older recipes—by Richard Napier and Grace Mildmay, for example. Anatomy did begin to be included in the curriculum of continental medical schools and gradually made its way to England. However, anatomies were not regularly practiced in England, even at Oxford and Cambridge, until after 1624, and their inclusion was gradual and spotty (Valadez 395–410). In my sources, these two movements are scarcely visible, perhaps because not obviously useful in understanding disorders of the mind. Following these, I deemphasize the anatomical body that Jonathan Sawday finds so important in *The Body Emblazoned* and the fragmented and deconstructed body parts that are the focus of *The Body in Parts*, edited by David Hillman and Carla Mazzio.

yellow bile or choler, phlegm, and blood) and the animal spirits through the
three unifying systems: the animal centered in the head, the natural centered
in the liver, and the vital centered in the heart.[5] Disorders of the mind, just
like other disorders, are believed to be caused by humoral imbalance and can
be cured by righting this. Madness's imprecise symptoms and terminology
make humoral theory an imprecise explanatory system for mind disorders;
hence the theory and practice of treating mental disorders may be especially
speculative and ad hoc. The route of transmission of the disordered humors
to the mind is complex and variously articulated, as are the links posited between organs, mind, and fantasy. Throughout this book, we will see many
ingenious ways to make these connections. An account by Lady Grace
Mildmay (1552–1620) provides an especially evocative description of distraction's etiological complexity. Melancholy, she says, "doth arise from the
putrifications of the stomach, liver, and matrix" and prevention must occur
there, but once it is found "working upon the spirits and senses," it varies
according to its origin:

> This melancholy . . . ariseth either first, from the predominance of that humour
> in the blood in the brains itself. Secondly, from the same in the veins sending
> vapours thither. Thirdly from the vapours arising from inflammations about
> the stomach and sides. The diaphram is called phrenitis because when it is in-
> flamed there follows a perpetual frenzy, for that part, . . . doth send up vapours
> of all kinds to the brain.
>
> The signs of the first cause here mentioned are fearfulness and strange imag-
> inations, the breathing long, pulse slow, voice base. The signs of the second is
> [*sic*] leanness of the body, blackness and roughness. . . . The signs of the third
> are rauves of the stomach, much windyness, sharp belchings, burnings, and
> pains in the sides. (121)

Mildmay further argues that melancholy is a "forerunner many times" of
frenzy and madness, distinguished because "the first is always accompanied
with a fever and the other is not" (119–120). Both frenzy and madness "pro-
ceed of the inflammation of the phlegms of the brain either by abundance of
blood, and then they will be subject to laugh and to conceive pleasant objects, or blood mixed with choler, and then they will be furious and angry.
And the more adust [burnt] the choler is, the more pernicious is the disease"

[5] Paster, "Nervous" esp. 112–113. Gail Kern Paster and Michael Schoenfeldt provide ex-
cellent analyses of the humoral body in the introductions to their books. Paster especially concerns herself with its engenderment, as do I. Schoenfeldt emphasizes how individuals, authors,
and works make use of the system's susceptibility to manipulation through the non-naturals
(diet, sleep, exercise, evacuation) to achieve self-regulation. But neither is concerned with perturbations of the mind that, while understood within the system of humoral theory, fit somewhat uneasily into it. Their emphasis on the literalness of the metaphors that describe the
materiality of the body is especially helpful, but literalism is somewhat less germane when considering explanations for perturbations of mind, even though they are always mediated through
bodily disease (see MacDonald, *Mystical* 182–183).

(119). To describe the links between humor and brain, Mildmay, like Bright, chooses metaphors of human intimacy: "If this disease sleep well and continueth ill, it is a sign the cause hath wrought a habit in the brain. The humour being gotten into the fantasy increaseth it and the fantasy working upon the humour increaseth it also, for befriending each other. Therefore at first expel the humour by violent evacuations" (119).

Grace Mildmay's account shows how inseparable are disturbances of body and mind, and how accurate diagnosis depends on patients' illness narratives. Since healers' only diagnostic methods were uroscopy and pulse-taking, patients' accounts of their own symptoms gained special consequence.[6] Since each story was different, and optimal humoral mixtures were unique to each patient, physicians were expected to provide highly individualized and creative diagnoses and therapies. Although most treatments consisted of some combination of blood-letting, purges, emetics, and cordials, both recipes and regimens varied widely and were targeted to the particular history and precise conjunction of symptoms in individual patients. Psychological healing often replaced or supplemented purgative regimens especially in the case of mind disorders.

One of the central influences on the development of humoral theory is the dynamic encounters between afflicted patients and healers that are my focus in this chapter. Interactions between theory and practice were increasingly important in medical schools.[7] Not only were licensed physicians growing more numerous, but they were supplemented in early modern England by many other unlicensed practitioners whose services were equally sought after: barber surgeons, apothecaries, midwives, cataract specialists, wise women, astrological healers, and skilled housewives like Lady Grace Mildmay. This array of practitioners created a competitive "medical market-

---

[6] Ronald Sawyer writes, "The taking of a case history formed the core of the clinical exchange. Nothing was as important in allowing a doctor to assess his patient" (247). He notes the long list of questions that typically Richard Napier asked his patients to assess their cases—about their biographical statistics, their symptoms, the periodicity of their disease, what they and relatives thought was its cause, their social and family relations, their bowel, urinary, and menstrual habits, their diet and exercise—in consultations that might last as little as fifteen minutes or as long as two hours. (See Sawyer 207–211 and MacDonald, *Mystical* 26–28 for records of a day's cases.)

[7] Andrew Wear, in "Explorations," concentrating on particular discussions of the disease of vertigo, shows how the *practica*, which served as textbooks for medical students and handbooks for physicians, were gradually transformed during the Renaissance due to physicians' experiences of particular diseases and encounters with contradictions in Galenic and Arabic medicine. Although Wear concludes, as do most of the essays in *The Medical Renaissance of the Sixteenth Century*, that Galen was a "strong conservative pull dampening innovation" (145), the article actually suggests otherwise. In his later summary article, "Medicine in Early Modern Europe, 1500–1700," he discusses many factors precipitating movement in the Galenic tradition. Jerome Bylebyl examines one source of innovative medicine in the Renaissance, namely the revised structures of the University of Padua medical school, which brought theory and practice together as professors of medicine began to lecture regularly at the bedsides of individual patients. Bylebyl argues that the return to Galen "ushered in some of the most significant innovations in Renaissance medicine, both in didactic techniques and in substantive content" (341).

place" in which patients shopped aggressively for therapies that worked and unsuccessful healers lost patients. They took active roles in their own diagnosis and therapy as did families, community, and other authorities.[8] Practitioners often shared ideas and recipes, and doctors listened to family members and sometimes used their remedies, as when John Symcotts (whose casebooks record his 1633–1660 practice) reports using a successful recipe he learned from the mother of a patient, and commends a cook-maid who staunched a child's potentially fatal nosebleed by making her sit on a cloth dipped in cold water (Lucinda Beier 102, 106). Under these conditions of practice, responsibility for healing was widely distributed, and the potential for innovative measures was great, as we will see in the Jailer's Daughter's treatment.

Lady Grace Mildmay's medical extracts, selected and analyzed by Linda Pollock, exemplify the period's wide dispersal of medical knowledge, its range of viable healers, the commonplace sharing of knowledge, and the etiology of mental disorder we have already seen.[9] In particular, her regimens for two cases of female madness beautifully exemplify the individualized remedies prescribed to heal women's reproductive bodies according to their ages and conditions. Her "practices of physic" show the precision of her regimens, their material specificity, and their careful calibration. They make clear that physical remedies are routinely prescribed for mind diseases, although we cannot view these on stage. They may also let us remember that we continue to diagnose disturbances of mind with imprecise and shifting terminology—schizophrenia, manic depression, bipolar, psychotic—and treat them with varying remedies such as insulin-coma therapy, electroshock therapy, psychoanalysis, strait-jacketing—and an array of drugs (Thorazine, Stelazine, lithium, Tegretol, Trilafon, Mellaril, Haldol, risperidone) that are

---

[8] Margaret Pelling and Charles Webster's discussion of medical practitioners, Ronald Sawyer's "Patients, Healers, and Disease," a nuanced study of the "patient shuffle" practiced by Napier's clients, and Lucinda Beier's *Sufferers and Healers* all show how patients sought therapy from widely varied healers on the "medical marketplace," as Beier titles a chapter, and made little distinction between "elite" and "popular" medicine or between licensed and unlicensed practitioners. These works and Roy Porter's edited collection *Patients and Practitioners* focus on the crucial role of the sufferer in constructing an illness attribution with family and friends, actively seeking cures from multiple practitioners, negotiating therapeutic encounters, and determining when healing has been accomplished. Arthur Kleinman's *Patients and Healers in the Context of Culture* usefully combines ethnography, clinical observations, and cross-cultural studies to create a model of culturally negotiated healing practices in which patients play an aggressive part.

[9] The published selections in Pollock represent just 40 percent of Mildmay's extant manuscript collection, which includes only that fraction of Mildmay's papers organized after her death by her daughter from what "was scatteringly and confusedly left to me in divers books and more than 2,000 loose papers" (110). The "divers books" include 1) "the structure of man's body"; 2) "the virtue of simples and drugs"; 3) "of the preparation of medicines"; and 4) diagnostics: "the conjectural signs of divers diseases with many experienced practices of physic for the same" (110).

no less brutal to the patient and rarely more successful than early modern therapies, as Jay Neugeboren's discussion of his brother's illness painfully demonstrates (4, 19).

Mildmay's two courses of medicine for madness include carefully sequenced doses of purges, emetics, and tranquilizing juleps in consort with elaborately sequenced top to bottom bloodletting through wide orifices. This begins with the head and proceeds downward to arm, then to womb or fundament (where leeches are to be used), and then to the soles of feet. The humors, first thinned by purges, then subdued by cordials, are gradually drawn down away from the head and out of the body. Two women patients, one "in years" and one "a maid," have different "courses" prescribed. The older woman is first purged for three days, then "let blood in the head vein about 3 ounces; not too much blood because she was in years." Afterwards she is to be given digestive cordials to settle vapors until "4 days before the full of the moon." At this time three more days of purging follow until, "the next day after the full, let her bleed in the arm in the liver vein about 6 ounces." Subsequently, a settling cordial is to be given until four days before the full of the next moon, when three more days of purging are followed by bleeding "in the spleen or matrix vein about 9 ounces." Then more cordial is to be administered (119).

Another "approved course" is used "upon a maid that was so outrageous for a quarter of a year, that her friends were making means to send her to Bedlam and she was something melancholy given 2 or 3 years before" (120). The young woman's condition is clearly associated with menstrual disorders for "she was exceeding costive and had other unnatural stoppings in her body" (119). The harsh treatment prescribed is obviously designed to open up all parts of her body. First she is treated for five days with suppositories with "trochisk alhandle" (laxative tablet) and additional strong purges, which "opened her obstructions so that she began to be a little more quiet" (120). Then she is switched to a regimen of morning purges and evening tranquilizing juleps (containing poppy), and a plaster is applied to her navel (to draw out humors). After taking "the opening drink" (for "obstructions of the matrix") for six days, she is finally ready to have the humors extracted. "Then she was let blood in the sasphena vein in the foot 8 ounces. Then she was very sensible and able to follow her work, God be thanked." However, three days before the next full moon, she again takes emetics and the opening drink and is "let blood in the other foot 8 ounces" (120).[10] The female

---

[10] The maid's purge consists of "an infusion of senna 1/2 ounce; agaric 1 ounce; in posset ale wherein is boiled primrose and cowslip leaves and roots, adding to the purge 2 spoonfuls of syrup magistral" (119–120). The julep recipe reads: "Take water of cowslips, poppy and dragon, of each 2 spoonfuls; syrup of poppy and cowslips, of each one spoonful and apply to her temples, wool dipped in oil of field poppy" (120). The purge prescribed to one of the two men treated for melancholy is much stronger and more complex (122).

deluded melancholics in the case histories will have perturbations of mind similarly rooted in their particular reproductive bodies, but their therapies will augment physic with psychological cures.

The History of Case Histories

The innovation made possible by the eclectic and patient-centered nature of medical practice is visible in the redeployment of the traditional cases of deluded melancholics by selection, expansion, revision, *and* by appending to them "late histories" of women patients from current practice. These cases are traditional *exempla* of diseases of the head passed down through medical history from Galen to the seventeenth century, but still open to reinterpretation: "This sort of passed-on tale counts as the folk-lore tradition of the profession, a tradition still alive, and it is of more moment which particular tales were circulating than that any of them were inauthentic or old" (Clarke 222). Their usefulness and availability for revision are increased because they are strikingly dramatic or comic, vividly characterizing patient delusions and ingenious healer stratagems. Revising these in the light of current cases answered pressing needs to reassess possibly supernaturally caused ailments as natural diseases and propose therapies. The result was new thinking about the parts played by mind and body in mental disorder, new constructs of gender difference, and new versions of cures. The delusions of Richard Napier's clients, Grace Mildmay's outrageous maid, Reginald Scot's Ade Davie, Edward Jorden's Essex gentlewoman, and the Jailer's Daughter—poignantly represented in fictional and nonfictional texts—participate in the invention of the modern case history (based in practice, not tradition) and in the construction of female melancholy.[11]

M. Andreas Laurentius or André Du Laurens, in a chapter titled "Histories of certaine melancholike persons, which have had strange imaginations" (100) in his treatise *A discourse of the preservation of sight: of melancholicke*

---

[11] Barbara Duden, in *The Woman beneath the Skin,* likewise describes how, in his medical observations of women's diseases, Johann Storch, practicing in Germany in the first half of the eighteenth century, recorded and confirmed women's experiences of their bodies and struggled to fit these into theoretical schemes (106 and passim). Recent scholarship has begun to explore how the women hysterics whose case histories were recorded in the late nineteenth century (for example, Blanche Wittmann, Anna O, Elisabeth von R, Dora) were not merely the subjects of observation and evidence for theory. They were active (and sometimes resistant) participants in and catalysts to Charcot's etiology of hysteria and Freud's and Breuer's development of the talking cure, the case history, the concepts of resistance, transference, and countertransference, and hence of psychoanalysis itself. See, for example, Martha Noel Evans; Charles Bernheimer and Claire Kahane's introduction and their essays; Barbara Sicherman 48–51; and Micale ("Future Perspective" 72–78; *Approaching* 139–149). Micale summarizes the scholarship that emphasizes the important participation in theory-making by the subjects of classic case histories. Obviously little is known about the patients in the brief early modern case histories I examine, but their role is no less productive for that.

diseases (1597, trans. 1599), provides an engaging introduction to the traditional figures of deluded melancholics that reveals their function, their emphatic maleness, and hints at new developments. He chooses cases "out of the Greeke, Arabian, and Latine writers" and cites Galen.[12] All exemplify the extreme disturbance of mind and imagination sometimes caused by disorders of the black bile and the ingenious therapies that have worked. Of the fifteen cases of deluded melancholics he enumerates (and exuberantly numbers in the margins), fourteen are men, twelve are handed down, and three are more current: "some such as I have seene with mine owne eyes" (101). All the cases but one involve male fantasies that encode anxieties about body configurations and boundaries, accompanied by grandiose notions of physical size (a man who believes his nose is huge) or responsibility (a man who thinks Atlas will pass on the world to him). The comic sufferers are terrified of bodily distortion or penetration: men imagine they are made of glass and will break, of earthenware and will dissolve, of butter and will melt, or that they have massively long noses, are crowing cocks, or have had their heads or arms taken away. The point of these cases is the comical oddity of the delusions and the equally comical but effective ingenuity of the physician's cures. In the most extended and oft-repeated of them, already cited in chapter 2—of the man who thought he was dead and would not eat, and of the voluntary retentive who refused to piss for fear of drowning the world—we see the two contradictory poles of these fantasies: a grandiose sense of power and an accompanying death wish in which the fear of the breaching of bodily boundaries is defended against by an extreme mortification of the body (not eating or pissing).[13] The cures ingeniously address both the particular delusion and the underlying suicide wish, healing body and mind. The doctor pretends an amputation and uses a chunk of animal flesh to convince the man his nose has been cut off. He places an iron cap on the head of the man who thinks he has none, and friends confirm that it is there. Friends pretending to be dead eat, and the melancholic does too. These cures are com-

---

[12] Galen, *On the Affected Parts*, book 3: "As for instance, one patient believes that he has been turned into a kind of snail and therefore runs away from everyone he meets lest [its shell] should get crushed; or when another patient sees some crowing cocks flapping their wings to their song, he beats his own arms against his ribs and imitates the voice of the animals. Again, another patient is afraid that Atlas who supports the world will become tired and throw it away and he and all of us will be crushed and pushed together" (Stanley Jackson 42). Here the delusions have not taken root as fully as in later citations of the exempla. Before Galen, Rufus cites instances of men who think they are earthenware pots, whose skin seems parchment, and who have no heads (Jackson 36) as does Avicenna later (Jackson 62). Du Laurens credits Aretaeus and Trallianus for some of his instances. During the Renaissance, selective citation is widespread, appearing in Bright (see my introduction, n. 19), Levinus Lemnius, *The Touchstone of Complexions* (1576; 2d book, 151–152), Felix Platter, *Praxeos Medicae* (1602; quoted Jackson 92), Thomas Walkingham, *the Optike glass of humors* (1607; chap. 13, 69–73), and Burton (1.2.3.2; 1:252). Basil Clarke discusses the tradition (222–223, 226–227).

[13] See Alan Walworth, "To Laugh," for a complex elaboration of the psychological dynamics of the cases that involve anxiety about bodily boundaries. I am indebted to his research and to his published and unpublished work on this topic.

passionate as well as clever and often involve servants or neighbors in the therapy.

Du Laurens narrates the "craftie devise[s]" (102) to testify to the "skil" (101) of doctors who will trick the imagination to cure its disorder and to "delight the reader" (101).[14] He not only summarizes the tradition but also adds the three "late" cases of his own. But because he omits the cures, these are not much fun: one is a standard man of glass, one a melancholic man who thinks he is nothing, and one a contemporary French Poet, who thinks that everyone is contaminated with an ointment, Populean (102–103). However Du Laurens's other innovation is more significant. By switching the gender of one traditional case from male to female, his catalog provides a hint that women too can suffer such delusions and require cures that are opposite to men's—both more material and more ignominious. Imagining penetration, not fearing it, the woman thinks she has swallowed a snake. Her cure is not the body's imagined repair but its expulsion of the offending part: a doctor prescribes an emetic and sneaks a serpent into the basin when she vomits. This therapy manipulates and breaches her bodily boundaries literally instead of, like those for males, creating the illusion of the body's protection or repair (e.g., the apparent cutting off of a long nose, the supposed reattachment of a head). This one case points to how women's bodies become increasingly the objects of analysis and manipulation in the following appropriations.

Reginald Scot, a justice, not a doctor, in his 1584 *Discoverie of Witchcraft* ingeniously selects, revises, and extends traditional "histories" (of the sort Du Laurens catalogs slightly later) to accomplish the aim of his treatise: the skeptical naturalizing and demolishing of the apparent supernatural powers of supposed witches. His method is to prove that what seems like witchcraft is usually the result of delusion, fraud, or false accusations. One strategy is to account for self-professed witches (a cornerstone argument for Scot's opponents, the witch-hunters, and a problem for skeptics) by representing them as ludicrous and credulous victims of melancholy who suffer, like traditional male melancholics, from diseased imaginations. In the course of his strenuous efforts to make this analogy stick, Scot naturalizes, medicalizes, and regenders melancholy by revising traditional case histories to locate its origin in women's reproductive bodies.[15]

[14] Schleiner, as we have seen, emphasizes doctors' compassion, and characterizes these strategies as the "therapeutic manipulation of melancholiacs" (233). Foucault sees them as symptomatic cures that silence madness by "theatrical representation" or "ruse" which "*continue* the delirious *discourse*" to "make it disappear in the non-delirious discourse of reason" (*Madness* 188, 189, 191).

[15] He is not of course the only one to do so. The tradition goes back to Hippocratic writings, to Aretaeus, and to Galen. See Veith 10–39. But although maids and widows had long been associated with uterine reproductive disorders, these were not often connected with melancholy, but we have seen earlier in this chapter that Grace Mildmay made the connection.

In book 1, chapter 3 of the *Discoverie,* Scot first attributes to supposed witches some of the traditional marks of melancholy: they are "old, lame, bleare-eied, pale, fowle, and full of wrinkles. . . . They are leane and deformed, shewing melancholie in their faces, to the horror of all that see them" (29). In book 3, chapter 9, "How melancholie abuseth old women, and of the effects thereof by sundrie examples" (64), Scot exploits the conventional cases of deluded male melancholics, selecting and regendering them to fit his argument's needs in a series of rhetorical moves in which we can watch the pressures of his rethinking. First, by shifting pronouns in midstream, he claims that excess of melancholy leads to brainsickness—even in women: "For you shall understand, that the force which melancholie hath, and the effects that it worketh in the bodie of a man, or rather of a woman, are almost incredible" (64). Having laid the groundwork with his insertion, "or rather of a woman," he innovatively splices witches onto the category of deluded melancholics—"as some of these melancholike persons imagine, they are witches and by witchcraft can worke woonders, and doo what they list: so doo other, troubled with this disease, imagine manie strange, incredible, and impossible things" (64). As proof of the analogy, Scot produces a revised catalog of deluded melancholics. The first cases noted, traditionally male, are ungendered in Scot's compressed references: "Some, [imagine] that they are monarchs . . . some, that they are brute beasts" (64). Six of his ten examples include traditional cases of delusions of grandeur or illusions about the outside world bypassed in Du Laurens but emphasized by Descartes: cases of men who believe themselves monarchs or ship owners, who imagine theatrical productions or music playing, who are deluded not about body configuration but, like self-proclaimed witches, about the external world and their power over it.

Having blurred gender distinctions and shifted the nature of delusions from vulnerability toward grandiosity and power, Scot can argue that witches only imagine the powers they confess to and that the witch who confessed at her execution that "she had raised all the tempests, and procured all the frosts and hard weather that happened in the winter 1565" makes a claim that is as incredible as those of melancholics with delusions of grandeur, though "manie grave and wise men beleeved hir" (66). In a key move with important consequences, Scot emphatically shifts the source of the mind's delusions from the male spleen to the female reproductive system, carefully citing authorities who support him. "Now, if the fansie of a melancholike person may be occupied in causes which are both false and impossible; why should an old witch be thought free from such fantasies, who (as the learned philosophers and physicians saie) upon the stopping of their monethlie melancholike flux or issue of bloud, in their age must needs increase therein, as (through their weaknesse both of bodie and braine) the aptest persons to meete with such melancholike imaginations: with whome their imaginations remaine, even when their senses are gone" (65–66).[16] Older women, formerly rare in or absent from the category of deluded melancholics, have become "the aptest persons to meete with such melancholike imaginations" (66).

Scot completes his refashioning and regendering of the deluded melancholic and culminates his attack on witchcraft confessions through the addition of a "familiar and late example," the drama of Ade Davie, wife of Simon Davie, husbandman, "yet alive, and dwelling in the parish of *Sellenge* in *Kent*" (66).[17] He powerfully characterizes the pain of the sufferer and the compassion of the husband healer. Ade, her husband reported to Scot, grew pensive and then her disorder deepened to "some perturbation of mind," sighing, lamentation, insomnia, and "extraordinarie moorning" (67). Eventually she confesses to her husband that, contracted to the devil, she has bewitched him and his children. She, like the man who thinks he is dead or the man who thinks he is nothing, is guilt-ridden and despairing. But Scot insists she is innocent, "howbeit she was brought lowe and pressed downe with the weight of this humor, so as both hir rest and sleepe were taken awaie from hir; & hir fansies troubled and disquieted with despaire, and such other cogitations as grew by occasion thereof" (67). Her husband, moreover, like the physicians and friends of deluded melancholics, proves to be an accomplished therapist whose comfort, like some of Napier's therapies, is spiritual. He offers, in Scot's gloss, the "christian comfort" which provides a context for healing (67). Taking Ade's "delusion" seriously, he fights it by arguing diligently that her contract is void and that Christ's mercy is available, and by praying with her to counter the devil's arrival to claim her. Patience and theological correctness achieve a cure. The only "devise" is a happy accident; the noises of a dog gnawing at a sheep carcass hung on a wall outside are thought to be the attacking devil who the couple believes is beaten back by prayer's efficacy.

The husband's successful therapy, assisted by the dog, is midway between approved Protestant exorcisms (achieved by prayer and fasting) and physi-

---

[16] Scot validates his display of medical expertise by a sarcastic dig at Bodin's lack of it: "Which *Bodin* laboureth to disproove, shewing himselfe as good a physician as else-where a divine" (66). In book 12, chap. 20, the fact of women's reproductive organs, Scot claims, is one means to account for why "women are oftener found to be witches than men" and "more capable of bewitching others." They are "monthlie filled full of superfluous humors, and with them the melancholike bloud boileth; whereof spring vapors, and are carried up, and conveied through the nosethrels, mouth and &c; to the bewitching of whatsoever it meeteth" (236–237).

[17] William Gulstad first drew my attention to this case, which he discusses in relation to Lear's madness in his dissertation on Scot and Shakespeare, 133–138. This is one of three contemporary cases Scot uses to exemplify each of the three explanations he advances to account for apparent witchcraft. Margaret Simmons is the victim of a false accusation; a maidservant of Westwell is an apparent fraud; and Davie is a melancholic. Scot emphasizes the recentness of the case ("and the matter not long sithence in this sort performed" 66), his direct knowledge of it from Davie's husband, and its validity: "Which I knowe is true, as proceeding from unfeigned lips, and from one that feareth God" (67).

cian-instigated treatments for deluded melancholics. Scot's polemical point is that the woman's confession does not prove her a witch and that sympathetic understanding for sufferers of melancholy is more appropriate than witch-burning. The effect of his ingenious argument to discredit witchcraft is to relocate melancholy in the actual bodies of contemporary menopausal women instead of in the fantasized male bodies of the traditional case histories, to focus on the "moorning" of lower-class women instead of the accredited melancholia of upper-class men, and to elaborate the drama of patient and healer. In this way he enlarges the traditional category of melancholy to include the disordered bodies and minds of women.[18]

The next author, because he was engaged in a different polemical battle, was led to characterize younger women also as melancholics. Edward Jorden, an eminent London physician, as we have seen, was called on to examine the patient and to testify as an expert witness in the trial of Elizabeth Jackson, accused of bewitching fourteen-year-old Mary Glover. He wrote his *briefe discourse of a Disease Called the Suffocation of the Mother* (1603) to distinguish between the causes and symptoms of supernatural bewitchment and those of natural disease and to vindicate his diagnosis of Glover's *hysterica passio* or the Mother in the face of Judge Anderson's scornful dismissal: "for if you tell me neither a Naturall cause of it, nor a naturall remedy, I will tell you, that it is not naturall" (MacDonald, *Witchcraft* xvii, and see introduction xix–xxvi). He retorts by locating the cause of Glover's diverse physical and mental symptoms in the suffocation of the Mother (B1r), the disordered uterus that, he explains, has more functions and more connections to all parts of the body than other organs and hence subjects women to manifold symptoms that look like bewitchment. By showing how disordered minds and bodies "befriend" and hence infect each other (Mildmay's phrase), his treatise blurs the boundaries between melancholy and the Mother and brings a new group, adolescent girls, under melancholy's capacious umbrella.

Jorden confirms his analysis not only "out of authenticall writers in our profession" but by the elaboration of current cases "cut of our own experiences" (B4v). One of these, the Essex gentlewoman, appears three times in the treatise and becomes, I newly suggest, a scarcely disguised stand-in for Mary Glover herself (whose case was probably too politically vexed to mention directly).[19] Like Glover's, her fits are both periodic, occurring every af-

---

[18] Ade Davie's age is not given. But the unfolding of the tale in the context of Scot's consistent characterization of supposed witches as old and his claiming menopause as a cause of melancholy, along with the fact that she (perhaps) has stepchildren from her husband's earlier marriage (hence her confession to her husband that she has bewitched "your" children) make her seem older rather than younger.

[19] The claim that the Essex gentlewoman has had the disease for fifteen or sixteen years may (like her Essex address) be a distancing device as well as a proof (to counter the judge's putdown) that lack of a cure does not prove the absence of disease. Glover's extraordinary array of symptoms (extended and elaborate convulsive fits, unconsciousness, numbness, choking,

ternoon, and additionally occasioned by eating meat (C2v, F1r, G2r). Like
Glover, she has "such violent convulsions as five or six strong men could
scarce hold her downe" (F1r).[20] Like Glover, "sometimes her limbes would
be contracted, sometimes perticular Muscles, which would cause swellings
in diverse parts of her bodie, sometimes she would be without all maner of
sense" (F1r). Most tellingly, Jorden indirectly accuses the doctors who as-
sessed Glover as bewitched of exacerbating her condition by his claim that
the Essex gentlewoman, "being made beleeve by a stranger Physition that
she was bewitched, her fits increased upon her, and grew to bee stronger then
before" (F1r).

The symptoms of suffocation of the mother closely resemble those of possession and bewitchment. Its source, like menopausal melancholy, is in
women's reproductive organs, which grow disordered by "want of due and
monethly evacuation, or the want of the benefit of marriage in such as have
beene accustomed or are apt there-unto" (G2v). This "breeds a congestion
of humors about that part, which increasing or corrupting in the place,
causeth this disease. And therefore we do observe that maidens and widowes
are most subject thereunto" (G2v). Innovatively, perhaps because Mary
Glover had not yet menstruated when her fits began, Jorden argues that "joy,
griefe, love, feare, shame, and such like perturbations of the mind" (G2v)
can likewise cause the fits of the Mother.[21] Hence in Jorden's analysis, the
condition closely resembles melancholy, also a disease of congestion and
coldness in which mind and body disrupt each other. It is akin to lovesickness, another disease of excess of unevacuated menstrual blood or sperma,
which is in this period becoming increasingly associated with women as we
will see in the next chapter.

The pressure of "experience" on theory and the merging of once separate
diseases that results is confirmed when Jorden triumphantly provides the
cure for the Mother that the judge had demanded (and the authority of tradition to support it) by revising the "divers sorts of fallacies" physicians use
"to encounter the melancholike conceits of their patients" (G4r). The three
cases he adduces *all* involve women who believe they are possessed, be-

---

paralysis, inability to eat) in her nine-month disorder are, however, dispersed among several
current cases. Three appear early in the treatise as examples of the crucial periodicity of the fits.
Two of the three, like Glover, have fits every day. One of these, like her, has them in the after-
noon (C2v).

[20] Stephen Bradwell, in his pamphlet "Mary Glover's Late Woeful Case," describes at great
length Glover's ordinary periodic fits elicited at times "for every substance that she tooke" and
her extraordinary fits in the presence of Elizabeth Jackson (5). The fits expanded, lasting from
2 to 6 P.M. daily in the early stages of her affliction and from noon to midnight daily in the later
stages. He also narrates the extreme violence of Glover's fits: "as that their paynes in keeping
her from receaving hurt against the bedsted, and postes, caused two or three women to sweat"
(5).

[21] Bradwell, in support of the bewitchment explanation, argues at length that fourteen-year-
olds before menarche—or even soon afterwards—are too young to suffer from congested or
corrupted blood or sperma, which takes time to accumulate (95–103).

witched, or have swallowed a serpent. Two are cured by somatic intervention—by providing purges and introducing nails and feathers or a serpent
"into the close stool" to make them believe they have evacuated it. Women's
uterine disorders are similarly caused by delusion and can be cured by a combination of devices and sex in marriage. Jorden's pamphlet contributes to the
emergence of a new category of women's melancholy, rooted in uterine disorders and revealed and theorized in his late patients.

The stories he revises and inherits allow Jorden to formulate and narrate
how patients and doctors create between them the conditions for healing and
to propose the usefulness of what we today call the placebo effect. Even "su-
perstitious remedies" may work cures, "not for any supernaturall vertue"
but "by reason of the confident persuasion which melancholike and passionate people may have in them" (H1r). Such confidence in healers, shared
by the community, provides the conditions for the Jailer's Daughter's eclectic healing in *The Two Noble Kinsmen*. Mary Glover herself, unfortunately
for Jorden's faith in doctors, was in fact subsequently successfully healed six
and a half months after her fits began not by a physician but by another version of a theatrical cure: an elaborate Puritan exorcism achieved by a day of
fasting, preaching, and praying by Puritan divines and laypersons. As they
ceased, "the maid felt something depart out of her; *and therewithall felt such
a freedom in all the faculties and instruments of her soule and bodie, as
caused her to spring out for joy,* and break out into this new and heavenly
note, *The comeforter is come. O Lord thow hast delivered me*" (Bradwell
115).

The Case of the Jailer's Daughter's Cure: *The Two Noble Kinsmen*

The representation of the Jailer's Daughter in Shakespeare and Fletcher's
Two Noble Kinsmen (1613) presents an enlarged case history of deluded female melancholy much like those just examined. Dramatizing at length a
woman's suffering and the negotiations over her therapy, it further increases
sympathy for the woman and foregrounds the Doctor's dilemma while
widely disseminating this emergent condition. Like the nondramatic texts,
the play appends to an inherited classical story of elite males—that of Palamon and Arcite's friendship and idealized love for Emilia set in ancient
Greece and adapted from Chaucer's "Knight's Tale"—a second plot featuring a lower-class madwoman who is characterized as English and
contemporary. This innovative addition with no identified "source" (Potter,
"Topicality" 78) places the classical material of the first plot in the context
of the contemporary tale.[22] The Daughter's role, far more extensive than that

---

[22] I interpret the Jailer's Daughter as representing emergent constructions of women and
madness and registering the increasing attention given to satisfying women's desires, perhaps

of women in the case histories, elaborates the blend of amusement and compassion that characterizes attitudes toward deluded melancholics, imagined
witches, or those with suffocation of the Mother in Du Laurens's, Scot's, and
Jorden's treatises. This case history continues to amalgamate the suffocation
of the Mother, delusional melancholy, and genital desire to construct woman's melancholy. It also dramatizes a yet more ingenious "cure," newly applied to a woman by family and friends under the direction of a doctor, which
merges the theatrical cure for deluded melancholics with the coital cure Jorden proposes for suffocation of the Mother.

In the extensive representation of the Jailer's Daughter's delusional melancholy, the conventions of stage madness are developed in the context of the
humoral pathology and therapy. She unfolds, as Lear does, the stages of her
deterioration of control; but unlike him she is given three long cogent soliloquies (2.3, 2.5, 3.2) to do so. In these she expresses her desperate love for
Palamon ("I love him, beyond love and beyond reason, / Or wit, or safety"
2.5.11–12), status barriers to her satisfaction ("to marry him is hopeless, /
To be his whore is witless" 2.3.4–5), and her decision to free him from prison
so he will sleep with her in return. By her fourth soliloquy, her altered speech,
now conventional for madness and hence in need of no special introduction,
marks her breakdown as it grows fragmented and italicized—like that of
Ophelia, Lear, and Poor Tom. She fantasizes journeys—on a ship at sea, in
a cockleshell with a frog, cross-dressed on horseback riding to seek her lover,
and quotes phrases and sings. This madness gives her commanding presence
and power. First the countrymen and later her relatives and neighbors listen
to her, and cooperate with her fantasies (for example that she is a fortune-
teller or sailor).

But she also enacts a tale of female desire and of bodily breakdown that
a doctor will cure. She describes herself as "moped" (a term less prestigious
than melancholy, used for mild, lower-class versions of the fashionable disease; MacDonald, *Mystical* 20, 160–163) and stops eating and sleeping—
causes and symptoms of melancholy: "I am moped: / Food took I none these
two days, / Sipped some water. I have not closed mine eyes / Save when my
lids scoured off their brine" (3.2.25–28). Her desire to die is more like that
of deluded melancholics since she wishes the dissolution they imagine:

---

especially characteristic of the growing middle ranks in which her father, the Jailer, is situated.
Richard Abrams goes even further in this direction, seeing the play as "Bourgeois drama" and
suggesting that "the Daughter, as a below-stairs denizen of Theseus's court, an advocate of de-
ceived maids, and the leader of the rustics' dance, serves a similar integrative function, amal-
gamating the dissident energies of the play's outsider factions and channeling them toward
release in the horse's violence" (159). Douglas Bruster's illuminating discussion in "The Jailer's
Daughter and the Politics of Madwomen's Language" asks similar questions about the Daughter's cultural functions but comes to opposite conclusions. He characterizes her as cut off from
the main plot, in a kind of backwater, and interprets her madness as representing nostalgia for
the past, the rural countryside, the mixing of classes, in short "a resistance to the historical pressures of the modern" (290).

"Alas, / Dissolve my life, let not my sense unsettle, / Lest I should drown, or stab, or hang myself. / O state of nature, fail together in me, / Since thy best props are warped!" (3.2.28–32). She desires a deathlike swoon like that identified in sufferers of the Mother (Jorden D2r–D3r), and later runs into the lake to evade the Wooer, nearly precipitating an "accidental" drowning like that of Ophelia.

The source of her disorder is thematized in her obsessive expressions of her desire for sexual satisfaction through images of violent penetration and excessive reproduction far more explicit than Ophelia's. Her reiterated images of an open, penetrable, metamorphic female body have more in common with the fantasy of the woman who imagines she has swallowed a serpent than with the rigidly bounded or terrifyingly fragile bodies of deluded male melancholics. She assumes (and hopes) that Palamon will be man enough to ravish her in the wood: "For use me so he shall, or I'll proclaim him, / And to his face, no man" (2.5.30–31). She fantasizes a ship going down when a rock "beats upon it" (3.4.7–8). She prays, "O for a prick now like a nightingale, / To put my breast against!" (3.4.25–26). She commands an imagined tinker to "Stop no more holes but what you should" and a "conjuror" to "Raise me a devil now" (3.5.84–86). She exaggerates Palamon's sexual prowess as so extraordinary that he will "tickle 't up" with at least twenty a night (4.1.137), and that "There is at least two hundred now with child by him" (4.1.128).

But the Daughter's fantasies also unfold a graphic critique of predatory male desire and its consequences in an underworld peopled with the images of Jacobean social life, not the remnants of a classical Hades. Her image of hell, like Lear's of the "sulphurous pit," is one of erotic burning. But, unlike Lear, she imagines herself one with those she excoriates, suffering punishment for love: "we maids that have our livers perished, cracked to pieces with love, we shall come there. . . . and there shall we be put in a cauldron of lead and usurers' grease" (4.3.21–23, 35–36). She also wittily satirizes both the men who ravish women and the women who fall, devising appropriate punishments for their respective perfidy and blindness. "Lords and courtiers, that have got maids with child," she says, "shall stand in fire up to the navel, and in ice up to th' heart, and there th' offending part burns, and the deceiving part freezes." Seduced women, however proud, also pay: "To hear there a proud lady, and a proud city wife, howl together! I were a beast and I'd call it good sport. One cries 'O this smoke!', another 'This fire!' One cries 'O that ever I did it behind the arras!' and then howls; th' other curses a suing fellow and her garden house" (4.3.40–44, 50–55).

The diagnosis and treatment of the Daughter's malady is undertaken (as in the case histories) by family, community, and the Doctor. All acknowledge responsibility and act compassionately and knowledgeably in concert. The Wooer saves her from drowning, her uncle and friends bring her home and understand, without any Doctor's instructions, that she must be humored:

"By no mean cross her, she is then distempered / Far worse than now she shows" (4.1.119–120). All play along with her fantasy when she asks them to set sail to the woods to search out Palamon, enacting a scenario like those in the case histories to steer her home:

DAUGHTER.   You are master of a ship?
JAILER. Yes.
DAUGHTER.   Where's your compass?
JAILER.   Here.
DAUGHTER.   Set it to th' north.
        And now direct your course to th' wood, where Palamon
        Lies longing for me. For the tackling let me alone.
        Come, weigh, my hearts, cheerly all! O, O, O, 'tis up!
        The wind's fair: top the bowling! Out with the mainsail!
        Where's your whistle, master?
BROTHER.   Let's get her in.
JAILER.   Up to the top, boy!
BROTHER.   Where's the pilot?
FIRST FRIEND.   Here.
                                            (4.1.141–148)

They all likewise collaborate in the more elaborately planned therapy directed by the Doctor.

He devises this based on the symptoms he extracts from her father, asking, for example, if "[h]er distraction is more at some time of the moon than at other some" (4.3.1–2), suspecting disturbed menstrual cycles and the Mother as a cause. He concludes, "'Tis not an engraffed madness, but a most thick and profound melancholy" resulting in a "perturbed mind" (4.3.47–49, 58), invoking the condition we have seen developing and providing one possible explanation of its etiology: "That intemperate surfeit of her eye hath distempered the other senses: they may return and settle again to execute their preordained faculties, but they are now in a most extravagant vagary" (4.3.69–72). This case of melancholy thus shares possible causes and symptoms with the traditionally separate diseases of the Mother and genital congestion. The play suggests that the root cause of the new illness is the emergence, at menarche, of women's (frustrated) sexual desire: "to marry him is hopeless, / To be his whore is witless. Out upon't, / What pushes are we wenches driven to / When fifteen once has found us!" (2.3.4–7). Like that of Mary Glover, who is a year younger, her disorder seems to arise from disordered reproductive functions that cause "Perturbation of mind" in maidens by "want of due and monethly evacuation or the want of the benefit of marriage" (Jorden G2v).

The Doctor's diagnosis leads to a remedy that dramatizes at length the folklore cures of the medical tradition and brings onstage a "late" case. Like those friends who staged a banquet to recover the melancholic man who believed himself dead, her friends are ordered to surround the patient with pleasant songs, flowers, odors, and food, a recommended treatment for melancholy or the Mother in Jorden and Bright. The Wooer, like the friends in the case history, is commanded to eat with the Daughter, encouraging the breaking of her fast. The therapy, exactly like those of deluded melancholics, requires complying with her delusion to end it. As the Doctor explains, "It is a falsehood she is in, which is with falsehoods to be combated. This may bring her to eat, to sleep, and reduce what's now out of square in her into their former law and regiment" (4.3.92–95). Furthermore, the Wooer must pretend to be Palamon and woo her ardently, rehearsing her friends so that they confirm his new identity: "The maids that kept her company / Have half-persuaded her that I am Palamon" (5.2.2–3).

Once the Daughter's perturbations improve, the Doctor prescribes the second part of his "appliance" (4.3.98): sex with the pretend "Palamon," which will cure the body's demands while feeding the melancholic fantasy. He discusses sex via bawdy innuendos ("And when your fit comes, fit her home, and presently" 5.2.11) and breaks into Latin just as Jorden, Burton, and Napier do when discussing sex: "*Videlicet,* the way of flesh—you have me? . . . Please her appetite / And do it home: it cures her *ipso facto* / The melancholy humor that infects her" (5.2.34–37). Traditionally the coital cure, like the delusion cure, was for men only. The social and moral difficulties that arise when it is reassigned to a woman are manifested as tension between her father, who objects to sex before marriage, fearing for his Daughter's "honesty"—"Ho there, doctor!" (5.2.20, 18); the Doctor, who argues that the cure his medical expertise prescribes is more important than "honesty" ("Ne'er cast your child away for honesty" 5.2.21); and the Wooer, who (naturally) sides with the Doctor, but fears to offend his prospective father-in-law and voices his agreement only when her father exits: "I am of your mind, doctor" (5.2.38). This tension dramatizes conflicting attitudes toward women and their sexuality in the discourses of medicine, romantic love, and the family and validates the satisfaction of desire over moral prescriptions. The issue of the Daughter's honesty is resolved dramatically (though not theoretically) when the Daughter, the Jailer, and the Wooer reenact (through their fanciful discussion of the magical horse 5.2.43–75) the agreement about dowry and jointure that the Wooer and the father arrived at in their opening conversation in the play. By means of the dramatization of the Jailer's Daughter's madness and its cure, women's delusions are now situated in their bodies and the "benefit of marriage" established as therapy. The difficult negotiations that attend this problematic consummation and marriage enact the cultural polarity between new views that wish marriage to promote friendship and sexual satisfaction between husband and wife and attention to women's desires (views lent support by medical treatises that urge marriage as therapy) and continuing demands by social authorities to control those desires in the interest of controlling marriage and reproduction.

The thematic contrasts and structural parallels that invite comparisons between Emilia and the Daughter serve to emphasize Emilia's role in the kinsmen plot and her lack of desire, thereby extending the play's representation of the disjunctive relation between sexual desire and marriage. As in the treatises, the addition of "late" cases puts the inherited material in a new perspective. Desire, which is necessary to propel subjects into marriage, may not be able to be satisfied or have its pain alleviated. Mostly the two marriageable women's relation to desire is contrasted. Hippolyta's sister, Emilia, an Amazon and stranger, refuses assimilation into Theseus's Athens, whereas the Daughter is entirely at home there. Emilia wishes to refuse the patriarchal heterosexual imperative that the Daughter embraces and that Hippolyta has been "subdued" to by Theseus (1.1.84). Instead she expresses a longing to remain in the all-female world of her Amazonian girlhood, arguing that "the true love 'tween maid and maid may be / More than in sex dividual" (1.3.81–82). Her encounters with women are intimate and those with men are indifferent or conflict-filled. The Daughter's interactions in the play are, however, entirely with men: her father, her Wooer, the Doctor, the schoolmaster, the countrymen. Whereas the Jailer's Daughter can fall in love passionately because (ironically, in view of the outcome) she sees "the diff'rence of men" (2.1.56), Emilia, unable to see or manufacture any difference between Palamon and Arcite (4.2), cannot choose either one though she once decisively chose her female friend, Flavia.[23]

In spite of these polarities, the two women have structural and symbolic connections that recent productions and criticism emphasize.[24] The Daughter's passion and Emilia's commitment to chastity are both introduced in act 2, scene 1. Emilia's resistance to Arcite's charms in scene 4 of act 2 ("I believe / His mother was a wondrous handsome woman: / His face methinks goes that way" 2.4.19–21) is framed by the Daughter's declarations of love for Palamon in scenes 3 and 5. Emilia's soliloquy agonizing over her inability to "run mad" for either suitor in act 4, scene 2 (1–54) is framed by the Daughter's growing madness for love in scenes 1 and 3. The structural and theatrical associations and contrasts between the two increase as the play continues. The Jailer's Daughter performs before Emilia in the Morris dance. Emilia's appearance to pray at Diana's altar, hair down and "stuck with flowers," parallels the Wooer's image of the Jailer's Daughter in madness with hair wreathed in bulrushes and stuck with flowers (4.1.83–88), her prayers all for Palamon. The moment when the rose falls from the tree on Diana's altar (signaling the rejection of Emilia's plea to Diana to remain a "virgin

[23] Laurie Shannon makes an eloquent case for Emilia's rational choice and defense of female friendship, chastity, and autonomy. She claims such persistent opposition to the tyranny of rulers and arranged marriages is rare in early modern texts.

[24] Margaret Shewring (121–125) discusses how their connections were emphasized in Barry Kyle's 1986 production. Clifford Leech, in his introduction to *Two Noble Kinsmen* (Barnet 1619), discusses their parallel appearances and situations.

flow'r ... [and] grow alone, unplucked" 5.1.167–168) is followed immediately by the initiation and success of the Daughter's coital cure. Finally, the Daughter's venture for Palamon makes possible Emilia's marriage to him. All the subsequent action is initiated by Palamon's escape from jail and, at the conclusion, Palamon is preserved from death for marriage because he stops on the way to his execution to inquire sympathetically about the Daughter's madness and to provide her with a dowry.[25]

That both women are manipulated into marriage to "Palamon" but neither one gets exactly what she desires extends the issues of the Jailer's Daughter's plot to the play as a whole.[26] In *The Two Noble Kinsmen*, Emilia remains to the end an object of exchange between the two unwanted kinsmen. Although Arcite gives her to Palamon as he dies: "'tis done. / Take her. I die" (5.4.93–94), his friend's death binds Palamon more closely to "One that yet loves thee dying" (5.4.89), and his desire for Emilia drains away: "That we should things desire which do cost us / The loss of our desire! That nought could buy / Dear love but loss of dear love" (5.4.109–111). Emilia expresses a few words of grief at Arcite's death, but says not a word about marriage to Palamon. Though the Daughter enters a marriage that pretends to satisfy her desire, she is more puzzled than happy to accept the substitute Palamon since she cannot believe the social gulf between them can be overcome: "Yes, but you care not for me. I have nothing / But this poor petticoat and two coarse smocks" (5.2.82–83).

The Jailer's Daughter's cure and Emilia's marriage resistance are central to the play's reiterated theme that while sexual desire and loss of maiden-

[25] *The Two Noble Kinsmen*, because of its collaborative authorship, its exclusion from the First Folio, its late publication in a 1634 quarto, and the apparent disparateness of its chivalric main plot and realistic subplot, has long been the subject of critical debates over who authored what and with what result. The Jailer's Daughter's supposedly dual-authored part has been one of the important "stakes" in this battle as Susan Green shows (121). My claims about the play do not depend on how the collaboration worked. My analysis shows the intricate connections between the equally weighted plots and implies that the Jailer's Daughter's plot is central to the play, as the prologue's identification with it suggests. No simple or absolute division of labor between the collaborators seems likely. (See Edwards, "On the Design"; Green; Jeanne Addison Roberts, "Crises"; Shewring.) For a comprehensive analysis of the authorship debate and a bid for Shakespeare's sole authorship, see Paul Bertram's *Shakespeare and "The Two Noble Kinsmen."* For revisionary views of the collaboration, see the essays by Charles Frey, Donald K. Hedrick, and Michael D. Bristol in Frey's collection. Much recent commentary such as that by Green, Bruster, Potter, and Shewring disclaims interest in the authorship question and focuses on connections among the strands of the play.

[26] Walworth ("Displacing Desires" 65–67, 72–74) analyzes within a Lacanian framework how, throughout the play, Arcite is represented as "following" Palamon as an object of desire, an imitative model for identity, and a deadly rival. Arcite's death, in this scenario, is "inevitable." "For the last time he 'follows' the lead of his condemned cousin, and for once, overtakes him in death. At the same time, by taking Emilia as his prize, Palamon will for once step into Arcite's place" (93). The two women, unknown to each other, follow each other differently. Emila gets marriage to Palamon without desiring it; the Jailer's Daughter achieves the satisfaction of her desires with a surrogate Palamon. The resolution of the main plot requires just one noble kinsmen; the resolution of both plots together requires two Palamons. The theatrical cure enables the play to have both.

head are essential to the social institution of marriage and reproduction of subjects, desire cannot be easily channeled into marriage without pain, and marriage does not necessarily satisfy the vagaries of desire as the medical texts claim. The theme begins with the prologue's comparison of the production of new plays with the laborious and perhaps never-achieved loss of maidenhead during "first night's stir" when "husband's pains" leave a new wife still modest and a "maid" (prologue 1–8). Identifying with the woman, the prologue shows that the translation of old material into new plays requires the sort of "tack(ing) about" (26) that the Daughter's fantastic journey to Palamon necessitated and may similarly meet with lack of success. This introduction is followed by the interrupted wedding ceremony of Theseus and Hippolyta, and the play concludes with three joyless and as yet uncelebrated marriages.[27] That unrequited desire kills is symbolized by the sudden distraction of Emilia's horse, which throws and kills its mistress's loving bridegroom. But its successful control through marriage is only comically embodied in the Daughter's narrative of the magical (but likely fake) educated horse, a gift from Palamon (5.2.44–66). He mechanically dances, reads, and does accounts and is imagined by the Daughter as a lover's gift and dowry negotiator—although the horse is entirely scornful of the chestnut mare who offers him love and a rich dowry (5.2.44–66). Still, whatever comedy there is in the tragicomedy is achieved through the Daughter's desires and the Doctor's cure, which will gain her some of what she wants: kisses, sexual intercourse, "many children," financial security, and a Wooer who is tender and attentive—all the quotidian satisfactions of marriage. But the ending of this story, which dramatizes the difficulties of assuring that "the benefit of marriage" will satisfy anyone's desires, is bitter, not comic.[28]

The Jailer's Daughter's story, extending a series of case histories that fo-

[27] Although my focus in this chapter is the Jailer's Daughter and her double, Emilia, the men are equally brutalized by love, compulsory heterosexuality, and arranged marriages. Theseus, who must loosen his deep bonds to Pirithious, views marriage as another martial challenge, "this daring deed / Of fate in wedlock" (1.1.163–164). There is no indication that Theseus and Hippolyta ever complete their interrupted ceremony, and their comical disagreements in *A Midsummer Night's Dream* have hardened to estrangement. Arcite loses his life for love, and Palamon expresses pain over the friend he has lost, not joy in the wife he has gained. Even the Wooer is miserable with the charade he must enact and has to be pushed into going off with the Daughter, in spite of his persistent affection for her.

[28] Much recent criticism focuses on the unrelieved painfulness of the play. Edwards ("On the "Design") analyzes the destructiveness of love and says, "*The Two Noble Kinsmen* seems to me to give the most cynical assessment of the progress of life since the writing of *Troilus and Cressida*" (105). Glynne Wickham, comparing the play to *A Midsummer Night's Dream*, notes its "pervasive sense of disenchantment and loss" (186). Barry Weller emphasizes its "revulsion from patriarchal marriage" and Shannon its political and marital tyranny. Even when the Jailer's Daughter's cure is seen as offering a comic antidote to the rest of the play, its efficacy is doubted. Wickham aptly notes: "And to this bitter-sweet conclusion to the main plot, the fate of the Jailer's Daughter supplies a gloss for the sub-plot like the play of 'Pyramus and Thisbe' does in *A Midsummer Night's Dream*—but as bitter in its tone and purpose as that is comic and sweet" (185–186). Potter ("Topicality") points out, however, that to modern audiences, the Jailer's Daughter's part is "easily the most successful and touching part of the play" (89), perhaps because it points toward the realistic, compromised marriages of modern bourgeois subjects.

cus, like the play, on women's sexual desire and sexual parts, poignantly registers the community pressure, parental interference, dowry negotiations, and compromises that accompany the transition to marriage. The Wooer and Daughter, before they go off to bed to cure the Daughter's illness, take hands before witnesses, staging a formal spousal that will become marriage proper at the consummation that follows:

> WOOER. That's all one, I will have you.
> DAUGHTER.   Will you surely?
> WOOER. Yes, by this fair hand will I.
> DAUGHTER.   We'll to bed, then.
> WOOER. E'en when you will.
>
> (5.2.84–85)

The scripted performance, dazed participants, and inevitable pain of this marriage and deflowering are its final note:

> DAUGHTER. And then we'll sleep together?
> DOCTOR.   Take her offer.
> WOOER.   Yes, marry will we.
> DAUGHTER.   But you shall not hurt me.
> WOOER.   I will not, sweet.
> DAUGHTER.   If you do, love, I'll cry.
>
> (5.2.109–111)

This plot, a development out of "late" case histories that began to concern themselves with the delusions caused by female bodies, enacts both the encounter with the doctor who prescribes a cure and the impossibility of that cure—for the Daughter, but also for all the couples forced into marriage by the heterosexual imperative: "That we should things desire which do cost us / The loss of our desire! That nought could buy / Dear love but loss of dear love!" (5.4.109–111). In this disturbing text, the mad Jailer's Daughter's cure becomes the vehicle for both the tying up of the plot and for whatever satisfaction ensues from it. Her history is a development out of the ongoing debate just as are the contemporary case histories of the Essex gentlewoman and Ade Davie. But whereas their suffering, though natural and medical, is cured by spiritual means, the Jailer's Daughter represents the difficulties of a therapy that is medical and sexual and hence caught up in the social exigencies and negotiations over women's roles that their brief stories leave out.

Practice into Theory

Robert Burton's *Anatomy of Melancholy* consolidates the new subcategory, women's melancholy, when he draws together all the associations we

have seen developing on stage and off by appending a new section, "Symptomes of Maides, Nunnes, and Widowes Melancholy," to the third edition
of the work in 1628 (1.3.2.4; 1:414–418). This new type of melancholy "differs from that which commonly befalls men and other women, as having one
onely cause proper to women alone" (1:414), and its symptoms and cures
differ accordingly from other kinds of "Head Melancholy." Its source is congestion of the female uterus or genitals, in "menstruous blood" or "corrupt
seed" (1:414). It creates or comes from "perturbation of mind" as a result
of unsatisfied sexual desire occurring in connection with women's life passages. It occurs in widows, "with much care and sorrow, as frequently it
doth, by reason of a sudden alteration of their accustomed course of life,"
to women in childbirth whose periods have stopped, to nuns, and "more ancient maids," as well as young ones, and barren women (1:414).

The many symptoms Burton enumerates have connections with melancholy (grieving and sorrowing without apparent cause) and are like "fits of
the mother": "dotage & griefe of some part or other, head, heart, breasts,
sides, backe, belly, etc., with much solitarinesse, weeping, distraction, etc.,
from which they are sometimes suddenly delivered, because it comes and
goes by fits" (1:414–415). Sufferers often think themselves bewitched or
possessed. They commune with spirits and are afraid of damnation or attempt suicide. But supernatural explanations are throwbacks and are not
credited. Like that of deluded melancholics, their condition is twice described as a "dotage" (1:414), a word that has associations with excessive
love, senility, folly, and mental disorder, and that Du Laurens's translator
uses to mean "funny story" (Clarke 226). Burton concurs with Jorden and
the Doctor in *Two Noble Kinsmen* that the "best and surest remedy of all,
is to see them well placed, and married to good husbands in due time"
(1:416). But here, as in the later partition on "Love Melancholy," Burton
worries, as does the Jailer in *Two Noble Kinsmen,* about the morality of the
coital cure for women and insists on marriage as its condition.

Although most of Burton's discussion is drawn from cited authorities, he
adds to these, not exactly a case history, but a piece of shrewd contemporary
social observation that shapes his views of causality and adds economic status to the conditions of age and sexual activity that experts claim increase
susceptibility to the disease: "For seldome shall you see an hired servant, a
poore handmaid, though ancient, that is kept hard to her worke and bodily
labour, a coarse country wench troubled in this kinde, but noble virgins, nice
gentlewomen, such as are solitary and idle, live at ease, lead a life out of action and employment, that fare well in great houses and jovial companies . . . ; such for the most part are misaffected, and prone to this disease"
(1:416–417). But, as the Jailer's Daughter anticipates and later seventeenth-
century casebooks show, this newly theorized disease continues to expand
its domain to women of many ages and classes.

In the seventeenth century, this new women's melancholy, a loose amalgamation of the suffocation of the Mother, melancholy, and genital pathology, became entrenched in medical theory and practice. In 1651, William Harvey in *Exercitationes de generatione animalium* affirms that the womb is the cause of the manifold symptoms maids at puberty display, "For the uterus is a most important organ, and brings the whole body to sympathize with it" (Hunter and Macalpine 131–132). This organ explains perturbations of mind, and supernatural explanations are viewed as mere similitudes or misrecognitions: "how dreadful, then, are the mental aberrations, the delirium, the melancholy, the paroxysms of frenzy as if the affected person were under the dominion of spells, and all arising from unnatural states of the uterus" (Hunter and Macalpine 132). The disease is entirely bodily: as it is with animals who conceive eggs, so it is "in young women when their uterus grows hot, their menses flow, and their bosoms swell—in a word when they become marriageable; and who, if they continue too long unwedded, are seized with serious symptoms—hysterics, furor uterinus, &c. or fall into a cachectic state, and distemperatures of various kinds. All animals, indeed, grow savage when in heat, and unless they are suffered to enjoy one another, become changed in disposition. In like manner women occasionally become insane through ungratified desire, and to such a height does the malady reach that they are believed to be poisoned, or moon-struck, or possessed by a devil" (Hunter and Macalpine 131). Harvey's theory determines his therapy. He is reported to have told the parents of an eighteen-year-old maid suffering from numbness "to take her home, and provide her a Husband, by whom, in effect, she was according to his Prognostick, and to many Mens wonder, cur'd of that strange Disease" (Hunter and Macalpine 132). Later in the century, Thomas Sydenham (1624–1689) accepted the uterine origin of women's mental disturbances and began subdividing the condition into several diseases with different symptoms (Katherine Williams 386–387) and subsequently claimed, "It should seem that no chronic disease occurs so frequently as this, for few women (which sex makes one half of the grown persons) excepting such as work and fare hardly, are quite free from every species of this disorder, several men who also lead a sedentary life and study hard are afflicted with the same" (quoted in Williams 383).

It is of course impossible to know how widespread the condition actually was. But the now subdividing disease with the associated symptoms of melancholy, uterine fits, and sexual frustration had several new names in addition to the Mother: "Clavus Hystericus," "hypochondriacal," "furor uterinum," "Hysteric fit." These conditions show up regularly in medical practice, as Katherine Williams's examination of seventeenth-century case records and manuscripts shows, and almost all those diagnosed are women. Nathaniel Johnston's casebook (1670–1690) includes ten women listed under "Hysteria," nine women and eleven men diagnosed as "hypochondriacal," and ten women and three men diagnosed as melancholy (Williams 387–388 and n 18); the women so diagnosed are maids, wives, and widows of all social classes. Edmund King's casebooks (1676–1696) include a woman who, like Mary Glover, has all the symptoms of suffocation of the Mother (Williams 393) and one Lady Betty Thomond, apparently married, who "fell into a violent passion . . . a love of R.E.S." She was thought likely to "fall into a furor uterinum or mania . . . was so raving extremely" and later had a "Hysteric Fitt" (Williams 394–395). The condition, which emerges in the late sixteenth century, becomes in the seventeenth century an established pathology that, in the encounters of medical practice, demands ongoing theorizing and therapy. Eventually, at the end of the nineteenth century, it will acquire a new name and a new theory, again one catalyzed by patient symptoms and suffering.

This selective case history of case histories shows how, because of pressure to find natural causes for conditions once thought caused by possession or bewitchment, a new disease emerges in witchcraft and medical treatises, is confirmed in doctors' diagnoses of women patients, and then picked up by the stage to further its own representation of madness and elaborate the drama inherent in theatrical cures of deluded melancholy. Of course, attributions of possession and bewitchment did not cease, and the larger process of secularization was carried far beyond this brief period, over several centuries and across many cultural locations. A brief comparison of visual representations in the seventeenth and nineteenth century can provide a companion example of the ongoing process of secularization and medicalization of women's conditions whose emergence I have traced. Hysteria, a new disease in the nineteenth century as women's melancholy was earlier, like it rose rapidly to prominence in the case histories—in particular those of Charcot and Freud. It disappeared just as rapidly, becoming diffused into separate disease constructions early in the twentieth century (Hacking, *Rewriting* 133–136; Micale, *Approaching* 169–173).

By comparing Baroque paintings of exorcisms (which continued in Catholic countries into the eighteenth century) with Brouillet's well-known portrait of Charcot, we can watch the iconography of possession transferred to representations of hysterics, whose symptoms are reattributed to natural causes while the visual power of spiritual healers is redrawn in figures of medical professionals. In Benedetto Luti's *St. Romuald Curing a Woman Possessed* (fig. 3, late seventeenth century) and Peter Paul Rubens's *The Miracle of St. Ignatius Loyola* (fig. 4, early seventeenth century), saints perform successful exorcisms. Their spiritual and healing power is represented by their elevation, their firm, tranquil uprightness, and their outstretched hands and visible halos. They preside over and orchestrate a cosmic drama in which the demonic, represented by tumbling ascending demons in the Rubens, is driven out of the body of the possessed. These bodies are in the traditional *arc de cercle* position signifying possession: eyes rolled back, mouth open and tongue sometimes out, limbs rigidly and powerfully askew. The possessed in their frightening fits must be sustained and/or restrained by the rel-

FIG. 3. Benedetto Luti, *St. Romuald Curing a Woman Possessed*, late seventeenth century. Courtesy of the Picture Library of the National Museum, Stockholm.

FIG. 4. Peter Paul Rubens, *The Miracle of St. Ignatius Loyola*, early seventeenth
century. Copyright Erich Lessing/Art Resource, NY, and the Kunsthistorisches
Museum, Vienna.

atives and neighbors who bring them to the healer (as the relatives of Mary Glover did). These onlookers gaze pleadingly at the saintly healer or at the heavens, supporting the possessed physically and emotionally.

This iconography of possession is reiterated and redefined in the iconography of hysteria available especially in the journal *Photographic Iconography of the Salpêtrière,* which, from 1877 to 1880 and again after 1888, published photographs that cataloged the stages of hysteric fits to exemplify the new disease. The visual signs of possession that were conventional in earlier periods are recapitulated in the visual representations of hysterics (Gilman 194–204). André Brouillet's painting *Charcot at the Salpêtrière* (fig. 5), drawing on this history, reiterates and reframes the iconography of possession and exorcism into that of hysteria and its diagnosis. In the painting, the hysteric fit of Charcot's most famous patient, Blanche Wittmann, allows the doctor not only to confirm but to teach his theory, as he lectures with his case on hand to dramatize the disease. The painting, like *The Two Noble Kinsmen,* disseminates to laypersons another new diagnosis.

Whereas in the Rubens painting, there are both male and female possessed persons, the majority of patients and of representations of hysteria in the later nineteenth century were female. Even in the earlier painting, the almost naked male possessed is represented as more powerful, violent, and in need

FIG. 5. André Brouillet, *Charcot at the Salpêtrière,* 1887. Courtesy of the National Library of Medicine, Bethesda, Maryland.

of restraint, whereas the possessed women in the two pictures appear less violent and muscular in their fits. This is partly because the women are more
fully clothed, although their arms and chests are bare and their clothes di-
sheveled. More clearly than the man, they are supported by sympathetic men
and women of their own class. In contrast, in the Brouillet painting, the up-
right and authoritative Charcot lectures to a large group of similarly black-
suited doctor colleagues. They are aligned with him instead of with the
patient as the crowds are in the earlier paintings. Neither he nor his audience
look at the patient, but her representation attracts the viewer's gaze as she
falls back into the arms of Charcot's assistant. This sole other woman present reaches out her arms in sympathy. Apart from this gesture, the communal support that was the center of the paintings of the possessed has
vanished, and Wittmann's suffering is a small part of the drama of medical
progress that is the picture's focus. She is represented in a modified version
of the iconography of possession that, in comparison with the possessed in
the seventeenth-century pictures, diminishes her power and her ability to
elicit sympathy from spectators. Her head is back, her eyes closed, her mouth
shut, her arms at her sides. She is passive and aestheticized compared to the
earlier possessed women and even more eroticized than they are. The doctor's power here, in contrast to that of the saints in the earlier paintings, is
directed toward making a diagnosis and imparting knowledge to others;
once Wittmann's usefulness as an exemplar is over, she will be carted away
on the waiting chair. Though her presence is crucial to Charcot's exposition
of hysteria, Wittmann in this representation, unlike the possessed in the earlier paintings and unlike Ade Davie, Mary Glover, or the Jailer's Daughter,
is offered no compassion and no therapy, though she does influence medical
history.

CHAPTER 4

DESTABILIZING LOVESICKNESS, GENDER, AND SEXUALITY

Twelfth Night and *As You Like It*

> Love is merely a madness, and, I tell you, deserves as well a dark house and
> a whip as madmen do; and the reason why they are not so punished and
> cured is that the lunacy is so ordinary that the whippers are in love too.
> *As You Like It*

In the last chapter, we watched how, in the cultural niche provided in the last decades of the sixteenth century and the first of the seventeenth, the case histories of deluded melancholics, and of Ade Davie, the Essex Gentlewoman, Mary Glover, and the Jailer's Daughter helped constitute a new category of women's uterine melancholy. In this chapter, we will see how a parallel condition, lovesickness, which has a long history stretching back to Galen, begins to be newly diagnosed in women, a shift that is visible in medical treatises, dramatic texts, and later in Dutch genre paintings. Lovesickness was named *amor hereos* in the twelfth-century medical renaissance; it is called "a melancholie which commeth by the extremitie of love" by André Du Laurens, termed "erotic melancholy" by Robert Burton, and, in translation, "lovesickness," in Jacques Ferrand's summation of the condition. Lovesickness is a somatic disease of inflamed and congested genitals leading to disordered fantasy and hence overlaps with the condition of female melancholy already examined. The disease, characterized by uncontrollable erotic desires for unconventional or unattainable objects, demands and deserves satisfaction—which the treatises advocate. It is the pathological underside of—and the antidote to—idealized and sublimated Petrarchan love. Because it can strike anyone and fasten on anything, it has the effect of making gender roles and erotic object choices fluid and the relation between

I want to acknowledge contributions to an early draft of this chapter by students in my 1996 graduate seminar "Shakespearean Subjectivities" and by members of the seminar "Reconsidering Subjectivity" chaired by Valerie Wayne and Akiko Kusunoki at the International Shakespeare Association Meeting in Los Angeles in 1996.

them unstable. Privileging satisfaction, the discourse of lovesickness licenses wayward desires, especially for women, newly deemed the most likely sufferers. Like the treatises that record this shift, *Twelfth Night* and *As You Like It* exploit lovesickness's comic potential and gender-bending effects.

Lovesickness Discourse

Examining lovesickness discourse in medical treatises and two Shakespeare comedies provides one way to think about how subjects act both through and against the rules that attempt to govern them and achieve the willfulness, momentum, and "insubordination" that Hugh Grady proposes for subjects in general and Linda Gregerson attributes especially to erotic subjects like Britomart in *The Faerie Queene*.[1] Although the condition enslaves humans to painful desires and strange fantasies, it also catalyzes passionate agendas. These drive sufferers to resist or disrupt status roles, rigid gender hierarchies, and binary constructions of sexual desire and object choice. An examination of lovesickness thus can clarify and help account for multiple and fluid early modern sexualities theorized by such scholars as Alan Bray, Jonathan Goldberg, and Valerie Traub and reveal what Jonathan Dollimore affirms as "a creative perversity in desire itself" ("Shakespeare" 484). As we have seen in the last chapter, medical discourse in flux again encourages theoretical and social change by opening up, outside of the institutions and prescriptions of the church and the state, a space for inquiry and debate about the body and its demands. And here, as in the last chapter, attention is especially devoted to the ordinarily restrained desires of women. Gender is less polarized and sexuality less normalized than usual in this discourse because it is concerned primarily with the satisfaction of desires, only peripherally with marriage, and not at all with reproduction. This occlusion and this emphasis permit tolerance for a wide and weird range of gender behaviors, erotic objects, and amorous styles, often viewed comically, and validate the satisfaction of desire, however obtained and even for women.[2]

---

[1] Hugh Grady usefully summarizes and analyzes the failure of Foucaultian and Althusserian theories to provide sufficiently nuanced conceptions of early modern subjects (34–40) and proposes drawing on theorists of the Frankfurt School and on psychoanalytic accounts of desire to allow for agency (40–48). Linda Gregerson suggests that the Lacanian subject "is one whose foundational instability is itself a form of momentum," one whose "very interpellation—whose ontological precariousness . . . provides the ground for *in*subordination, which is to say for agency and change" (93), and adds, "The same might be said (and often was in sixteenth-century England) of erotic love" (94 n 38). Her primary literary example of specular momentum is Britomart, whose love for Artegall propels her into an epic quest in books 3 and 4 of *The Faerie Queene*. Other critics find other potentials for agency within subjects or created by contradictions within ideology. Louis Montrose finds subjects "loci of consciousness and initiators of action" ("Professing" 21); Catherine Belsey and Jean Howard discover possibilities of change in the "contradictions" and "gaps and discontinuities" in ideology (Belsey 8–9, 149–160; Howard 93ff.); as does Alan Sinfield who explores its "faultlines."

[2] Other scholars likewise show how medieval and early modern medical discourse, because

In medical traditions from the second to the seventeenth century, love-sickness is associated with the melancholy humor and characterized as a disease of the head, heart, imagination, and genitals. Its powerful somatic symptoms, the most agreed-upon aspect of the malady, are summed up in Jacques Ferrand's *Treatise of Lovesickness* (1623, trans. 1640): "a pale and wan complexion, . . . a slow fever, . . . palpitations of the heart, swelling of the face, depraved appetite, a sense of grief, sighing, causeless tears, insatiable hunger, raging thirst, fainting, oppressions, suffocations, insomnia, headaches, melancholy, epilepsy, madness, uterine fury, satyriasis, and other pernicious symptoms that are, for the most part, without mitigation or cure" (229). André Du Laurens in his rich succinct chapter on the condition, "Of another kinde of melancholie which commeth by the extremitie of love" (1597, trans. 1599), further explicates the (for him male) sufferer's maladies and their long-standing connection with melancholy, whose main symptoms are fear and sorrow: "feare buffeteth him on the one side, & oftentimes dispayre on the other; he is (as Plautus sayth) there where indeede he is not; sometime he is as hot as fire, and upon the sudden he findeth himselfe as colde as ice: his heart doth alwaies quake, and his pulse keepeth no true course, it is little, unequall, and beating thicke, changing it selfe upon the sudden, not onely at the sight, but even at the very name of the object which he affecteth" (118). These symptoms, especially the revealing pulse, allow the disease to be diagnosed, brought under the care of doctors, and cured—the outcome that lovesickness treatises advocate.

Although lovesickness's symptoms were agreed upon by theologians, philosophers, and poets, the disease's exact progression was much debated. Medical treatises, claiming bodily origins to secure their own authority over lovesickness, proposed a complex somatogenesis, articulating intricate relationships among its disparate sites and symptoms. It might originate in the head, imagination, or genitals—or all of the above, as Peter of Spain's 1250 treatise argues: Love is "a disease of the testicles . . . a disease of the brain . . . a disease of the imaginative faculty" (quoted, Wack 235–241; cf. Ferrand 257, 263–265). Du Laurens provides the most explicit Renaissance etiology of lovesickness that, entering through the eyes, rapidly corrupts the subject:

Love therefore having abused the eyes, as the proper spyes and porters of the mind, maketh a way for it selfe smoothly to glaunce along through the conducting guides, and passing without any perseverance [*sic*] in this sort through

---

it is tolerant of erotic love, counters sexual repression, licenses women's desires, and promotes changing and varied representations of gender and sexuality. See also Ian Maclean, *The Renaissance Notion of Woman* 29–30, 45–46; Danielle Jacquart and Claude Thomasset, *Sexuality and Medicine in the Middle Ages* 1–6; and Mary Frances Wack, *Lovesickness in the Middle Ages* 7–8, 68–72. Exploring a different use of medical discourse, Michael Schoenfeldt usefully emphasizes how male subjects may draw on medical knowledge to discipline themselves: to, for example, "dampen" "the overheated instability of erotic passion" (95; see also 39, 72, and passim). The discourse contains both potentials.

the veines unto the liver, doth suddenly imprint a burning desire to obtaine the thing, which is or seemeth worthie to bee beloved, setteth concupiscence on fire, and beginneth by this desire all the strife and contention: but fearing her selfe too weake to incounter with reason, the principal part of the minde, she posteth in haste to the heart, to surprise and winne the same: whereof when she is once sure, as of the strongest hold, she afterward assaileth and setteth upon reason, and all the other principall powers of the minde so fiercely, as that she subdueth them, and maketh them her vassals and slaves. Then is all spoyled, the man is quite undone and cast away, the senses are wandring to and fro, up and downe, reason is confounded, the imagination corrupted, the talke fond and sencelesse; the sillie loving worme cannot any more look upon any thing but his idol: al the functions of the bodie are likewise perverted, he becommeth pale, lean, souning. (118)

Although the disease's creation of a "sillie loving worme" is comic, its progression may be fatal; indeed some writers report that in it, the adust melancholy humor burns up the liver, heart, brain, and genitals (lightes), ravages said to be visible in anatomies of the lovesick.[3]

Since the primary symptom of lovesickness is unsatisfied desire, and its "immediate cause" for men or women is *sperma* needing evacuation (Ferrand 327), the most efficacious cure is therapeutic intercourse, "the injoying of the thing beloved" (Du Laurens 121). This is ideally to take place within marriage. If not, sex with the loved object or with any available substitutes is traditionally recommended: with prostitutes, slaves, or widows—preferably more than once or with more than one partner so as to evacuate both sperm from the genitals and the beloved's image from the brain. But since this coital cure may be unobtainable (especially for women) or morally problematic, other methods of prevention or remedy are offered. Friends, doctors, or the beloved may try aversive therapy, or what I call the misogyny cure—which is the first line of prevention for Ferrand (314). The doctor or a friend is to expose the physical ugliness and moral flaws of the (female) beloved, or, more graphically, an old crone is to wave a bloody menstrual rag in the face of the lovesick nobleman, or reveal her own diseased genitals and her cankered breasts to signify the repulsiveness of women's bodies.[4] So, in Shakespeare's *As You Like It,* Jacques puts down Orlando's mistress to dispel his Petrarchan love and Rosalind too offers Orlando lessons on the wayward bodies of women (a variation perhaps designed rather to elicit desire than to avert it). Physicians also propose therapies to ameliorate the

---

[3] "I have seene a Aanatomie [*sic*] made of some of those that have dyed of this malady, that had their bowels shrunke, their poore heart all burned, their Liver and Lightes [*sic*] all vaded and consumed, their Braines endomaged, and I thinke that their poore soule was burned by the vehement and excessive heat that they did endure when that the rage of love had overcome them" (Boaistuau 192).

[4] On misogyny cures, see Ferrand 318; Burton 3.2.5.2; 3:214; Wack's discussions of coital cures in treatises from Africanus (ca. 1180) to Bona Fortuna (ca. 1300), 41, 66–70, 103, 142, and of aversive therapy, 70, 103.

body's heat through control of diet or environment; they distract the lover through music (like Orsino), exercise, and travel (like Rosalind), or prescribe traditional purges, opiates, and bloodletting (Du Laurens 123–124; Ferrand, chaps. 30–37; Burton 3.2.5.1; 3:201–207). But only the coital cure is sure to succeed—at least temporarily.

As the presence of coital and misogyny therapy suggests, women were traditionally subordinated as subjects in a disease generally construed as male—as in the quotation above from Du Laurens (see Wack 149–152, 174–176). Both in Galen and in the twelfth-century medical renaissance in Italy, examined by Mary Wack, lovesickness is usually characterized as a disease of upper-class heterosexual men, men like the doctors who theorized and treated it in mostly male patients, many medical students themselves. Its male associations are explicit in its designation in those treatises as *amor hereos*, a term resulting perhaps from a confusion of *eros* (love), *heros* (hero), and *herus* (lord). It is thought to refer to the love of noble men "who, on account of riches and the softness of their lives, are more likely to suffer this disease" (Wack 203, translating Avicenna; and see also 60–61). Burton traces and continues this male-centered tradition, claiming of the disease, "It rageth with all sorts and conditions of men, yet it is most evident among such as are young and lusty, in the flowre of their yeares, nobly descended, high fed, such as live idly and at ease" (3.2.1.2; 3:56).

But from the beginning, women, though not the typical sufferers, appear occasionally as subjects as well as objects of desire, providing impetus for later developments. A lovesick woman is the subject of one of Galen's (130–200) rare case histories, and her tale circulates down through medical tradition into the late Renaissance (cf. Du Laurens 119, Ferrand 266). But even in this originary case history, her desires get short shrift. Its point is the physician's diagnosis. The diagnosed woman is known only as the wife of Justus; unlike the doctor, her husband, and her love object, she has no name and no satisfaction. Her symptoms are insomnia without fever, a refusal to answer questions about her condition, and the absence of physical disease. Although she keeps her love hidden, Galen diagnoses her condition accurately after discovering that her pulse races when a certain dancer, Pylades, enters the room. Since she is an upper-class woman whose love is adulterous and crosses class boundaries, therapeutic intercourse is probably unacceptable, and no cure is proposed (Wack 9).

A second Galenic case history has a different ending. Galen picks up the story from Valerius Maximus (early first century A.D.), Plutarch, and others, and it circulates through medical treatises and literary works well into the eighteenth century (Beecher and Ciavolella 50). Antiochus falls madly in love with his stepmother, Stratonice, and his father, Seleucis, generously gives his wife to his son in marriage to prevent the son's demise; to conceal his desires, Antiochus has decided to commit suicide by starving himself. In Plutarch's rendition, the physician Erasistratus, suspecting the cause, remains in the

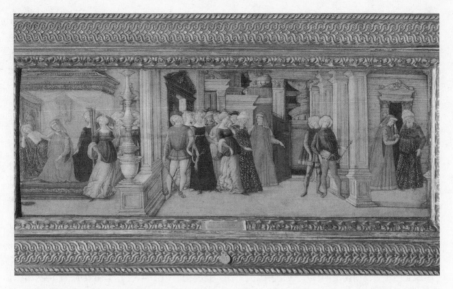

FIG. 6. *Antiochus and Stratonice,* two panels by the fifteenth-century Sienese
painter known as the Master of the Stratonice Panels. Courtesy of the Huntington
Library, Art Collections, and Botanical Gardens, San Marino, California.

youth's chamber to watch his reaction to all the beauties of the court who
enter, "male or female." At Stratonice's entrance, Plutarch writes, "lo, those
tell-tale signs of which Sappho sings are all there in him: stammering speech,
fiery flushes, darkened vision," heart palpitations, pallor (Beecher and Ciavolella 50, translating Plutarch). When the doctor informs the boy's father,
as Maximus says, "Without hesitation the king gave his beloved wife to his
son"—who was immediately cured (Beecher and Ciavolella translation 49).
This paradigmatic tale introduces into the medical tradition unfulfilled love
as a disease, pulse-taking as a diagnostic method, and sexual gratification,
however transgressive, as therapy (49). In one sympathetic Renaissance
retelling by a late fifteenth-century Sienese painter, the story is narrated as a
comedy in six scenes (fig. 6).[5] These represent 1) the pulse-taking; 2) Antiochus's response to Stratonice; 3) the physician's report of the son's dire condition to Seleucis; 4) his giving of his wife to his son in marriage; 5) the

[5] These representations, by an artist known only as the Master of the Stratonice Panels, dec-
orate the fronts of two quattrocento cassoni (chests). They are discussed in Wack (15–18) and
in Wolfgang Stechow (224), who recounts the circulation of the story through literature, visual
art, and opera. When Thomas Rogers retells the tale in the sixteenth century (1576) as an exemplar of lovesickness, he omits the physician and emphasizes Seleucis's diagnostic skill and
compassionate willingness to save his son's life. The father, "because he tendered his welfare,
joygned his wife to his sonne in mariage, and was content that his Queene, & wife shoulde be
a daughter in law unto him." "A strange Love, & a rare pittie," Rogers exclaims sympathetically (20r).

youthful couple dancing exuberantly at their wedding; and 6) Stratonice enjoying the wedding feast with her women. She, like Antiochus, is represented as revived by the second marriage. She loses her subordinated posture and no longer wears a sober black overblouse but elaborately decorated gowns, and she has the last panel to herself. Her centrality, confirmed in the standard designation for these, the Stratonice Panels, anticipates the attention to women's lovesickness that begins to emerge.

Cultural conditions in early modern Europe provided opportunities for women to become increasingly prominent in lovesickness discourse and encouraged elaborating and adding to these inherited stories. As we have seen in chapter 3, increased numbers of doctors, seeking professional recognition, are treating more women, and diseases of women's reproductive tract are becoming increasingly associated with erotic melancholy. Clinical practice produces case histories of women, and as lovesickness becomes "an issue in practical medicine" (Beecher and Ciavolella 103) new theorizations arise.[6] At the same time, the translation of Arabic treatises (though sometimes bowdlerized) and their incorporation into western medicine, encourages at-

---

[6] Francois Valleriola, Jean de Veyries, and Ferrand all report on cases in their practices of young men who are mad from unrequited love (Beecher and Ciavolella 105 and 375 n 13, 110, 273). Earlier, in 1565, Pieter van Foreest introduces a woman's case history. She suffers from convulsions—a symptom more explicitly somatic than the men's. When van Foreest diagnoses lovesickness and identifies the object of desire, he gets her parents to arrange the match; she is the only subject in these cases who is cured (Wack 175).

tention to women's pleasures.[7] Additional women's stories became available through the Renaissance's rediscovery and translation of ancient literature. These translations circulate female exemplars of the disease, as do Galen's newly recovered works with their initiating case of Justus's wife.

A woodcut representing Galen's diagnosis, chosen to illustrate the 1541 Venice edition of Galen's collected works, is symptomatic of these new developments because it is markedly sympathetic to the wife's plight (fig. 7). She and the dancer gaze into each others' eyes at one side while Galen takes her pulse and looks at Pylades with awareness and tolerant interest. The elegantly attired and coifed wife is young and charming, faintly smiling. The dancer, who frames the right side of the woodcut, is young, tall, and handsome, with graceful stride and a heavily muscled (and prominent) arm and leg. In sharp contrast is a satiric representation of Justus, the husband, which frames the left side of the woodcut. He is a senex figure: old, with withered face, sunken eyes, a tight little mouth, tiny beard, and shriveled, bowed legs. The appropriate match for the wife is clear—as in the Stratonice Panels. An old tale is given a new reading sympathetic to women's desires and she, not the doctor, has become central to it.

Renaissance discussions of lovesickness increasingly take women into account, using ingenious strategies to do so. Although more men then women serve as examples, classical and mythological women—Phaedra, Iphis, Persephone, Dido, Semiramis, and Sappho—are deployed so as to emphasize that this disease is gender-blind. Some treatises begin by providing paired male and female exemplars: Du Laurens names first Antiochus and Justus's wife, and John Bishop (*Beautifull Blossomes* 1577) opens with a harlot and two men who were sexually promiscuous at early ages (51v). Another strategy occurs in Thomas Rogers (*The Anatomie of the Minde*, 1576). Although, like most treatise-writers, he names more male than female victims, he achieves a degree of gender equity by providing paired cases in which Semiramis is exploited as an all-purpose example. First, like Vitellius, she exemplifies a ruined reputation (20v); then, it is noted, she commits incest with her son as Clodius does with his sister (22r); later, she loves a horse, Persiphaea loves a bull, Cyparissus, a hart, and Aristomachus, bees (22v); finally, her love leads to violence as she murders her friends so they will not

---

[7] Although marginalized in western medicine's discourse of lovesickness, women are more prominent in Arabic treatises that, outside of the restrictive context of Christian theology, promote an erotics of pleasure. They include detailed instructions for coital cures for sexual frustration, frigidity, impotence, and infertility for men *and* for women. They instruct in foreplay to enhance women's orgasms and hence fertility. Although they condemn voluntary male masturbation, they prescribe it for women as a reliable cure for excess of uterine blood, sperm, and heat, especially for fourteen-year-old girls with no available sexual partners (Jacquart and Thomasset 152–155). According to Jacquart and Thomasset, these treatises appear tolerant of same-sex liaisons (124), containing detailed nonjudgmental comparisons of vaginal and anal receptacles and of sex with women and men. One identifies a kind of woman so elegant, literate, and libidinal that she is (naturally and rightly) drawn to Sapphism (124).

FIG. 7. Galen's diagnosis of *amor hereos,* from *Omnia Opera Galeni* (Venice, 1541). Courtesy of the National Library of Medicine, Bethesda, Maryland.

reveal her passions, just as Catiline murders his son to please his new wife (23r).

Women's growing visibility in lovesickness discourse not only brings their desires to the forefront but importantly stimulates rethinking about all aspects of the condition. This is graphically illustrated in Jacques Ferrand's *Treatise on Lovesickness* (1610; revised and enlarged 1623; trans. 1640).[8] Because this treatise is the period's most comprehensive compendium of medical lovesickness discourse, it is an especially acute barometer of the changes wrought in the symptoms, signs, causes, and cures of lovesickness when women's condition is attended to. The repeated use of Sappho as an exemplum of lovesickness is one indication of Ferrand's (and the age's) new emphases.[9] Ferrand's second chapter, "The Symptoms of Erotic Melancholy," immediately gives women's lovesickness prominence and focuses on their organ of pleasure. At the climax of his opening catalog of those mad for love he tells us: "Sappho the poetess, forlorn for her love of Phaon[,] hurled herself from the Leucadian rock into the sea, for women are more frequently and more grievously troubled by these ills than are men" (229). The rest of Ferrand's chapter and treatise is driven by this new claim that women are the majority of the lovesick; this view undoes their prescribed role as chaste, silent, and subordinate.[10]

Ferrand accounts for the ubiquitousness of women sufferers by arguing, in chapter 12, that two causes of erotic melancholy are satyriasis in women

[8] Ferrand's treatise, which was not translated into English until 1640 (by Edmund Chilmead), does not directly influence medical discourse or drama in England until then. But it is a remarkably complete record of developments in lovesickness discourse in the late sixteenth and early seventeenth century. It was published in its first version in 1610, seven years after Ferrand started practicing medicine; a second edition, doubled in size, appeared in 1623. Its main influence was Du Laurens's succinct chapter on lovesickness, part of his longer treatise on melancholy. This was published in Paris in 1597 and translated into English in 1599, making available in England the core of material that Ferrand elaborated. Ferrand's debt to Du Laurens, Beecher and Ciavolella show, was "global in nature." Du Laurens's treatise was for Ferrand, "matter entirely digested, memorized, and absorbed," affecting the structure and emphases of his arguments (104). Similar ideas were available in other medical, cultural, and satiric discussions, including Burton's partition on Lovesickness in *The Anatomy of Melancholy,* which first appeared in 1621. Since direct influence is not at issue, I quote from the modern translation of Ferrand's 1623 treatise by Donald Beecher and Massimo Ciavolella.

[9] In the six references to Sappho in his treatise (229, 231, 250, 270–272, 337, 347), Ferrand draws on both classical (Ovid, Suidas) and Renaissance (Belleau, Muret) sources to circulate several of the "fictions" of Sappho that Joan DeJean identifies as prominent in France in the period. In Ferrand's treatise, as elsewhere in sixteenth-century France, Sappho's homoeroticism is acknowledged, and she is figured as a writer ("poetess" 229) and an authoritative figure ("learned" 231, 270). She is also represented as the suicidal victim of heteroerotic love for Phaon, the primary representation of Sappho in the first half of the seventeenth century, notes DeJean (29–42). See also Harriette Andreadis, who traces increasing anxiety and evasiveness in representations of Sappho's tribadism in England in the sixteenth and seventeenth century, but does not give examples from lovesickness discourse.

[10] Although the woodcut of Justus's wife serves as cover and frontispiece for their indispensable edition of Ferrand's treatise, Beecher and Ciavolella overlook his new emphasis on female sufferers and re-exclude women. Instead, in their discussion of literary and social contexts, they hypothesize a male lover, an erotic recluse who is the opposite of a Don Juan figure (165).

("an itching or tickling of the private parts"), and, especially, uterine fury ("a raging or madness that comes from an excessive burning desire in the womb, or from a hot intemperature communicated to the brain and to the rest of the body through the channels in the spine, or from the biting vapors arising from the corrupted seed lying stagnant around the uterus" 263). Chapter 14, "Diagnostic Signs of Love Melancholy," continues the emphasis on women through its many female exempla and its lengthy testimony to Sappho as a "learned and amorous poet" who both experiences and diagnoses the signs of love. After quoting her in Greek, Latin, and French ("for those who hate Greek and like Latin no better"), Ferrand asks, "Does it not appear that Sappho was as wise and as experienced in this art as our Greek, Latin, and Arab physicians in light of the fact that they mentioned no indisputable signs that this lady did not already know?" (271–272), making her the central sufferer of and the primary authority on the condition.

The privileging of women is still more evident in Ferrand's unambiguous new resolution to an old debate concerning who takes more pleasure in intercourse, men or women, and hence who is more prone to the disease— women, because more irrational or men, because hotter. Many treatises compromised, attributing to men more quality of pleasure and to women greater quantity, as does Peter of Spain (ca. 1250): "pleasure is greater in men than in women. And this is because they emit more and are more consumed in intercourse. But pleasure is double on women's part (in emitting and receiving), yet it is not of such a quality" (in Wack 247). Ferrand, however, decisively argues that "the woman experiences more violently this brutal desire, and not unreasonably so, since nature owes her some compensating pleasures for the suffering she endures during pregnancy and childbirth" (312). This explanation from nature's justness compensates women for Christianity's imposition of pain in childbirth as their punishment for Eve's fall. Ferrand further affords women's genitals, often viewed as inferior versions of men's, privileged access to desire. Women's desires are greater because their reproductive organs are contained inside and curled around each other, not outside and straight like men's (312). The concealed and self-touching aspect of women's organs causes them to experience greater intensity, quality, and frequency of desire. Ferrand supports his theory by observation: "This opinion is confirmed by daily experience which reveals to us a greater number of women witless, maniacal, and frantic from love than men—for men are far less often reduced to such extremities, unless they are effeminate courtiers, nourished on a life of riot and excess and on the breast of courtesans" (311). Although women's suffering is more somatically rooted, more prevalent, and more extreme, neither misogyny, therapeutic intercourse, nor even marriage can dependably effect a cure (Ferrand 334–335, Du Laurens 122–123). Ferrand's response is to stress prevention (chaps. 29–32) and cures for married couples (336–341).

Ferrand's generalization, although it can't be proved by statistics from his own practice in France (1603–1623?) or elsewhere, is corroborated by Richard Napier's contemporaneous practice in England (1597–1634). As MacDonald documents, and we have seen, 40 percent of the patients who saw Napier for social stresses did so for anxieties about courtship and marriage, and more women than men (two to three times as many) consulted Napier about such problems (89, 240–241 for tables). The cases reported, though brief, often conform to Ferrand's delineations of the disease's widespread symptoms and advocate his recommended cures. Mary Blundell, who pays Napier three visits in 1606, took "much grief and sighing touching a young man that promised marriage of his own accord, and after . . . broken off by his father that would not consent" (MacDonald, *Mystical* 94). The first visit she suffered "Rising up her stomacke . . . ready to stop her wynd" (Ashmole 215 fol. 21). Six days later her symptoms were mental, not somatic. She "Dreameth fearful dreams of climing up to the top of churches . . . ready to fall" (Ashmole 215 fol. 31). Three months later she still suffers "much greefe for on[e] that she would have" and has new symptoms: "Pricking and shooting . . . pricking betwixt her shoulders and the small of her backe" (Ashmole 215 fol. 100). She is purged, not married.

The case of Mr. Fettyplace illustrates the sufferer's capacity to use the condition to his own advantage—and the physician's sympathetic complicity. (We have seen this in the Jailer's Daughter and will shortly see it in the two comedies.) When Fettyplace's mother refuses to marry him to her servant, he grows mopish and stops talking. After three visits in four months and no improvements from the prescribed medications, Napier queries "whether good for Mr. Fettyplace to marry the poor maid, his mother's maid, though but poor, or to continue still foolish and idle-headed for lack of one." He answers: "purge him well . . . and then let him marry where his mind is set" (Ashmole 414 fol. 187). Napier's comment can sum up the attitude toward the satisfaction of desire that was characteristic of lovesickness theory as well as practice and of the plays that drew on it.

Sexualities

Because of its emphasis on the extremes to which lovesickness drives its victims, medical discourse overrides sharp distinctions between normative and transgressive desires and between heteroeroticism and homoeroticism. In the latter half of Ferrand's ground-laying second chapter, Sappho is the exemplar not only of heteroerotic but also of homoerotic love. The disease's several effects on women—suicide, organ changes, or Sapphism—emphasize the instability of women's bodies, desires, and love objects. Although Ferrand records the view current among some of his contemporaries that sexually frustrated women may produce penises when, in the heat of passion, their genitals reverse themselves, he argues instead that what seems to

be a penis is a descended clitoris, enlarged through passion (230). Women
need not become men to desire aggressively. He authorizes their own organ
of pleasure by providing seven different Latin and Arabic names for it from
as many different authorities: *queue, tentiginem, symptoma turpitudinis,
nympham, clitorida, amorem et dulcedinem veneris,* and *albatram, id est
virgam* (231). Ferrand represents the female homoerotic practices that this
organ makes possible as (unfortunately) widespread. The condition is
"known to many other women who unhappily abuse that part, women
called *fricatrices* by the Latins, *tribades* by the Greeks and *ribaudes* by the
French—among whom Suidas and Muret place the learned Sappho" (231).
Women's love for women and women's bodily transformations are cited in
this chapter—with only mild censure. Men's love for men, usually more fully
acknowledged in early modern legal, theological, and literary discourses
(Traub, "(In)Significance" 62–65), is downplayed here and elsewhere in this
treatise.

In many treatises, there is no sharp distinction between homo- and heteroeroticism. Gendered object choice does not centrally define the boundary
between acceptable and unacceptable sexuality, for reproductive sexuality is
not valorized and gender and sexuality are detached. Indeed the acts that
these discussions record are "unstable, resistant to codification, and defiant
of limits" (Traub, "(In)Significance" 64). For men to love men is not represented as much different from their loving prostitutes, stepmothers, sisters,
beasts, or disdainful maids. Women loving women, if no better, is also no
worse. John Bishop, in his especially moralizing discussion, shows the torments of love "both before, after, and against nature" (50v) and condemns
with equal fervor "heynous incest" (51v) in which a mother sleeps with her
son and they beget a daughter, whom he later marries; men who "against nature doe filthily abuse men, and women, women" (51v); and the madness
and shame of those who love beasts or statues (51v–52r). In contrast,
Tomasso Garzoni's satiric treatise, *The hospitall of incurable fooles* (trans.
E. Blout, 1600), humorously recites the equal folly of those who love con-
cubines, boys, corpses, bulls, and she-goats (85).

Robert Burton's *Anatomy of Melancholy* (1st ed. 1621), not a medical
treatise but a moralizing encyclopedia of pathology, does indulge in a Latin
diatribe, "for the learned only," which salaciously catalogs the worst excesses of love melancholy to reveal just what an "utterly confused category"
sodomy is (Goldberg 18, following Foucault). Under the notion of sodomy,
Burton includes bestiality; sex of "man with man"; sex "in the married state,
where an opposite part is used from that which is lawful"; masturbation, the
"other uncleanness" of "self-defiling monks" (Burton's favorite satiric tar-
get); and the actions of "wanton-loined womanlings, Tribadas, that fret each
other by turns, and fulfill Venus, even among Eunuchs with their so artful
secrets" (trans. Floyd Dell et al. 3.2.1.4; 2:651–653). The climactic and most
derogated example in the catalog is that of a woman who, disguised as a

man, married another woman, hence transgressing simultaneously normative gender roles, normative heterosexuality, and the institution of patriarchal marriage (653). We can see here how the new inclusion of women
increases the disease's destabilizing potential.

Neither particular acts nor human or animal objects, however, constitute
the greatest excess to which lovesickness drives its victims; this place is filled
by the love of inanimate objects. Fetishism, attributed only to men in the
treatises, regularly occupies the climactic place in the catalogs of sufferers
and is the love most vigorously condemned.[11] It is the ultimate pathology
because it shows "how love corrupteth the imagination, and may bee the
cause of melancholie or madnes" (Du Laurens 119). Driven by fantasy alone,
it can't be satisfied.[12] Rogers declares the "most horrible" of the loves he has
recited (including incest, same-sex, and bestiality) is that of men who dote
on images (22v). The primary example is the man of Athens who Bishop declares doth "farre exceede for raging follie" (52r). This Athenian fetishist, in
love with a statue, appears in most discussions (including Du Laurens and
Ferrand) and provides the only extended case history in Pierre Boaistuau's
treatise *Theatrum Mundi, the Theatre or rule of the world* (trans. J. Alday
1581, 199). The noble young man falls in love with a marble statue; frantic
with love, he embraces and kisses it and offers to buy it at any price from the
Senate. When refused, he decorates "her" with a robe, binds "her" hair with
fillets and garlands, and offers himself up as a suicidal sacrifice to unrequited
love (Boaistuau 199–200). The desire to use a public object for private satisfaction and the sacrifice of his male authority and his life to an inanimate
object who can't satisfy him physically make the case extreme. Men also fall
in love with other inanimate objects: with a picture of good Fortune (Rogers
22v), with statues of naked Cupid or naked Venus, or naked boys (Bishop
52r), with a tree, or their own shadows (Ferrand 260); with none of these is

[11] In "Women/Utopia/Fetish," I discuss how women have been customarily excluded as
fetish-makers from anthropological, economic, and psychoanalytic theories of fetishism (esp.
60–63 and nn 5 and 6). Lovesickness treatises display an early instance of this exclusion.

[12] Ferrand, discussing how love melancholy can lead to deluded imagination, is explicit
about this: "the Prince of the Peripatetics in his *Ethics* teaches that the affection felt for inanimate objects is not true love because there is no possibility of reciprocal affection, and that therefore the well-wishing that is the essential nature of love is pointless in such cases" (260).
Masturbation is not explicitly associated with fetishism in this discourse and, although alluded
to in Burton's diatribe against "the other uncleanness of self-defiling monks, scarce to be
named" (652), is not mentioned elsewhere in the treatises I have looked at either as a symptom
of or a cure for lovesickness. This supports Thomas Laqueur's provocative thesis that masturbation was newly "invented" as a medicalized disease in the early eighteenth century. Moreover, the treatises' belief in the potentially fatal consequences of a corrupted imagination when
obsessed with objects who cannot give satisfaction provides a medical context out of which
masturbation could emerge as a new disease of the corrupted imagination. Its danger lies in its
instigating desires that can't be satisfied but only perpetually exacerbated. Laqueur identifies
analogous sites where the imagination is thought dangerous, namely the new extension of financial credit and the increase in fiction reading.

satisfaction possible.[13] Garzoni, in his parody of the discourse, mocks it by using as his climactic terrible example (following those in love with bulls, she-goats, and corpses), the story of a man who loves a fish he names Il Gobbo and who becomes suicidal when it is eaten (85).

Far from being repressive technologies of the self, Renaissance lovesickness discourses and their offshoots partly contest theological, legal, and moral prescriptions to provide a space in which conventional gender and erotic roles and styles are loosened. Love may make men, like the man of Athens, vulnerable, passive, irrational, and subordinate—that is, more like normative women. Or it can render men insatiable tyrants. Love can banish women's modesty and turn their bodies hotter and their actions more aggressive, making them, like Semiramis, more like normative men. Or love can silence them as it does the wife of Justus. Love can give and take away power. Since lovesickness, the inability to satisfy desires, springs invariably from the love of inappropriate or unobtainable objects, whether these objects are homoerotic or heteroerotic is not of great importance. These discourses display a mixture of pity, tolerance, and appalled amazement at the "strange capers" that lovers indulge in (*AYL* 2.4.52), authorizing non-normative desires.

In lovesickness discourse, erotic stances do not always have fixed alignments with gender enactments, making it a site that perfectly exemplifies Eve Sedgwick's claim, in *Epistemology of the Closet* (22–27), that gender and sexuality are not identical and that differentiations in desire exceed gender difference and object choice and have "unaccounted-for potential to disrupt many forms of available thinking about sexuality" (25). In particular, the discursive operation of lovesickness in *Twelfth Night* and *As You Like It* elucidates Sedgwick's remark that "Some people, homo-, hetero-, and bisexual, experience their sexuality as deeply embedded in a matrix of gender meanings and gender differentials. Others of each sexuality do not" (26). Similarly, some comedies do, some don't. Valerie Traub's tripartite definitions of gender and sexuality likewise can be clarified and extended through lovesickness discourse. She differentiates gender into core gender identity ("the persistent experience of oneself as male, female or ambivalent"), gender role ("the degree to which one complies with societal expectations of 'appropriate' behavior"), and gender style ("the personal choices one makes daily to assert agency within the confines of gender") ("Differences" 87). Following

---

[13] Sometimes, however, the imagination *can* provide satisfaction. Often reiterated is the story of an Egyptian man who loved a courtesan who spurned him; but his dream of satisfaction with her cured him "of his inward fire" (Du Laurens 121–122; cf. Ferrand 333–334). This cure for lovesickness is parallel to the theatrical cure for deluded melancholics discussed in chaps. 2 and 3. And like those case histories it has a witty turn at the end when the realistic courtesan sues the beloved, complaining that although he has been satisfied, she has not been paid. The judge rules that her fee is to be the sound and sight of money—as her lover was satisfied by a dream of sex.

and revising Traub, I will analyze the two comedies to make a similar tripartite distinction within eroticism, differentiating among erotic identification (e.g., homo-hetero-bi-erotic), erotic role (e.g., aggressive or passive,
playful or serious), and erotic style/practice (e.g., particular sex acts or
fetishism). Using the terms hetero- and homoerotic (in place of the terms heterosexual and homosexual) helps defamiliarize early modern concepts and
displace twentieth-century assumptions of "heterosexuality" and "homosexuality" as fixed identities rooted in genital relations with gendered objects. And it facilitates a focus on desires, not sexual acts—which are not
explicit in either lovesickness treatises or Shakespearean comedies.

Lovesickness in Shakespeare's Comedies

The history of lovesickness brings women's desires to the forefront, and
the drama mines the narrative and comic potential of this development. In
fact, in Shakespeare's comedies, from *Love's Labor's Lost* through *All's Well
That Ends Well,* they are routinely represented as erotic, urgent, aggressive,
and acted on. In contrast men's love is more often passive, Petrarchan, and
fetishistic. To be sure the comedies are tamer than the treatises, for in them
love objects are not pictures or beasts. But in them, too, the gender of love
objects may be less important than their age, class, or erotic roles or styles.
Or it may be central. As in the nondramatic works, desire grants both male
and female characters urgency and agency, especially manifested in ubiquitous puns on "will," meaning genital organs (male or female), desire (usually sexual), and also purpose, intention, determination, and resistance.[14]
The urgency of desires and the agency of women also complicate the capacity
of the concluding moment of marriages to reproduce patriarchy and secure
normative gender hierarchy (Traub, *Desire* 120). Formalist critics such as
C. L. Barber and Northrup Frye have celebrated the reconciliation brought
about by the comic conclusions, and more recently materialist and feminist
critics have lamented the ideological containment and women's subordination they impose. But comic endings and happy marriages, like unhappy families, are not all alike; they are not all equally conventional, hegemonic, or
subordinating of women and erotic possibility. Every Shakespearean comedy arrives at marriage by different routes and performs it differently or dis-
sonantly. Especially in *As You Like It* and *Twelfth Night,* Shakespeare's ninth

[14] The lady of sonnets 127–152 is "will-full" in multiple interconnected senses and gets her
will throughout, not just in sonnets 135 and 136. The women in *Love's Labor's Lost* puncture
the men's shifts from misogyny to idealization and discuss being "hit"; Titania in *A Midsummer Night's Dream* desires everything in sight including a woman, a boy, and an ass. Helena in
All's Well That Ends Well undertakes a specular quest like Britomart's and secures her cross-
class marriage by means of a coital and reproductive cure that allows her to reframe the man
who "hates" her into one who is "wondrous kind" (1.1.98; 4.4.22; 5.3.310)—as I show in *Broken Nuptials* 58–104.

and tenth romantic comedies and the last of this type he would write, marriage, as the lovesickness discourse insists, assures neither permanent satisfaction, nor women's subordination, nor social harmony.

Examining *Twelfth Night* and *As You Like It* side by side with lovesickness treatises reveals the interaction of the discourse with comic form. Like the treatises, the plays represent the somatogenesis of love through eyes, heart, imagination, and liver as well as its conventional symptoms. They include debate about who loves most, men or women, and seem to agree with the treatises that women do—portraying them as pursuing desire more aggressively. They explicitly seek sexual therapies for the condition. Most tellingly, the plays intensify the treatises' attitude of amusement, titillation, and sympathy for the lovesick. Because these are romantic stage comedies that unfold extended characterizations instead of citing brief examples, they elicit extended identification with lovers and considerable investment in their satisfaction.

But the two plays use this discourse's disturbance of the gender/eroticism equation in opposite ways. The contexts in which love explodes are different: in a space without (viable) rulers, fathers, or politics in *Twelfth Night*, in a patriarchy governed by all three in *As You Like It*. The cross-dressed heroines function differently. Viola/Cesario blends gender roles; Rosalind, as Ganymede, enacts them sequentially. The first mirrors others' ungendered desires back to them, while the second elicits desire by representing several gendered stereotypes of it. Because inheritance and reproduction are not at issue in *Twelfth Night* but are in *As You Like It*, the relationship between gender and erotic desire is loosened in the former, but cemented in the latter. The marriages at which the two plays arrive underline their differences: the ending of *Twelfth Night* extends triangular circulations of desire and subordinates gender differences, while the ending of *As You Like It* eliminates triangles of desire and proliferates heterosexual couples.

Twelfth Night

I begin with *Twelfth Night* because its subtitle, "What You Will," and its three symbolically named willful characters, Viola, Olivia, and Malvolio (their names all anagrams of their "volition"), designate it a site of unruly desires. Yet influential discussions by Jean Howard, Cristina Malcolmson, Valerie Traub, and Dympna Callaghan qualify earlier claims for the liberating potential of comedies with cross-dressed heroines by arguing that *Twelfth Night* subordinates women and erotic possibility. Howard, focusing on the implications of cross-dressing, maintains that Viola's "properly feminine subjectivity" (113) makes her masculine attire nonthreatening while the genuinely unruly woman, Olivia, is humiliated and punished by "being made to fall in love with the crossdressed Viola" (114), leading to the "containment of gender and class insurgency" (112). Malcolmson claims that the play displaces class anxieties and struggles onto marriage to reestablish gender hierarchies underwritten by loving female service and subordination ("What You Will" 50–51). Traub, finding, as I do, circulations of homoerotic desire in *Twelfth Night,* asserts that these are displaced onto Antonio and decisively eliminated (*Desire* 123). Callaghan contends that *Twelfth Night* curtails women's power by circulating denigrating representations of their bodies and desires, most prominently through Malvolio's references to Olivia's C's, U's, T's, and great P's (436–440).

Although indebted to these feminist critics, I find erotic and gender irregularity remarkably untrammeled in *Twelfth Night* as in lovesickness discourse. Cesario's role and the shifting triangular identifications of lovers tease apart gender and eroticism so that status, not gender, becomes the primary modality that incites and circulates unruly desires—instead of class anxiety being displaced onto gender as Malcolmson suggests. Erotic desire is a function of age, status (economic and social), and body type more than of gendered objects. Because Viola/Cesario, the cross-dressed character at the center of the triangles (Kott, "Gender" 115–116), remains in disguise throughout virtually the entire play, her "masculinity" and "femininity" are simultaneous and inseparable, not polarized (Howard 113).

This character's gender and erotic identifications, roles, and styles are nuanced but sustained. Viola/Cesario identifies as a woman in love in brief soliloquies, but plays the role of a boy in company; her "masculine" gender style oscillates between wistfully boyish (with Orsino) and cheekily adolescent (with most others)—between passive resignation and assertive wit. These qualities are as apparent out of disguise as in it (in act 1, scene 2). Her/his erotic identification is female, her/his erotic (and bi-gendered) role is service, and his/her erotic style is to express desires covertly and elicit them from others through specularity. Hence she/he can elicit by mirroring (in cross-gendered fashion) different modalities of desire from differently gendered lovers/love objects whom he/she similarly serves self-interestedly. The servant's supposedly subordinate position, like that of the patient in lovesickness discourse, mobilizes erotic power.

Cesario/Viola uses her own "contemned" desires to specularize those of others as she travels back and forth between the two households. She engenders Olivia's desires (for him/her) by anticipating their urgency in the promise to act and speak—to "Make me a willow cabin at your gate. . . . Write loyal cantons of contemnèd love. . . . Hallo your name to the reverberate hills" (1.5.266–270). Here Cesario ventriloquizes Orsino's romantic desires for Olivia in a note that enables Viola to voice her own more demanding ones for Orsino. These reverberations spur Olivia's desires as she responds immediately, "You might do much. What is your parentage?" (1.5.275). Later, Viola/Cesario mirrors and elicits the desires that underlie Orsino's fetishistic love for Olivia by speaking her own for him, relayed through those of an imaginary sister who dies of erotic melancholy: "She pined in thought; / And, with a green and yellow melancholy, / She sat like Patience on a monument, / Smiling at grief" (2.4.112–115). This self-projection of standard erotic melancholy represents Orsino's and her own frustration whereas the willow cabin builder represents Olivia's and her initiative-taking. The effects of these two scenes are to release desires that are not "definitively homosexual or heterosexual. . . . Its relays are complex, its circulation endless, its field practically boundless" (Crewe, "Field of Dreams" 111).[15]

Most characteristically, Cesario forcefully enacts Viola's desire for erotic service. On first hearing of the Duke's love for Olivia, her response is to "serve" one or the other (1.2.41, 55), and she becomes page to Orsino. Later, in act 3, Cesario is "votre serviteur" to Andrew, vows "most humble service" to Olivia, and is said to be "servant" to the Count Orsino: "Your servant's servant is your servant," quips Cesario/Viola (3.1.73, 97, 99, 101, 103–104). "Service" here connotes a status, a bi-gendered role, and an erotic style, one that perhaps is an incentive to disguising and that the disguise facilitates. The reverberations of desire that Viola exudes and elicits undo polarized gender roles, represent permeable subjectivities, and loosen boundaries between homoerotic and heteroerotic desires as they are loosened in the treatises.

Gendered object choice seems to play only a small part in Orsino's and Olivia's attachments as well. Their wealth, aristocratic status, and power as heads of households give both a similar habit of command and love for servants, although their erotic styles are differently expressed.[16] Olivia likes to "command" (2.5.103) and is drawn to youthful subordinates of either gender, but not to the perhaps older and more socially powerful Malvolio and Orsino (Sinfield 70). Sir Toby tells Maria that Olivia won't marry the Count because she has sworn not to "match above her degree, neither in estate, years, nor wit" (1.3.105–106). She admits Cesario/Viola to her only on learning that he is "Not yet old enough for a man nor young enough for a boy" (1.5.155–156). She is attracted to his poor, but gentlemanly state ("'Above my fortunes, yet my state is well,'" she quotes, 1.5.288) and to attributes that are not gender specific: "Thy tongue, thy face, thy limbs, actions, and spirit" (1.5.290). She "catch(s) the plague" conventionally, as in the treatises, when she feels "this youth's perfections/ With an invisible and subtle stealth / To creep in at mine eyes" (1.5.293–296). Since Sebastian has

---

[15] See also Martha Ronk, who explicates the significance of these speeches in relation to Viola's unsettled position in the play as a whole.

[16] Alan Bray (esp. 46–57) analyzes the social and institutional settings in which homoerotic relations were situated in early modern England, emphasizing especially relations between master and servant in the patriarchal household. Bruce Smith further explores how "Renaissance Englishmen, like the ancient Greeks and Romans, eroticized the power distinctions that set one male above another in their society" (194).

the same adolescent attributes, the same face and limbs, more pliability, and less money, he is an equally apt object of Olivia's desires.

Sebastian, like Olivia, seems more turned on by age and economic markers than by gendered attributes. What he wants is to be kept, and he is perhaps willing to sleep with anyone who will do so.[17] Like his twin, Viola, he finds protective possessiveness in older men and in rich women especially attractive. So he easily slides from dependence on Antonio's power and purse to dependence on Olivia, who has more rank and money and is equally dominating. She runs her household and Sebastian with a firm hand. "Would thou'dst be ruled by me!" Olivia demands. "Madam, I will," replies Sebastian, combining volition with subordination. "O, say so, and so be," she replies (4.1.65–66), completing a traditional spousal that reverses prescribed gender hierarchies.

Orsino, even more than Olivia, likes giving orders to servants (see especially 1.4 and 2.4). In Viola/Cesario, Orsino is attracted to the same adolescent and subordinate qualities as Olivia is; indeed it is his awareness of the potential appeal of Cesario's "youth" to Olivia (1.4.27) that triggers his own eroticized perception: "Diana's lip / Is not more smooth and rubious; thy small pipe / Is *as* the maiden's organ, shrill and sound, / And all is semblative a woman's part" (1.4.31–34). As my italics suggest, Orsino is attracted to Cesario because he is appealingly *like* a woman but not a woman—that is, not like imperious Olivia. Although the tender "part" Cesario plays for and with Orsino is less witty than the one he plays for and with Olivia, it is equally obstinate and not necessarily more "feminine." He responds to his master's and his mistress's needs differently, just as he reverberates differently to each the shapes of their own desires. Her/his layered erotic and gendered style enables Olivia to desire a woman and Orsino to desire a man, consequences of lovesickness the treatises record.

Orsino's love for Olivia, in contrast to his intimate exchanges with Cesario, partakes of the fetishism and narcissism, the love for an idealized, unobtainable object that, in the treatises, only men exhibit. His opening speeches document, as critics have long noted, his absurd fixation on his own fantasies and his lack of interest in any contact with the disdainful Olivia. They also delineate all the symptoms of lovesickness that he fantasizes Olivia catching. Love fills his "liver, brain, and heart" (1.1.38), as it may hers. His "fancy" is "full of shapes"; his "desires" "pursue" him (1.1.14, 23–24); and the solitude and music, recommended as cures in treatises, only exacerbate them. Proud of his grandiose love, he argues, as do some earlier treatises, that men's capacity for love is greater than women's—because women's hearts are too small and their palates only, not their livers, are infected. He

[17] Joseph Pequigney 205. He makes a plausible case that Sebastian and Antonio, during their three months together when Sebastian assumes the name Roderigo, have been engaging in sexual relations that Sebastian now tries to terminate; hence his resumption of his own name and dismissal of Antonio (204–205).

also claims they "lack retention"—both the genital capacity for love and the ability to remain constant—thus responding to an old debate about genital pleasure (resolved in favor of women in Ferrand) with a new argument for male psychosomatic capacity (2.4.93–103). But Viola, who earlier claimed that women's "waxen hearts" and "frailty" make them more susceptible to love than men (2.2.30–31), articulates and acts out in the play, as does Olivia, the culture's growing belief that women's lovesickness is greater than men's.

It is Antonio, however, who is the play's most passionate, expressive, and constant lover; his beloved object, Sebastian, is unconventional only in his gender. Their intimacy is well established, and Antonio's passion is equally romantic and erotic. His gender and erotic roles are complex. He is a sea captain and a pirate, a romantic hero who will brave anything for love, declaring his "devotion" and "sanctity of love" to his beloved's "image" (3.4.364–366). But he also expresses his body's demands: "My desire / (More sharp than filèd steel) did spur me forth" (3.3.4–5). He is older and richer than Sebastian, yet he also begs to be his beloved's "servant" (2.1.36)—an erotic stance consonant with his lower status role. His scenes (2.1, 3.3, and 3.4) provoke relief through their directness and poignancy, a sharp contrast to the romantic fancy and triangular suggestiveness of adjacent parallel love scenes between others. Like Olivia, who is his replacement and whose erotic roles are comparable, he is represented sympathetically. He is baffled by confusing the identical twins but is not humiliated (as is Malvolio) by either the characters or the play itself.

At the play's ending, his relationship with Sebastian (whatever its precise nature) must now be shared; but it is not decisively ended by the youth's marriage, and Antonio is not excluded from the ending (Pequigney 206). After his first encounter with Olivia, Sebastian immediately seeks out Antonio: "His counsel now might do me golden service" (4.3.8). His exclamation, when they are reunited after his marriage, is passionate: "Antonio, O my dear Antonio, / How have the hours racked and tortured me / Since I have lost thee!" (5.1.217–219). Although Sebastian's reunion with Antonio is displaced by his longer one with Viola, he exchanges no more words with Olivia after this—and has exchanged none as passionate as these. The ending leaves open the possibility that marriage and a homoerotic attachment can coexist, as Bray and others have claimed they could in early modern culture (69–70).

The "specific anxiety about reproduction" that Valerie Traub "hypothesize[s] as a *structuring* principle" for these comedies (*Desire* 139) is, as she is aware, virtually unacknowledged in them. Indeed in *Twelfth Night* it is absent altogether, just as in lovesickness discourse. There is no older generation, no emphasis on lineage, indeed no represented family or political order at all. Unlike the conclusions of a majority of Shakespeare's comedies, including *Midsummer Night's Dream, Much Ado About Nothing, Merchant*

of Venice, and *As You Like It, Twelfth Night* contains no concluding antici-
pation of reproduction or of the accompanying fear of cuckoldry. These are
missing even from Feste's final disillusioned song, which narrates a man's
progression through life—although his protagonist does "wive" (5.1.398).
The lack of projection of a social order or of a reproductive or political future allows the circuits of desire to remain open at the ending. *Twelfth
Night*'s irregular matches are further made acceptable—structurally, thematically, and ideologically—by the humiliation of Malvolio for desires that,
like those of the others, are incited by status difference and social ambitions.
Malvolio's maddening, as punishment for his desires, will be treated in the
next chapter.[18]

The marriages that the play anticipates or completes do not reestablish
conventional erotic pairings or gender hierarchies or promise children. Instead the fluidity of desire and gender is reemphasized at the conclusion by
the "large residue of bigendered and bisexual subjectivity" which remains
(Crewe, "Field of Dreams" 112). As we have seen, Sebastian remains loved
by Antonio and Olivia and Viola and loves all three. Although Cesario is revealed as Viola, the twins share "one face, one voice, one habit" (5.1.215).
Their many similarities of looks, desires, and roles make their nominally different genders of scant importance. Orsino's affections easily enlarge to em-
brace Viola along with Cesario. He effortlessly moves Viola into the place
formerly held by Olivia as "Orsino's mistress and his fancy's queen"
(5.1.389). At the same time he offers his "boy" and "lamb" his hand for service already tendered and continues to call him Cesario; s/he continues to
"over swear" the "sayings" Cesario formerly swore (5.1.266–273). S/he remains in male dress and the retrieval of her "other (female) habits" is de-
ferred (5.1.272–277, 388), as is her movement into a normative gender role.
Like the Duke, Olivia is "betrothed both to a maid and man" (5.1.262). She
likewise embraces her surrogate love object with equanimity since he has all
the qualities she desired in Cesario and continues to be subordinate to her:
"I am sorry, madam," he apologizes after besting Sir Toby in a sword fight
(5.1.208).

Olivia, still entirely in control, interrupts the unfolding ending to free
Malvolio and assess blame. While waiting for his appearance, she occupies
herself by arranging a double wedding:

---

[18] The trick on Malvolio precipitates another marriage. In the play's third match, Maria,
Olivia's waiting woman (of borderline gentility), marries Sir Toby Belch, Olivia's impoverished
aristocratic uncle, "in recompense" for her "device"—the insubordinate trick she plays on
Malvolio (5.1.360–364). She remains a woman on top throughout the play, curbing and incit-
ing Toby and Sir Andrew, feigning her mistress's hand and signature, offering to Malvolio an
image of an antic lover that he cannot help but don. The unruly cross-class match will provide
Toby with the security he needs, but like the other marriages in the play, it fails to fulfill the primary early modern functions of marriage: to prevent fornication, ensure legitimate procreation,
and subordinate women.

My lord, so please you, these things further thought on,
To think me as well a sister as a wife,
One day shall crown th'alliance on't, so please you,
Here at my house and at my proper cost.

(5.1.316–319)

Her offer to pay for Orsino's marriage forces his hand—literally—for her words generate his explicit offer of marriage to Cesario and the giving of his hand: "Here is my hand; you shall from this time be / Your master's mistress" (5.1.325–326). But Olivia concludes the line—"A sister; you are she" (5.1.326)—translating her affection for Viola/Cesario into a new configuration. Hence the play that begins in the household of Orsino ends at Olivia's; she displaces the Duke as the primary authority figure in Illyria.[19] Neither marriage is represented as conventionally gendered or even exclusively heterosexual, and bonds and pleasures other than marital ones explicitly persist and are acknowledged in the final scene.[20]

As You Like It

As You Like It circulates desire through a cross-dressed heroine and elaborates the discourse of lovesickness still more directly than does *Twelfth Night*—but with very different effects. Some critics have found the play more transgressive than *Twelfth Night* in its representations of gender and sexuality. Jean Howard, for example, argues that the epilogue reopens and makes visible "the contamination of sexual kinds and the multiplication of erotic possibility" the play has intimated (121). Valerie Traub shows how the performance of the mock marriage of Rosalind/Ganymede/Rosalind with Orlando has the effect of "appropriating the meaning of matrimony for deviant

---

[19] Alan Sinfield's analysis of what Olivia desires in Sebastian is almost identical to mine except that he sees Olivia's "silence," when confronted with the twins, as signaling the sacrifice of her desires and her character's consistency to the ideological project of the play's closure, which entails that she "cannot be allowed to have a man who will not dominate her" (72). But Sebastian's ability to win an (offstage) fight against the drunken Sir Toby and the pathetic Andrew does not render him as straightforwardly "manly" (71) as Sinfield claims. He continues to be subordinate to Olivia as she dominates and controls all the characters in the last scene. The "faultlines" that do emerge under the pressure to achieve closure seem especially visible in the Duke's acceptance of Viola as a "mistress" in spite of her boy's clothes. The "dissidence" (Sinfield's useful term, esp. 35–51) in both relationships is concealed by the intrusion of the Malvolio subplot into the denouement; it functions throughout to displace attention away from the main couples, as I will show in chap. 5.

[20] A Chicago Repertory Theater production of *Twelfth Night,* directed by Michael Pennington in 1996, concluded with Olivia and Orsino exiting arm in arm, dressed in matching upper-class whites, followed by Cesario and Sebastian, still in identical pages' garb and embracing. This graphic signal that Olivia and Orsino remain twinned, as do Viola and Sebastian, kept the circuits of desire open within and between the marriages. Equally appropriate would be an ending in which Olivia and Viola, and Orsino, Sebastian, and Antonio exit together arm in arm.

desires" and "exposing the heterosexual imperative of matrimony as a reduction of the plurality of desire into the singularity of monogamy" (*Desire*
127). The play, however, represents eroticism as more deeply "embedded in
a matrix of gender meanings and gender differentials" (Sedgwick 26) than
does *Twelfth Night* and circulates more stereotyped representations of gender and eroticism and their connections than does that play. But the prolif-
eration in *As You Like It* of stereotypes of desire, gender, and marriage and
the abruptness with which the characters shift their roles or their love objects ultimately call into question, in this play too, the possibility of normative desire, fixed gender roles, or stable marriages. As is characteristic of
pastoral romance, the movement to Arden precipitates shifts in roles and desires and undoes conventions.

Alterations of character and allegiance are the rule. The usurping Duke
Frederick, an irascible textbook villain, converts to meditative pleasures. The
bad older brother, Oliver, turns filial when Orlando saves his life. Desire, as
in lovesickness discourse, causes equally sudden transformations. Touchstone, a mocker of love's conventions, desires the "poor thing" Audrey
enough to marry her. Audrey abandons her swain William for Touchstone
and the prospect of becoming a courtier's wife. Phebe veers from disdain for
Silvius to desire for Ganymede to a resigned marriage to Silvius; Orlando
from a heroic wrestler to a pupil of love. Rosalind and Celia give up their affection for each other to become lovers of men.

The character of Rosalind/Ganymede, of course, undergoes the most radical changes of role and desires; she also precipitates changes in others by
putting into circulation multiple stereotypes of masculinity and femininity,
of love and marriage. As these are ventriloquized through Ganymede/Ros-
alind, they are rendered comic and unstable. Her quadruple role of the boy
actor (or "ganymede") playing Rosalind playing Ganymede playing Rosalind is sequentially unfolded rather than layered like that of Viola/Cesa-
rio—because Rosalind has a confidante in Arden whereas "Viola" exists
throughout most of *Twelfth Night* only under and through her Cesario role,
and the boy actor never emerges as he does in the Epilogue to *As You Like
It*. This sequential role-playing makes it difficult to conceptualize for *As You
Like It*'s central character a unified identity or stable "femininity." The play
unfolds a series of "Rosalinds" and "Ganymedes" that never coalesce, and
these shes and hes generate instability in others.

The first act of *As You Like It* represents the romantic (and in performance
potentially homoerotic) love of Celia and Rosalind in a more extended way
than any such affections cited in lovesickness discourse or performed elsewhere in Shakespearean comedy. It is vowed permanent. It is more fully represented than that of Antonio and Sebastian in *Twelfth Night* although not,
in the text, as passionately eroticized (but see Traub, "(In)Significance" 71).
Before we meet the two we learn that "never two ladies loved as they do"
and that Rosalind remains at court after her father's banishment because

Celia (like Antonio) "would have died to stay behind her" (1.1.105–110). To each other they are, "my sweet Rose, my dear Rose" (1.2.21–22) and "Dear Celia" (1.2.2). Celia's greater resources and greater affection make her Rosalind's protector: "Rosalind lacks then the love / Which teacheth thee that thou and I am one. / Shall we be sund'red, shall we part, sweet girl? / No, let my father seek another heir" (1.3.95–98). She possessively spurns Rosalind's suggestion that they play at the sport of "falling in love" (1.2.24) and, although equally taken with Orlando's youthful charm, never falls for him. The trip to the forest with Rosalind as Celia's protector continues their intimacy while reversing its power dynamics. Rosalind, whether because of her disguise, her lovesickness, or the change in venue and status, now takes the lead. Celia, abandoning endearments, is increasingly subordinated; she is reduced to watching, mocking, and eventually mimicking Rosalind's lovesickness. Both the Celia characterized in act 1 and the love between women performed there gradually evaporate from the play (DiGangi 52–53).

Lovesickness overtakes Rosalind and Orlando simultaneously as both "fall" in love at first sight (1.2.245–251). Neither, however, acknowledges their sexual desires until Rosalind plays Ganymede playing, sometimes, "Rosalind." Rosalind exploits the conventions of the discourse of lovesickness to draw Orlando's attention away from his fetishizing poems on trees: "From the east to western Ind, / No jewel is like Rosalind. / Her worth, being mounted on the wind, / Through all the world bears Rosalind" (3.2.87–90) and to incite his desires. Pretending a cure for love, Ganymede induces lovesickness by modeling for Orlando its bodily affect, a material wooer, sexual practices, and a misogyny cure. She teaches him the conventional bodily symptoms: a "lean cheek," a "blue eye and sunken," a "beard neglected," as well as the "careless desolation" of dress that will result (3.2.371–379). Next she incites Orlando to a rehearsal of wooing, a desire for kissing, and a walk through the marriage ceremony. The "cure" (3.2.400, 401, 415, 419, 420) she undertakes is precisely the standard misogynistic denigration of women recommended in the treatises. Du Laurens, for example, advises accusing the lover's mistress of being "light, inconstant, foolish, devoted to varietie, mocking and laughing to scorne this his griefe and corrosive, disdainful as not acknowledging his deserts" (122–123). Ganymede improvises on this scheme by playing to the hilt the stereotypical woman's role the misogynists construct; she will, she says "grieve, be effeminate, changeable, longing and liking, proud, fantastical, apish, shallow, inconstant. . . . now like him, now loathe him; then entertain him, then forswear him" (3.2.405–411). By playing these roles, he/she deploys misogynist stereotypes and uses lovesickness discourse to incite heteroerotic desire.

Rosalind, playing Ganymede playing "Rosalind," subordinates Orlando. To catalyze his desires, she replaces the unthreateningly static, asexual "Rosalind" of his poems with another "Rosalind," a specularized image of a powerful, sexually promiscuous woman and wife. In doing so, Ganymede/

Rosalind perhaps imagines herself into the role of this "Rosalind," in order to alleviate her own anxieties about being subordinated to a lover or husband. To cure romantic love, she maps out for Orlando (and herself) the oft cited dangers of marriage; like Burton she proffers to cure love melancholy by adducing "Women's Faults, Miseries of Marriage, Events of Lust" (cf. Burton 3.2.5.3; 3:229–240). Just as Burton advises husbands to see their prospective wives, "angry, merry, laugh, weepe, hote, cold, sick, sullen, dressed, undressed, in all attires, sites, gestures, passions, eat her meales, &c. And in some of these you will surely dislike" (3:227), Ganymede represents a "Rosalind" that will be a wife, "more clamorous than a parrot against rain, more newfangled than an ape, more giddy in my desires than a monkey" (4.1.147–149). As Burton warns that marriage means infidelity and financial ruin (3:235–236), so Ganymede warns penniless Orlando of penury and cuckoldry: a snail is an apt wooer because he "carries his house on his head; a better jointure, I think, than you make a woman" (4.1.52–53), and also of the demands of child-bearing and child-rearing: "let her never nurse her child herself, for she will breed it like a fool" (4.1.171–172). "Rosalind's" italicized commonplaces, like those of Burton, remind both the couple and the play's audience that marriage does not necessarily provide a cure for love, produce a stable gender hierarchy, or lead to a happy ending.

"Rosalind's" ventriloquizing of misogyny reveals it to be the discourse in which the Renaissance most fully acknowledges women's power, voice, and eroticism.[21] "Rosalind" especially represents to Orlando her uncontainable wit, a metonymy for her "will," sexual and otherwise: "the wiser, the way-warder. Make the doors upon a woman's wit, and it will out at the casement; shut that, and 'twill out at the keyhole; stop that, 'twill fly with the smoke out the chimney." If a husband were to meet "your wife's wit going to your neighbor's bed," she'd say, "she came to seek you there" (4.1.157–160, 164–168). Rosalind here attributes aggressive sexual promiscuity to herself and, perhaps, homoeroticism to herself or her future husband—depending on who is imagined with whom in that neighbor's bed (DiGangi 58). She wittily insists, as Burton does, on "the inconstancy and lightnesse of women" (229). No wonder Orlando flees: "For these two hours, Rosalind, I will leave thee" (4.1.174–175). Meanwhile Celia executes a milder version of this debunking strategy, criticizing Orlando's looks, his kisses, his fidelity (3.4.1–43).

Rosalind's appropriation of misogyny does not eliminate desire but induces it. Talking about sex is titillating for the couple, as perhaps reading lovesickness discourse or misogyny tracts or attending comedies would have

---

[21] Here, as in the preface to the 1993 edition of *Broken Nuptials* (xii–xiii), I emphasize the denaturalizing effects of Rosalind's performative re-citation of misogyny in *As You Like It*. Joan Kelly likewise sees the discourse of misogyny as an incitement to early feminist theory. Linda Woodbridge finds that misogynists' representations of women as aggressive, lusty, and powerful emphasize stereotypical attributes congenial to contemporary feminism (8, 323).

been for early modern audiences. For Rosalind as for Orlando, acting out marriage and talking bawdily about sexual organs and going to bed gives body to romantic imaginings and arouses desire. Since Ganymede/Rosalind's mockery is playful and italicized, it promotes interchange and intimacy. Such witty exchanges, as Stephen Greenblatt shows, generate erotic friction (*Shakespearean* 88–90). Celia accurately recognizes Rosalind's mockery as a "love-prate" that exposes female genitalia/desires: "We must have your doublet and hose plucked over your head, and show the world what the bird hath done to her own nest" (4.1.200–202). Rosalind, in response to the couple's extended witty intercourse, passionately expresses the erotic depth of her love. "O coz, coz, coz, my pretty little coz, that thou didst know how many fathom deep I am in love! But it cannot be sounded. My affection hath an unknown bottom, like the Bay of Portugal" (4.1.203–206). This avowal of the genital excess that treatises circulate is an acknowledgment of insatiable desires, not an expression of "properly feminine subjectivity" as Howard suggests (118).

Ganymede/Rosalind's passion and witty role-playing likewise induce erotic desires in others by example and design. Her angry denunciation of the static Petrarchan affair of Phebe and Silvius again counters one set of idealizing gender stereotypes with another kind, denouncing Phebe and praising Silvius to reverse the Petrarchan power dynamics of the relationship. Her attack on Phebe's ugliness ("inky brows," "black silk hair," "bugle eyeballs" 3.5.46–47) and low value ("Sell when you can, you are not for all markets" 3.5.60) and her challenge to Silvius's subordination ("You are a thousand times a properer man / Than she a woman" 3.3.51–52) are conventionally recommended cures (see Burton 3.2.5.3; 3:220–227). Her attack jolts both, but in fact deepens Silvius's desires and attracts Phebe's to Ganymede. Here again, a dose of misogyny serves to empower Phebe—in the short run. And Touchstone everywhere insists on the drive to copulation of sheep, goats, cats, and humans: "If the cat will after kind, / So be sure will Rosalind" (3.2.102–103). Celia and Oliver, who must both endure the love prates of their "sister" and brother, mimic their siblings and plunge into lovesickness with textbook regularity: in the space of a single sentence they "looked," "loved," "sighed," diagnosed their condition, and "sought the remedy"— immediate marriage to avoid being "incontinent" before (5.2.33–39). In turn, the recital of Celia's and Oliver's movement toward satisfaction, made first by Orlando and then by Rosalind (5.2.1–4, 30–41), reverberates back to them. Their mirrored narrations precipitate Orlando's comment that he "can live no longer by thinking" (5.2.50) and Ganymede/Rosalind's movement beyond role-play and foreplay: "I will satisfy you if ever I satisfied man" (5.2.114).

While all the erotic styles and gender roles circulated in the play through characters and text are conventional, their multiplicity and transience are unsettling. The changes in gender roles, erotic styles, and power inflections that mark Rosalind's role deconstruct any simple notions of gender and desire. The boy actor playing the character plays: the dependent girlfriend with Celia in act 1, "coupled and inseparable" (1.3.75); the protective youth, Ganymede, who parodies the self-importance adolescent boys project hopefully around girls: "I must comfort the weaker vessel, as doublet and hose ought to show itself courageous to petticoat" (2.4.5–7); another Ganymede with Orlando—the youthful misogynist, wise in the ways of women and love; the aggressively promiscuous wife, Rosalind; the woman in love who weeps and faints (3.4 and 4.3); and the self-subordinating daughter and wife who recites "To you I give myself, for I am yours" to father and husband in the last scene (5.4.116–117). With the addition of the homoerotic vibrations potentially aroused both by the name "Ganymede" (that of Jove's page and the standard slang term for a youthful homoerotic object of desire—especially a boy actor) and the presence of the boy actor playing multiple bi-gendered roles, the play circulates images of genders, genitals, and drives to copulate as do the lovesickness treatises. The play, even more than the treatises (which lack the resources of performance or disguise), makes visible contradictions in the multiple gender roles prescribed for women and for men.

As the treatises sometimes advocate, the play's fluid desires are channeled by Rosalind, Hymen, and the play into a highly ritualized and apparently conventional set of marriages. These are explicitly situated within a social context emphatically marked as patriarchal in which economic, political, and marital power are expressly controlled by men (Montrose, "Place" 51–54). The hymn of the male god Hymen imposes the social, community-building, and reproductive functions of marriage, absent from *Twelfth Night:* "Tis Hymen peoples every town" (5.4.143). Hymen's blessings on "you and you," perhaps introduce some mutuality into these marriages. But while, in the body of the play, the women characters establish positions of power over their lovers—Phebe by disdain, Audrey by resolute chastity, Rosalind by role-playing deferral, and Celia as heir to the ruling Duke—this power is eliminated in the last scene through the performance of the marriages and the Duke's abdication. Whereas bonds between Antonio and Sebastian, Orsino and Cesario, Viola and Olivia were reasserted at the moment of marriage, those of Celia and Rosalind, Phebe and Ganymede, Orlando and Ganymede are suppressed in the text of the last scene. When, in *Twelfth Night,* Viola emerges out of her Cesario role, she retains aspects of it, as Orsino acknowledges. But the decorous re-habited bride who appears in the final scene of *As You Like It* contains few traces of former Ganymedes or former Rosalinds.

What are powerfully represented here, unlike in *Twelfth Night,* are conventionally gendered heterosexual unions enunciated in Jaques's concluding blessings. These assert the political and economic as well the sexual functions of marriage; their order delineates a hierarchical society from Duke down to fool. They emphatically position the four husbands as subjects, relegating their unnamed wives to possessed objects:

[To ORLANDO.]	You to a love that your true faith doth merit;
[To OLIVER.]	You to your land and love and great allies;
[To SILVIUS.]	You to a long and well-deservèd bed;
[To TOUCHSTONE.]	And you to wrangling, for thy loving voyage
	Is but for two months victualled.

(5.4.188–192)

But viewed in the light of the play as a whole, the ending may be interpreted as less than perfectly hegemonic and normative. The highly formalized and ritualized enactment of the weddings hints that this is just yet another donning of roles. They may be no more permanent than any of the others we have seen enacted or circulated. Rosalind's stereotypes of powerful wives remain salient, challenging the view that marriage permanently subordinates women. The lack of acknowledged affection between Celia and Rosalind in the last act reminds us that love can disappear. Jaques's precisely differentiated blessings make clear that the four marriages serve different functions and that Touchstone and Audrey's will not last. The same may be true for the rest. Like Shakespeare's audience, we know from lovesickness discourse and experience, that marriage, while the approved strategy for satisfying inordinate desires, does not always work. As Burton says, "If women in generall be so bad (and men worse than they) what a hazard is it to marry, where shall a man finde a good wife, or a woman a good husband? A woman a man may eschue, but not a wife: wedding is undoing, (some say) marrying, marring; wooing woing" (3.2.5.3; 3:229–230), and, like Ferrand, he judiciously includes a chapter on the prevention and cure of lovesickness in the married (Burton 3.3.4.2; 3:316–329; Ferrand, chap. 34, 336–341).

The epilogue encourages such uncertainty by reopening erotic possibility and circulating it to the audience, whether men or women, married or unmarried. The actor playing Rosalind claims, while still in his female costume, that if he were a woman he would kiss men, and if a man would kiss women. The epilogue, like the play, continues to suture eroticism to gender by making the play's success depend upon "the love [women] bear to men" and "the love [men] bear to women" (epilogue 12, 14). The boy actor's female role-playing, however, renders even this mapping less secure and reminds us of the multiple possibilities for "masculinity," "femininity," and "marriage" that the play has put into circulation. Would early modern playgoers, leaving the theater after a performance of *Twelfth Night* or *As You Like It,* find their own lovesickness hegemonically contained? Or might it have been elicited? Did they go home to court their beloveds? to kiss their spouses?

Might they leave the theater to solicit the actors as the Citizen woman so-licited Richard Burbage in John Manningham's reported anecdote?[22] Or are they like those theater audiences Stubbes, the antitheatrical polemicist, fan-tasizes in which "everyone bringes another homeward of their way verye freendly, and in their secret conclaves (covertly) they play the Sodomits, or worse" (quoted in Goldberg 118)? In the examples of the lovesickness trea-tises, in the eroticized intercourse between performers on the stage, in the charged exchanges between performers and audiences, and in the exchanges within the audience that may continue after the play is over, a heterogeneous, volatilely erotic and gendered subject with unpredictable agency emerges from both these Shakespeare comedies as from the treatises. The plays, even more than the developing lovesickness discourse, teach us to hope for satis-faction of all subjects' desires, however untoward—but most especially for those of the women protagonists.

Women's Lovesickness Visualized

The trends that have been emerging in medical and dramatic discourses of lovesickness early in the seventeenth century are wonderfully visible in en-gaging paintings of the Doctor's Visit, which were wildly popular in mid-cen-tury Dutch genre painting. Jan Steen paints the scene at least eighteen times (Sutton et al., *Masters* 313; Westermann 130 n 63). Women, who by now have become the primary sufferers of the formerly male-coded condition of lovesickness, are the protagonists of each picture. The paintings, like the dra-mas, seize on (and perhaps encourage) medical interest in uterine diseases, while popularizing and sympathizing with women's condition. These comic paintings, like the treatises and Shakespeare plays, grant women agency and engender sympathy and hopes for their satisfaction. There are no bars to this since doctors are comically redundant, fathers and husbands are absent, and the successful therapy is acknowledged by patient and viewers alike.

The paintings wittily represent the conventional symptomatology of lovesickness, its diagnostic techniques, and its proven therapy—as Laurinda Dixon has shown in *Perilous Chastity*. In all of them, and especially those by Jan Steen that will serve as my examples here, the youthful women patients are beautiful, elegantly attired, and well-to-do (which makes them, as we have seen, especially prone to the disease). They are displayed in poses of dreamy melancholy, with heads characteristically resting on hand, and they

---

[22] "Upon a tyme when Burbidge played Rich[ard] 3. there was a Citizen grewe soe farr in liking with him, that before shee went from the play shee appointed him to come that night unto hir by the name of Ri[chard] the 3. Shakespeare, overhearing their conclusion, went before, was intertained, and at his game ere Burbidge came. Then message being brought that Richard the 3d. was at the dore, Shakespeare caused returne to be made that William the Conquerour was before Rich[ard] the 3" (Manningham 75).

FIG. 8. Jan Steen, *The Lovesick Maiden,* ca. 1661–63. Courtesy of Bayerische Staatsgemäldesammlungen, Alte Pinakothek, Munich.

FIG. 9. Jan Steen, *The Doctor's Visit*, ca. 1663. Copyright Victoria & Albert Museum, London/Art Resource, NY.

FIG. 10. Jan Steen, *The Doctor's Visit*, ca. 1663–65. Courtesy of the John G. Johnson Collection, Philadelphia Museum of Art.

suffer from many of the symptoms of lovesickness Ferrand lists, especially "pale and wan complexion," "a sense of grief," "sighing," "fainting," "melancholy," and "uterine fury" (229). The attending doctor gazes at the patient's urine or looks astonished as he recognizes the pulse's palpitations, as in *The Lovesick Maiden,* likely the earliest and also the most explicitly titled of Steen's renditions (fig. 8). The patient has sometimes swooned on the floor or bed. The woman's afflicted part is graphically and bawdily represented by the womb-shaped baskets, bowls, pitchers, mandolins, flasks, and bed warmers that abound. Its overheated condition, Dixon suggests, is particularly symbolized by the prominent foot warmer bases—coals in a clay pot that sit outside of the perforated box on which feet would rest (figs. 8, 9, and 10). Sometimes the instrument that assures the woman's satisfaction is figuratively present, represented by a clyster, a candle, a herring. Interim therapies are also visible: a glass of wine, music, a prescription, or sometimes a recently burnt string whose noxious smell supposedly drives the rising womb back into place, what Westermann calls "folksy aroma therapy" (103, and see Dixon 143–147). Surer remedies are sometimes at hand when the lover appears in the doorway (figs. 8, 10). Visual quotations—paintings of lovers embracing (cf. Venus and Adonis in fig. 9) or boy Cupid with bow and arrow (fig. 9)—further emphasize that heterosexual intercourse is the desired and desirable cure.

These paintings draw on developments in the medical tradition and may have piqued further medical interest in women's uterine diseases and hastened shifts in terminology already underway. The decade of the 1660s, when this topic was suddenly and wildly popular in Dutch painting,[23] was followed by an increase in dissertations on the condition through to the end of the century and beyond. As we have seen in this chapter and the last, at the beginning of the seventeenth century, the reproductive disease of the suffocation of the mother, with its multiple causes, began to coalesce with erotic melancholy with its single cause in the congested genitals. The reciprocal influence between artistic and medical innovation is easier to trace in mid-century Holland than earlier in England since the paintings flourished so briefly and dissertation titles from Dutch medical schools are available. The Leiden medical school was a prominent center for the study of uterine diseases (Dixon 218–219), and the first dissertations on the topic appear between 1650 and 1655 (6 titles), anticipating the paintings. But the topic becomes even more popular in Leiden *after* the paintings have been completed and hung, suggesting their influence on medicine.[24] A gradual shift in medical

[23] Franz Van Mieris initiated this genre or topic in 1657 and, after flourishing for a decade, it waned in popularity after 1670 (Westermann 130 n 63; Dixon fig. 14). Although Dixon notes a few late seventeenth-century instances and imitations, almost all of the paintings she discusses are in that thirteen-year period—including Steen's major contributions to the genre.

[24] Dixon's useful appendix shows that, following the 6 dissertations in Leiden between 1650 and 1655, there were 5 coinciding with the production of the paintings (between 1658 and 1665). These were followed by 10 dissertations in Leiden between 1671 and 1680 and 7 more

terminology signals new understandings of a once general condition, now associated specifically with women's bodily desires. The once standard designation for uterine disorder, *De suffocatione uterina* (Jorden's "suffocation of the mother"), almost disappears as a dissertation topic by the end of the seventeenth century, and two new designations gain favor—*hysterica passio* (passions of the womb) and *De chlorosi* (greensickness). These emergent terms eventually replace the older designations, emphasizing the discrediting of the womb's wandering and the disease's narrowing associations with erotic desire. Both paintings and dissertations participate together in changes in medical nosology and cultural attitudes toward women.[25]

In particular, the paintings greatly enhance the agency we have watched being granted to desiring women. Everything in them conspires to elicit sympathy with the woman and hope for her satisfaction: the bawdy objects, the representation of knowing onlookers and clueless doctors, and the suitor's arrival frame these pictures as little comedies looking toward a happy ending.[26] In most paintings, sympathetic older women (who may be maidservants, nurses, mothers) gaze either dubiously at the foolish doctor or compassionately at the woman whom they sometimes support or comfort with music or wine (see figs. 8, 9, and 10). An analogue to the supporters of the possessed women whose visual representations were viewed in the last

---

between 1681 and 1691 (Dixon 251–252). In Utrecht, where study of the disease was likewise popular, there are 3 relevant titles before 1667; but the greatest cluster of titles (9) occurs later, between 1690 and 1697 (Dixon 253–254).

[25] Because Dixon chooses (unusually) to term the patients' condition uniformly *furor uterinus* or uterine fury, and because she usually represents the medical tradition as unified and static to "show how the art of this period revealed, justified, and perpetuated an ancient medical belief in the innate instability of the female sex" (3), she overlooks the regendering and the changes in diagnoses and attitudes that medicine, drama, and paintings participate in together. In Dutch medical dissertations, *furor uterinus* is a late and infrequent designation for lovesickness. Of the 131 medical dissertations on uterine diseases published between 1575 and 1699 that Dixon lists in her appendix "Female Hysteria" (249–256), only one 1685 Leiden work titles the disease *furor uterinus*. Of the 49 dissertations between 1700 and 1750, only 5 use this title. The plethora of designations (well over 30) reveal different emphases and shifting constructions of the disease. The most common title, *De suffocatione uterina*, appears 35 times before 1700, but more often earlier than later (6 of the 7 dissertations published in Leiden before 1655 have this title). The second most popular title is *De hysterica passione* and its variants (e.g., *De passione hysterica*), with 24 appearances before 1700. While not new (Lear famously uses "*hysterica passio*" of his madness 2.4.56), this designation grows more prominent at the end of the century. *De chlorosi* (chlorosis or greensickness) is the third most popular title before 1700, with 14 instances. It too gains ground, but then disappears after 1700, and *passio hysterica* and its variants become the usual designation (18 appearances). The terminological shifts point to the gradual disappearance, toward the century's end, of the explanatory power of the wandering womb and manifest new etiologies of a disease increasingly situated in the passions, genitals, and fantasy. When this condition becomes routinely titled with some derivation of *hysteria*, women's lovesickness begins its journey toward becoming the condition eventually made famous under that title by Charcot and Freud.

[26] Dixon interprets these representations as containing and subordinating women, claiming that the disease of the raging uterus inevitably requires and allows doctors to control unruly women; as she puts it, "A sick woman was also a safe woman" (220). But the pictures may have different—or contradictory—messages.

chapter or to Glauce, Britomart's invaluable nurse, these figures sanction the woman's desires, solicit the viewers' sympathy, and provide an alternative to the doctor's inept diagnosis. Similarly, "laughing prompt[s]" break the frame to directly solicit the viewers' indulgence for the desired comic climax (Westermann 113). These include the bawdy jester holding up the phallic herring—who has Steen's features (fig. 10); the laughing boy cupid preparing to shoot his arrow (fig. 9); the grinning boy gesturing with the clyster (Dixon fig. 66); and the boy giving the finger knowingly to the viewer in Schalcken's more explicit representation of pregnancy (Dixon fig. 63). Even the little dogs are sympathetic to their mistress's condition and imitate her excitement, dejection, or desired copulation (figs. 8 and 9). Only the doctors are clueless. Their old-fashioned clothes, their unnecessary diagnostic tools (urinanalysis and pulse-taking), and their worthless prescriptions are redundant, for it is clear to all but them that the only cure is intercourse with the approaching lover (figs. 8 and 10 and Dixon fig. 65). The pictures' theme is driven home in the motto inscribed on love letters in four Steen paintings: "No doctor needed there since it is the pain of love" (Sutton, "Jan Steen" 21, and nn 4 and 5 and fig. 8).[27]

These paintings develop and consolidate trends we have watched emerge in medical treatises and English drama earlier in the century. Lovesick women are the center of attention, and support for their satisfaction is elicited. The representations perhaps influence medical research, which is continuously revising its conceptions of and terminology for women's diseases of desire. In the pictures not only are doctors redundant, but fathers and husbands are absent. Hence there are none of the usual social barriers to women's satisfaction (no Justus, Jailer, or Duke Senior to negotiate with). The narrative thrust of the pictures, their bawdy images, and the incorporated portraits of lovemaking all point toward a traditional comic happy

[27] Mariët Westermann analyzes Steen's parodic uses of pictorial traditions and comic markers, placing his paintings in the contexts of jestbooks, satire, and stage farce and emphasizing their invitations to laughter. She interprets these doctor visit paintings as comic narratives and identifies the old-fashioned costumes of the doctors as the borrowing of a stock satiric stage device (101–105). Henry Meige, a physician himself, analyzed Dutch paintings of "La Mal d'Amour" in a series of chatty articles that compared Steen with Molière, who sees physicians as "ignorant pedants, often pretentious and almost always grotesque" ("Medicins" 189, trans. Dixon 185). Like Westermann and Meige, Peter Sutton, in a catalog for a 1983 Steen exhibition usefully subtitled "Comedy and Admonition," emphasizes the comic portrayals of the doctors (21–23). In addition to imitating jokebooks and stage satire, these figures parody earlier representations of the doctors diagnosing lovesickness—including the 1541 woodcut of Galen diagnosing Justus's wife (see fig. 7). Like Galen there, the doctors in Steen's paintings usually wear long robes/capes with collar showing, and tall "stovepipe" hats. The features of Steen's doctors sometimes resemble Galen's sharp nose and small pointed beard: compare fig. 7 with figs. 8 and 9. Likewise the pulse-taking doctor and lovesick youth in the cassoni panels of Antiochus and Stratonice (fig. 6) anticipate the poses of Steen's doctors and lovesick maidens— and of his own (now lost) representation of the legendary pair. Stechow claims that Steen's "Antiochus and Stratonice" differs radically from earlier versions "in that it shows none of the classical dignity usually bestowed on the subject but makes it appear like a low comedy affair, with the burlesque aspect rather predominating over the serious" (229 and fig. 7).

ending in sexual congress. Marriage may be a subtext, but it is never explicitly gestured toward.[28] Since the women's desires are always represented as heterosexual, and their suitors appropriate, there is none of the fluidity of gender or of love objects that we have seen earlier—except perhaps in the viewers. The luminously painted maidens are certainly objects of desire for male viewers and objects of identification for women viewers; but these two viewing positions need not be mutually exclusive. There is no telling what variety of desires might be incited by these beautiful, titillating, and witty pictures. They might have been as various as those represented in lovesickness treatises and elicited by dramatic performances.

---

[28] Simon Schama's work on the social history of the Netherlands in this period shows how such renditions might be useful in mediating contradictions between traditional prescriptions for women's chastity and emerging concerns for their satisfaction in marriage. He notes that local customs and sympathies often sided with couples who used courtship and, especially, prenuptial pregnancy as a means to get parents—whatever their nominal veto power—to consent to desired matches. He notes that "tender sentiment was regarded as indispensable for a solid match" (444) and therefore "parents were not supposed to stand in the way of matches that were by most lights at all suitable" (441).

CHAPTER 5

CONFINING MADMEN AND TRANSGRESSING BOUNDARIES

The Comedy of Errors, The Merry Wives of Windsor, and Twelfth Night

I am as mad as he,
If sad and merry madness equal be.
Twelfth Night

In chapters 3 and 4 we saw how the early modern discourse of erotic melancholy, or lovesickness, provides a context in which unruly desires, especially women's, are tolerated and promised satisfaction—at least within the context of marriage. In *Twelfth Night,* however, not only women desire, and not all desires go unpunished. Malvolio's dream of marrying Olivia leads to his maddening, confinement, and mock exorcism. This is the third Shakespearean comedy in which a farcical confinement occurs. In the first of the three, Shakespeare develops an episode found in his Plautine source; in his two reiterations, he extends and darkens the scene. In *The Comedy of Errors, The Merry Wives of Windsor,* and *Twelfth Night,* the maddening and brief restraining of Antipholus of Ephesus, Falstaff, and Malvolio—sexually errant, socially aggressive, and greedy men who commodify women—serve as a farcical climax to growing misidentifications. The self-absorbed misogyny of the maddened man is punished, and his scapegoating permits the unions of romantic or lovesick couples: Antipholus S. and Luciana, Anne and Fenton, Olivia and Sebastian. However, the brutal exclusions of farce provide unfestive release that darkens comic conclusions. In these scenes, women and servants successfully adapt religious exorcism rituals, medical confinement protocols, and social Skimmington practices (usually shaming unruly women) to madden men. The effect of the scenes is to discredit first Catholic, and later Puritan, exorcism, and to consolidate comic community. But unlike the tragedies that, by newly articulating madness, enlarge human subjectivity, and unlike the comedies that elaborate lovesickness to license women's desires, these plays mock both the mad and the authorities (whether doctors or exorcists) who are expected to treat them. Hence they circulate emergent attitudes toward the mad that dehumanize and punish them, instead of treating them with the compassion and therapy we have seen before and will view in Napier's medical practice at the end of this chapter. Farce and dehumanization will be carried even further in the scenes of Bedlamites that are staged first in 1604 and 1605, three years after *Twelfth Night*.

The Protocols of Comedy and the Uses of Madness

The titles of the three plays under discussion deliberately showcase their genre by emphasizing errors, lightheartedness, and misrule: *The Comedy of Errors, The Merry Wives of Windsor*, and *Twelfth Night*. Although only one of the three (*Twelfth Night*) is included by C. L. Barber in his *Festive Comedy* category, all three are laced with the stuff of contemporary social rituals—the licensed mocking and reversals of holidays like Twelfth Night and the spontaneous community performances of exorcism or Skimmington rides. Hypotheses about early performances seem to support the connection with authorized festive release. *The Comedy of Errors* is known to have been presented as part of Christmas revels at Gray's Inn on December 28, 1594. *The Merry Wives of Windsor*'s English setting and locale and Garter reference have led to assumptions (unproved) of a performance during Garter festivities at Windsor, perhaps in 1597 (see Green). *Twelfth Night,* whether acted on its name day or not, was performed at the Inns of Court in 1602 and at Court in 1623.

All three plays are festive, in the definition of the term made popular by Barber, but include farcical scenes that provide what I term unfestive release.[1] In each, the farcical scene brutalizes one or more individuals to enable release and community building for others, darkening the reconciliations and unions that the farce helps make possible. As Barbara Freedman says, "farce is committed to the discontinuous and the dysfunctional," its aims are "subversive rather than festive" (*Staging* 105). It creates the condition of nightmare: "the terrors of humiliation—of being, say, unable to remember the simple answer to a leading question; of being found in a stranger's bedroom without pants on; of being taken for a notorious criminal or a lunatic without a scrap of evidence to support one's identity" (Albert Bernal quoted in Freedman, *Staging* 106). Farce's punishment breaks its targets instead of releasing them. It is increasingly relentless in each successive play: only narrated in *The Comedy of Errors,* the punishment is dramatized briefly in *The Merry Wives of Windsor,* and elaborated in two scenes in *Twelfth Night*.

[1] Leo Salinger astutely groups them as blends of farce and romance, whose double plots have roots in Italian comedy, either classical (Plautine) or Renaissance (300), and Barbara Freedman, Jeanne Addison Roberts, and John Astington, among others, concur.

All three of the maddened characters are *pharmakos* or scapegoat figures who are punished in excess of their own flaws for the inadequacies of themselves and of others; their confinements and exorcisms benefit the community, not the confined men. In *The Comedy of Errors,* Antipholus of Ephesus is confined and threatened with exorcism by Doctor Pinch, not only for his violent choler and his own marital and financial debts but also for those of his father, Egeon, his servant, and his brother (Freedman, "Egeon's" 370–373). In *Merry Wives,* Falstaff is duped and humiliated for the third time with a mock exorcism of not just his own lust and greed, but the similarly impotent and/or mercenary misprisions of Shallow, Slender, Caius, the Pages, and, especially, Ford (Roberts, Hinely). In *Twelfth Night* the misogynist and mercenary self-absorption for which Malvolio is gulled and confined is shared by Sir Toby, Sir Andrew, and Orsino. In *The Comedy of Errors* the maddened figure, Antipholus of Ephesus, resumes his place in his society. But in *The Merry Wives of Windsor* and *Twelfth Night,* Falstaff and Malvolio, marked as outsiders, are excluded.[2]

The attribution of madness central to these scenes is not present in most of their literary sources or analogues, or in traditional social rituals of inversion or humiliation, but derives from one brief scene in which madness is diagnosed in Plautus's *Menaechmi,* the source for *The Comedy of Errors.* In each of the plays, the invented scene of farcical confinement is enacted as a parody of exorcism. Unlike in humoral discourse or in the other plays we have examined, the behavior deemed mad is caused not by somatic imbalances, but by errors or practices—by the baffling presence of Antipholus's identical twin in Ephesus and by the absurd behaviors prescribed in the other plays: hunter with horns for Falstaff, and lover with smiles, yellow stockings, and cross-garters for Malvolio. Because these characters are not mad but maddened, they lack the self-representation and sympathy we have earlier seen granted to Ophelia, Lear, Lady Macbeth, and the Jailer's Daughter. And whereas in the early modern period the diagnosis of madness and warrant for confinement were ultimately under the male authority of doctors, parsons, or quarter-session judges, in the plays these are undertaken by witty wives and servants and their allies. Because confinement's compassionate intentions are reversed, and its institutional protocols are eschewed, the theatrical diagnoses have punitive, not therapeutic, consequences. Madness is used as a (fraudulent) label to mock and exclude—and to madden.

When madness is imposed as ascribed devil possession or bewitchment, and is imagined "cured" by fake exorcisms, the discourse of possession and bewitchment is harshly discredited. As we have seen in earlier chapters, the

[2] For discussions of scapegoat figures, especially in connection with farce, see Eric Bentley and Russ McDonald on *Comedy of Errors*'s techniques of farce, Jan Hinely's discussion of Falstaff as alazon/pharmakos in *Merry Wives of Windsor,* and John Astington's of Malvolio as well as Barbara Freedman's three essays, "Egeon's," "Errors," and "Falstaff's," theorizing farce as punishment dream.

relationship of possession to distraction and the validity of exorcism were topics of intense debate during the time these plays were written. Five instances of multiple possessions and exorcisms were sensations between 1585 and 1599, followed in 1602 by Mary Glover's case. In 1585–1586, in Denham, Catholic priests performed exorcisms for six demonics. In 1586 John Darrell, a Puritan minister, attempted dispossessions of Katherine Wiley and Thomas Darling, the latter successful. In 1585–1587, seven children in Lancashire, said to be possessed, were cured only when the male witch held responsible was executed. In 1597–1598, Darrell repeatedly exorcised William Sommers of Nottingham who later (repeatedly) confessed to fraud and then (repeatedly) reneged on his confessions. In May 1599, on evidence from three supposed demonics (including Sommers) who accused him of teaching them how to feign possession, Darrell was "condemned for a counterfeyte" by the Commissioners for Ecclesiastical Causes and jailed (Walker quoting Harsnett 64). Between late 1598 and 1601, Darrell's guilt or innocence and the politics of possession and exorcism were vigorously debated in print in at least thirteen items, taking many sides. By first representing Catholic exorcism practices farcically in *The Comedy of Errors* and later parodying Darrell's Puritan exorcism through Feste in *Twelfth Night,* these comedies mock the credibility of possession and exorcism to play into the hands of the established church's and state's battle against both Catholic and Puritan exorcists. But they likewise represent the social usefulness of attributions of possession, bewitchment, or madness and the grassroots diagnosis and management of these that developed independently of elite hierarchies. By mocking the healers but not the social efficacy of such rituals, the plays resituate them within community social practice.

In such dramatic scenes and enacted rituals, certain kinds of transgression are enabled at the expense of others. By punishing aggressive misogyny with comic attributions of madness, these plays legitimize and reward the loss of self attendant on erotic love. The situating of the scenes of confinement draws negative attention away from scenes of romantic satisfaction. Antipholus of Ephesus violently rages against his diagnosis at the same time that Antipholus of Syracuse gives in and "entertains the offered fallacy" (2.2.180–186) of romantic love. While all on stage are distracted by the humiliation of Falstaff for seeking an adulterous cross-class liaison for financial reward, Fenton can elope with Anne, entering a cross-class marriage for similar purposes. Malvolio is punished for pursuing his dream of marriage to his rich mistress, Olivia, at the same time that Sebastian is passively being seduced by her. Thus, in these comedies, the farcical maddening and confining of a sexually errant man (who serves as a scapegoat) permits (structurally, thematically, and ideologically) other kinds of unruliness and sudden matches of the lovesick—of the sort we have already examined. In particular, by punishing those who commodify women, the mockery confinements let women protect their power and marriages. But the unfestive scene, repeated three times, increasingly casts its shadow over the more festive matches. The first time around, Shakespeare works to better his source—and succeeds.

Improving on Plautus: *The Comedy of Errors*

As is well known, in *The Comedy of Errors* Shakespeare adapts and elaborates Plautus's tightly constructed farce, *The Menaechmi,* which was published in a translation by William Warner in London in 1595, probably after the Shakespearean play was already on stage. This source was early identified in the *Gesta Grayorum*'s narrative of the hilarity and disruptions that accompanied the play's performance at the Gray's Inn festivities on December 28, 1594: "after such Sports, a Comedy of Errors (like to *Plautus* his *Menechmus*) was played by the Players. So that Night was begun, and continued to the end, in nothing but Confusion and Errors; whereupon, it was ever afterwards called, *The Night of Errors.*"[3] It is appropriate that this play became immediately synonymous with errors since it systematically multiplies those in Plautus by adding to his twin Menaechmi a second set of servant twins, a sister-in-law for the local twin, incidents taken from Plautus's *Amphitruo,* and a frame plot involving the twins' father and mother, Egeon and Emilia; hence the seventeen misrecognitions in *Menaechmi* grow to over fifty in *The Comedy of Errors.*[4] By moving the play's locale from Epidamnum to Ephesus, a place of magic and exorcism, rather than lechery and debauchery (Kinney 157–165; Maguire 360–366), and by insistently "feed[ing] Elizabethan life into the mill of Roman farce" (Barber, *Whole Journey* 68), Shakespeare lays the groundwork for a farcical confinement that skewers English Catholic exorcists and their rituals. In both plays, escalating confusions, debts, and violence lead to the confinement of an alleged madman. In *The Comedy of Errors,* however, the scene itself is doubled, and every aspect—the instigators, the healing figures, the diagnoses, the therapies—are caricatured. As healers and madmen are punished for errors, farce precipitates out romance—barely.

In Plautus's *Menaechmi,* a doctor's restraint literalizes an escalating series of accusations of madness rooted in mistakings. When, in act 5, Mulier, the unnamed wife of Menechmus the Citizen, rages at Menechmus the Traveller and misaccuses him of her husband's philandering, he calls her "bitch" and "mad." She and her father return the accusation and corroborate it, report-

---

[3] R. A. Foakes's Arden edition, appendix 2:116, includes relevant parts of the *Gesta Grayorum,* which use the language of the play in a mock indictment of the disorderly events of December 28 at Gray's Inn. Douglas Lanier provides a keen analysis of the parallel uses of mock ritual, sorcery, and scapegoating to restore order in the theatrical indictment and the play.

[4] Rouse's calculations in his parallel edition of Plautus and Warner's translation. He also provides a useful comparative summary of the two plots (xiv). Cf. Miola, *Shakespeare* 22.

ing that "his eies sparkle, . . . his colour goes and comes, he lookes wildly" (Bullough 1:31). Having been declared mad, Menechmus the Traveller (in Plautus, unlike in Shakespeare, the more choleric of the two twins) deliberately feigns madness to escape his abusers (Bullough 1:131–132). His feigned mad discourse can be seen, in Warner's translation, to follow its Plautine precedent, as well as earlier madmen like Hieronimo and Titus, by calling wildly on classical gods to aid revenge. The Traveller raves: "*Bachus, Appollo, Phoebus,* do ye call mee to come hunt in the woods with you? I see, I heare, I come, I flie, but I cannot get out of these fields," and abuses Mulier as "an old mastiff bitch" and her father as "an olde goat."[5] Upon being declared a "Bedlam foole" (Warner's colloquial translation of a Latin phrase meaning, "woe to you"), Menechmus escalates his threats: "Harke, *Appollo* commaunds me that I shoulde rende out hir eyes with a burning lampe," "yea *Appollo,* I will sacrifice this olde beast unto thee: and if thou commandest mee, I will cut his throate with that dagger that hangs at his girdle" (Bullough 1:31, 32). He escapes and the Citizen twin is later treated in his stead.

Since the madness scene is split between the two twins in Plautus and is represented briefly and straightforwardly, it has little psychological or satiric force. Medicus, the doctor, undertakes a conventional examination of the Citizen twin, asking all the appropriate questions about his senses, his diet, his eyes, his stomach, and his sleep. Finding most of the answers satisfactory (Menechmus of Epidamnum, though confused, is not enraged), he cautiously notes: "He speakes not like a mad man in that" (33) and promises to "order him" with medications at his house (34). The Citizen twin immediately escapes, encounters his brother, and the play concludes.

In *The Comedy of Errors,* this brief episode is exuberantly doubled and exaggerated. First, instead of the twins sharing the diagnosis of madness made by family and doctor, they are treated by different healers. Their differentiated "cures" fit their contrasted situations and characterizations. Antipholus E., in Shakespeare the more "choleric" and misogynist of the twins, is represented as beating his servant, raging at his wife, and genuinely acquiring debt for a chain bought for his Courtesan. He attributes madness to all those who misrecognize him, never for a moment doubting his own rectitude and sanity. So his punishment is to be accused of madness, an extreme of the choler he exhibits; he is treated violently as he treats others. Dr. Pinch diagnoses possession; he has Antipholus E. bound and carried to his own house, where his exorcism causes "deep shames and great indignities" at the site of his misdemeanors—"in a dark and dankish vault at home" (5.1.254,

---

[5] Plautus's twin calls only on Bacchus, but Warner translates: "*Bachus, Appollo, Phoebus,* do ye call mee to come hunt in the woods with you?" (Bullough 1:31). In *The Spanish Tragedy,* Hieronimo calls on Pluto and a "troop of Furies and tormenting hags" to aid his revenge (3.13.110, 112) and in *Titus Andronicus* the protagonist, "distract," solicits both hell and heaven for justice, calling on Pluto as well as Jove, Apollo, Mars, Pallas, Mercury, Saturn (4.3.26, 13, 54–57).

248). Antipholus S., his part greatly enlarged from that of the Traveller, becomes the more sympathetic of the two brothers. He is represented as habitually "melancholy" (1.2.20), yearning, and dissatisfied, not settled and
self-satisfied like his twin. He seeks his mother and brother; he befriends his
servant rather than beating him; he is a romantic lover, not an irascible husband. Rather than regularly attributing madness to others, he fears for his
own stability—both in the early soliloquy when he falls in love (1.2.33–40)
and in his amazed responses to mistakings.[6] Believing Ephesus to be a town
of "nimble jugglers that deceive the eye, / Dark-working sorcerers that
change the mind, / Soul-killing witches that deform the body" (1.2.98–100),
he fears he may be possessed or bewitched or that he and his servant are "distract" (4.3.40). Although he himself attempts to exorcise the Courtesan
(4.3.46–75), his anxious melancholy is promised treatment with soothing
potions by an Abbess in a Priory.

But both therapies take the form of farcical punishments that beget more
confusion. Luce, the Police Officer, and Dr. Pinch represent the punitive conscience that must have its way before reconciliations can occur (Freedman,
"Egeon's" 374–375), and the Abbess can be added to this list. Both healers
are also caricatured and themselves subjected to their own medicine. The farcical retribution against Pinch exacerbates rising tensions. While Pinch may
partly represent the punitive superego, he has more material and historical
resonances. His representation is a mockery of three early modern male authority figures—a Doctor, a "Schoolmaster" (following 4.4.37), and a Catholic exorcist; any of these might use "pinches" to diagnose or treat their
hapless clients. But his claims to supernatural or natural authority are caricatured as grandiose and groundless.[7] Without any diagnosis of Antipholus
E. beyond thwarted pulse-taking, Pinch mechanically produces the proper
form of (Catholic) exorcism: "I charge thee, Satan, hous'd within this man, /
To yield possession to my holy prayers, / And to thy state of darkness hie
thee straight; / I conjure thee by all the saints in heaven" (4.4.52–55). After
contradictory testimony from all present, Pinch again summarily declares:
"Mistress, both man [Dromio E.] and master is possess'd, / I know it by their
pale and deadly looks; / They must be bound and laid in some dark room"
(4.4.90–92). Then, when a police officer arrives to take Antipholus E. to jail
for debt, Pinch diagnoses possession a third time: "Go bind this man [Offi-

---

[6] He has one hundred lines more than his brother (Foakes xxv) and the soliloquies his brother
lacks. Alberto Cacicedo characterizes their two humoral temperaments as melancholic and choleric (25–32). Alexander Leggatt contrasts their situations and experiences ("Shakespeare's"
140–142). In Barbara Freedman's complex interpretation, they are fantasy aspects of their
father's divided identity and of identity more generally. Antipholus of Ephesus represents identification with a past self whom others forget and Antipholus of Syracuse represents dis-identi-
fication with a present self whom others mistakenly view as a repressed past self ("Egeon's"
365–370).
[7] "His practice remains a bizarre compound of schoolmasterly pedantry, of quasi-religious
conjuration, . . . and of confidently propounded truisms" (Crewe, "God" 221).

cer], for he is frantic too" (4.4.111). This sequence brilliantly satirizes the contagion of possessions and Catholic exorcisms in Denham in 1585–1586 (Walker 43–49) and the satisfaction the community takes in them. Adriana and the Courtesan, who have together sought Pinch's help after they both diagnose Antipholus as "lunatic" (4.3.92), are relieved when he is bound and taken away.

The Syracusan pair, mistaken for their local counterparts and declared mad too, seek succor in a priory where another spurious diagnosis is proffered by a nun, a similarly anachronistic Catholic authority figure. Like Pinch, the Abbess diagnoses without evidence and insistently claims her prerogative to treat the "distraction" she inaccurately interprets and cannot heal. She parodies medical formula as Pinch does those of exorcists. For example, her claim that "Unquiet meals make ill digestions; / Thereof the raging fire of fever bred, / And what's a fever but a fit of madness?" (5.1.74–76) directly contradicts the well-known doctrine that madness (as distinct from delirium) was diagnosed by *absence* of fever. She diagnoses the wrong man. She manipulates Adrianna into revealing that she is a nagging wife, then uses that against her, denying her wifely right to help heal her husband. Her diagnosis of madness as a result of "the venom clamours of a jealous woman" is another error. Nagging is decidedly not the cause, as the audience well knows, of confusion in Ephesus or of the behavior even of the right Antipholus, let alone the wrong one. The Prioress's proposed humoral treatment by "wholesome syrups, drugs and holy prayers" (5.1.104) would, however, have been approved by Dr. Napier, but is never tried.

Both healers beget anger from those they pretend to help and both, in effect, have their diagnoses turned against them; Pinch is bound and violently exorcised, and the Abbess is returned to the subordinated wifely status she prescribes to Adriana. The climactic violence of the play is visited, offstage, on Pinch (and the maids) by Antipholus E. and Dromio E., who have, a messenger narrates:

> Beaten the maids a-row, and bound the doctor,
> Whose beard they have sing'd off with brands of fire,
> And ever as it blaz'd, they threw on him
> Great pails of puddled mire to quench the hair;
> My master preaches patience to him, and the while
> His man with scissors nicks him like a fool;
> And sure (unless you send some present help)
> Between them they will kill the conjurer.
>
> (5.1.170–177)

This narrated humiliation by fire, excrement, preaching, and nicking turns Pinch's name, his diagnosis, his profession, and his own treatment back on him. He must endure the regimen that might be used in the period to heal those believed to be witches, possessed, or bewitched. He is bound, he is covered with excrement, and he is burned and nicked, a stratagem for discovering witches or healing bewitchment.[8] But this retaliatory violence does not purge the play of delusion and rage. Antipholus E.'s anger at his wife intensifies: "He cries for you, and vows if he can take you / To scorch your face and to disfigure you," the messenger reports (5.1.182–183). His litany of grievances to the Duke, suppressing his own faults, blames Adriana. He never apologizes to her or to Dromio E. for his mistakes. The farcical exorcism is less cathartic than some critics suggest.[9]

The Abbess's role reiterates that farcical confinement cannot banish madness, although it does lead to plot resolutions. The Abbess/Emilia is a second comically punitive figure when she dresses down Adriana for flaws that she may share. Freedman suggests that Egeon cooperated with fate or even sought separation from his wife, Emilia: leaving her for business, "unwilling" to return home, passively accepting their separation in the shipwreck, and never seeking her until his son wishes to do so (1.1.43, 58–60, 124–126; "Egeon's" 374–376). Might we see in his recital of Emilia's insistent demands a hint of why he did so? Was *she* a nagging wife once? Will she be that "same Emilia" (5.1.345) again? It is she who "made provision" for following him, she who "Made daily motions for our home return," whose "incessant weepings" encouraged him to try to save his family in the storm (1.1.47, 59, 70). Once she entered the Priory, Emilia, like Antipholus E., seems never to have been melancholy nor to have sought her family ("What then became of them I cannot tell" 5.1.360). She has been satisfied with celibacy and her Abbess's authority. At her reappearance, she continues to be both long-winded and peremptory. She lectures Adriana, blaming her for confusions that are not her fault. She demands reunion with her grudgingly compliant husband, "Speak old Egeon, if thou be'st the man. . . . O, if thou be'st the same Egeon, speak— / And speak unto the same Emilia" (5.1.341–345). At the play's end, Emilia, losing none of her authority, commandeers all to come into the abbey for a "gossip's feast" (5.1.406). The representa-

---

[8] For discussions of how fire, nicking, and occasionally excrement figured in the searching out of and testing of witches and the counteractions taken against them to promote healing, see Robin Briggs 118–120; Alan Macfarlane 103–113, esp. 108–109; and Keith Thomas 497, 530–531. For example, in 1604, 94-year-old Agnes Fenn alleged that those who suspected her of witchcraft, "punched, pricked and struck her, threatened her with firebrands and gunpowder, and finally stabbed her in the face with a knife," and Andrew Camp, suspecting that Goodwife Bailey had bewitched his children, "dragged her out of her house into the street, bruising her back, and pinching her, and then kneeled upon her breast; 'and when he had her so under him his wife came and clawed her by the face and said she would claw her eyes out of her head, and her tongue out of her mouth'" (Thomas 530–531). Burning a cake made with the suspected victim's urine was a test for bewitchment, and burning the witch's thatch or a piece of her hair or her animals or pieces of clothes was a test for witchcraft.

[9] For Barber, Pinch is burned as a "comic effigy" to revenge "notions of madness and magic" and signal "the end of the delusions" (*Whole* 70). For Freedman, "The self is finally freed from the superego's sadistic action as Antipholus of Syracuse [*sic*; her "error" for Antipholus of Ephesus] . . . revenges himself upon this pinching, punishing parasite" ("Egeon's" 378).

tion mocks her outmoded role as Catholic healer by making her a nagging wife. Her final lines do, however, move the play beyond farce, sounding the note of romance: "After so long grief, such nativity" (5.1.407).[10]

In the plot, concluding with farcical confinement, money and chains as well as wives and servants are returned to their proper owners. But no character seems transformed and no one apologizes or is forgiven. The debate about the proper role of women in marriage is left up in the air when, in response to the Abbess's lecture, Adriana and Luciana switch their positions on wifely roles, with the wife rebuked into subordination and the sister urging denial of false accusations (5.1.86–89). But Antipholus S. remains the eager romantic in love with Luciana. In surpassing Plautus, Shakespeare multiplies twins, healers, and farce, and leaves in doubt who can prescribe for madness.

Exploiting Elizabeth: *The Merry Wives of Windsor*

The Merry Wives of Windsor, usually thought to have first been performed in 1597, a few years later than *The Comedy of Errors,* is anomalous among Shakespeare's comedies in ways its title telegraphs. It has no known sources. It is the only Shakespeare play set in contemporary England amongst the middling ranks with wives (one a mother) as protagonists. It is also—uniquely—a play in which women's social power goes virtually unchallenged. In the play, wives give commands, manipulate men, and are well pleased at Falstaff's fate. Their power is deployed, like Queen Elizabeth's own, by their appropriation of popular and elite rituals traditionally used against them.[11]

In spite of its anomalies, *The Merry Wives of Windsor* has several con-

[10] Critics mostly ignore the gaps and the comedy in Emilia's story. Leggatt says that as she "takes centre stage away from the Duke, so the fussy legalism he has represented is swept away by a deeper authority, the spontaneous force of life" ("Shakespeare's" 150), perhaps an unfortunate choice of metaphor given this family's history. According to Cacicedo, she is the opposite of Pinch; she is the good doctor who restores humoral balance, a religious icon, and an undivided mother who participates in the "oceanic imagery of the play" (33). According to Crewe, she is a better physician than Pinch but not "infallible," not as good as the playwright himself who uses theater as a place of healing ("God" 222). Even Laurie Maguire, who lucidly unfolds the play's production and deconstruction of dualisms (especially the contradictory female roles and contradictory marital paradigms it represents), stops short of finding, in the Abbess, contradictions between the "independent pagan amazon" and the "submissive Christian servant" (378).

[11] A later and probably apocryphal story (1702) about the play's creation gives authority to a woman as well. The tale claims that Queen Elizabeth wished Shakespeare to "shew" Falstaff "in love" and so "This Comedy was written at her Command, and by her direction," and "she was so eager to see it Acted that she commanded it to be finished in fourteen days; and was, afterwards, as Tradition tells us, very well pleasd at the Representation." The first comment is from Nicolas Rowe's biography of Shakespeare in his 1709 edition of the plays, and the second is from John Dennis's dedication of *The Comical Gallant.* Both are quoted by Oliver, in his Arden edition of *The Merry Wives of Windsor* xliv–xlv.

nections with *Comedy of Errors:* its generic mix (farce with a dash of romance), its double plot (encompassing marriage in two generations), its richly detailed urban setting, its thematized ideological debates over the nature of marriage and the roles of husbands, wives, and parents, and its punishments for misogyny.[12] When the play reworks the scene of scapegoating exorcism from *The Comedy of Errors,* women not only instigate but perform it. There are no accidental misrecognitions and no traditional figures of authority; no doctors, exorcists, parsons, or rulers are called in. No supernatural or natural explanations of inappropriate behavior are credited—not witchcraft, possession, or madness. The management of aberrant behavior takes place entirely in the realm of the domestic and local.

This realm, as in *The Comedy of Errors,* is that of the emergent heterogeneous category of "the middling sort," one characterized in the play, as recent scholarship has emphasized, by proliferating conflicts over money, marriage, and status.[13] The play manifests how variously status may be gained—by family name (Shallow), by economic success (Ford and Page), by professional attribution (Evans, like parsons in the period, receives the honorific title, Sir), by marriage (Fenton)—and how uncertain it is. Characters must fight to stay in place. Settlements of their resulting rivalries are not sought through the institutional channels of the church, the law, or the local or central government, although in early modern England these were regularly venues for addressing conflicts.[14] The male authority figures who might have been expected to mediate—Justice Shallow, Knight Sir John Falstaff, Doctor Caius, Parson Sir Hugh Evans, and Master Ford—have their masculinity and professional expertise ridiculed. In particular the doctor and the parson are caricatured by their accents; are shown up as cowards through their aborted duel; and have their professions derided: "he gives me the potions and the motions"; "he gives me the proverbs and the no-verbs"

[12] Throughout her book and especially in her last chapter, Jeanne Addison Roberts places *Merry Wives* in the context of other Shakespearean comedies, including *Errors* (119–136).

[13] Much current scholarship analyzes the precise status dynamics of the play. In two earlier essays ("Constructing Female Sexuality" and "Shakespeare's Women"), I have discussed the relation of the play to gender and class dynamics in Shakespeare's Stratford. Peter Erickson claims that the middling sort in Windsor is subordinated to the authority of the Court by the allusions to it (124–128). Leah Marcus emphasizes how the additional allusions to the Court, to Windsor, and to money in the Folio text diminish the power of community, and especially of women visible in the Quarto edition. Stephen Foley, while acknowledging the suspension of aspects of Court culture in the play, argues that these are circumscribed by materials from popular venues (237–239). Rosemary Kegl analyzes the conflicts that divide the middling sort in Windsor, although acknowledging that overlapping oppressions make possible short-term alliances (80–105). My emphasis is on how middling-status women use both community rivalries and Court rituals to achieve their ends.

[14] Church courts, assizes, and local guilds and governments (often intersecting) kept order in early modern England by taking complaints, deciding cases, and punishing offenders. But, as Kegl points out, these avenues for retribution are rejected or suppressed in the play. I interpret this refusal as a mark of local independence from centralized and elite institutions, whereas Kegl interprets it as the result of the "nation's conflicted relationship to absolutism" (94, 87–96).

(3.1.97–100). All the men strive for advantage. Marriage to Anne Page is hotly contested by suitors who explicitly want her money, and by parents interested in the status that her prospective husband might bring: Mr. Page and Shallow (with Parson Evans's support) back Slender's suit in the hopes of joining the two estates. Mistress Page backs Doctor Caius for his money and "friends potent at court" (4.4.87–88), and he seeks the incorporation into the community that his French accent hinders. Fenton, an impoverished courtier (especially in Folio text), woos Anne at first for her money. Falstaff, out of funds, seduces the wives for gain and is punished for the aggressive impotence that the local men share.

With status so vulnerable, retaliations against insults are swift, but the only successful ones are the shaming rituals engineered by the wives and Mistress Quickly. They devise farcical punishments to fit exactly Falstaff's social, sexual, and financial abuse of them. He is dumped into the river in a basket of dirty laundry for his invasion of the domestic space and his pretensions to aristocratic panache; he is dressed as an old woman and beaten for his claims of youthful phallic potency; he is exorcised by Windsor fairies for his exploitation of desire. More clearly than Antipholus, Falstaff is a scapegoat figure who is punished not just for his own transgressions but for the greed, impotence, and misogyny of other men: Dr. Caius, Parson Evans, Slender, and Ford, who is closely identified with Falstaff and jointly humiliated when he pays Falstaff to cuckold him (Carroll, *Metamorphoses* 185–190, and Parten 191–192). The wives succeed by self-consciously manipulating the discourses of the supernatural, the popular, and the courtly—all routinely used to contain women.[15]

Madness, possession, and witchcraft are employed as figures of speech or parodic attributions to expose Ford's and Falstaff's delusions as pathology and eventually to exorcise them (Carroll, *Metamorphoses* 186–189). First Master Page (3.3.201–210) and later Mistress Page characterize Ford's textbook misogyny as madness: "Why, woman, your husband is in his old lunes again. He so takes on yonder with my husband, so rails against all married mankind, so curses all Eve's daughters—of what complexion soever, and so buffets himself on the forehead, crying, 'Peer out, peer out!' that any madness I ever yet beheld seemed but tameness, civility, and patience to this his distemper he is in now" (4.2.19–26). As Ford's frenzy increases, Master Page offers a remedy "You are not to go loose any longer; you must be pinioned," and Evans concurs: "Why, this is lunatics, this is mad as a mad dog" (4.2.119–121). The wives lay a similar charge against Falstaff, suggesting that he would not continue his assault if not possessed: "If the devil have him not in fee-simple, with fine and recovery" (4.2.204–205). The wives farcically identify Falstaff as a witch when they dress the fat knight in clothes said

[15] Parten (195–196) places the play in the context of the literary controversy over women. Kegl (107–122) discusses its participation in social debates over the role of women in marriage.

to be those of "the fat woman of Brainford," whom Ford wildly accuses of being "A witch, a quean, an old cozening quean!" who "works by charms, by spells, by th' figure" (4.2.166, 170–171).

As in *The Comedy of Errors,* metaphorical madness and trumped-up possession and bewitchment climax in a mock exorcism and witch-finding in which Falstaff, twice gulled, is "publicly shamed" for "public sport" (4.2.216, 4.4.13). This ritual takes its form from the popular protocols for identifying a witch (by burning and scratching), extracting a confession, and reconciling estranged participants (see note 8 above). No doctors, witch-hunters, or exorcists are consulted, but the whole community participates; just so, in the period, most accusations of witchcraft and possession emerged from and were managed at the local level.[16] The ritual is emptied of super-natural claims when children and servants, playing fairies in a play within a play, simulate exorcism to frighten and punish Falstaff. He is comically tested for lust by "trial-fire" as suspected witches were; torches will burn him if he is guilty and "back descend" if he is not, exposing the "flesh of a corrupted heart" (5.5.86–89). Burning and pinching are also punishment for his "fantasy," "luxury," and the "bloody fire" of lust (5.5.95–97). The feigned exorcism unites the community, provides a scapegoat for their flaws, drives out the feigned lust that possesses Falstaff, and forces a "confession" which, as in witchcraft rituals, instigates healing: "I do begin to perceive that I am made an ass" (121). The pageant shames Ford as well, who again confesses he has wronged his wife (136–137).

These resituated rites appropriate as well the form of Skimmington rituals used to control behavior within the community and protect it from unwanted incursion.[17] Such rituals, like witch-findings, emerged spontaneously from the lower ranks (Underdown, *Revel* 103). Skimmingtons, although diverse, typically imitated and punished inversions (especially women on top) through parodic reversals. Shrewish women who scolded, beat, or cuckolded their husbands were punished indirectly by a husband stand-in who rode backwards on an ass, carrying a Skimmington label, and was beaten by the "wife," a man dressed as a woman (Underdown, "Taming" 126–133, and *Revel* 100–103). In *The Merry Wives of Windsor,* the form and features of the Skimmington-like practice are inverted; they are deployed by women to mock and discipline phallic men. Falstaff's costume as

[16] Thomas, Macfarlane, and Briggs emphasize this dimension of witchcraft, and Clive Holmes sorts out, through examination of judicial proceedings, the popular and elite strands that combine in English witchcraft beliefs.

[17] Much recent criticism discusses this connection; see Parten, who first argues at length that the climactic scene is shaped "by the same attitudes and folk traditions that produced ceremonies such as the skimmington" (185, 185–187, 198–199). See also Roberts 149–150, n 63; Foley 229; and Kegl 102–103. Underdown explains that Skimmington rituals were sometimes intended to rid the community of a "skimmington," that is "something undesirable brought into the village by outsiders that, like an unruly woman, must be dealt with by communal action" (*Revel* 110), a characterization applicable to Falstaff.

Herne the Hunter, his horns, and the lure of assignation, construct him as ludicrously hyper-masculine. The large horns that are a prominent feature of Skimmington rides traditionally mock cuckolds or henpecked husbands. Here they signify and mock the would-be cuckolder by first exaggerating, then stripping away, his phallic pretense when he is "dis-horn[ed]" (Roberts, *English Comedy* 114, Parten 196–197). Likewise the cross-dressing episodes in the play, reversing their import in Skimmington rides, farcically expose male impotence and cowardice. Ford, as we have seen, beats a (supposed) woman and his wife as well. Caius's and Slender's "arranged" marriages to low-status boys disguised as brides mock their desire to marry up *and* subordinate their wives.

To secure women's and citizens' power, the climactic pageant not only manipulates the exorcism and Skimmington rituals of the lower ranks but also incorporates and transforms elements of courtly Garter rituals. The brief allusions to Windsor Castle and its chapel (the site of the installation of Garter knights) function along with the mock exorcism to scorn Falstaff's pretense of knighthood and courtly love, and perhaps mock courtly ostentation more generally. The lines in context do not idealize the Court, the Garter ritual, or the queen, as those scholars who would valorize the play's picture of Merry England and those who condemn its elitism assume.[18] The play wittily appropriates Garter rituals as it has exorcism and Skimmington rituals. The allusions are multiply displaced as they are spoken, in a play within a play, by Pistol and Mistress Quickly, characters pretending to be fairies who are at the very bottom of Windsor's middling ranks—where they have migrated from the different genre and historical period of the Henry plays (Neely, "Constructing Female Sexuality" 220–221). Pistol's aggressive prescriptions for domestic morality are especially hilarious:

> Elves, list your names; silence, you airy toys!
> Cricket, to Windsor chimneys shalt thou leap.
> Where fires thou find'st unraked and hearths unswept,
> There pinch the maids as blue as bilberry.
> Our radiant queen hates sluts and sluttery.
>
> (5.5.44–48)

[18] Critics used to admire the Garter references as a gracious compliment celebrating the queen, the installation of Lord Hunsdon as Garter knight, and the Garter as an emblem of English unity. See Oliver lxix–lxx and Green. More recently critics lament how the allusions subordinate the middling sort to the aristocracy or the Court or the queen. See, for example, Erickson, who says: "the harmony represented by the bourgeois townsfolk's participation and assimilation into the aristocratic rites of the Order of the Garter promotes royal power and thus ratifies, while palliating, the existing class structure" (129) and Marcus: "The women's triumph in Q [without Garter allusions] is unallayed by larger patriarchal forces, while in F., Windsor, the court, and the Order of the Garter loom over the antics of the townspeople" (78). Wall, however, claims that characters "mock the ceremonial Order of the Garter" (34) and that "the play's inscription of Windsor largely signals the court's irrelevance and underscores instead the domestic politics of shared language" (32).

This attack on sluttery frightens "slutty" Falstaff (Wall 34) and cues the "radiant queen's" witty elaboration and the fairies' punitive actions. Although Quickly, an unmarried woman and household servant, is low on the Windsor status ladder, she is precisely the good housekeeper the castle needs.[19] Her appropriation of Garter imagery refers only indirectly to Elizabeth, to Garter knights, or to installation ceremonies; it brings these down into the theater, domestic space, and local culture. Her order to the pretend fairies to strew Windsor Castle with good luck and blessings is a self-referential allusion to the ceremony Shakespearean fairies had recently performed in the final scene of *A Midsummer Night's Dream*. The chapel needs a good cleaning and the Garter emblem (rendered ludicrous because worn below "Knighthood's bending knee," like Malvolio's yellow garters, instead of around the neck as was customary) is translated to a fairy ring:

> Search Windsor Castle, elves, within and out.
> Strew good luck, ouphs, on every sacred room,
> That it may stand till the perpetual doom,
> In state as wholesome as in state 'tis fit,
> Worthy the owner, and the owner it.
> The several chairs of Order look you scour
> With juice of balm and every precious flow'r.
> Each fair instalment, coat, and several crest,
> With loyal blazon, evermore be blest.
> And nightly, meadow-fairies, look you sing,
> Like to the Garter's compass, in a ring.
> Th' expressure that it bears, green let it be,
> More fertile-fresh than all the field to see;
> And "Honi soit qui mal y pense" write
> In emerald tufts, flow'rs purple, blue, and white—
> Like sapphire, pearl, and rich embroidery,
> Buckled below fair knighthood's bending knee—.
>
> (5.5.58–74)

Although the speech certainly implies loyalty to the "worthy owner" of Windsor Castle, the values it celebrates are specifically those of the Windsor community: property management, good housekeeping, lineage, and honesty, especially marital chastity. The Garter motto, "evil be to him that thinks evil," serves as a warning to Falstaff, a mockery of his false knighthood, and a description of the retaliation under way against him. The resituating of the ritual links it with farcical reenactments of exorcism, bewitchment, and Skimmington rituals—all part of Falstaff's punishment.[20]

---

[19] "I keep his house; and I wash, wring, brew, bake, scour, dress meat and drink, make the beds, and do all myself" (1.4.92–94).

[20] Contemporary popular audiences were more apt than present day scholars to pick up mocking allusions to the (perhaps racy) origin of the Garter symbol, to Elizabeth's politic habit

These punishments not only protect the women but also permit romance to flourish. Anne Page and Fenton arrange to slip away and marry while Falstaff is being exposed. The farcical climax modulates to a festive conclusion as all apologize and Mistress Page implicitly is reconciled with her husband and invites Falstaff home to dinner. But the unfestive shaming of Falstaff reverberates. The Pages are accused of "shamefully" trying to marry off their daughter "where there was no proportion held in love" (5.5.220–221) and must accept the love match. (Or is it another cross-class match secured for money with a woman in charge?) The two farcically matched and disgruntled suitors react violently, not penitently, to the status insult of marriage to boy brides. Slender would have "swinged" his bride, a "postmaster's boy," and the court-aspiring Caius, horrified to find himself married to "un garçon, a boy; un peasant," threatens he will "raise all Windsor" (5.5.187–210). In spite of the farcical scapegoating, rivalries persist in Windsor. The play suggests that no permanent harmony is possible but that attributions of madness, possession, and witchcraft used in unfestive shaming rituals are a potent resource for managing conflict.

Gulling Puritans: *Twelfth Night*

The tensions and hostilities that erupted within the community in *The Merry Wives of Windsor* recur in *Twelfth Night* within two households where no one is in charge because, as we have seen in chapter 4, the master and the mistress are distracted by lovesickness. Intersecting with the primary, multifaceted, erotic intrigues is the Malvolio subplot in which a self-serving courtship (like Falstaff's) is deliberately incited and farcically punished. Malvolio's maddening, confinement, and exorcism are more extended and more brutal than the earlier two. Having enraged Sir Toby Belch, Sir Andrew Aguecheek, Maria, and Feste in 2.3, Malvolio is tricked by their feigned letter in 2.5; his elicited lover's antics produce a diagnosis of mad possession in 3.4; he is confined and tested by a counterfeit exorcist in 4.2; later he is released and exits vowing revenge in 5.1. These strategically placed scenes have no specific antecedents in the multiple sources and analogues adduced for the play.[21] The scenes' placements and farcical action draw both laughter and condemnation onto Malvolio, and away from the erotic unruliness, gender fluidity, and willful marriages examined in the preceding chapter. They

---

of deferring Garter nominations to consolidate her power, and to her transfer of the Garter feast to London to ensure greater crowds. I discuss contested Garter origins and the play's parodic ceremonies in "Constructing Female Sexuality" 222–224 and passim.

[21] The original source is the Italian play *Gl'Ingannati,* presented in Siena in 1531 and circulated through Bandello and Belleforest to Barnabe Rich, *Riche his Farewell to Militarie profession* (1581), where it becomes the tale of Apolonius and Silla, the direct source of the play. See the Arden edition of *Twelfth Night,* xxxv–l; Bullough 2:269–374.

pathologize Malvolio's status-seeking match to elicit tolerance for those driven by erotic desire. More extensively than in the other plays, Malvolio serves as a scapegoat who is punished for flaws others share.

As in the other farcical comedies, Malvolio is gulled partly in revenge for his own hubris and contempt for others—for attacking the "uncivil rule" of Sir Toby, Andrew, Maria, and Feste, terming them "mad" (2.3.124, 87)—and partly for his misogynistic exploitation of Olivia to achieve money and power. Like Falstaff, he desires her place, not her, as his soliloquy *before* reading the letter shows. He imagines his new power after this marriage: "Calling my officers about me, in my branched velvet gown; having come from a daybed, where I have left Olivia sleeping," and then rehearses the contempt he will display for those who have disdained him: "And then to have the humor of state; and after a demure travel of regard, telling them I know my place, as I would they should do theirs" (2.5.45–52). His reasons for wanting Olivia are to be found not in the missive's C's and U's and T's that signify her penetrable sexuality, an enticement for the lovesick, but in its M. O. A. I., letters that signify his name and his own palpable "self-love" (1.5.90).[22]

The feigned letter merely fans this self-love so that when crossed, "he must run mad" (2.5.190). The resulting performance of lovesickness—smiling, cross-gartering, yellow stockings—is punished by an attribution of madness that is triply apt. It turns Malvolio's insults to others back on him. It assaults the self-righteousness of the "time-pleaser" and "affectioned ass" (2.3.147) by inscribing the loss of control characteristic of the devil-possessed, the bewitched, the mad. Maria and Toby claim the "fiend speaks within him!" suggest he is "bewitched," and propose to "carry his water to th' wise woman" (3.4.95, 105–106), running through the period's diagnostic options. Finally, as in the earlier farcical comedies, the tricksters punish Malvolio for desires and flaws they share. They mock his ambiguous authority as a steward, his impotence as an unmarried, unloved, anti-festive man, and his nastily aggressive status hunger. Like Malvolio, three of his tormenters are single, impotent men of ambiguous status who seek advancement. Sir Andrew is tricked into playing a pathetic suitor to Olivia; Sir Toby is an impecunious parasite advocating Sir Andrew's suit for his own advantage; Feste is a licensed, placeless, unmarried, dependent fool who resents Malvolio's charge that he is a "barren rascal" (1.5.84; 5.1.375), perhaps because it hits too close to the mark. Maria, whose position of intimacy and dependency as Olivia's waiting woman most closely resembles Malvolio's, may initiate the trick against him out of rivalry for her mistress's favor and possibly to disavow the sort of cross-class marriage she herself desires (Osborne 144–145).

---

[22] Many critics read Malvolio and the letter scene in related ways: See Barber, *Festive* 254–257; Malcolmson, "What You Will" 38–39; Astington, "Eunuchs"; Osborne 137–163; and Edward Cahill.

The violent commentary of Andrew, Toby, and Feste in the letter scene shows how by humiliating Malvolio they compensate for their own cowardice. "Pistol him, pistol him," "Fire and Brimstone!" "Out, scab," "Ay, or I'll cudgel him and make him cry O," they taunt (2.5.35, 48, 72, 130).

As in the two earlier comedies, scapegoating helps validate romance when attributions of madness distract those on stage from other liaisons underway and siphon off spectators' disapproval from them. Compared with Malvolio's illusions in the letter scene (2.5), Orsino's self-absorption and Cesario's and Olivia's desires, manifested in the two flanking scenes, 2.4 and 3.1, appear benign. In act 3, scene 4, attributions of madness escalate as disguise and misrecognition precipitate multiple crises. Sir Andrew and Cesario are tricked into a duel neither wants. Antonio, enraged when (in the first misrecognition) the youth he believes to be Sebastian fails to acknowledge him, is next declared "mad" by the Officer who seizes him (3.4.374). Sebastian, attacked by Andrew, then unaccountably rescued by Olivia, puzzles, "Are all the people mad?" "Or I am mad, or else this is a dream" (4.1.28, 62). Olivia, in love and pressing her suit with Cesario, upon hearing that Malvolio is "tainted in 's wits," immediately identifies with him: "I am as mad as he, / If sad and merry madness equal be" (3.4.12–14). Malvolio's exorcism in act 4 scene 2, takes attention away from the precipitous union of Olivia and Sebastian, which is occurring simultaneously offstage. He enters her house in 4.1, and in 4.3, believing he is "mad" (4.3.15–16), he goes off with a priest to marry her. Exorcism by a false parson keeps the members of Olivia's household from noticing her marriage by a true priest. For the audience, the broad farce of the scene attracts censure and laughter onto the scapegoat, Malvolio, and in this way promotes acceptance of other transgressive liaisons, not only Olivia and Sebastian's but, we learn later, Toby and Maria's.

In the scene of Malvolio's confinement in a dark room, Feste, counterfeiting a parson, Sir Topas, exorcises the steward's demons. The scene seems excessive in every way—too long, too hard to stage, gratuitously brutal. However, it "chime[s] in" with the debates about possession and exorcism that had heated up again between 1597 and 1601 (Schleiner 273) when John Darrell's guilt or innocence and the politics of possession and exorcism were vigorously debated in print, notably in Samuel Harsnett's *Declaration of the Fraudulent Practices of J. Darrell concerning the pretended possession and dispossession of W. Somers* (1599) and John Darrell's *Detection of that sinnful, shameful, lying, and ridiculous discourse of Samuel Harshnet* (1600). In April 1602, soon after *Twelfth Night*'s Candlemas performance, Mary Glover's "possession" would commence.

The confinement scene, by playing with multiple elements of exorcism—the exorcist's motives, the possessed's behaviors, the spectator's pleasure, and the terms of the elite debates—does not just discredit exorcism, but credits the social efficacy and scapegoating functions of the practice. As we have seen in the earlier comic scenes, intricate parallels and reversals mock the qualities the "exorcist" shares with and displaces onto the "possessed." Just as Falstaff, the would-be cuckolder, is punished as a cuckold, Malvolio, the socially aggressive "puritan," is framed as a devil-possessed religious fanatic and then exorcised by a mirror of himself. Feste, like his victim (and like Darrell in the state's eyes), is a "counterfeyte," who assumes spiritual power. By donning the gown of "Sir Topas" and "Master Parson," he elevates his status as Malvolio had dreamed of doing (4.2.2, 12, 16). But the scene shows that the supposed possessed are likewise fakes—or dupes. Malvolio's cross-gartering reveals how easily behaviors can be cued, lending support to opponents who argue that possession is a rehearsed performance. The comic dialogue between the clown and the parson parodies the debate between devils and better selves in "good" possessions (4.2.101–103).[23] Feste's mocking question in his own person, "are you not mad indeed, or do you but counterfeit?" (4.2.115–116), satirizes his assumed role of exorcist as it does the attributed madness of Malvolio. If the scene suggests that exorcists and their clients may both be fakes, so may be the opponents of exorcism whom Feste also ventriloquizes and satirizes (Schleiner 266–270). The scene represents the debate over possession and exorcism as unresolvable. As we have seen elsewhere, distinctions between madness, possession, and fraud are almost impossible to make.[24] When Malvolio claims sobriety and victimization, the "hyperbolical fiend" (26) can be blamed; his repeated denials only confirm his condition.

It is only partly true that, as Stephen Greenblatt claims, "By 1600, then, Shakespeare had clearly marked out possession and exorcism as frauds" (115). The multiple effects of the scene are more complex. The audience is invited to participate in a farcical diagnosis of the differences between madness, possession, and fraud, distinctions that are devilishly difficult to make. It does not exactly drain exorcism of power, but transfers that power to theater—as the scene's lasting success (and exorcism's incipient decline) suggests. Theater in turn circulates that power back into social life. Although

---

[23] Thirteen-year-old Thomas Darling (who wanted to be a preacher) had just such a possession, which took the form of dialogues "between the godly Thomas and the devil, whose speech he reported" (D. P. Walker 54). Such possessions are said to be "good" because they reveal the power of God being marshaled against the Devil.

[24] As accusations and counteraccusations of fraud multiplied in the Darrell case, determining credibility became increasingly difficult. Darrell drove out devils and Harsnett claimed that they were false, but that the true Devil might counterfeit a possession (Greenblatt 105). William Sommers was repeatedly possessed and dispossessed. Eventually he blamed witches, and one of them, Alice Freeman, after she was convicted by two juries and acquitted by a third, counterattacked, accusing Sommers of having bewitched one to death. Arrested, Sommers (to save himself?) confessed to fraud and demonstrated his simulated convulsions. Subsequently, he withdrew the confession and produced genuine fits for the Church Commission's investigation. Later he reaffirmed that he was a fraud, and again produced simulated fits for a judge. It was on Sommers's testimony that Darrell was convicted (Walker 62–65). Such claims and counterclaims made the truth about that condition supremely elusive.

the supernatural underpinnings of exorcism are parodied and theological debates about possession are turned into a joke, the social, exclusionary uses of such a ritual in everyday life are affirmed. Confining madmen can be used to punish disruptive or non-normative behaviors, to disavow or mitigate one's own, and to get ahead.

John Manningham's well-known diary entry in February 1602 reports on the performance of *Twelfth Night* he saw at the Inns of Court. His response shows how and why the farcical scenes of Malvolio's humiliation could provide "pleasure," draw attention away from other more threatening love intrigues, and let Manningham disavow the vulnerabilities he shares with Malvolio. Characteristically terse, Manningham first distances himself from the main plot by learnedly cataloging its analogues and sources, then relishes the farce of the Malvolio subplot.

> At our feast wee had a play called [mid-canceled] "Twelve night, or what you will"; much like the commedy of errores, or Menechmi in Plautus, but most like and neere to that in Italian called Inganni.
>
> ---
>
> A good practise in it to make the steward beleeve his Lady widdowe was in Love with him, by counterfayting a letter, as from his Lady, in generall termes, telling him what shee liked best in him, and prescribing his gesture in smiling, his apparraile, &c., and then when he came to practise, making him beleeve they tooke him to be mad. (fol. 12b, 48)

Manningham's interest in Malvolio makes sense since his own situation, like that of many aspiring young men, is comparable to that of the tricksters and their victim. In 1602, he is a twenty-six-year-old unmarried orphan (adopted by his childless uncle Richard) at the Inns of Court who is anxious about status and money (although he was his father's and uncle's heir). In 1605 he will make a financially and socially advantageous match with Anne Curll, the sister of Edmund Curll, his Inns of Court roommate for ten years, and the daughter of William Curll, gent, and Auditor of court of Wards, a lucrative job (Sorlien 268). Henk K. Gras thinks that Manningham occludes the Orsino plot "because it was unfamiliar and in the way he experienced it, almost unacceptable to him" because of its homoerotic elements (148), and focuses on the Malvolio story because it includes topics and themes the diary everywhere incorporates: jokes and practices, rivalry between men, castration anxiety, misogyny, and bawdy. More explicitly, Manningham's pleasure in the scapegoating of Malvolio demonstrates the uses of farce I have proposed. It allows him to scorn Puritans, distance himself from erotic intrigue and women's power, and disavow the marital/economic ambition he shares with Malvolio. He, like the trickers, relishes "practices" that advance status by putdowns of opponents.

In the *Diary,* Puritans are regularly mocked, not for their theology (although Manningham was a conventional Anglican), but as in the play for their social hypocrisy: "A puritan is a curious corrector of thinges indiffer-ent" (29), reads the first entry and later entries concur: "A puritane is such a one as loves God with all his soule, but hates his neighbour with all his heart" (fol. 117b, 219). Like the play, he sides with those who find Puritan exorcism a joke. He defends Bishop Bancroft when Thomas Overbury sneers at the propagandist for exposing Darrell's exorcism of thirteen-year-old Thomas Darling as a fraud.[25] He reports a joke about the spectacle of a cel-ebrated (but not credited) possession, likely Mary Glover's: "A gentlewoman which had bin to see a child *that was sayd* to be possessed with the Divel [my italics], told howe she lost hir purse while they were at prayer. 'Oh,' said a gent[lemen], 'not unlikely, for you forgott halfe your lesson: Christ bad you watch and pray, and you prayed onely; but had you watched as you prayed, you might have kept your purse still'" (fol. 58, 120).[26]

Enjoying the joke on Malvolio allows Manningham to distance himself from his own obsession with the precise remuneration gained by an advan-tageous marriage. In January 1602, a month before the *Twelfth Night* entry, Manningham reports approvingly two such marriages: that "Sir Moyle Finche of Kent married Sir Frauncis Hastinges daughter and heir, worth to him 3,000£ per annum," and, that of Sir Francis Vane, "a young gent. of great hope and forwardnes," whose "possibilitie of living by his wife verry much, shee beinge daughter and heire to Sir Antony Mildmay; and thought hir mother will give hir all hir interitance alsoe; the father worth 3,000£ per annum, the motheres 1,200£" (fol. 10, 42–43). A series of canny marriages could build family fortunes: "Jo. Vermeren, a Dutchman, of kin to my cosens first wifes sisters husband, had issue a daughter, married to one Niepson. Their daughter was married to one Hoofman, a notable rich man, whoe in his beginning was but a pedler of pottes, yet after by his good fortune and industry he proved soe wealthie that he gave 10,000£ with his daughter in marriage to Sir Horatio Polivizena, now deceased, and the widdowe married to Mr. Oliver Cromwell, the sonne and heir of Sir H[enry] Cromwell [and father of the Protector]. This marriage and certaine land he had from his Un-cle Warrein cleared him out of debt." He is now, Manningham marvels, "the

[25] "He [Overbury] spake bitterly against the Bish[op] of London, that Darling, whoe was censured for a slaunderous libellor in the starchamber, and had bin convict for a counterfaitour of passes[?] [or, more likely, "posses[ion]"], was a better scholler then the bish[op]; that the bish[op] was a verry knave. I contradicted" (fol. 128, 235). Sorlien's note on this passage (401) quotes from John Chamberlain's letters, February 28, 1602: "'The last starchamber day one Darling a youth of Merton Colledge, (that pretended heretofore to be dispossessed of a devill by Darrell) was censured to be whipt and loose his eares, for libelling against the vice-chauncel-lor of Oxford and divers of the counsaile.'" Manningham's anecdote, and Chamberlain's, show that Darling's six-year-old possession is still well known, assumed to be counterfeit, and that later, at seventeen, his unruly behavior continues. In context, it would seem likely that the dif-ficult-to-decipher word in the manuscript that Sorlien transcribes as "passes?" and that a note suggests may be "posts" is in fact "posses[ion]," following Manningham's standard habit of contraction (see Sorlien 401).

[26] MacDonald connects the diary entry and the Glover case (*Witchcraft* xiii).

greatest esquire in those partes, thought to be worth neere 5000£ per annum" (fol. 37 and 37b, 85–86).

Manningham's (false) assumption that Olivia is a widow (an error usually attributed to his mistaking her mourning dress for widow's weeds) probably reflects his assumption that a rich woman in charge of her money is inevitably a widow—and an especially good catch.[27] He reports, "I heard that the old Earle of Hartford maried Alderman Parnels [Pranell's] sonnes widdowe; shee was the daughter of Viscount Bindon" (fol. 17b, 55). He records with special glee a practice that won a widow when "Mr. Bodly [a merchant's son], the author, promoter, and the perfecter, of a goodly library in Oxford, wan a riche widdowe by this meanes." During a card game, he asked the favored rival suitor to hold his cards, sought out the widow in a garden, "courted, and obteined his desyre; soe he played his game, while an other held his cardes" (fol. 46, 100–101). This strain in the *Diary* suggests his potential identification with Malvolio's ambitions; but the sexual danger in such a match results in ambivalence about marriage and pleasure at Malvolio's discomfiture. Rich women might make men fools.

The *Diary* anecdotes, many cited in Gras, routinely represent marriage as a dangerous sexual battleground that challenges men's capacity to please wives, especially when they are rich and sexually experienced widows. Manningham's friend Hoskins, newly married to a widow (380, note), reports that: "One told Sergeant Harrys howe many there were newe prickt sergeantes, 'Would I were neweprict to,' q[uoth] he; 'it would be the better for my wife then'" (fol. 98, 187).[28] Many jokes record men's loss of power to women. For example, "A gent. Of Nottinghamshire called an other whore maister. 'Why,' said the other, 'I had rather be a whore maister than maistered by a whore as thou art'" (fol. 15, 52). Since marriage in the *Diary* is associated with financial pleasure and sexual danger, Manningham can use the Malvolio plot to disavow the status-elevating but potentially dangerous marriage he longs for and to mock Malvolio for the humiliation he fears from strong women. He can then ignore other threats to male advancement in *Twelfth Night*'s main plot: romantic love, homoerotic desires, and women on top. Manningham tellingly fails to mention that the "good practice" he so admires is engineered by Maria, a serving woman, and results in her own upwardly mobile marriage. Other differently placed audience members, especially women, servants, and those drawn to homoerotic relationships, might have applauded different parts of the play in accord with their own very different desires, fulfilling the promise of the subtitle: "What You Will."

Such responses are not, however, recorded for us. But the prominence

---

[27] Greenblatt sees Manningham's widow mistake similarly—as "a sign, I think, of the normalization of the fantasy" of marrying rich widows (176, n 4).

[28] When Gras catalogs the jokes Manningham reports, the majority (63) are misogynist jokes about women's promiscuity or power; there are also many about male sexual dysfunction or phallic prowess (137ff.).

given to Malvolio's maddening and exorcism and the subordination of the main plot, visible in Manningham's *Diary,* would characterize allusions to the play for more than a century. These hint that, as Mad Hieronimo came to signify *The Spanish Tragedy* (see above, chap. 1), so maddened Malvolio came to stand for *Twelfth Night,* circulating a comic construction that scape-goats madness. In 1623, the *Office Book* records that "At Candlemas Malvolio was acted at court, by the Kings servants" (Chambers 2:346). In 1640, Leonard Diggs, in commendatory verses to Shakespeare's *Poems,* placed the steward at the apex of his catalog of audience-pleasing characters that include "Honest Iago and the jealous Moore," Falstaffe, Hal, Poins, and Beatrice and Benedicke: "The Cockpit Galleries, Boxes, all are full / To hear Malvoglio that crosse garter'd Gull" (Chambers 2:233). Charles I, in agreement, wrote "Malvolio" next to the title in his Folio, and Rowe, in 1709, in the first edition after the Folio, found "something singularly Ridiculous and Pleasant in the fantastical Steward Malvolio" (quoted in Lothian and Craik, ed., l) and illustrated the play with the scene of Malvolio confined in the dark room (fig. 11).[29]

These scattered allusions cannot stand in for all spectators' responses. But they help us to understand how the scenes of gulling, confinement, and exorcism could be received with pleasure and put to social use and how unfestive farce can serve to draw off audience disapproval from the excesses of lovesickness. The theatricalization of madness and possession that the play picks up from the culture undoubtedly contributed to the period's increasing denial of charisma to the Catholic and Puritan challengers of the Anglican middle way. By translating accusations of witchcraft, bewitchment, and devil possession into diagnoses of distraction and farcical exorcism, the plays shift power from elite authorities to resourceful communities, demonstrating how those of varying gender, status, and power can use attributions of madness to advance their own interests. By scapegoating the mad and farcically punishing them, the plays run ahead of contemporary social attitudes toward distracted persons and feed into the representations of Bedlam and Bedlamites that make their first appearance on stage in 1604.

The Protocols of Confinement

Although these plays draw on period protocols of treatment and confinement, their farcical scenes do not represent the compassionate attitudes to-

---

[29] The reception history of Malvolio is beyond the scope of this discussion. Laurie Osborne traces changes to his part and hence changed responses to him in eighteenth- and nineteenth-century performance editions and later productions and films. Recent editions continue to emphasize the theatrical pleasure his humiliation gives in spite of the fact that critical attention at the end of the twentieth century had shifted to the class, gender, and erotic exchanges of the main plot. In Roger Warren and Stanley Wells's 1994 Oxford edition, five of the eight production pictures are of Malvolio, and in Elizabeth Story Donno's 1985 Cambridge edition, twelve of the sixteen illustrations feature or relate to him.

ward the mad visible elsewhere. I turn now to offer glimpses from period records to emphasize their utter disjunction from the plays' treatments. The diagnosis of distraction, always communal and complex, is made by discerning the condition's onset, its possible internal and external causes, and its documentable behaviors, which often unfold episodically over a period of weeks, months, or years. When, as rarely, confinement is sought, it forms one of a continuum of strategies for "relief" and compassionate management of the distracted, designed to aid their recovery and protect the community. Recovery of memory and business, followed by full reintegration into that community, is always the goal. We can discern the outlines of this process in case notes of Richard Napier's distressed patients.[30] Although most of Napier's case notes, as we have seen in earlier chapters, document minor disorders, they also show us more severe cases and their management. For such clients, onset and development are precisely specified: e.g., Ann Smith, 30 and "12 days sick," "behaveth like a Bedlam" (Ashmole 230, fol. 177); Elisabeth Hurrell has been "distracted of wits since Midsummer" (Ashmole 227, fol. 216); William Cras, 31, was "taken with a spice of lunacy Oct 22" (Ashmole 230, fol. 71); William Iremonger has been "1 year ill" (Ashmole 227, fol. 65). Symptoms are unfolded in their social contexts, and onset often corresponds to the kinds of emotional traumas the plays represent: unrequited love, childbirth trauma, bereavement, marital breakdown, suspicion of bewitchment or possession. Chrystopher Nueman "lost his wits loving one (a waiting gentlewoman) that drew him on" and "mocked him and despised him" (Ashmole 227, fol. 150v). Elisabeth Wats, 41, had the falling sickness for three months after the death of a child and experienced "a great flushing heat rising from the bottom of her belly, with a great heat into her head benumbing and frighting her." A year later when her breast milk killed another child and the two sightless "puppes" which she used to relieve her breasts, she believed that "some planet doth blast her" and became "wild and unruly" (227, fol. 150). Alice Maryot, 45, is diagnosed by Napier as "Brain light and wild—very furious." She is, on her husband's report, "Full of pride and jealousy. Suspecteth her husband to be naught with [have sex with] women. Possessed as it is thought with some evil spirit. This woman hath been twice at Bridewell. On Tuesday night last had a spit in her hand to thrust into her husband" (235, fol. 9).

Some of Napier's more extensive case histories provide vivid illness narratives, revealing the causes, developing behaviors, and characteristic attitudes. For example, over three visits, in March, April, and June 1613, we discover Elizabeth Piddenton's most recent bout of "a swounding." She "will spoil her cloathes," and "will talk idly," will "fling at her husband" and "fling anything abroad," in the fourth episode of an illness. This "took her"

---

[30] I reiterate my gratefulness to Michael MacDonald for many conversations, suggestions, and criticisms and especially for the loan of his transcriptions of Napier's notes, which I quote from below. Napier's case notes are in the manuscripts of Elias Ashmole in the Bodleian Library, Oxford, which, following MacDonald, I cite.

first at age fourteen for three months, then "vanished of itself" for five years, "took her again with a mopishness, sighing, weeping and it held her for about a quarter of a year," then she was "well for five years, after took her again and continued somewhat longer," and "holdeth her the fourth time on Shrove Monday night." The most recent episode coincided with the birth of a child that is "testy and choleric"; it is exacerbated by the fact that her husband "hath beaten her in her fits" (199, fols. 107v, 139). Napier designates her "lunatick" (used to describe only 2 percent of his patients: MacDonald 247) and prescribes bleeding and various medications (199, fol. 73v).

Chrystopher Nueman's extensively documented case is especially interesting for its striking parallels—and contrasts—with Malvolio's. Nueman, twenty-six at his first visit and unmarried, was brought by his mother to Napier nine times between February 1627 and January 1629. It emerges that some years before, he "set his mind on a wench" who "cared not for him" and "never intended to marry, she being a waiting gentlewoman" and he only a lowly tile-maker (224, fol. 358; 227, fol. 135). His mother also opposed the match for financial reasons, "because he could not maintain her"—the beloved (227, fol. 39). At each visit, Nueman's ever-worsening symptoms are documented. The primary one is "wild, mad fits": he "did stamp and talk to himself and praying twice a day," but "thinks he seeth the devils at his prayers" (224, fol. 358). As time passes, he "will curse and swear and fight with his father" and "knock sorely" his tiles (410, fol. 186v), and he also turns his violence against himself. In "strange fits of melancholy," he "will moan and ready to pull his tongue out," and "will bite his clothes" (407, fol. 23). He talks of the devil, "sayeth that he is damned," and that he has "something speaking in his belly" (224, fol. 358). In spite of so many symptoms that are congruent with possession via bewitchment, Napier always designated the broken match the cause of illness, and prescribed his entire repertoire of somatic remedies: bleeding, emetics, and various juleps. Once, however, he gave Nueman's mother a "sigil" for him, a metal emblem that, as we have seen (chap. 2) was used to ward off supernatural affliction (227, fol. 39). Even in such a violent and recalcitrant case, the young man continued to be cared for by his parents in the home and continued to visit Napier in search of a cure, although none is recorded.

In the cases above, as in all of the texts I am using, extreme cases of distraction are not represented as medically or morally different from milder ones or as incurable. Nowhere in the records available to me are there signs of moral condemnation or dehumanization of the mad or the desire to segregate them permanently from society—Foucault's meaning for "confinement." Restraint, in the few cases in which it is used, is one in a series of strategies for managing distracted persons, used reluctantly as a complement or catalyst to healing. Restraint for the mad is a necessary expedient to protect the ill and the community from arson, glass breaking, violent attacks, or suicide attempts; it is sometimes prescribed specifically for its calming influence. Elizabeth Hurrell, a widow of 60, probably with no one to care for her, "will be doing of some ill except she be tyde." Widow Lovet, 50, also presumably without family, is "mopish and senseless by fits," "well and then furious," and "was thought urged? [ ] to be wanton" (a widow stereotype), is "by fits worse than ever," and is "bound with fetters." Jone Savage, 36, unmarried, and "a very poor woman," suffering from unrequited love for sixteen years, has been "mad since Whitsuntide" (when she happened to see the object of her love), and "hath ever since been tied up in chains," reports the cousin who consults Napier for a remedy. Sybill Fisher, 24, grew ill following a "hard delivery," marred by one "unskillful midwife" and a second who was froward and refused to come because she was not called in first. Hence Fisher suspects that she is bewitched. Fisher exhibits a variety of mad behaviors—weeping, laughing, dancing, cursing, fleering—and "knows nobody." Hence "they bynde her hands and feete. When she is loose she is so strong that they cannot deale with her." Napier prescribes medication for her, and five years later he reports that she "now is well God be thanked." But at 39 she is back to consult him, "distracted" again and "will cry out she is damned." We see in these case histories the maladies of earlier chapters reiterated: the despair of love melancholy, the lusts of lovesickness, the terror of bewitchment.[31]

Since very few of Napier's distressed patients are bound, have hired keepers, or are institutionalized, one must turn for evidence on such cases to quarter-session and other records, analyzed by Fessler, Suzuki, Rushton, and Pelling.[32] These records provide evidence about those who are seeking help (for themselves or relatives) in the form of financial assistance for caretaking. When institutional restraint is used, it is most often initiated by families at the end of their financial and emotional resources. Three conditions are prerequisites for receiving "relief and mayntaynence," including restraint, from the parish. First, the distressed do or threaten senseless harm to themselves, or others, or to property (MacDonald, *Mystical* 142); second, no family members or servants are available to provide the high level of care needed; third, they or their families lack funds to pay for care. Petitions to the parish required demonstrations of economic need, so most cases where confinement was requested involved poor petitioners. The relief offered to the poor distracted was the same as that provided for other needy parishioners unable

[31] In Ashmole manuscript. Hurrell: 227, fol. 216; Lovet: 237, fol. 80v; Savage: 402, fol. 75; Fisher: 207, fol. 113v, 229, fol. 140, 230, fol. 141.

[32] The work of these scholars has been indispensable to me although the wide geographical, chronological, and generic disparities in the records they draw on render my statistical analysis speculative. Margaret Pelling analyzes records from the town of Norwich concerning treatment of the sick poor, 1550–1640. Peter Rushton examines quarter-sessions records along with those of hospitals, infirmaries, and parishes for management of idiots and lunatics in two northeast counties, 1600–1800. A. Fessler examines lunacy cases in seventeenth-century Lancashire quarter-sessions records. Akihito Suzuki examines lunacy cases in seventeenth- and eighteenth-century quarter-sessions records from Middlesex.

to care for themselves: orphaned children, the sick, disabled, infirm (Andrews, "Hardly a Hospital" and "Bedlam"). It consisted of payment to the family or, if necessary, to local caregivers to shelter, feed, clothe, and watch over the infirm. In the scattered records I draw on, women and men equally suffer extreme distraction, and are equally likely to be bound, to have keepers hired, or to be candidates for institutional confinement.[33] Family responsibility is still predominant in such cases; sufferers who are bound or "tabled" with others remain integrated in the family and community, and restraint is always seen as temporary. A brother, asking for an allowance to pay a keeper or friend to sit with his violent and suicidal sister, reports that he is "*compelled* sometymes to bind her" (Fessler 903, my italics). A woman begs "relief" from charitable people for her husband who became lunatic when wounded and "doth remayne bound up in Iron Chaynes at this present . . . nor any none to looke to him—beinge lockt to a post" (Fessler 903). One young man in a "lunatic frensie" is "lyinge bound in Cheanes and ffeathers" (Fessler 903).[34] Few would come near him except his aged father, "who adventures himself into him to keep him in some awe and subordination," attempting to restore him to health by returning him to his proper place in the family (Fessler 903). Justices also ordered the disposition of one who was "a poore distracted woman and hath lately pulled out one of her Eyes and is wandering about—and offers violence to her owne Children," urging that she "may be kept by some person to be appoynted by the overseers of the poore when she shalbe found" (Fessler 903). Another case where restraint seems cruel, but allows treatment to occur, is the securing of Jane Ovington in a stable. The parish paid for her confinement there for twelve weeks—for food, straw, men to clean the stable, replace straw, shave her head (perhaps to facilitate bleeding from the head?), doctors' fees, and the cost of medications and bleeding. She recovered (Rushton 44).

In only six extreme cases did petitions urge that friends or relatives be sent to a House of Correction; in these, other alternatives had been exhausted. One husband urged it for his wife since she was a "daily nuisance to her neighbors" and "he had done what he can to help her both by Doctors and by chaining her" (Fessler 904). One man was sent to the House of Correction after he had been tabled with a parishioner, broke his chains, pulled

---

[33] Scattered records do not permit much statistical accuracy. Out of 48 severely disturbed Napier patients I culled out (35 women and 13 men), 4 women are bound; 1 is sent twice to Bridewell; 1 is brought in a cart to Napier. Two men have to be held down. Of the 30 cases from the quarter-session records reproduced by Fessler (16 men and 14 women), 3 men have keepers hired for them; 3 are chained; and 3 are urged sent to a House of Correction; 2 women have keepers hired; 2 are chained; and 3 urged sent to House of Correction. In Suzuki I, which stresses the dispositions of families and parishes to care for the distressed, of 11 men and 15 women discussed, 1 man has keepers; 1 is sent to a local House of Correction; 1 is "ruled in house"; 1 woman is released from a House of Correction; and 1 is maintained there.

[34] Probably because, as I learned from Jonathan Andrews's dissertation, feathers were preferred to straw as more comfortable, although more expensive and less easy to keep clean from the incontinence that made them necessary.

down slates at a neighbor's, and threatened arson, so "is a person not fitt to go loose" (Fessler 904). Even in an anomalous case where the court orders the inhabitants and constable of Crowley to confine a lunatic and dangerous Hughe Thrustanes, the emphasis is on care and recovery—"they [the "whole inhabitants of Crowley"] shall maynteyne and keepe him in stronghold, geving and fynding him sufficyent meate and dryncke untill he be restored unto his former remembrance" (Suzuki I 452).

Placing case histories of the mad side by side with farcical representations of the maddened reminds us that, although some historicist criticism of literature appears to assume otherwise, literary representation and social history can diverge as well as converge. The play's farcical and punitive ascriptions of madness are contrary to the period's protocols for reintegrating the mad into the community. Such disjunctions between representation and practice suggest how play texts and performances, with their many agendas, can produce rather than reproduce attitudes and ideology. As Shakespeare strives to surpass Plautus, to provide additional theatrical pleasure, and to displace censure from lovesickness; and as he reworks the scene of confinement, drawing on popular witchcraft beliefs, Skimmington rituals, and exorcism practices, his plays circulate debates and images that promulgate new attitudes toward the mad. We may have a hard time seeing these changes since we have inherited their consequences. In the rest of this chapter, and the next, I will take a fresh look at the emergence of attitudes on stage that newly segregate and dehumanize the mad.

A glance ahead and a comparison of two visual representations of confinement suggest how stage attitudes toward Malvolio's madness came to influence attitudes toward patients in Bethlem Hospital. The engraving of Malvolio's confinement included by Nicolas Rowe in his 1709 edition of Shakespeare's works (fig. 11) bears startling resemblances to the 1710 engraving of Bedlam by Bernard Lens and John Sturt in the fifth edition of Jonathan Swift's *Tale of a Tub* (fig. 12). Taken together, the engravings show how Shakespeare's scenes of confinement help produce the attitudes toward madness that were emerging in early eighteenth-century culture. On the left of Rowe's illustration, Malvolio, like the madmen in the Swift illustration, is sitting uncomfortably on straw on the floor of a bare dark chamber with a spilled slop bowl by his side, his mouth open and his hand out, pleading. On the right, Maria, elegantly garbed, and Feste, smug in priest's gown and elaborate wig, are brightly lit and smile complacently. The scene represents an artist's rendition, not a stage production where Malvolio may be hardly visible (Astington, "Dark" 55), and it renders Malvolio subhuman.

The second engraving, illustrating Swift's brutal satire (which uses the metaphor of madness to signify human corruption and religious fanaticism) utterly segregates and dehumanizes the mad. Six madmen in a bare Bedlam cell perform antics for visitors, who gawk through grates on the right. Several madmen are nearly nude, including the central figure, who is chained on

Fig. 11. *Twelfth Night*, act 4, scene 2: Malvolio in the dark room,
from Rowe's edition of Shakespeare, 1709. Courtesy of the University
of Illinois at Urbana-Champaign Library.

FIG. 12. "Bedlam," from an engraving by Bernard Lens and John Sturt for Jonathan Swift's *Tale of a Tub*, 5th edition, 1710. Courtesy of the Division of Rare and Manuscript Collections, Carl A. Kroch Library, Cornell University.

hay in the foreground. In an abjected version of Malvolio's twisted pose, he flings his slop angrily at the visitors. Both engravings circulate the assumption, increasingly prominent in the eighteenth century, that the madpersons in the newly enlarged Bethlem at Moorfields are inhuman spectacles to be separated from and gawked at by the healthy. The farcical use of the exorcism of the maddened in the three comedies produces attitudes toward the mad that would not take hold until over a century later. But the correspondence between stage and hospital, seen in these engravings, continues to haunt the imaginations of literary critics and historians, as we shall see in the next chapter.

CHAPTER 6

RETHINKING CONFINEMENT IN EARLY MODERN ENGLAND

The Place of Bedlam in History and Drama

If others had not been mad, then we should be.
SHOSHANA FELMAN QUOTING GEORGES BATAILLE QUOTING WILLIAM BLAKE

As earlier chapters have shown, most management of mad persons in early modern England and in theatrical representation between 1576 and 1632 takes place within the family and local community. However, for literary critics, historians, and students of the period, assumptions about madness misleadingly center on confinement in tiny Bethlehem Hospital and rest on an apparently ineradicable analogy between the hospital's patients and the confined Bedlamites that first appears in five Jacobean plays. Theatrical and therapeutic confinements are imagined to be analogous spectacles of excess, performativity, and "incontinence" (Mullaney 49). This analogy continues to be supported by the belief that, in the early seventeenth century, Bethlem Hospital was regularly visited by spectators for amusement and titillation, and that, in the absence of documentary evidence, this practice is confirmed by mimetic stage representations of Bedlamites. The monumental scholarly work, *The History of Bethlem* (1997), recycles the image of Bethlem as spectacle in its third paragraph (with typical chronological vagueness): "For over a century [which?] Bethlem was one of the sights of London on any serious tourist's itinerary, along with the Tower and Westminster Abbey" (2). Natsu Hattori's well informed essay, "'The Pleasure of Your Bedlam': The Theatre of Madness in the Renaissance" (1995), links the two sites as analogous and contiguous sites of entertainment: "In fact, the hospital and its mad folks were considered one of the chief amusements of Tudor and Stuart London. . . . The old Bethlem Hospital, at Bishopsgate, was a stone's throw away from two of London's main playhouses near Moorfields, the Theatre and the Curtain, thus making a convenient stop to or from the theatre for entertainment-seekers" (287). Both her article and *The His-*

tory of Bethlem continue to support long-standing assumptions that play-wrights' representations record the practice of visiting the historical Bethlem for entertainment: "Bethlem's early and growing popularity as a resort for curious and idle visitors, out for fun or diversion, [is] powerfully attested by the Bedlam scenes of Jacobean literature" (*HB* 152). This chapter chal-lenges the analogy and the importance of such visiting (before 1632) by analyzing the huge differences—geographical, institutional, historical, and functional—between the charitable hospital and the early modern stage. I seek to understand why, since hospital documents and stage plays represent madness and attitudes so differently, the analogy persists and what purposes it continues to serve for us today. I propose that, by certifying the horrors of Bedlam and the unruliness of early modern drama, it supports our discipli-nary and ideological agendas. The analogy may satisfy our need to see the mad (both then and now) as our Other—as spectacles distanced from us, ob-served for our titillation or instruction.

We can see with special clarity in this chapter how attitudes toward mad-ness undergo heterogeneous changes at different cultural locations, driven by divergent institutional struggles and consequent innovations. The first two of the mere five plays with brief self-contained Bedlamite scenes are per-formed in 1604–1605, soon after the appearance of *Twelfth Night* with its farcical domestic confinement and just before *King Lear* (1605) and *The Two Noble Kinsmen* (1613) with their representations of psychologically devel-oped and potentially curable madness. The representations of Bedlamites represent a dramatic innovation and circulate emergent attitudes toward the mad whereas the tragedy and romance, like the routine practices of confine-ment at Bethlem Hospital, tap into the currently dominant views. The long-established hospital is a sought-after resource for charitable treatment whose goal is the reintegration of the distracted into the community from which they have temporarily become detached. In contrast, the plays, in the newly built theaters, represent Bedlamites as performative caricatures permanently segregated from the onstage and offstage spectators—for whom they pro-vide momentary theatrical pleasure. At the hospital, men and women are ad-mitted, treated, and released for similar reasons and in equal numbers, but in the plays' representations of Bedlamites, gender distinctions sharpen. Mad-women (who represent only two of the twenty-one madpersons in the plays) are reduced to eroticized female bodies. The old Bethlem Hospital and the new representations of Bedlamites must be uncoupled to dispel the myths of correspondence that distort both. Only then can their intersections and their contributions to changing constructions of madness be understood.

The Purposes of Confinement at Bethlem Hospital

Bethlem Hospital's function as a charitable hospice for the sick poor re-mains essentially unchanged from its origin as a religious foundation, the Priory of St. Mary of Bethlehem, in 1247 until its move to a larger building at Moorfields in 1676. My brief history of the hospital emphasizes its institutional and geographical embeddedness in the fabric of the City of London and its long-standing commitment to providing treatment for the poor distracted persons, and reveals attitudes toward the hospital and the distracted. I quote liberally from early modern comments about Bethlem to provide vivid accounts of the attitudes displayed by those who managed and used it.[1]

The hospital was already accepting distracted persons at the beginning of the fifteenth century and came to serve only this function by the mid-sixteenth. Although its commitment to treatment of the sick poor remained constant, it was managed first by the Catholic Church, then by the Crown, then by the City of London. Its administration and funding were first under the auspices of the Church of Bethlehem, which initiated the Foundation to house its representatives and succor the needy. In the second half of the fourteenth century, responsibility for it was gradually assumed by the London Fraternity of St. Mary's, by the Skinners' and Drapers' Guilds, and by private citizens like Sir John Crosby, Grocer, Woolman, Sheriff, Alderman and knight (Stow 1 172–173) who, when he died in 1475, left a bequest to benefit "the distract peple being thanne within thospitall of Bedleem" in whatever way was best: "outher in redy money or in vitailles good and holsom for thaim or in other wise, necessary for thaime" (*HB* 98). In 1534, at the Reformation Suppression of Catholic properties, Henry VIII took over Bethlem. After years of negotiations between Crown and City over patronage and administrative control, Henry ceded governance, but not ownership, to the City in 1547, just before he died. Ongoing negotiations over the patronage, appointment of keepers, and administrative control of Bethlem continued until 1633 when the City gained complete authority over the hospital, having been its de facto caretaker since at least 1574, when it came under the auspices of the Bridewell Board of Governors. In spite of these administrative battles, the hospital's charitable and therapeutic functions, its space, its protocols of admission, and its desirability as a refuge for indigent distracted persons remained unchanged from the early fifteenth to the late seventeenth century. Close attention to these matters shows that at no time were madpersons who sought entry viewed as less than or other than human, deemed incurable, or considered spectacles.

The process whereby Bethlem Hospital, which served the ill, the poor, and travelers, came to specialize in the care of the mentally disordered was grad-

---

[1] I draw extensively and gratefully on Patricia Allderidge's and Jonathan Andrews's archival scholarship, and I am profoundly indebted to both for conversations and generous assistance of many kinds. This chapter also relies on the magisterial *History of Bethlem* (*HB*) by Jonathan Andrews, Asa Briggs, Roy Porter, Penny Tucker, and Keir Waddington, which meticulously traces the hospital's development from its inception in 1247 through its fourth relocation up to 1994. Patricia Allderidge's *Bethlem Hospital, 1247–1997: A Pictorial Record* provides a wonderful visual overview of that history.

ual and apparently spontaneous.[2] A report of a visitation in 1403 first documents this development when it finds six men *"menti capti"* (seized in mind) and three other infirm persons in the hospital (Allderidge, "Management" 141). Later references confirm that the poor distracted were given care and therapy, but were often subjected to administrative neglect. In 1436, William Mawere, a tailor and later an alderman, was discharged from his jury and other civic duties "owing to his constant attention to the poor mad lunatics of the Hospital of St. Mary de Bedlem without Bishopgate" (*HB* 57). But in 1437, an incoming Master of the Hospital reported that neglect threatened the "worship of God there, and alms and other works of piety and the succour of demented lunatics and other poor and sick persons resorting thither" (*HB* 73). Although little is known about the kinds of therapy offered, the hospital probably provided the standard purges, emetics, and bleeding. Although many of its masters were aldermen who were not by trade physicians, this does not mean, as we have seen, that they all lacked medical knowledge, and three fifteenth-century masters appointed by the king were in fact physicians or surgeons (*HB* 85). A 1519 advertisement, perhaps exaggerating to gain funds, offers indulgences to donors to the inmates of Bethlem "who are there kept and nurtured with great care and diligence, and are cured by the doctor [medicus] and unceasing solicitude" (*HB* 114). Additional evidence that medication was provided (even in the absence of a resident physician or apothecary) is a report of a salary of 8s a week paid in 1589 to a Mrs. Thomson who claimed experience in curing the distract. She "hath given medicine to the poor at Bedlem" (O'Donoghue 129) and is paid to look after two lunatics "in Bedlem in romes ther provided for her she to finde them diett and medsens" (*HB* 89).[3]

In a much cited passage in his "Apology" (1533), Thomas More alludes to another kind of treatment—outside the hospital—of a man who was formerly "put uppe in Bedelem, and afterwarde by betynge and correccyon gathered hys remembraunce to hym, and beganne to come agayne to hym selfe" (118). The treatment is harsh because More, like others, assumes that distraction is a temporary invasion of a recoverable self. After being discharged, More tells us, "hys olde fansyes beganne to fall agayn in his hed," and he disrupted churches and harassed praying women. Hence More, at the time likely undersheriff of London, had him bound and whipped before the whole town; constables "stryped hym with roddys therfore tyl he waxed wery and somwhat lenger" and afterwards, More reports, "Veryly, god be

---

[2] Similarly specialized hospitals for the distracted were likewise being founded on the continent from the fourteenth to the sixteenth century (*HB* 111–113).

[3] While both Edward O'Donoghue (129) and the authors of *The History of Bethlem* (114) express amused doubt that this entry could mean what it says, it is perfectly credible that this woman could have been paid for and been successful at dispensing the same sorts of medications that were used by many other unlicensed and licensed practitioners and housewives in the period and that were restorative for the patients of Lady Grace Mildmay and Richard Napier.

thanked, I here none harme of him now" (O'Donoghue 107; *HB* 99–100, 112, quoted from More, "Apology" 9:118).[4] Chaining, like whipping, is rarely mentioned but may have sometimes been a necessity. A 1446 indulgence which mentions that many of the "miserable persons dwelling there . . . are so alienated in mind and possessed of unclean spirits that they must be restrained with chains and fetters" (quoted *HB* 114), is the only reference to existence of possessed at Bethlem or to chaining the inhabitants. However, as we have seen in the discussion of domestic confinement, chains or some form of restraint were often necessary; those admitted were the most violent and recalcitrant cases, and there may have been no locked rooms or doors at the facility, which was sandwiched into an increasingly crowded business and residential district.

Bethlem was by far the smallest and the least well endowed of the City's hospitals. The building, labeled Bedlam on the ca. 1559 Copperplate Map (figs. 13 and 14), is unchanged from its inception in 1247 until the move to Moorfields in 1676 and so was therefore sometimes overcrowded and often in disrepair. Its exact size and disposition are not known, but Patricia Allderidge estimates, based on the late 1677 ground plan (fig. 15), that "the long building running from east to west in the c. 1559 map is the hospital proper, apparently including the small north/south wing at the west end. Taken together with the two tenements at the east end (which by then were occupied by the steward and porter respectively) the whole measured 200 feet in length in 1677 and was 51 feet wide at the west end" ("Management" 145).[5] All that is known of its interior in its first four hundred and thirty years of existence is a 1632 entry quoted in a nineteenth-century report that lists on the ground floor "a parlour, a kitchen, two larders, a long entry throughout the house, and 21 rooms wherein the poor distracted people lie, and above the stairs eight rooms more for servants and the poor to lie in" (Allderidge, "Management" 145). How the patients were dispersed, what the rooms were like, and whether the entry was east/west or north/south are not known. Whatever the facilities, they were not well maintained. The 1598 inspection finds the kitchen sink stopped up, the floor and ceiling in the keeper's lodge falling down, and tiling everywhere in need of repair (fig. 16). Although the precinct was increasingly built up with rent-producing tene-

---

[4] Neither this reference nor More's later analogy comparing one "thou shalt in Bedleem se[e] . . . laugh at the knocking of his own hed against a post" with a fool who laughs when doing wrong to his neighbor (More, "Last" 1:131) need suggest (as *History of Bethlem* notes) that More visited Bedlam for amusement (O'Donoghue 107; Allderidge, "Management" 144). He had multiple reasons to be in the area in the course of his duties and daily life. He lived in Bishopsgate Ward not far from the hospital; John Calvalari, a Bethlem Master, was a close friend (*HB* 60); and More was responsible, first as undersheriff and later as chancellor, for keeping peace in the ward and the City (*HB* 132), which likely accounts for his administration of the whipping to the disruptive recidivist patient.

[5] This late plan may "correlate well" with the original building, as Allderidge proposes ("Management" 145), or may incorporate renovations undertaken after the hospital moved and provide no clues at all to its layout, as the *History of Bethlem* suggests (48).

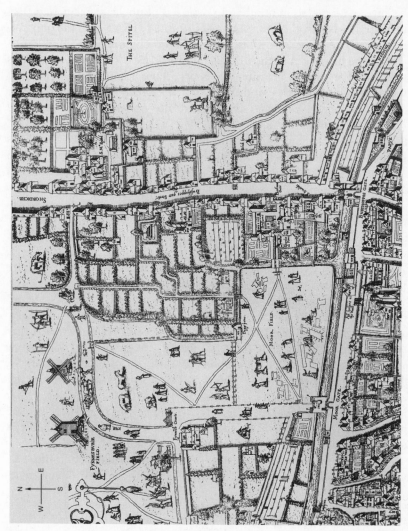

FIG. 13. Moorfields and neighborhood, ca. 1559, Copperplate Map. By permission of the Museum of London.

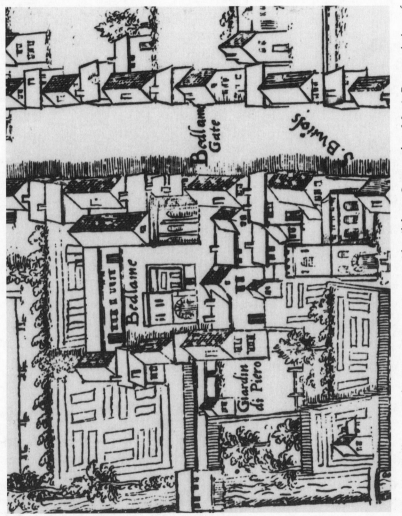

FIG. 14. Bedlam on Bishopsgate Street, ca. 1559 (detail from Copperplate Map). By permission of the Museum of London.

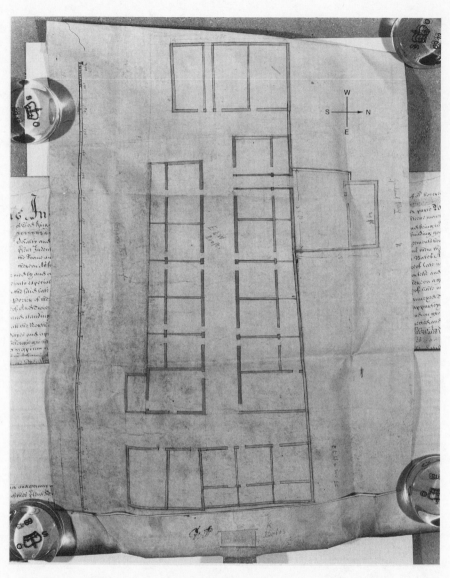

FIG. 15. Groundplan of Bethlem Hospital, 1677. Courtesy of the Bethlem Royal Hospital Archives and Museum.

ments crowded near the hospital and large mansions along the north and south boundaries of the ward, no other comments on its interior or complaints about disruptions have survived.[6] The lack of complaints, indeed of *any* information whatsoever about the building's interior or its inhabitants suggests that few visitors went there.

Perhaps because Bethlem was so small and was the only hospital without its own Board of Governors, it received scant attention even from the aldermen. But records provide some indication of Bethlem's protocols of confinement, types of residents, and, most important, of attitudes toward them. The Court of Aldermen's primary business with Bethlem, as its records between 1551 and 1599 reveal, concerned the property's money-generating rents and leases (7 items), the always fraught assignments of keepers (11 items), miscellaneous business usually about provisions (8), and referrals of individuals (8). Admission to Bethlem Hospital was selective and much sought after, available only with a warrant certifying the petitioner to be distracted *and* poor, but not diseased, feigning, criminal, or simple-minded. Those the period termed idiots, fools, or simple (those we would characterize as developmentally delayed) were believed congenitally ill and hence inadmissible. Warrants for admission could be granted by the Governors of Bridewell and the Court of Aldermen who oversaw the Governors, by the lord mayor, and by the keeper, who could and did admit patients who could afford to pay (Allderidge, "Management" 150; *HB* 119–126). For those less poor or admitted on request of private parties, an "obligor" or "surety" was required—someone who guaranteed to pay weekly or annual graduated fees to "allow" or "maintaine" them. In the Court of Aldermen's records, those seeking admission were most often characterized as "distraught" (8 times), but also as "lunatic," "mad," "frantic," and "idle-headed" (1 each). Those certified ill but not incurable were allowed admission. "And the Chamberlain by the order of the court received XXVI *s* Viii d. delivered here by the friends of a woman distraught brought unto Bethlem to keep in the mean season." "Item it is ordered by this Courte at the request of Mr Steven Shawe & others the inhabitants of St. John Street by their bill of petition that Ellen Barnes wife of George Barnes Cook shall be received into Bedlam there to remain until such time as God shall restore her to perfect memory paying forthwith to the keeper there Vis. VIIId. And every week so long as she shall remain there VIs. which the said Shaw & others have promised to pay."[7]

---

[6] The theaters, in contrast, were regularly closed down for plague control and censured for the disruptions their crowds caused. For example, complaints permanently closed the first Blackfriars Theater when its neighbors generated a petition that stopped Burbage from opening a new playhouse there in 1596. It argued that the "comon playhouse . . . will grow to be a very great annoyance and trouble, . . . both by reason of the great resort and gathering togeather of all manner of vagrant and lewde persons that, under cullor of resorting to the playes, will come thither and worke all manner of mischeef, and allso to the great pestring and filling up of the same precinct, yf it should please God to send any visitation of sicknesse as heretofore hath been" (Gurr, *Shakespearean Stage* 144).

[7] Repertories of the Court of Aldermen, transcribed by Allderidge: Rep. 12, no. 2, fol. 482b,

Because of high demand and overcrowding, admittance was difficult
and those cured were supposedly promptly discharged to make room for
the many others seeking admission. Frauds, like John Langton, "a rouge
fayninge hym selfe to be made" were committed to the less desirable
Bridewell for work rather than cure (*HB* 118). Katherine Comy in 1620 was
first thought to be a "lewd counterfeite vagrant" and hence kept in Bridewell
(the standard repository for bawds and prostitutes), but later, when "found
to be Lunatique" was sent to Bethlem (*HB* 118). Once five aldermen were
assigned to "take the pains to examine and try whether certain poor persons
lately sent from the hospital in Smithfield [St. Bartholomew] to Bethlem be
distraught or not and agreed that if they be no distraught that they shall be
put out of the said house of Bethlem."[8] When, in 1576, Thomas Dowsinge
was found in "well & in perfecte memorye," he was ordered discharged (*HB*
121). Although some stays were long, other patients recovered quickly. In
the 1598 census, for example, nine patients had been there for under three
years and eleven for longer stays (see *HB* on turnover and length of stay,
124–126).

    We receive our fullest glimpses of the house and its inhabitants and atti-
tudes toward them in the Bedlam censuses of 1598 (fig. 16) and 1624 (fig.
17), and in the list of patients granted apparel (shirts and smocks) in 1607.[9]
These reveal its avenues of admission, guarantees by surety, type of patients,
length of stay, and conditions of removal. The largest group of patients was
sent and maintained by Bridewell (6 warranted by Bridewell in 1598, 14 in
1624). Other petitions and warrants were by the lord mayor or the aldermen (2 in 1598, 6 in 1624); by corporate groups such as parishes, guilds,
Inns of Court (5 in 1598, 3 in 1624); or by individuals (4 in 1598, 2 in 1624).
It is clear that by 1624, as the City was solidifying its administrative control,
official admissions increased and private ones declined. Most of the inhabitants were poor, but a few of higher standing had wealthy patrons (*HB*
121–124). The population in 1598 included the very poor such as Welch
Elizabeth, Rosse an Almswoman, several widows, and a servant. In 1607,

---

19th May Edward VI; Rep. 18, fol. 24 (25 original numbering) 4 June [1573]. These fees may
have been characteristic. Fees for guaranteeing the entrance of private persons seem to have
been on a sliding scale and not exorbitant. Other guarantees recorded in the 1598 census were
16 pence a week, 20 pence a week, 4 pounds a year (7 shillings a week), and 20 nobles a year.
Six shillings was the average amount earned by an "industrious artisan" in a week (Gurr, *Shakespearean Stage* 12), and we have just seen Mrs. Thomson paid 8s. a week to care for the distracted. About sixpence a day or 3 shillings a week was required for a subsistence diet. Luxuries
like a pair of silk stockings (2£.) or books (6s. to 10£.) cost more.

    [8] Repertories of the Court of Aldermen, transcribed by Allderidge: Rep. 13, no. 1, fol. 100b,
28 November 1554.

    [9] These censuses, reproduced in Allderidge, "Management," 152–153, 158–160 and in figs.
16 and 17, have been invaluable to me. I am grateful to Patricia Allderidge for publishing these
documents, for her lengthy and instructive tour of the Bethlem archives and museum, and for
providing me with her transcripts of items dealing with Bethlem Hospital in the fifteenth-, six-
teenth-, and seventeenth-century Repertories of the Court of Aldermen and allowing me to
quote from them.

three of the same women, Jone Bromfeild, "Mother kempe," and "Mother Claye" were still there, as now were Edward Booth (the Earl of Shrewsbury's page), Welsh Harry, and Black Will—all given smocks or shirts. But there were higher status inhabitants as well. In the 1598 census we find "Anthoney Greene fellow of Penbrooke Hall in Cambridge sent in by the L: of Canterbury," and "Edmond Browne one of the Queenes Chappell sent in by the L. Chamb[er]leyn" and maintained by "his wages wch he hath of the Queene." In 1624 we find Thomas Hackett, by warrant from the mayor, and Sir Thomas Middleton, Knight, and John Gibbins who owned on the Banke side "a play house & pyke gardens."

Although the hospital favors poor patients over rich ones and those warranted by officials over private patients, there is no evidence that either men or women are more likely to be confined—although we might expect women to be poorer and hence more appropriate objects of charity than men were.[10] The evidence shows the institution serving equal numbers of men and women—just as we have seen (in the previous chapter) that nearly equal numbers of distracted men and women were candidates for local confinement or caretaking. In the 1598 census, 9 men and 12 women are resident. In 1607, 5 men receive shirts and 5 women receive smocks. In 1624, 18 men and 13 women are resident. But that census was taken to reduce overcrowding and "to see the warrants how they were taken in, whether they be fit to be kept, and if they be found simple idiots, or recovered, to send them to the places whence they came" (Allderidge, "Management" 158). As a result, 8 of the men were designated "fit to be kept" and 9 "to be removed." Eleven women were fit to be kept and 4 were thought "not fitt to be kept in this house," terminology that underlines the desirability and difficulty of getting into Bethlem Hospital.

However, the 1624 census, like other findings in this book, may hint at the emergence of differential attitudes toward ill men and women (but *not* differential treatments). Unlike the earlier one, the second census of patients is segregated by gender, perhaps because when patients were being culled, gender balance was thought desirable (although there is no evidence that the facility was gender-segregated at this time). The designations for the 18 men speak only to their administrative status; they are termed "fitt to bee kepte," "not fitt to bee kepte," or "to be sent to . . . some other hospital," "home to his wife," "to Hull from whence he came." Only two of the men, both "simple fellows," have their illness specified. No man is designated "mad." In contrast several women are explicitly characterized as "very ill" (3), "madd" (1), "very madd" (1), "a mad woman" (1), "something idle-headed" (1), and "fell madd" (1). One woman is termed "a poor idiot not fitt to bee

---

[10] In the first census, those who have been there longest are all women (1 for 25 years, 1 for 13 years, and 2 for 10 years); in the second census they are all men (3 for 20 years and 2 for 18 years—all "to be kept"). *The History of Bethlem* finds little evidence in the records that women (or political troublemakers) were confined to control them (116–118).

The Fowerth daye of December 1598

A view of Bethalem [in margin]

Whereas it was ordered at a Court holden the Second daye of this instant December before the governors of this Hospitall that certayne of the sayd governors should view and p[er]use the default[es] and want of rep[ar]ac[i]jons in Bethalem where the lunatick people are kept Whereuppon we whose names are heerunder subscrybed have accordinglye viewed and p[er]used the
default[es] and want of rep[ar]ac[i]jons in the sayd howse and we do fynd as followeth

Inprimis the flower over head in the Keepers lodge must be trused higher wth a long peece of tymber to gecrosse over thwart the lodge and a post to be sett at one end of it to barre upp the crosse
peece and a ground plate to be layed crosse the lodge toward[es] the street syde thorowghout the whole frame and the seeling and walls are to be repayred.

Item the sinck in the Kitchen is stopped by reason of a garden wch ioyneth to it wch one Mrs. Colte or her assignes holdeth of the Cittye and by that meanes there is no sinck to passe the water
awaye wch hath bine heertofore used for that the water did passe thorowgh the garden to the com[m]on sewer the [blank] in the sayd Kitchen over head is broken in sonder and is to be taken
downe and a new to be putt in.

Item a new reason peece [*sic*] is to be putt in the romes over the lodge for that the old is rotten and readye to fall.

Item the great vault is to be empryed for that it is full.

Item the tyling thorowghout is to be repayred

We do also fynd in the sayd house theis prisoners heerunder named sent in as well by this Hospitall as by other men whereof the Keeper doth receive the profites

Salvado Mendes about three yeares past
Neme Barker about Fyve & twenty yeres past
Elizabeth Androwes about Tenn yeares past
Jone Bromfeild about A yeare past
Rose Bromfeild in January last
Henrye Richardes in November last   theis were sent in
Elizabeth Dicons sent in by Mr. Oliver Skinner Salter at the request of the parishioners of East Ham in Essex and the sayd parishe doth allow for her.   by this Hospitall
Elizabeth Kempe Widdow who was taken in by Mr. Sleford tenn yeares past and doth still continew there.
Anne Claye sometyme dwelling in Aldermary parish Widdow sent in by warrant from the Lord Mayor who hath remayned there about Thirten Yeares and Mrs. Wood her sister is bound to pay
fower poundes yearly towardes her maintaynaunce.
Johan Brockehurst Widdow sent in by St Wolsey Dixey L. Mayor at the request of the Company of Skinners and hath allowance of xvi^d. A weeke.
Barbara Heron sent in by the Ladye Stafford who hath remayned there some viii or ix yeares and is allowed for by her
John Somerskall sent in by Mr Swaldell when he was Treasorer at the request of the Benchers of Grayes Inn about three yeares past and is allowed for by them.
Barwick Constable sent in by St John Hart about two yeares now past and is maintayned by Xptopher Willoby gentleman dwelling in Kent.
Welch Elizabeth sent in from St Bartholomewes Hospitall about A yeare now past the sayd Hospitall alloweth Twenty pence A weeke
Anthoney Greene fellow of Penbrooke Hall in Cambridge sent in by the L. of Canterbury about half A yeare now past and Doctor Androwes paieth twenty Nobles A yeare for him.
James Cliterbooke sent in by Mr. Mannsfeild dwelling by Maydenhead about half A yeare now past and he maintayneth him.
Hawnce A Dutchman sent in by the governors of the Dutch church about fower monthes past and they maintayne him.
Rosse an Almeswoman sent in [by] Mr. Bromeskill Vyntner dwelling at St Mary Hill about fower monthes past and is maintayned by the Company of Vyntners.
John Dalton sent in by the Lord Admirall in October last and his Honor maintayneth him.
Edmond Browne one of the Queenes Chappell sent in by the L. Chamb[er]leyn in October last and his wages wch he hath of the Queene payeth his chardges.
We do fynd divers other default[es] in the sayd house in such sorte that it is not ffyt for anye man to dwell in wch was left by the Keeper for that it is so loathsomly and filthely kept not fitt for
anye man to come into the sayd howse

Thomas Box Thresorer	John Pollard
Florens Caldwall	George Southake
Thomas Harding	Symon Bowrman
James Austen	

FIG. 16. "A view of Bethalem," December 4, 1598. Transcribed by and courtesy of Patricia Allderidge, Bethlem Royal Hospital Archives and Museum, and Cambridge University Press.

Bethlem   28 January 1624

By order of the Court teis Committees mett att Bethlem to veiwe the prisoners and to see the warrants howe they were taken in-whether they bee fitt to bee kepte, and if they bee found simple Idiots or recovered to send them to the places where they came either in London or the Country, for that the house is overcharged and wanteth roome there being nowe 31 att the house ['s] charge w[hich] groweth soe highe as the Revenewes are not able to keepe them, the usuall number heretofore being not above 20 att ye most, there being nowe no more roome than form[er]ly.

Hamon John Hamon hath beene in the house theis 20 yeares att least, and is thought fitt to bee kepte. Brought from Camberwell

Whetston Will[ia]m Whetstone hath beene there about 18 yeares & is fitt to bee kepte; was sent from the Court.

Flack James Flack hath beene here about 6 yeares by warr[t] : from S[r] George Bowles Maior fitt to be kepte.

Fludd Walter Fludd hath beene here about 18 yeares to bee kepte.

Bicknar Will[ia]m Bicknar hath beene here about 20 yeares, to bee kepte.

Shaller Gabriell Shaller hath beene here about 20 yeares, a simple fellowe, to bee returned to S[t] Peters att Peters att Paulswharfe.

Hobson Henry Hobson hath beene here about 4 years by warr[t] : from Bridewell to bee kepte.

Burcott Charles Burcott hath beene here about 4 years by warr[t] : from Bridewell sonne to Burcott the shoemaker in Bedlem, not to bee kepte w[th]out mainten[a]nce from his father or the p[ar]ishe.

Teddar Robert Teddar al[ia]s Bennett hath beene here about 9 yeares by warrant from Bridewell a simple fellowe to bee kepte & doth s[er]vice in the house.

Bond John Bond hath beene here about two yeares by warr[t] : from Bridewell to bee sent to Barwick from whence hee came.

Will[ia]m Robertson hath beene there about 5 yeares by warr[t] : from S[r] Will[ia]m Cockaine Mayo[r] : was taken up in the sheet to bee sent to Hull from whence hee came./Mr Jackson a drap[er] in watheling street his brother.

Kite Hugh Kite hath beene here about one yeare by warr[t] : from Bridewell penc[i]oner to y[e] marchanttaylors, to bee sent home to his wife, or to some other hospitall not fitt to bee kept here.

Manger Phillip Manger hath beene here three yeares by warrantt from Bridewell, hee is recov[er]ed and to bee sent to some other hospitall being onely lame of his feete.

Hackett Thomas Hackett hathe beene there 5 monethes by warr[t] : S[t] Martin Linnley Maior and S[r] Thomas Middleton Knight to bee sent to some other hospitall, hee came from S[t] Dunstans in the East.

Gibbons John Gibbins hath beene here about 4 yeares borne att Barington in Oxford shire neare Burford hee hath land att the Banke side a play house, & pyke gardens Henry Elmes in Fleetstreet did begyre him.

Felday Will[ia]m Felday hath been there about 6 week[es] by warr[t] : from my lo : Maior & Mr Tr[easur]er. recomended by M[r] Recorder Fynch not fitt to bee removed.

Pearson Frauncis Pearson hath beene here about 4 monethes came out of the minorites & recomended hether by Captaine Milward being bound unto him as his Apprentice, & well recov[er]ed.

Denham Tho : Denham hath beene here 14 dayes sent thether by Deputy Whitwell, and to bee kept no longer then the p[ar]ishe will pay his charg[es].

Browne Jone Browne hath beene here about two yeares and a quarter by warr[t] : from Bridewell out of Hampshire qre [query] what allowance Bridewell hath for her, some say the p[ar]ishe from whence shee came doth allowe ii[s] vi[d] weekly towards her mainten[a]nce, very ill.

Ellis Margarett Ellis hath beene here about 16 yeares from the p[ar]ishe of S[t] Mary Monnthawe London in reasonable case some course for her remove, beinge willinge to goe unto Woodstock where shee was borne.

Royden Anne Royden hath beene here about 3 yeares ½ by warrant from Bridewell borne att Coventrey or Lichfeild sent from S[t] Zacharies p[ar]ishe very madd.

Baylie Phillis Baylie hath beene here two yeares by warr[t] from Bridewell dated the 25th of March 1622. a mad woman sometime a servant to the Matron of Bridewell.

Bygrave Rebecca Bygrave hath beene here 3 yeares and ½ by warr[t] : from Bridewell from the p[ar]ishe of S[t] Giles Criplegate very ill.

Whitehead Anne Whitehead hath beene here three monethes by warr[t] from Bridewell Recomended by M[r] Acourt from S[t] Martins Ludgate very ill.

Killingham Katharine Killingham hath beene here about two yeares in Aprill last by warrant from Bridewell under 7 governors hand[es].

Parratt Anne Parratt hath beene here about 14 yeares divers times putt out of the house and returned first by the Court of Ald[er]men. 2. by S[r] Will[ia]m Cockaine Maior & S[r] Rob[er]t Heath Recorder. something idle headed, to bee removed sister a M[r] Panters wife.

Floid Mary Floid hath beene here about 4 yeares by warrant from Bridewell her husband liveth about Westminster very ill.

Rathbonn Eliz[abeth] Rathbonn hath beene here about 18 monethes by warrant from Bridewell shee came from S[t] Thomas Hospitall when shee was cured of the fowle disease and fell madd not yet fitt to goe abroade.

Hardick Margarett Hardick hath beene here about 4 yeares and ½ sent by S[r] Will[ia]m Cokaine Maio[r] not knowne from whence shee came & must bee kepte.

Silvester Anne Silvester hath beene here about 40 weekes warr[t] : from Deputy Whitwell who is her Uncle, and lieth att the charge of the house fitt to bee removed.

Mary Thompson hath beene here allmost two yeares by warr[t] : from Bridewell 5th Octob[r] 1622. qe [query] from whence shee came, beinge a poor Idiot not fitt to bee kepte in this house. hir mother dwelleth w[th]in Bishopsgate & doth allow her 12[d] weekly towards hir mainten[a]nce.

FIG. 17. Bethlem Census, January 28, 1624. Transcribed by and courtesy of Patricia Allderidge, Bethlem Royal Hospital Archives and Museum, and Cambridge University Press.

kepte in this house," and the dispositions of one man and one woman are not specified.

The designation of women, but not men, as "mad" is difficult to account for. Here we may notice that the term "madness" seems to be just beginning to replace "distract," "lunaticke," and "frantic" as the general term for the condition of the inmates. But why should it be applied specifically to women? The women may in fact have been more acutely ill. But it seems more likely that they were *viewed* as more acutely ill—perhaps because frantic madness was a more violent disruption of normative femininity than of normative masculinity. Or perhaps women's madness generated more sympathy and hence more rhetorical exaggeration. We cannot know. It may not be just coincidence that whereas the first *OED* citation for "madman" is dated 1377, the first one for "madwoman," as one word, is at this same time—1622. Perhaps this new designation signals that madness's diagnoses are becoming more sharply differentiated by gender (although since the phrase "mad woman" had long existed, the citation cannot provide a reliable index to shifting oral usage). These puzzling differentiations reinforce other instances where women's madness is becoming increasingly visible and differentiated—by doctors who generate diagnoses of female melancholy and lovesickness, by witchcraft skeptics, and on stage. In the five plays with Bedlamites between 1604 and 1623, the gulf between representations of madmen and madwomen widens yet more—as we will see. These scattered signs make visible the earliest beginnings of a long process that would result, by the late nineteenth century, in the clear-cut emergence (and rapid disappearance) of the mostly female malady of hysteria.[11]

None of these records, however, provides a shred of evidence that (*pace* Foucault) the sick, the disruptive, and the seditious were warehoused indiscriminately and left abandoned and silenced (*HB* 111–129; Porter, *Mind-Forg'd* 6–15, and chap. 6; A. L. Beier, "Foucault"). Instead, highly specialized charitable institutions gradually emerge out of all-purpose medieval foundations and provide therapy or work within the range of period competence. Stringent admission protocols are designed to screen out all but the most distracted and needy. Distracted people are not viewed as essentially or permanently different from those who are healthy. Far from being condemned or mocked, characterized as inhuman, as animal-like, or as outside humanity, they are attended to with concern and compassion. The assumption is that they have temporarily lost a self that can be "recovered" or "restored to memory." When this happens, they are sent home into the care of a relative or parish, sometimes with a stipend to pay for continuing care. These ill persons are never represented in period records as spectacles for en-

---

[11] The history of hysteria—its rise, gendering, and fall—is discussed in Showalter, *Female*, Micale, *Approaching* and his review essays, and Hacking, *Mad*.

tertainment; nor is the hospital ever seen as a theatrical site for amusement-seekers. Theaters are another story.

By 1575, just before the first theater opened, Bethlem Hospital, like each of the four other specialized charitable hospitals managed by the City of London for relief of the sick poor, was situated on a major thoroughfare near one of the City's nine gates: Bethlem Hospital for the distracted poor (outside Bishopsgate); Bridewell, a workhouse for the vagrant poor (outside Ludgate); Christ's Hospital for Orphans (inside Newgate); St. Bartholomew's (outside Aldersgate); and St. Thomas's (across London Bridge in Southwark), both hospitals for the sick poor. Managed for its needy, these complementary institutions are, for London citizens, a source of civic pride, an emblem of civic responsibility, and the most visible manifestations of the City's extensive interlocking network of charitable relief for the poor, the sick, and the otherwise disadvantaged dispensed through the mayor and Court of Aldermen and by parishes, wards, guilds, and private donors and supplemented by the Crown (Porter, *London* 49–54; Andrews, "Hardly" 63–67; Archer 149–203). A glance at so-called Aggas Map of London (fig. 18) and my modification of it (fig. 19), which includes the newly built theaters, at first suggests that hospitals and theaters are similarly ringed around the City outside its walls. But, unlike the hospitals, most theaters are outside of City wards as well. Bethlem and the other hospitals are thus quite differently situated, not only historically but also institutionally from the theaters that encircle the City. The hospitals, although sometimes outside the City gates, are within its expanding wards and administrative structures; they are centuries old and have long staying power. At their inception, the theaters are entirely outside of the City's administrative wards in the suburbs; they are new and are far from being permanent. Of the seventeen theaters "new made" after 1576, only six were still extant by 1629. These were all second-generation houses, built after 1599 (outdoors: the Globe 1599, the Fortune 1600, and the Red Bull 1605, and indoors: Blackfriars 1600, the Cockpit 1617, and Salisbury Court 1629).[12] The City does not manage these, but does regulate them and the companies who play there. Hence companies seek protection from its hostility with licenses from the Crown. The hospitals are ancient public charitable institutions administered and supported by the City of London; the theaters are newly erected for private gain and patronized by

[12] A late reviser of Stow's *Annales* reports: "In the yeere one thousand six hundred twenty nine, there was builded a new faire Play-house, neer the white Fryers. And this is the seaventeenth Stage, or common Play-house, which hath beene new made within the space of threescore yeeres within London and the Suburbs, viz. Five Innes, or common Osteryes turned to Play-houses, one *Cockpit*, S. *Paules* singing Schoolle, one in the *Black-fryers*, and one in the *White-fryers*, which was built last of all, in the yeare one thousand six hundred twenty nine, all the rest not named, were erected only for common Playhouses, besides the new built Beare garden. . . . Before the space of threescore yeares above-sayd, I neither knew, heard, nor read, of any such Theaters, set Stages, or Play-houses, as have beene purposely built within mans memory" (quoted from Chambers 32 in Gurr, *Shakespearean Stage* 120).

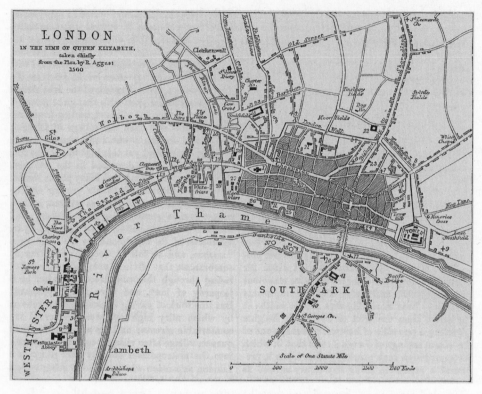

FIG. 18. Map of London, 1560, from the plan by R. Aggas. Courtesy of Mary
Evans Picture Library.

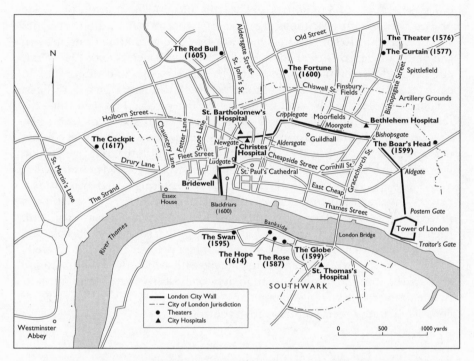

FIG. 19. A plan of London based on Aggas map, 1560, modified to show
hospitals and theaters in use after 1576.

the Crown. The hospitals are for "reliefe" while the theaters are for "recreation" (Stow passim and 2:262, 1598 edition).

John Stow's pervasive affirmation of the hospitals and other charities and his disapproval and excision of the theaters from his *Survey of London* (1598, revised 1603) reveals the sharply contrasting attitudes of at least the older generation of Londoners toward the old and new institutions. He praises both extant charitable organizations and former Catholic charities suppressed at the Reformation in his ward-by-ward perambulations, in a roll call of donors (1:104–117) and in his laudatory enumeration of "Hospitals and Leper Houses in the City and Suburbs" (2:143–147, and see Jordan). In contrast is his virtual occlusion of the newly built theaters, which he dislikes. The one reference in his 1598 edition to the Theatre and the Curtain—described as "two publique houses for the acting and shewe of Comedies, Tragedies, and Histories, for recreation"—is eliminated in the 1603 edition, perhaps because by then the Theatre had been torn down and the Curtain was not much in use for plays.[13] His only other brief reference (retained in 1603) regrets, characteristically, that private enterprise and professional players have replaced communally mounted performances: "Of late time in place of those Stage playes [i.e., those performed on civic occasions], hath been used Comedies, Tragedies, Enterludes, and Histories, both true and fayned: For the acting whereof certaine publike places have beene erected" (1:93).[14] Stow's attitudes reflect the unease with which the new institution was viewed and the more general anxiety or hostility the City administration felt toward the new—and popular—spaces outside their walls and never completely under their administrative control.

Theater History and the Innovation of Bedlamites

Although the new purpose-built playhouses, emergent institutions, begin their history when Bethlem and the other City hospitals have been in existence for centuries, and although they seek private gain, not public dona-

---

[13] See Stow 2:262 n 73, l. 36, for footnote inclusion of quotation omitted in the 1603 edition. See Gurr, *Shakespearean Stage* (118) on the demolition of the Theatre (whose timbers were used for the Globe) and the abandonment of the Curtain as a playhouse.

[14] Stow regularly regrets the replacement of public spaces and institutions for communal or charitable use by buildings erected for private economic advantage and show. He laments the gentrification of small houses with gardens, formerly leased to the poor for one penny a year, but subsequently rebuilt and dearly leased by an entrepreneurial Draper (2:74–75). He decries the eating up of the once public recreational grounds at Moorfields by the encroaching gardens of private summer houses that he condemns as "like Midsommer pageants, with Towers, Turrets, and Chimney tops, not so much for use or profite, as for shewe and pleasure, bewraying the vanity of mens mindes, much unlike to the disposition of the ancient Cittizens, who delighted in the building of Hospitals, and Almes houses for the poore, and therein both imployed their wits, and spent their wealthes in preferment of the common commoditie of this our Citie" (2:78). Steven Mullaney, seeking "ambivalent spectacle and cultural license" (23) in the suburbs, reads this passage as Stow's lament for the loss of "marginal spectacle" (46).

tions, they too are driven to negotiate their institutional survival amidst the conflicts of City and Crown and to seek gate receipts from London citizens. As their story is relatively well known, I will only recap it briefly to emphasize how the innovative Bedlamite scenes grew out of the theaters' struggles to survive in the highly competitive first decades of the seventeenth century. Although the new theaters had to compete for audiences, their popularity and independent financial base enabled them to turn the City/Court rivalry to their advantage, as Bethlem had not been able to do. The Court, in order to use the players' services, licensed and controlled the building of the playhouses, the authorization of companies, the texts of the plays, and the times of playing: restrictions forbade playing on Sundays or religious holidays, or after or near dark, or when the plague roll was over 50. In return for players' adherence to these restrictions, the Court protected them from the hostilities of City officials, who feared the potential licentiousness and sedition of the plays as well as the potential violence and spread of plague by the playgoing crowds. Playhouses and players were also attacked in the sermons of City preachers, who inveighed against the unreality and immorality engendered by playing. The City's restrictions were administered unevenly, but the theaters were always under threat of closure.

The first decade of the seventeenth century was precarious as well as prosperous for the growing number of companies and their shifting venues (Knutson, "Repertory" 478), which led to a demand for new plays and for innovation like that which had marked the first decades of playing. The emergence of the two new boys' companies, Paul's and Blackfriars, created additional competition, and the transition from Elizabeth I to James I in early 1603 was an anxious one until patronage was assured. When it was, the four companies who were preferred instead of the earlier two had to vie for spaces and spectators (Gurr, *Shakespearean Playing Companies* 105–119). Bad outbreaks of plague shut down playing for long periods in 1603–1604, 1608–1609, and 1609–1610. The players, playwrights, and companies were in an ambivalent relationship to the London inhabitants whose attendance they sought and whose officials' hostility they feared (Gurr, *Playgoing* esp. 63–65). The emergence of "city" or "citizen" comedy and innovative shows of Bedlamites in houses of confinement can usefully be understood in the context of company rivalry, demand for new material, and ambivalence toward citizens.[15] These newly farcical, satiric, metatheatrical scenes are designed to amuse *and* thumb their nose at those professionals and City officials who object to, but frequent, plays.

Just four plays—over an eighteen-year period—stage scenes in houses of confinement where groups of madpersons perform: Dekker and Middleton's *Honest Whore Part I,* acted by the Princes' company at the Fortune (1604),

---

[15] See Muriel Bradbrook, *Growth* (141), and Brian Gibbons (11) on "city comedy"; Alexander Leggatt, *Citizen* (4, 8–11), on "citizen comedy"; and Jill Levenson (282–295) on "urban designs."

Dekker and Webster's *Northward Ho,* acted by Paul's Children at Paul's (1605); and, fifteen years later, Fletcher's *The Pilgrim,* performed by the King's Men at Court in 1621–1622 and at Blackfriars; and Middleton and Rowley's *The Changeling,* licensed to be acted by Lady Elizabeth's Men at the Cockpit in 1622. In a fifth, Webster's *Duchess of Malfi,* acted by the King's Men at Globe/Blackfriars in 1614, madpersons put on a brief performance before the imprisoned Duchess. These are only 1.5 percent of the 318 plays in Andrew Gurr's "Select List,"[16] and they cannot be seen as constituting a vogue for or an obsession with Bedlam on the Jacobean stage as is commonly claimed. But they do introduce a new motif into early modern drama. The rivalry that drove the repertory, encouraging imitation, one-upmanship, pastiche, and parody, is especially visible in these five plays, authored by different playwrights and performed by different companies in several theaters.[17]

These metatheatrical Bedlamite scenes appear in several genres—two city comedies, two tragedies, and a romance. When closely attended to, they tell us not about practices at Bethlem, but about companies' competition, playwrights' defiantly farcical self-representation in response to antitheatrical hostility, and playhouses' counterattacks on the elites who strive to regulate them. The self-contained metatheatrical scenes are isolated from the main action of the plays. The handful of madpersons who perform briefly in them are static caricatures who are (increasingly) cordoned off from the principal characters. Their routines satirize, especially, City professionals with more prestige and authority than playwrights and players, skewering doctors, lawyers, merchants, and scholars for ambition, lasciviousness, and stupidity. The heightened theatricality of the mad scenes exaggerates those very characteristics for which plays are attacked: unreality, violence, bawdiness, sexual license. When these threatening characteristics of theater are concentrated in the mad and played for laughs, they counter attacks on theater. By exploiting the mad for self-defense and profit, these scenes widen the gulf between the mad and the healthy.

One clue to the Bedlam scenes' metatheatrical, rather than mimetic, functions and effects is the tiny restricted part that the house, the scenes there, and the mad performers have in these five plays. In the first three, just one

[16] Andrew Gurr's "Select List" of 318 plays includes only plays known to us today that "can reasonably be positively assigned to particular playhouses and companies" (*Shakespearean Stage* 216ff.); hence it represents nowhere near the total number of plays performed in the period.

[17] See Roslyn Knutson, "Repertory" passim; R. A. Foakes, "Playhouses" 24–32 (on "antimimetic"); Lee Bliss, 237–248 (on parody). The success of Dekker and Middleton's *Honest Whore I* precipitated part II (with its scene in Bridewell) the following year. Dekker and Webster's *Westward Ho,* by the children of Queene's Revels at Blackfriars in 1604, provoked the rival boys' company to stage Chapman, Jonson, and Marston's *Eastward Ho* at Paul's in 1605 (which was countered with Dekker and Webster's *Northward Ho* in 1605). Middleton and Rowley's *Changeling,* licensed to a different company just five months after Fletcher's *Pilgrim* was performed, may be a retort to that play's social politics.

scene is set in a house of the distracted. *The Pilgrim* includes two such scenes
and *The Changeling* three. Act 5, scene 2, the comic denouement of *The
Honest Whore I*, is set in "Bethlem monastery" (near Milan), an "Inne" for
travelers whose Friar (or Father) Anselmo performs marriages in the "chappell (which) stands hard by, / Upon the West end of the Abbey wall."[18] Three
mad performers appear in 207 of the scene's 517 lines. Act 4, scene 3 of
Northward Ho includes a spontaneous visit to London's Bedlam, accurately
located on Bishopsgate Road across from the Dolphin Inn; two madpersons
speak 47 of its 170 lines. In *The Duchess of Malfi*, set in Italy, eight madmen
are introduced; four speak and all sing, dance, and perform for the Duchess
in prison in 67 lines of act 4, scene 2. The later comedy and tragedy, both set
in Spain, develop the motif at greater length. In *The Pilgrim*, Pedro visits a
"house" "where people of all sorts, that have been visited / With Lunacies,
and Follies wait their cures" (3.5, p. 190), and three distracted persons speak
61 of the 220 lines of act 3, scene 6. Subsequently Alphonso seeks his daughter there in act 4, scene 3, and two new madpersons join the first three to
speak 60 of the scene's 281 lines. In *The Changeling*, also set in Spain, the
discrete subplot action unfolds in three extended scenes—1.2, 3.3, and 4.3—
set in a "house" for mad folk that, while unnamed, may well allude to contemporary negotiations over Helkiah Crooke's keepership at Bedlam in the
1620s. In this play three offstage madmen speak just 8 lines. Of the total of
twenty-one mad characters in the five plays, seventeen have just about 300
lines. Only two madpersons are women. These seventeen comic caricatures
confute assumptions of hordes of Bedlamites on stage and Salkeld's claim
that these texts specialize in the "confinement of women" (124).

These self-contained performances by Bedlamites are explicitly framed as
plays within plays that are performed for the amusement and sympathy of
onstage spectators as well as for offstage audiences. They decisively segregate
the mad from the plot, from the other characters, and from the sympathy of
the plays' audiences. Their metatheatricality is emphatically highlighted in
Honest Whore I, the first play with such a scene, when the mad folk are introduced by a sweeper who describes himself as a recovered "mad wag"
(5.2.111–112) and whose stage directions ("Enter Towne like a sweeper"
following l. 106) and speech prefixes ("Tow") consistently identify him as
Thomas Towne, a popular comic actor. His routine, applauded we can assume by audiences familiar with him, introduces the mad folk with a comic

---

[18] (4.4.100, 101; 5.1.67; 5.2.17–18). As the presence of a friar suggests, this house resembles a pre-Suppression religious foundation more than the contemporary hospital. Bethlem's
church and chapel were never in this location (*HB* 136); they were used for secular purposes
after the Suppression; and by the seventeenth century had long since been torn down (Stow
1:165; Allderidge, "Management" 145; *HB* 43–44). In *Honest Whore II*, also set in Italy, the
parallel concluding scene in Bridewell specifically laments the loss of the building's former charitable function as a palace bequeathed to citizens for use as a richly endowed hospital and condemns its relatively new function as a "Worke-house" which practices punishment as well as
charity (*HWII* 5.2.1–54).

patter declaring he is an ex-inmate and all are mad: if "all the mad folkes in *Millan*" were brought to the monastery, "there would not be left ten men in the Citty" (5.2.120–122). The Master, Friar Anselmo, introduces his first madman to his audience with a theatrical flourish, registered in a stage direction that reads: "Discovers an old man, wrapt in a Net" (following 5.2.177). Performative aspects are further emphasized in *Northward Ho*, when Bellemont, a poet and playwright, seeks material in Bedlam for his "Commedie"—as he does in the plotting he and his friends enjoy (1.1.39–55; 4.1.208–215). In the tragedies, the scenes are even more emphatically staged as performances segregated from the plays. In *The Duchess of Malfi*, the "wild consort of madmen," sent to the Duchess as "sport" and therapy, performs comic monologues and sings and dances before being taken away (4.2.2–5, 39, 62–73, 113ff.). In *The Changeling*, the mad are seen just twice: once costumed as birds and animals, and once rehearsing a dance to perform at wedding festivities. The self-conscious staginess of these vaudeville routines calls attention to the pleasures of theater, not to practices at Bethlem.

Framing devices work to elicit from audiences new and unaccustomed laughter at the mad—side by side with calls for the sympathy elicited in earlier plays or visible in period records. They urge onstage (and hence offstage) spectators to find the mad not only pitiably moving (like objects of charity) but also hilarious (like stage performers). Father Anselmo, in *The Honest Whore*, announces "we have here some, / So apish and phantastike, play with a fether, / And tho twould greeve a soule, to see Gods image, / So blemisht and defac'd, yet do they act / Such anticke and such pretty lunacies, / That spite of sorrow they will make you smile" (5.2.156–161). Yet more explicitly in *The Pilgrim,* a Gentleman encourages Pedro to visit the house to experience pity and pleasure: "There's fancies of a thousand stamps and fashions, / Like flies in several shapes buz round about ye, / And twice as many gestures; some of pity, / That it would make ye melt to see their passions: / And some as light again, that would content ye" (3.5, p. 190). Onstage spectators in both plays respond when cued, "melting" and laughing in unison just like the theater audience whose responses they elicit. In *Honest Whore I,* when the old madman performs his undersea fantasy, "Omnes" respond, "Ha ha ha" (5.2.200); but when he complains he is so starving that: "you may looke through my ribs,—see how my guts come out—," they respond, "A very piteous sight" (237–238). In *Northward Ho,* "Omnes" respond sympathetically to the bawd's story of miscarriage, "O doe not weepe," but laugh at the tales of her profession, "Taylors! ha ha" (4.3.79, 85). These solicited communal responses protect audiences from individual engagement with particular madpersons. In the last of the plays, *The Changeling*, the roles of keeper and theater impresario explicitly converge when the Keeper, Alibius, trains his madmen to perform for profit.

The otherness of the Bedlamites and the metatheatrical aspect of these scenes are heightened because the madpersons who perform comic routines in them exist in a separate register from the characters in the plays proper.

Not really "characters" at all, they have no development or role outside of their contained performances and virtually no interactions with characters or plot. In this they differ from the performers of earlier plays within plays like the Pyramus and Thisbe play or the Wedding Masque in *The Spanish Tragedy*. Even the actors in Hamlet's "Mousetrap" appear as characters outside their staged play. But in these plays' Dramatis Personae, the mad are lumped together with nonspeaking parts as generic "Madmen" in *Honest Whore* and *The Changeling* or "Bedlamites" in *Northward Ho*. They are nameless, designated only as 1. 2. and 3. Mad. (*HWI*) or by their professions, Musition and Baud (*NH*), Mad Doctor, Mad Lawyer, Mad Priest, Mad Astrologer (*DM*). As these designations reveal, almost all are satiric caricatures of early modern professions—further reductions of the humor characters popular in the drama at this time (Levenson 284).

Ventriloquizing the play's satire, the mad are removed from human subjecthood. Mad caricatures act out satires on women, ethnic others (Welsh madmen), and, predominantly, early modern professions: lawyers, doctors, parsons, merchants, scholars—the very professionals who are regular playgoers (Gurr, *Playgoing* 67–68). Types are recycled from one scene to the next. The old merchant in *Honest Whore*, the pricking Musician in *Northward Ho*, the doomsday-obsessed astrologer in *Malfi*, and the Scholar who thinks he's Neptune in *Pilgrim* are, like the lawyers and doctors, parodies of impotent professionals or intellectuals whose grandiose ambitions have come to naught and who are mocked for their losses—lost love, ships, virginity, or cheese. Reminiscent of the deluded melancholics in medical texts we have examined in chapter 2, they receive no comically appropriate cures. The monologue delivered by the jealous husband, Madman 3, in *Honest Whore I* provides a characteristic (and influential) example of the mix of satire on London professions, titillating sexual allusion, and witty misogyny that is ventriloquized through the mad:

> Gaffer shoomaker, you puld on my wives pumps, and then crept into her pantofles: lye there, lye there,—this was her Tailer,—you cut out her loose-bodied gowne, and put in a yard more then I allowed her, lye there by the shomaker: ô, maister Doctor! are you here: you gave me a purgation, and then crept into my wives chamber, to feele her pulses, and you said, and she sayd, and her mayd said, that they went pit a pat—pit a pat—pit a pat,—Doctor Ile put you anon into my wives urinall:—heigh, come a loft Jack? this was her schoolmaister, and taught her to play upon the Virginals, and still his Jacks leapt up, up: you prickt her out nothing but bawdy lessons, but Ile prick you all. (*HW* 5.2.258–268)

These caricatured types bear no resemblance to the range of persons we have seen inhabiting Bethlem Hospital, who are mostly poor, mostly old, half women—and include no whores or bawds, as those are sent to Bridewell.

The only two madwomen in the scenes, the bawd in *Northward Ho* and the she-fool in *The Pilgrim*, perform misogynous fantasies of female lasciviousness and exaggerate the hostile associations of theater with prostitution. The bawd's long monologue, extensively referencing contemporary London, represents the City of London as sex-obsessed. She has never been in Bridewell, is a virgin who miscarried her child on Shrove Tuesday when apprentices rioted, prides herself on selling maidenheads thrice over, and claims her best customers are "taylors": "I Taylors: give me your *London* Prentice; your country Gentlemen are growne too polliticke" (4.3.86–87). If the bawd trades in flesh, the she-fool in *The Pilgrim*, "as leacherous too as a she-Ferret" (3.6, p. 191), seeks to seduce patients, keepers, and onstage spectators indiscriminately, caricaturing women's lovesickness. She also provides a vignette of women's sexual means to upward mobility when she joins with the drunken English madman in a shared fantasy of erotic, reproductive, and economic satisfaction:

> ENGL. I'le get thee with five fools.
> FOOL. O fine, O dainty.
> ENGL. And thou shalt lie in a horse-cloth, like a Lady.
> FOOL. And shall I have a Coach?
> ENGL. Drawn with four Turkeys,
>   And they shall tread thee too.
> FOOL. We shall have eggs then;
>   And shall I sit upon 'em?
> ENGL. I, I, and they shall all be addle,
>   And make an admirable Tanzey for the Devil.
>   Come, come away, I am taken with thy love fool,
>   And will mightily belabour thee.
>
>   (3.6. p.191–192)

Her fantasies parody those of the Jailer's Daughter in *Two Noble Kinsmen* (and Fletcher may have penned both characters). They demonstrate the lack of causation, social context, and psychological development that strips the Bedlamites of subjectivity and makes identification with them impossible.

Similarly, the comic violence of the Bedlamites parodies and dilutes that of revenge tragedy. Although the mad mostly deliver monologues, tepid disagreements break out, represented as playground arguments rather than the frantic acts characteristic of the distracted. In the first such exchange, in *Honest Whore,* two madmen have an escalating 'tis/'taint battle over porridge:

> 2. MAD. Give me some porridge.
> 3. MAD. Ile give thee none.
> 2. MAD. Give me some porridge.
> 3. MAD. Ile not give thee a bit.
>   .   .   .   .
> 2. MAD. Ile shoote at thee and thow't give me none.
> 3. MAD. Wut thou?
> 2. MAD. Ile run a tilt at thee and thow't give me none.
> 3. MAD. Wut thou? doe and thou dar'st.

2. MAD.   Bownce.

3. MAD.   Ooh! I am slaine—murder, murder, murder, I am slaine, my braines
          are beaten out.

.   .   .   .

ANS.   Take em in both: bury him, for hees dead.

                                        (5.2.272–297)

"Bounce," used repeatedly to mimic the sound of guns—as in our "bang, bang, you're dead," is the note of comic violence. It appears earlier in the mad merchant's fantasy of doing battle with the Turks and is reiterated in the silly fracas in *The Pilgrim* between the drunken Englishman who rules the bottle, the scholar who rules the sea, a Welshman mad for cheese (named Jenkin like the Welsh Captain Jenkins in *Northward Ho*), and a parson "run mad for tyth Goslings" who threatens excommunication (4.3, p. 209). Violence, like desire, is ludicrous in these scenes.

Along with affirming theatrical pleasure, blunting antitheatrical attacks, and satirizing rival professionals, these Bedlamite routines function, like the comic scenes of confinement we examined in chapter 5, to draw moral censure away from the unconventional reversals and resolutions of the main plots. In the plots proper, those who are falsely confined and those who feign madness have their health confirmed. Middling-sort characters, satirized in the Bedlam scenes, win out over lascivious aristocratic gallants and raging Dukes. Women unconventionally take control, and misogynists are discomfited (Leggatt, *Citizen* 112–116). An honest whore, a disobedient daughter, and an unruly wife expose misogyny and get what they want. Although three men are gullingly maddened and three women and two men feign madness, only in *The Pilgrim* is there a hint of distraction in primary characters. In the others, the maddened or feigning characters are, in contrast to the Bedlamites, utterly sane.

Three male characters (as in Shakespeare's farcical comedies) are falsely declared mad and confined (at the warrants, respectively, of a wife, friends, and a witty waiting woman). These mock confinements serve, as they did in Shakespeare's plays, as climax to a series of deceits, disguises, and reversals, described in *The Honest Whore I* as "Comedy of errors" (4.3.24). But in these plays the mad, not the maddened, are scapegoated; two of the victims have their stability vindicated and the third reforms instantly. Most thoroughly validated by his fake confinement is Candido in *Honest Whore I,* a draper and a *very* patient husband, who is committed to Bethlem Monastery on the warrant of his shrewish wife, Viola. Seeking to rupture his infuriating calm, she feigns an affair with her brother, encourages gallants to ruin his goods, refuses him his Master's gown, and dresses his apprentice in it, turning his world upside down. When these stratagems fail, she has him arrested and taken to the madhouse "to turne a tame man into a madman" (5.1.17). Once there, he perfectly maintains his exemplary calm, marking the absolute gap between the mad and the sane, and easily convincing the Duke of their shared sanity: "Then may you know, I am not mad, that know / You are not mad, and that you are the duke: / None is mad here but one"—that is, his wife (5.2.467–469). Finally, satisfyingly, he speaks out against Viola, accusing *her* of being, metaphorically, a "mad-woman" and eliciting her contrition and reform: "Forgive me, and ile vex your spirit no more" (5.2.479). All the reversals that occur in Bethlem Monastery in the last act emphasize the improbabilities around which the plot revolves: a dead daughter is alive, an honest whore marries, and a husband is impervious to jealousy.

Northward Ho's reprise of the earlier scene resituates the hospital in a realistic London cityscape. The briefly faked confinement of the play's most stable and sympathetic character, Bellemont the poet/playwright, affirms the sanity of playwrights in spite of the fantasies they draw on, extending the self-authorizing function of the Bedlamite scenes. As in its predecessors, *Westward Ho* and *Eastward Ho,* courtier gallants try to seduce a City wife. They are thwarted when her husband, Mayberry, with the help of Bellemont's plot expertise, reveals to the would-be cuckolder, Greenshield, that he is being cuckolded by his fellow seducer, Featherstone, and tricks him into marrying the courtesan, Doll. As all ride toward the appropriately named Ware, a site for assignations north of London where the final scene unfolds, Bellemont proposes a lark, a stop-off at Bedlam: "lets bee mad once in our dayes" (4.3.33). This allows the play to imitate the Bedlamite scene in *Honest Whore I* and to insert the requisite north London landmark that its title demands. But it also proves Bellemont's—and playwrights'—sanity even though they traffic in fantasy. He describes himself as "sometimes out a my wits" (4.1.22–23) and talks of identifying with his characters, even becoming them (4.1.8–10). He is identified as one who "talkes besides to himselfe when he's alone, as if hee were in Bed-lam, and he's a Poet" (4.1.19–21). Playwrights' harmless traffic in unreality is represented when Bellemont seeks rapport with the mad musician in Bedlam, going off to speak Italian with him. But Bellemont has nothing in common with the comic bawd and musician; he merely draws on them for matter, self-reflexively like his author. Like Candido's, his brief false confinement shows his self-control. He sees the trick, frees himself with an attack on the keeper, then accepts good-naturedly the practice by his fellow travelers to confine him—"for your best Poets indeed are madde for the most part" (4.3.192–193). The scene proves his sanity and sangfroid and represents playwrights/poets not as distracted or melancholy, but as wittily successful plotters who exploit fantasy and madness.

Fletcher's *Pilgrim*'s mock confinement is more punitive and also transforming. Alphonso, a brutal, violent father, is briefly held as mad on a warrant feigned by Juletta, his daughter Alinda's trickster servant and champion. His violence and rage are rendered comic when he identifies with confined madpersons, precipitating his contrition and reformation. Alphonso is enraged at Alinda's bounteous charity and marital choice. When she flees, he calls her whore and hunts her down, tries to seduce Juletta her maidservant, and misrecognizes Alinda disguised as a she-fool: "'Pox o' your fools, and Bedlams" (4.3, p. 210). Seeking Alinda in the house of confinement, he instantly identifies with the anger of the four feuding madmen—who comically reprise his rage. He especially admires the Welshman's threats of violence such as "I will peg thy bums full of Bullets" (4.3, p. 211). His decision to free the fettered mad and confine the keeper (4.3, p. 213) plays into Juletta's plan to incarcerate him on a feigned warrant. But when Alsemero comes to bind him, Alphonso, deflated, immediately accepts the diagnosis: "Indeed I am angry, / But I'le contain my self: O I could burst now, / And tear my self, but these rogues will torment me, / Mad in mine old days? make mine own afflictions? . . . I will go in, and quietly, most civilly. . . . 'Twill starve me Sir; but I must bear it joyfully" (4.3, pp. 214–215). Threatened with subduing by whips and reduced diet, he reforms immediately, confirming his difference from the bickering inhabitants who are chained and removed.

The three men, gullingly confined, prove sane, and so do three women who self-consciously disguise themselves as mad to defend their chastity, reform their lovers, and transform others. In the initiating play, Bellafront, the titular honest whore, disguises herself as a wandering madwoman in order to defeat the planned secret marriage at Bethlem Monastery of her beloved Hippolyto (who scorned her as contaminated) and to marry Matheo, who first stole her virginity. At the house, her thin veneer of distraction and canny fortune-telling do not stop the wedding, but Matheo *is* ordered to marry her. Misrecognizing her, he agrees to, "when her wits stand in their right place" (5.2.421, 430)—and immediately discovers they do. In this play, the antics of performing madpersons make feigned madness, gulling internment, and unconventional marriages seem normal.

In the two later plays, John Fletcher's romance, *The Pilgrim,* and Middleton and Rowley's tragedy, *The Changeling,* the role of the disguised madwoman gives Alinda and Isabella yet more theatrical and thematic authority. Alinda, in *The Pilgrim,* moves from poignant distraction to efficacious feigned madness in which her speech is constructed of quotation, proverb, and fragmentation like that of Shakespeare's madpersons. Like the Jailer's Daughter, but disguised as a boy, she seeks her lover in the woods and, on becoming lost, hungry, and sleepless, she feels her wits "wavering": "These wild woods, and the fancies I have in me, / Will run me mad" (3.3, p. 185). She is brought, "a little crazed; but much hope of recovery" to be succored in the house for the mad (4.3, p. 208) where she is quickly cured by food and rest and a brief encounter with her lover, who runs away again. In response to his defection, Alinda adopts feigned madness by exchanging garments with the house's she-fool and using her pied coat as a disguise to confront and convert others. She speaks telling parables to Alphonso her father, which caricature his arrogance by urging him to fly over the moon, and predict his fall by picturing him sinking into a river (4.1, pp. 197–198). Next she barrages Roderigo with fanciful songs, sayings, and fortune-telling that, by representing his abandoned goodness, initiate his repentance: "Sure 'tis a kind of *Sibyl,* some mad Prophet; / I feel my wildness bound, and fetter'd in me" (4.2, p. 201). After her own reconciliation with Juletta, their subsequent disguises as old women and then shepherds enable them to instigate multiple conversions. For Alinda, as for Alphonso, a brief encounter with madness leads to sanity, transformation, and a romance ending. But the play's recycled Bedlamites—a Welshman, parson, scholar, English drunk, and she-fool—are immune to change.

Middleton and Rowley's tragedy, *The Changeling,* shares with Fletcher's contemporary romance a Spanish locale, a prominent house of the mad, and a feigning madwoman who exploits madness and brings her husband to contrition and reform. Ken Jackson usefully suggests that *The Changeling* is a direct retort to *The Pilgrim:* "Like so much Protestant charitable discourse, Middleton's play responds to a valorization of good works (by Alinda in *The Pilgrim*) by exposing the perversion or potential for perversion underlying those works and, in the process, offers a subtle critique of James's intervention in London's charitable offices and a bitterly satirical look at Catholic charity generally" ("Bedlam" 381).[19] *The Changeling* elaborates many of the motifs of madness treated in this chapter and in this book in ways that withdraw sympathy from the mad, hence rendering unnecessary the charity that supports them. It exploits the deadliness of uncontrolled lovesickness to damn Spanish aristocratic wives and affirm London middling-sort citizen wives like Isabella, who only play with madness and lovesickness. It uses counterfeit madness for comic turns and removes confined Bedlamites to the margins of representation. Their role and resonance are limited by the near absolute segregation of the house for the mad from the characters and events of the main plot and of the mad themselves even from the subplot.[20]

The play's two plots are set in a Spanish castle in the realistically depicted port of Alicante, in the region of Valencia, and in a madhouse that, although in the same city, alludes unmistakably to London's Bethlem and, through Al-

---

[19] Whereas the earlier play, Jackson argues, validates the Catholic doctrine of indiscriminate charity as grounds for salvation and "hollows out" Protestant critiques like Alphonso's, the latter play critiques (by perverting) such charitable intentions through refiguring Alinda as Beatrice and Anselmo, the good keeper, as Lollio, the bad one (383, 384–387). Jackson emphasizes that Beatrice is a revision of Alinda, but I read Isabella as Alinda's successor. *The Changeling* also provides a broader critique of James and of the Spanish whose alliance the king has just dissolved Parliament to preserve, one that supports Jackson's reading. Dale B. J. Randall (189–216) analyzes the realism of the Alicante setting and discusses the political context of James's battle with Parliament over his alliance with Spain and the anti-Spanish sentiment of the source story, John Reynolds's *Triumphs of God's Revenge against the Crying, and Execrable Sinne of Murther* (1621), and of other Reynolds publications.

[20] The only intersections are when two men of Lord Vermandero, the protagonist's father, enter the madhouse in disguise to woo Isabella and appear briefly at the Citadel in the last scene. Alibius and Isabella come to the Citadel to report them in act 5, scene 2, and remain there for the denouement. The madmen, hired to entertain at Beatrice's wedding festivities, never do so for the bride is murdered.

ibius the ineffectual Keeper, to Helkiah Crooke, its famously corrupt and absentee master from 1619 to 1633. Much commentary focuses usefully on how Isabella's role in the subplot parallels and contrasts to Beatrice-Joanna's in the main plot.[21] But it has not been noticed that these contrasts are established by using the discourse of lovesickness to identify Spanish Catholics with hot-blooded promiscuity and the discourse of madness to protect Isabella from such identification. Each woman is isolated within an enclosed space controlled by well-meaning but baffled older men—Vermandero, Beatrice's father, and Alibius, Isabella's husband. Each woman negotiates with her three suitors (two aristocratic and one a servant) to achieve her desires, but employs opposite strategies. Beatrice-Joanna, an aristocratic daughter, unself-consciously manipulates her suitors; the satisfaction she gains consumes her and her suitors in spreading lust and violence. Isabella, a married, middling-sort woman, like the citizen wives in Jacobean city comedy (the genre this plot belongs to), self-consciously exploits her three suitors (two counterfeit madmen and the Keeper) and the mad inhabitants, controlling them *and* her jealous husband to test and deflect her own desires. Isabella and the play exploit the mad, and her own counterfeit madness produces not compassion and reform, but disillusion and retaliation.

The Changeling's two plots represent parallel solicitations to desire, viewed as an illness, and the contrasting responses of the two women. In act 1, scene 2, Alibius protects the "ring" of his wife's chastity by locking her in the madhouse and deputizing Lollio his keeper to watch her "treadings" and "thrustings" and "supply my place"; she declines his advances (1.2.26–31, 39, 31, 40). In the following scene, Beatrice tries to regain control of her own chastity by deputizing Deflores to murder her first fiancé. When he does so and cuts off Alonzo's finger encircled by Beatrice's "ring," he symbolically (and soon actually) deflowers her. In both spaces, coitus, as in the lovesickness treatises, is (ironically) proposed as the "cure" for the disease of desire. Diaphanta links the plots when she wittily proposes that the madhouse doctor can "cure" Jasperino's mad desires; but he offers a substitute physic: "we two would compound together, and if it did not tame the maddest blood, . . . I'll ne'er profess physic again" (1.1.136–145).

Those who desire or couple in the castle plot—Beatrice-Joanna and her three suitors, Alonso, Alsemero, Deflores (as well as Jasperino, Alsemero's servant, with Diaphanta, Beatrice's waiting woman and bride substitute)—are all condemned by the discourse of lovesickness and genital heat that, as we have seen, proved more enabling in the comedies treated in chapter 4. Alonso, Beatrice's first fiancé, is "hot preparing for his day of triumph" (1.1.187). Alsemero with unconscious irony talks of his "hidden malady,"

---

[21] Joost Daalder, *Changeling* xxi, xxiv–xxxiii; Patricia Thomson xxiii–xxiv; Muriel Bradbrook, *Themes* 214–217. Christina Malcolmson, "Tame," analyzes how both women are misused by patriarchal control.

and even his luggage carriers understand that "this smoke must bring forth fire!" (1.1.24, 50). Beatrice, likewise unconsciously, offers to treat Deflores's disfigured skin, which she attributes to "the heat of the liver" (2.2.80). Lovesickness is graphically tested and staged when Diaphanta, the serving maid, passes and Beatrice fakes a virginity test that releases the blockage of the virginally contained humoral body. Virgins who drink the liquid in glass M yawn, sneeze, and laugh, achieving a substitute orgasm that displaces upwards the congestion of unsatisfied genitals. Nonvirgins, with no need for release, do not respond—but can fake it. When Beatrice substitutes the proven virgin Diaphanta in bed for herself on her wedding night and finds her all too apt, Deflores sets the fire that symbolically represents the sexual heat that engulfs the castle and punishes Diaphanta for coupling with Alsemero: "Now the flames / Are greedy of her: burnt, burnt, burnt to death" (5.1.107–108). At the play's conclusion, Beatrice-Joanna sacrifices herself to quench desire. She is (misogynistically) represented as the carrier of impure blood, which, "taken from you for your better health," must be purged and flushed away in the "common sewer" (5.3.150–153).

Unlike Beatrice, but like the City wives in citizen comedy, Isabella shrewdly manipulates and mocks her three lovesick suitors and fake and actual madmen to test her desires, protect her marital chastity, and reform her jealous husband. The counterfeit fool, Antonio, the parodic lunatic, Franciscus, and the bawdy steward, Lollio, who court her supply the farcical comedy that was provided by the Bedlamites in earlier plays when she puts them through their turns. By teasingly flirting with all three, Isabella tries out "the pleasure of your bedlam," to stave off boredom. She encourages the counterfeits to deflect Lollio's advances (3.3.21). Then she uses the steward to fend off the madmen, encouraging him to set up a duel between them. She also plays mad herself and derides the inhabitants of the house. Like the plays themselves, Isabella, by performing madness, inoculates herself against it.

Franciscus's high-flown romantic "lunacy" is performed through parodic classical and folklore allusions reminiscent of now outmoded representations like that of Hieronimo or of Plautus's feigning Menechmus the Traveller: "Hail bright Titania! / Why stand'st thou idle on these flow'ry banks? / Oberon is dancing with his Dryadës; / I'll gather daises, primrose, violets, / And bind them in a verse of poesy" (3.3.50–53), which Lollio mocks. Isabella dismisses him abruptly when he grows insistent and "dangerous" (3.3.89). When the counterfeit idiot, Tony, reveals his disguise and makes advances, she terms him a "parlous" and "froward" "fool" and puts him down:

ANTONIO.   This was love's teaching:
A thousand ways he fashioned out my way,
And this I found the safest and [the] nearest
To tread the Galaxiá to my star.

ISABELLA. Profound, withal! Certain you dreamed of this;
Love never taught it waking.

(3.3.129, 134–139)

Subsequently Isabella tests Antonio's desires (and her own inclinations) by briefly disguising herself as a madwoman and adopting mad speech that self-consciously imitates his and that of Franciscus, but lays down a real challenge to him. Is he willing, as his high-flying rhetoric suggests, to risk a fall like that of Icarus into the "lower labyrinth" or the "wild rebellious waves," a fall into sexuality and danger (4.3.108, 123). She pleads: "Stay in the moon with me, Endymion, / And we will rule these wild rebellious waves / That would have drowned my love" (4.3.122–124). Ignoring her cryptic images of flight and fall, Antonio contemptuously shuns her: "I'll kick thee if again thou touch me, / Thou wild unshapen antic; I am no fool / You bedlam!" (4.3.125–127). Disillusioned by his blindness, denial of madness, and refusal of the release solicited, she bitterly renounces him, and the instability and performativity of her own desires: "Come not near me! / Keep your caparisons, y'are aptly clad; / I came a feigner, to return stark mad" (4.3.134–136). In retaliation, she unflinchingly exposes her two absurd suitors to Alibius and the Duke at the Castle, where she witnesses the consequences of choosing otherwise: the violent spectacle of Beatrice-Joanna's and Deflores's deaths. Sobered, she uses the revelation of Alibius's jealous folly: "Your change is still behind, . . . You are a jealous coxcomb"—to extract her husband's promise of reform: "I see all apparent, wife, and will change now/ Into a better husband" (5.3.209–214).[22]

Isabella's ability to make others a spectacle to protect herself is also apparent when she exploits actual madpersons even more brutally than she uses the counterfeits. The madmen appear "above" in act 3, scene 3, when Tony, having kissed her, presses his suit. Her denigration of the inhabitants deflects Tony's solicitations and dispels her own awakening desires. Implicitly projecting onto the mad her own wildness, she characterizes their emotions as merely performances, and reduces them to beasts, denying them subjectivity and humanity:

> Yet are they but our schools of lunatics,
> That act their fantasies in any shapes
> Suiting their present thoughts: if sad, they cry;
> If mirth be their conceit they laugh again;
> Sometimes they imitate the beasts and birds,

[22] Isabella's manipulations of emotion protect her from becoming a spectacle as Beatrice-Joanna does—a "deformed" madwoman with a keeper, performing with her lover for an audience first on stage, and afterwards in hell: "rehearse again / Your scene of lust, that you may be perfect / When you shall come to act it to the black audience / Where howls and gnashings shall be music to you" (5.3.114–117). Isabella, instead, is an audience to others' spectacles.

Singing or howling, braying, barking—all
As their wild fancies prompt 'em.

(3.3.193–199)

The play further reduces the mad from satiric spectacles (that role taken over
by the counterfeits) to speech fragments and speechless costumed performers.

The Changeling completes the representation of confined mad persons,
emergent throughout these five plays, as the permanent opposite of the
healthy. Counterfeit and real madpersons are exploited by Lollio for laughs,
by Isabella for amusement, by Alibius for "trade" and "bounty," and most
of all by the play itself. The scenes in the madhouse, extending their predecessors, exploit the mad for comic effect, provide contrasts with the main
plot, and defend citizen wives. But the effect is still deeper and long lasting.
The Changeling exiles the mad from subjecthood and, almost, from representation. Just three madmen in the play speak only six offstage lines rant-
ing for food and later commenting metatheatrically on the plot.[23] When
seen, they are speechless. Once they appear "above," costumed as birds and
beasts (stage direction following 3.3.191). At the conclusion of act 4, scene
3 and the madhouse scenes, "The MADMEN and FOOLS dance," rehearsing
their wedding show. But, unlike others who rehearse shows on stage, they
never get to perform it. In the last of these plays with madhouses, the mad
are those Foucault imagines: silenced, dehumanized, exiled to the margins of
representation. Distilling earlier comic representations of those in houses for
the mad to their logical precipitate, *The Changeling* banishes the mad to the
very edge of the play-space and so effectively ends the vogue for madness on
the Jacobean stage.[24]

In these five plays, the confinement episodes and routines of madpersons
feed on theatrical predecessors as playwrights seek to match their rivals' hits
or embellish their own earlier successes. The popular metatheatrical scenes
authorize theatrical excess and neutralize opponents of theater by representing bawdy punning, satire on other professionals, and farcical violence
as the antics of the mad. The farce of the scenes takes the heat from the unruliness in the main plots, and their reduction of women to sex objects is a

---

[23] In act 1, scene 2, the four hunger-driven lines of three madmen echo earlier Bedlamite
scenes: "Put's head i' th' pillory, the bread's too little," "Fly, fly, and he catches the swallow."
"Cat-whore, cat-whore, her permasant, her permasant!" (197–204). Later tags comment on
the main action. When Antonio enters to court Isabella in act 3, scene 3, an offstage madman
cries (derivatively): "Bounce, bounce! He falls, he falls!" (3.3.110). When Isabella seems attracted to Tony, a madman's allusion to the game of barley break serves as a warning: "Catch
there, catch the last couple in hell!" (3.3.166), and contrasts their aborted flirtation with the liaison of Deflores and Beatrice-Joanna when he uses the game to symbolize their union as they
die: "Yes; and the while I coupled with your mate / At barley-break. Now we are left in hell"
(5.3.162–163).

[24] A couple of later masques of the mad (in, for example, Ford's *Lover's Melancholy*, 1629,
and Brome's *Antipodes*, 1637) are theatricals performed by those who are not mad for those
who are easily cured.

counterweight to the authority some women characters gain. The scenes displace onto madpersons and the houses where they reside those offenses for which antitheatrical polemic attacked the stage: salaciousness, immorality, and unreality. In this way brief shots of madness permit theatrical excess and inoculate the plays. Making Bedlam look bad makes the stage look good. Hence these dramatists become the first in a long series of groups who use Bethlem Hospital to secure their own agendas, prestige, and sanity.

The Hospital and the Plays: The Myth of Bedlam

Once the metatheatrical, satiric, and self-advancing functions of these scenes are understood, it becomes clear that they do not imitate and cannot document inhabitants at Bethlem Hospital, conditions there, or visitors who laughed at their antics (*HB* 130–131 and ff.). To be sure, certain characteristics of the stage representations correspond to certain practices and conditions at Bethlem Hospital likely well known to Londoners: the protocols of admission, the hunger of inhabitants, the assumption that the hospital was a place of cure. Confinement in the plays, as in the period records, occurs by warrant from high-placed authority figures (the Duke in *The Honest Whore I*) or by requests of private parties who offer support and provision for entrants as do Bellemont's friends (who give "a crowne to provide his supper," and promise to send "bedding," "a gowne," and "straw" *Northward Ho* 4.3.142–147).[25] Although in these stage houses the mad are never cured and the counterfeit mad don't need to be, it is everywhere assumed that inhabitants go there to "wait their cures" (*Pilgrim* 4.1, p. 196), that they will "recover" (*Honest Whore* 5.2.137; *Pilgrim* 4.3, p. 212), or be "converted" to health (*Northward Ho* 4.3.143). Likewise, in all of the plays, patients complain of hunger. This comically exaggerated motif clearly has connections with the lack of provisions that hospital visitations regularly report—in spite of the routine charitable donations of food from many parties.[26] Other as-

[25] In *The Changeling,* the friend who secures entrance for the counterfeit madmen by promising to defray "the charge of diet, washing, and other necessities" (1.2.89–90) may be a specific allusion to the well-known extortion of fees and donations by Helkiah Crooke; he was finally removed in 1633 after investigations revealed his neglect of the hospital and the money and goods he and his underlings siphoned off for their own benefit. The allusion is often remarked (Reed 49–51; Jackson, "Bedlam" 380–381, 384).

[26] This was not due to policy but to corruption and mismanagement. As Allderidge points out, the care of patients was supported not only by rents and bequests, by a stipend from the Crown, and by fees paid by relatives but also by large quantities of donated food as enumerated in the April 1632 Commissioners' report she quotes from: "From the Lo: Mayor Of bread every Munday 6 penny loaves, besides broaken bread when they will come for it. Of beefe 2 Stone at the Least every Munday, and a pott of pottage made with halfe a peck of oatmeale. From the 2 Sheriffes Of bread, beefe, and pottage the like p[er] porton, from the one upon Wensday, from the other upon Thursday. . . . Besides allsoe divers charitable gifts sent in weekely by some honorable, and other well disposed p[er]sons, as sometimes by the M^r of the Rolles, sometimes by the Lady Dudley, by Sr Hen: Martin, Sr Paull Pindar, and others" ("Management" 161).

pects of the scenes, like the whips that are regularly brandished on stage, make for good theater but are only occasionally corroborated in period records (*Honest Whore* 5.2.230–241; *Pilgrim* 4.3, p. 213; *Changeling* following 3.3.55).

The fact that visitors enter the stage houses and laugh at performances does not prove that early modern subjects did so at Bethlem. Theatrical necessity requires such visitors; for mad plays within plays to function, onstage audiences must be present. No visitors appear in *The Changeling*, although Alibius worries they may (1.2.53–54). The characters who seek out the Inne and Chapel at Bethlem Monastery in *The Honest Whore I* have diverse motives independent of the madpersons there, as do those who enter the house in *The Pilgrim*—except Pedro, who goes reluctantly. The only character who explicitly seeks the mad for entertainment is Bellemont, the poet in *Northward Ho*. As we have seen, he enters to enhance his fantasy—significantly, not by watching a spectacle, but by conversing with the mad there. On this comic, self-reflexive visit rests the myth of Bedlam "visits" onstage. These plays, however, provide the primary evidence that early moderns visited Bethlem for theatrical spectacle, along with a handful of satiric allusions in other plays (likely themselves inspired by the scenes in *Honest Whore* and *Northward Ho* in 1604 and 1605).[27] These fictions, each with their own specific agendas, cannot provide independent evidence for a historical practice in the absence of corroborating documents. And in the period of my study, 1576–1632, there are none at all.

Obviously many people went to Bethlem Hospital throughout its long history, and in this period, for many reasons—to bring in distracted persons and take them home when recovered, to visit and provision friends and relatives there, to leave charitable donations, to examine the property or the inhabitants for the Court of Aldermen—and perhaps to be morally instructed (Andrews, "Bedlam" 11–133, the basis for *HB* 178–199). But a single (ubiquitously cited) entry in the nonfictional records before 1632 provides the only documentation for Bethlem Hospital as a spectacle and tourist attrac-

---

[27] The first allusion cited as evidence for visiting, in Middleton's *Mad World My Masters* (1605–1606) 5.2, asks, "When was the wedding kept? In Bedlam?" perhaps remembering the wedding there in *Honest Whore I*. (Actual weddings no longer take place there in the absence of a chapel or religious personnel.) Satiric allusions in Ben Jonson's comedies all disseminate the view, as do the madhouse scenes, that the mad are spectacles or commodities—and so can be bought. The first, in *Epicene* (1609–1610), presents madness as a "sight" without reference to the hospital. Truewit babbles to Morose, "Alas, sir, do you ever expect to find a chaste wife in these times? now? When there are so many masques, plays, Puritan preachings, mad folks, and other strange sights to be seen daily, private and public" (2.1.86–89). Elsewhere, the Collegiate Ladies wittily counsel Epicene to make her husband allow her every extravagance, including tours of the City with them: "And go with us to Bedlam, to the china-houses, and to the Exchange" (4.2.25–26). In Jonson's *Bartholomew Fair* (1614), Dame Purecraft the husband-hunter, it is said, "has been at Bedlam twice since, every day, to enquire if any gentlemen be there, or come there, mad!" (1.2.49–50) and Wasp jests to Mistress Overdo, "How sharp you are! With being at Bedlam yesterday" (1.5.22–23).

tion.[28] This entry, read closely, seems unlikely to refer to Bethlem Hospital at all. The crucial reference is quoted (or more often paraphrased) by contemporary scholars from the 1877 *Sixth Report of the Royal Commissioners on Historical Manuscripts: Part I Report and Appendix,* a nineteenth-century collection of documents.[29] The list of disbursements in the Northumberland papers—by an unknown hand—is as follows: "1609, Feb. 6–1610, Feb. 6. Expenses of housekeeping at the Tower, and board of servants at the Tower and at Syon.—Rewards: To Franceso Petrozani, for reading Italian to the Earl, 7£.—To Dr Turner, 40s.—to Mr. Fenton, the chirurgeon, 10s.—In reward by Lord Percy, viz., for seeing the Lions, with Lady Penelope and his 2 sisters, 6s.; the show of Bethlehem, 10s.; the place where the Prince was created, 2s.; and the fireworks at the Artillery gardens, 10s" (229).

As this entry gets paraphrased and the paraphrases are re-cited, its origins are concealed, and its meaning is transformed.[30] What can we learn by looking squarely at this cryptic bookkeeping entry? The surrounding entries in the report provide clues. Algernon, Lord Percy, was the oldest son of Henry

[28] For the fullest and most nuanced discussion of various motives for visiting, including the didactic, charitable, pietistic, and pleasure-driven, and for careful assessments of its gradual increase, see Andrews, "Bedlam" chap. 2, 11–133, and *HB* 178–199. Although there are many references to visiting cited in this chapter, they are not organized chronologically, and their dates are hard to discover. But I find no documentary evidence (other than the Percy visit) of visiting cited before 1632 when there is a reference to "money given at the hospital door by persons that come to see the house" (quoted in Alldridge, "Bedlam" 21). This could refer to official visitors. Of course I may have missed something and other references may exist, unexamined, in the archives. There may have been visitors and they may have enjoyed the spectacle, but there is no evidence of this that I can find. The few references before the move to Moorfields in 1676 are from hospital regulations (*HB* 180–181) or from satires like Donald Lupton's *London and the Country Carbonadoed and Quartred into Severall Characters* (1632), and Ned Ward's *London Spy* (1703). Most are after the move, and the great majority are from the eighteenth century.

[29] The reference occurs among the 160 paper account rolls of the Northumberland Household—entries made by various stewards from the reign of Henry VIII to 1629 and extant in regular series from 1578 to 1617; only "selections of interesting items" are printed in the Report's appendix (226). The notation under consideration is from a series of items dated (old-style) "1609, Feb. 6–1610, Feb. 6" hence referring to the period from February 7, 1610 to February 6, 1611 (new style).

[30] For example, Reed (23) quotes O'Donoghue's paraphrase of the Report: "Lord Percy with Lady Penelope and her [*sic*] two sisters 'saw [*sic*] the lions, the show of Bethlehem, the place where the prince was created, and the fireworks at the Artillery Gardens'" (405, note to p. 235). *The History of Bethlehem* that, with Alldridge, refutes the larger claims made for visitors, calls this "the first undoubted reference to a real-life visit" and likewise misquotes it to good effect: "Lord Percy and company 'saw the lions, the shew of Bethlem [*sic*], the places [*sic*] where the prince was created, and the fireworks at the Artillery Gardens'" (187); the book refers to the passage three times, thus enlarging its importance (*HB* 133, 180, 187). Natsu Hattori likewise misquotes and misattributes the reference the better to prove that "In fact, the hospital and its mad folks were considered one of the chief amusements of Tudor and Stuart London, well-frequented by native Londoners as well as by provincial sightseers. . . . in 1610, Lord Percy records [*sic*] that on a visit to London with the Lady Penelope and her [*sic*] sisters they saw 'the Lions [in the Tower], the shew of Bethlem [*sic*], the place where the prince was created, and the fireworks at the Artillery Gardens'" (287). The *History of Bethlem* further extrapolates proof of donations from the visit, averring that "wealthy or charitable visitors evidently left more, Lord Percy giving 10s in 1610" (180).

Percy, the ninth Earl of Northumberland. During the period of the entry (which must be between June 4, 1610, the date of Prince Henry's investiture, and February 6, 1611, new style, the terminus of this set of disbursements), the earl was imprisoned in the Tower of London, where he resided from 1605 to 1620 (for suspected complicity in the Gunpowder plot in which his steward, Thomas Percy, was a conspirator). Lord Percy, born in 1602, was eight years old. His two sisters, Lady Dorothy and Lady Lucy (born 1598 and 1599), were twelve and eleven (*DNB*). Lady Penelope, their cousin, was most likely Penelope Rich (or Blout), the daughter of Penelope Rich possibly by her lover, later husband, Blout, Lord Mountjoy. Born in 1589 (Ringler 444 and n 2), she was twenty-one and an appropriate chaperone for her three young cousins. Their mother, Dorothy Devereux, and her mother, Penelope Rich (by now deceased), were sisters.

The entry suggests that the three Percy children came to visit their father in the Tower (where he lived palatially with many servants and extensive provisions of books, maps, food, drink, and tobacco) and were provided with London entertainment (on one or more visits). Other accounts record payments for the earl's amenities and for the children. With their father living in the Tower, the children sometimes resided in Essex House, their mother's family palace on the Strand (as Lady Penelope likely did) and sometimes, as this entry shows, at Syon House, the Northumberland estate up the Thames near Hampton Court. Either way, visits to the Tower may have been frequent. In surrounding records covering this and other years, disbursements are recorded at both locations and at the Tower, for example in 1608–1609 for "Boat hire of sundry servants between Syon and the Tower" (229). "Rewards" in the accounts means either payments (as, in the entry, to doctors and tutors) or gratuities. The Tower's Keeper of the Lions was often given such payments; in 1608–1609 he received 12d (229). Certainly the children would like to see the lions in the Tower when they visited their father. The earl would surely want his son and heir to visit "the place where the Prince was created"—the Court of Requests at Westminster where Henry, elder son of James I, was invested as the Prince of Wales on Monday June 4, 1610, in an elaborate ceremony that the earl likely attended (Strong 154; Palmer 102). Fireworks at the Artillery Gardens are a plausible entertainment for pre-adolescents.

But what might the "show of Bethlehem" mean in this context? It is likely to have nothing whatever to do with the hospital. A visit to Bethlem by the four aristocratic cousins seems improbable considering the likely condition of the house and the inhabitants in 1610. In 1598, the house was in disrepair and "so loathsomly and filthely kept not fitt for anye man to come into the said howse" (Allderidge, "Management" 153). The inhabitants in 1610 probably included the three elderly women who had been taken in, as widows, before 1598 and given smocks in 1607: Jone Bromfield, Mother Kemp, and Mother Clay. Kemp would have been there for 22 years and Clay for 25. The three poor men, Welsh Harry, Abraham, and Black Will, who were all given shirts, were likely still there too. It seems impossible that these very old, very poor, and very ill patients could have put on a "show" for children who were eight, eleven, and twelve.

Another clue that the hospital is not referred to here is the fact that the spelling "Bethlehem" is almost never used to refer to the hospital in either the period's drama or official documents. In drama it is always called Bethlem or Bedlam. In Court of Aldermen's Repertories from 1503 to 1617, the institution is referred to 24 times as "Bethelem" (including variants "Bethelym," "Bethelam," and "Betheleme"), 16 times as "Bethlem," and 9 times as "Bedlam" (including variant "Bedleem"). It is called Bethlehem in a single entry of 1550 (during the reign of Edward VI) which asks for "the relief of the poor in Bethlehem." This entry might refer to the city in Judea, not the hospital. The Northumberland entry might well refer to some kind of "show" *about* the city of Bethlehem, perhaps a Christmas play, pageant, diorama, or a puppet show (Shershow 45–47, esp. n 6). Even in the unlikely event that these three young children did visit the hospital for amusement, a dubious interpretation of the evidence, this sole entry cannot provide proof, as it is routinely claimed to do, for habitual visiting of Bethlem Hospital by adults in the early seventeenth century. But it is on this single, thin, and misrepresented archival reed that the documentation of visiting before the mid-seventeenth century rests. Apart from it, all those supposed visitors left not a single trace in the period I am examining. There are no drawings, like DeWitt's sketch of the Swan, no reports of a "performance" in memoirs, no complaints about the disruptions crowds caused, like those directed at Blackfriars, no jokes in circulation, like that in John Manningham's *Diary* about the spectator at Mary Glover's fits. Except in drama.

The Bedlam scenes in Jacobean drama first initiate and disseminate emergent ideas of Bethlem as a place of comic spectacle where caricatured madpersons are visited for amusement. They perhaps encouraged the practice, which seems to have increased after their representations, showing how "life can be influenced by art" (*HB* 131). Visiting seems to have begun (or increased) gradually in the middle decades of the seventeenth century.[31] It accelerates in the Restoration. It is not until then that "Bedlam" comes to refer not merely to this hospital and to madpersons but to houses of confinement in general and figuratively to a world gone mad.[32] The term "Bedlam" (like

---

[31] In 1650, 1657, and 1663, hospital regulations show restrictions on visiting (*HB* 190). Well-known recorded visits around this time are John Evelyn's in 1657 and Samuel Pepys sending his cousin's children there in 1669 (*HB* 187).

[32] *The History of Bethlem* and Natsu Hattori distinguish the hospital Bethlem from its "alter ego," Bedlam, a figurative name for a world gone mad, and place this development earlier in the sixteenth century, attributing its emergence to the stage plays (*HB* 131–135; Hattori 283, 293). But I find no evidence that the period routinely made such a distinction or used the word in this way. As we have seen, in the records the most popular designation for the hospital is Bethelem, the second Bethlem, the third, Bedlam. Five of Shakespeare's six uses of "bedlam" refer to persons, usually figuratively, and the sixth, in 2 *Henry 6*, refers literally to the London hospital (5.1.131). We have seen both uses—referring (figuratively) to madpersons or (literally)

"Bethlem") had been a colloquial contraction for the city of Bethlehem since at least 971 (*OED* 1) and was used in reference to the hospital named after the city as early as 1528 (*OED* 2). The use of "a bedlam" as a synonym for a lunatic (literal or figurative) emerges at the same time in the early sixteenth century (*OED* 5, 1522). But the first use of "Bedlam" to mean "a lunatic asylum in general" cited in the *OED* (3) is 1663, and the next is 1713. The first *OED* citation of its figurative use to mean "a scene of mad confusion or uproar" (4) is 1667—after the Restoration and just before the hospital's move to Moorfields in 1676. But this shift in terminology is already anticipated in the first play with such a house. In *Honest Whore I,* the house is regularly referred to as Bethlem Monastery. But when the Duke uses it figuratively in the last line to underwrite his claim that the upside-down world of the play must be righted, the changed spelling signals the emergence of "Bedlam" as a symbolic place, opposed to normative order: "Wives (with meeke husbands) that to vex them long, / In Bedlam must they dwell, else dwell they wrong" (5.2.516–517).

The newly emerging attitudes that segregate the mad and the hospital from normalcy, revealed in this shifting usage and new representations, are likely accelerated by the association of madness with religious enthusiasm and political radicalism during the Civil War and the Interregnum, an exploration beyond the limits of this book. Whenever visiting for amusement began, its pace was certainly much accelerated following the institution's enlargement when it was rebuilt at Moorfields in 1676 as an architectural showcase for over 200 patients (fig. 20), became gender-segregated, perhaps took in more middle-class patients, and eventually, in the 1720s and 1730s, included wards for incurables.[33] Other Restoration developments that encouraged visiting the hospital for amusement may have been the pride at the impressive rebuilding of London after the Great Fire in 1667, the rapid growth of the City, the increased secularization of madness, and, especially, the backlash against religious enthusiasm after the Civil War, which went hand in hand with the Enlightenment's new validation of reason (and see *HB* 145–147). By 1704, in Swift's *Tale of a Tub,* the mad in Bedlam became the central metaphor for the excesses of religious zeal, political corruption, and professional arrogance and incompetence—as the book's frontispiece manifests (see fig. 12 in chap. 5). One antecedent of Swift's use of Bedlamites as vehicles of satire is the caricatured madpersons on the Jacobean stage.

---

to this hospital—earlier in this book. William Warner's 1595 translation of *Menaechmi* included the exclamation, "Out upon him Bedlam fool" (87). Lady Grace Mildmay's papers (before 1620) refer to the melancholy maid whose friends were collecting resources to send her to "Bedlam" (119). Drayton uses the term in a generalized figurative sense in 1627 to claim "This isle is a mere Bedlam" in his elegiac familiar letter "To My Noble Friend Master William Browne, of the evill time" published in *The Battaile of Agincourt.*

[33] See *HB* 145–155 for a summary of developments from 1633 to 1783 which part II of the book unfolds more fully.

FIG. 20. "Hospitium Mente-Captorum," engraving of Bethlem by Robert White, 1677. Courtesy of the Guildhall Library, London.

Our Uses of Bedlam

My concern is not simply to expose scholars' inadvertent errors. I am sure that this book contains its fair share. What I am interested in exploring is why we (historians, literary critics, and the public at large) continue to reinvent and depend on the myth of Bethlem Hospital as a spectacle and the analogy between stage and hospital that sustains it. What are the investments in Bethlem, in the drama, and in the early modern period that continue to require it? Visiting for amusement, no matter how flimsily substantiated, remains the lynchpin that proves the early modern hospital a theatrical spectacle mirrored by stage representation. This analogy is firmly cemented in the twentieth century in two studies—Edward O'Donoghue's *Story of Bethlehem Hospital* (1915) and Robert Reed's *Bedlam on the Jacobean Stage* (1952)—and it has stuck. In spite of historians' debunking and radical changes in critical fashions, the claims of these books continue to be recycled or reinvented right up to the century's end (see, for example, Twyning 28–31). First, this has happened because, as both Jonathan Andrews and Patricia Allderidge demonstrate, the idea of Bedlam as a spectacle of horror serves the needs of "an overly retrospective and Whiggish historiography" (Andrews, "Hardly" 63). Historians wishing to trace a progressive history of psychiatry and of asylums need the horror of an earlier Bedlam as "the ultimate symbol of all that is evil" (Allderidge, "Bedlam" 18). The central evidence of this horror, even more than imagined chains, whips, and indiscriminate long-term confinement, is that the mad were visited for amusement (Andrews, "Bedlam" 11).

O'Donoghue's book conspicuously displays this agenda in its efforts to laud the miraculous effects of the "moral treatment" instituted in the nineteenth century. Since O'Donoghue was the chaplain at Bethlehem and not a historian, the *Story* he tells is, not surprisingly, characterized by "whimsy," "anecdote, and supposition" (Andrews, "Bedlam" 2–3; Allderidge, "Bedlam" 17–18). It is driven by O'Donoghue's personal investment in "our hospital" and is a celebration of its "transformation" (the title of the penultimate chapter) from a "noisy, fetid" space (367) where prisoners were starved, whipped, and gawked at to a high-class mansion for the genteel. He conjures up a picture of Webster, Jonson, Dekker, and Middleton downing Rhenish wine and pickled herring just before they "lurch into Bedlam for an hour's diversion" (145–146), and he concludes the book by taking his readers (visitors) on a tour of the improved modern hospital. It has become a place in which the ladies' drawing room might be that of "a ladies' club in Piccadilly" (350), in which the social status of the patients has (thankfully) been raised (353), and in which, most tellingly, the recreation hall includes "a stage equipped with dressing-rooms and all the accessories of a theatre, and once a fortnight a company from outside puts on a comedy, and the hospital band serves as orchestra" (358). The hospital could hardly be more progressive; the patients are no longer spectacles but theater-goers.

Robert Reed is, with O'Donoghue, the primary purveyor of the myth of Bedlam as a stage spectacle—but his investments are different. The first sentence of his *Bedlam on the Jacobean Stage* suggests why critics of Jacobean drama thrive on the analogy: "When I think of the temper of the Jacobean stage, I sometimes picture a patient in the psychopathic ward running amuck with fever, his brains afire, as Robert Burton might have diagnosed him. Without undue exaggeration this mental image portrays the excitement, the temperature, and the precipitate career of Jacobean drama for the critic, who . . . habitually compares it with the more conventional, and sometimes much less interesting, periods of dramatic literature. . . . The Jacobean stage was, and remains, distinguished by unusual abnormality, extravagance, and bombastic utterance; its average temper, figuratively speaking, was not a good deal short of madness" (1). The historian uses the analogy to represent a bad old Bedlam against which subsequent progress can be gauged. The literary critic needs the analogous spectacles to extol the excitement, excess, and uniqueness of a mad Jacobean theater and to measure subsequent cooling off and decline.

The reasoning Reed uses to affirm the analogy of house and stage that promotes both unparalleled drama and benighted Bedlam seems almost laughable, but his conclusions remain popular. In the absence of evidence other than O'Donoghue's, Reed proves visitors enjoyed the spectacle at Bedlam by collapsing together the reports of eighteenth-century "journalists" (actually satirists) and "Jacobean dramatic presentations of Bedlamites" (7) so that, "by putting two and two together . . . we shall have some idea of the inmate that the Elizabethan or Jacobean visitor may have witnessed within the reception hall or, more probably, within the cells themselves of the original Bethlehem Hospital" (7). The dramatic "copy" proves what the "original" is like, and the "original" substantiates the mimetic realism of the copy—which in turn proves that playwrights visited Bedlam and recorded "first-hand observation" (29). Reed argues, for example, that the division of the insane into lunatics and fools in *The Changeling* "not only suggests a direct knowledge on the author's part of the separated wards of Bethlem Hospital, but conversely indicates that the mad folk at Bethlehem were similarly segregated" (35). The fact that idiots were expelled from Bethlehem Hospital has no impact on the fantasy of correspondence. Reed even claims that visitors *caused* the agitation that generated the inmates' spectacles that provided matter for dramatists. And, like many later scholars, distressed perhaps by the lack of evidence for individual visitors, Reed manufactures thousands, extrapolating from entrance fees supposedly paid by eighteenth-century visitors. On his count there were likely 96,000 visitors a year in the eighteenth century and a third as many in the Jacobean period, or about 75 visitors a day (25–26). Patricia Allderidge has decisively exposed the multiple false assumptions and historical inaccuracies on which this figure is based, and Jonathan Andrews's dissertation extends her critique (Allderidge, "Bedlam" 21–24; Andrews, "Bedlam" 14–16). But the figures and the assumptions they conveniently support have not disappeared.[34] If no visitors can be traced, thousands must be fabricated, for without audiences, Bethlem can't be a spectacle, and if it isn't, dramatists can't imitate it.

The myth of hordes of paying visitors to the hospital's dramatic spectacle is still revived, even by non-Whiggish historians who continue to conflate the patients in the hospital with stage representation of confined and unconfined madpersons, a conflation barely emergent in the period but now irresistible. Thus Michael MacDonald, when he talks of Bethlem (in a meticulous book largely concerned with nonconfined disordered persons), writes: "Renaissance Englishmen were fascinated by fools and madmen. The Jacobean stage teemed with idiots and lunatics. . . . It is impossible to think about madness in early modern England without hearing Lear rage; Webster's *Duchess of Malfi* and Fletcher's *The Pilgrim* contain whole troops [or troupes?] of Bedlamites. In the greatest age of English drama, the longest running show in England was Bedlam itself" (*Mystical* 121). Thus Roy Porter, collapsing two hundred years of early Bedlam's history into a few paragraphs, waxes Shakespearean: "But the true lure of Bedlam was the *frisson* of the freakshow. . . . Spectators thronged to see unaccommodated man. And largely because Bethlem housed the only collection of mad-people in the nation, it achieved a sort of concentrated notoriety; it became an epitome of all that people fantasied about madness itself. . . . Chaos is come again" (*Mind-Forg'd* 122–123). Even Jonathan Andrews implicitly lends credence to a picture that his scrupulous scholarship on Bethlem systematically refutes when he opens his impressive dissertation: "As the only public institution for the insane in early modern England for over three hundred years, Bethlehem or Bethlem Hospital (popularly known as Bedlam) occupied an unrivaled place at centre stage for contemporaries when conceptualizing and responding to madness in all its Protean forms. . . .[B]eing located in the very heart of the city, with its doors laid open in welcome to the visiting public, the hospital and its in-

---

[34] Reed's figure is reiterated, as Allderidge notes ("Bedlam" 21–24), by both Michel Foucault and Michael MacDonald, whose seminal books, taken together, provide the basis for most late twentieth-century scholarship on madness in the early modern period. Paraphrasing creatively and without acknowledgment, Foucault gets Reed's "facts" mixed up and transposes them to the nineteenth century (when visiting had been eliminated): "As late as 1815, if a report presented in the House of Commons is to be believed, the hospital of Bethlehem exhibited lunatics for a penny, every Sunday. Now the annual revenue from these exhibitions amounted to almost four hundred pounds; which suggests the astonishingly high number of 96,000 visits a year" (*Madness* 68). That's 1,846 visitors each Sunday! MacDonald reiterates Reed's figure of 96,000, citing him and correctly ascribing the figure to the eighteenth century although assuming, as Reed does, that it held true earlier in the Elizabethan and Jacobean periods when conditions did not "deter the public from coming to gawk at the small company of lunatics" (*Mystical* 122). The figure will not go away; the *History of Bethlem* quotes from Robert Youngson and Ian Scott's *Medical Blunders* (London: Robinson, 1996), which simply plagiarizes Foucault, omitting his qualifications: "As late as 1815, the Bethlehem madhouse exhibited lunatics every Sunday, admission one penny. The annual revenue from these visits amounted to 400£, which amounts to an astonishing 96,000 visitors a year" (286). Reiterating this figure to refute it only further perpetuates it—as this note will no doubt do.

mates were seen and experienced at first hand by all and sundry (at the expense of a measly donation)" ("Bedlam" 1).

Even *The History of Bethlem,* committed to exposing "pseudo-facts" about the hospital and to separating the state of "Bedlam" from the institution, Bethlem, cannot completely abandon the analogy between the theater's and the hospital's spectacle and the visitors who underwrite it. The introduction touts the international reputation of its subject by insisting that "for over a century Bethlem was one of the sights of London on any serious tourist's itinerary, along with the Tower and Westminster Abbey" (2). Subsequently, however, it exposes exaggerated numbers (see n 34) to exemplify hand-me-down falsehoods that demand refutation (4). The *History* claims circumspectly that the 1610 reference to the Percy children is "the first undoubted reference" (133). But a page earlier it employs a speculative close reading of the last sentence of the 1598 visitation, which says the hospital was "not fit for any man to come into" (probably referring to the just-mentioned keeper who had decamped) to suggest, tentatively, that the hospital may have begun to encourage visitors to the "spectacle" still earlier. This speculation elsewhere in the book becomes a certainty: "It is possible that it was partly as a result of a decision taken by the Governors in the 1590s to encourage visiting that Bedlam, the metaphor for a world gone mad (as opposed to the familiar name for the place, or a word for madhouses generally), developed at all" (11, and see Jackson, "I Know Not" 223–224). With Natsu Hattori, *The History of Bethlem* proposes new support for Reed's claim that playwrights visited Bethlem, suggesting that the proximity of the hospital to the theaters north of the City may have encouraged this, since playwrights "had more cause than most to be in the area of Bethlem" (133). But only two theaters, the Theatre and the Curtain, were ever north on Bishopsgate Street near the hospital, and by the time plays with madhouses appeared, the first had been torn down, and the second was antiquated, disreputable, and rarely in use. No author of any play with Bedlamites had a work mounted on either of these rapidly superseded stages.[35] But historians of Bethlem want "their" hospital to be the source of the dramatic rep-

---

[35] Hattori exaggerates the physical proximity, noting that old Bethlem Hospital was "a stone's throw away from two of London's main playhouses, the Theatre and the Curtain, thus making a convenient stop to or from the theater for entertainment seekers" (287). Actually, as my recent trek from the plaque commemorating the site of the original Bethlem to that commemorating the original Theatre proved, it is a good hike from one to the other, even now along paved streets. The Theatre, opened in 1576, was torn down by 1597, and its materials were used to build the Globe south of the City. Although the Curtain was in existence at least until 1627, it was rarely used by resident companies after the turn of the century when the Rose, the Globe, and the Swan were built to the south and the Fortune to the west (Gurr, *Shakespearean Stage* 118). No plays with houses for the mad were produced until 1604. No play with a madhouse scene was performed in either of the original theaters north of the city, and none of their authors had any connections with Bishopsgate ward or with any plays produced at the Curtain or the Theatre. (See Gurr's appendix, *Shakespearean Stage* 216–228 for companies and venues; and fig. 18 for the site of these theaters.)

resentations so, like Reed, they make drama both effect and proof of hospital practices and spectacles.

Recent literary criticism from diverse theoretical perspectives similarly reaffirms the analogy supported by the same circular mimetic claims. Duncan Salkeld's 1993 cultural materialist book, *Madness and Drama in the Age of Shakespeare,* wishing to substantiate a broad assertion that "The increased use of confinement as a political strategy for social control is reflected in early-seventeenth-century drama," insists that Bedlam, "as a kind of theater-space itself . . . furnished dramatists with a resource of spectacular material" (123). Alexander Leggatt in 1996 aptly contrasts the madness of the unconfined Lear, Edgar, and Ophelia with that of Richard Napier's unconfined patients, but slips inevitably into the durable analogy: "Controlled, contained, and on display, the madmen of these plays are like the inmates of Bethlehem Hospital, better known as Bedlam, who were among the sights of London" ("Madness" 124). William Carroll, in his 1996 *Fat King, Lean Beggar* concurs: "The 'Bedlam poor' are thus just another form of popular entertainment, culturally equivalent to various urban curiosities, or to such theatricalized spectacles as bear-baiting or 'stage-plays'" (100). Ken Jackson, in a more knowledgeable and nuanced fashion, insists, as I do, that stage and Bethlem are "distinct cultural institutions," but continues to credit "the theatrical practices of Bethlem, the hospital's practice of showing the mad to elicit charity" ("I Know Not" 216). Even Joost Daalder's resolutely new critical close reading of *Honest Whore I* and *II* employs the historical Bethlem to ground his claims for the universality of stage madness: "As the asylum was much visited by curious spectators, we can surmise that the dramatists [not only Dekker but Middleton, Rowley, and Fletcher] knew it at first hand; anyway we cannot fail to be impressed by the skill with which they conjure up an image of a madhouse in the Renaissance" ("Madness" 72; see also his introduction to *The Changeling*, xiv). Natsu Hattori concludes with Daalder that the period conceives of madness as "universal," and that the stage representations blur the line between madness and sanity (308, 294). But as I have shown throughout this book, constructions of madness are complex, shifting, and heterogeneous onstage and off. The line between madness and health is conceived as permeable but distinct in the early modern period, and individuals can cross it in both directions; only in plays with Bedlamites is it absolute.

Scholars persist in portraying Bethlem Hospital and Bedlam on stage as analogously universal spectacles of madness because this analogy heightens the intensity of the Jacobean theater and the horrors of Bethlem Hospital. So lunacy becomes a "trade" for academics. For historians, Bedlam as a place of violence, cruelty, and drama-like spectacle is a more lively object of study than Bethlem Hospital, one small unprepossessing house among many institutions for relief of the sick poor. For critics of early modern literature, Jacobean drama is admired as unusually powerful, intense, violent, and out of bounds; the analogy with Bedlam neatly confirms this. Contemporary criticism's historicizing has, if anything, intensified the analogy. Steven Mullaney, in *The Place of the Stage,* situates early modern playhouses as places of marginal spectacle: "The dramaturgy of the margins was a liminal breed of cultural performance, a performance *of* the threshold. . . . The vehicles for such a performance ranged from hospitals and brothels to madhouses, scaffolds of execution, prisons, and lazar-houses" (31). Duncan Salkeld not only collapses stage confinement and political seizures but analyzes theatrical representations of madness as a "metaphor for sedition and the subversion of authority and reason" (2). Stephen Greenblatt, as we have seen, analyzes how the theatricalization of exorcism, onstage in *King Lear* and offstage in Harsnett, empties out belief and cedes to the theater the power "to unsettle all official lines" (128). Nor am I immune to the desire for an unruly, oppositional theater for which madness provides an irresistible metaphor, as my analogy between playwrights and the mad at the end of chapter 2 demonstrates. I suspect that the durable analogy between Bethlem Hospital and the stage as comparable spectacles serves our even deeper need to imagine the mad as irredeemably other. We do not want to accept, as early moderns were usually able to do, that the mad are like us, only momentarily distracted from the human selves still intact and recoverable. As long as we are visitors to Bethlem and audiences to drama, we are safe because the mad are not like us. *"If others had not been mad, then we should be."*

The representations of the mad in Bethlem Hospital and in the playhouses are more complex and more disjunctive than this ineradicable analogy can represent. The effect of the stage plays studied in this final chapter is not to universalize madness but rather to circumscribe, caricature, and specularize it. In them the mad are dehumanized. The staged scenes of confinement promote an emerging attitude that the mad are spectacles and thus predict and perhaps catalyze future attitudes toward Bethlem Hospital and toward madpersons and perhaps later practices. We inherit these attitudes and practices, as my epilogue will show. But *The Honest Whore I* and *Northward Ho* are staged prior to *King Lear* and *The Two Noble Kinsmen* in which madness, feigned possession, and women's melancholy are explored and responded to with discernment, compassion, and therapy. The topic of early modern madness can make us acutely aware of the complexities of reading representations, of the difficulties of situating drama within larger histories, and of the uneven process of historical change evident in the multiple discourses that flourish in the ecological niches of early modern England from 1576 to 1632. This book has shown that representations of the mad and the attitudes these represent undergo heterogeneous change in this period. Further developments are anticipated in the plays with Bedlamites and consolidated during the Restoration with the move to the new Bethlem Hospital at Moorfields. But these changes are neither as instantaneous, monolithic, or absolute as Foucault's proposed epistemic break and silencing of madness implies. Likewise this book suggests that his unification of all distracted subjects under the emergent term "madness" is premature and falsely reifies both the condition and its sufferers. Beyond particular periods or competing time lines, we need to reconsider our investment in both a romanticized universal madness and a specularized excluded madness, and guard against any easy assumptions about the mental distraction that troubled early modern society and continues to distress our own.

EPILOGUE

Then and Now

If we go mad—so what? We would come back again
if not chased away, exiled, isolated, confined.
KATE MILLETT, *The Looney-Bin Trip*

Our own images of, contests over, and attitudes toward madness have both continuities and discontinuities with those of the early modern period. At the turn into the twenty-first century in England and America, our formulations of madness have undergone rapid transformations across a range of cultural locations including the medical and the literary. Our representations of madness often appear as mirror images of early modern ones, as we change direction and move back toward the earlier concepts that have shaped us. This epilogue therefore mirrors the book, revisiting its issues in reverse order by means of their contemporary recapitulations. I can only suggest some of the ways that we wrestle with issues that early moderns did and use madness to articulate the pain and possibility of the human. In this book, especially in chapter 6, we saw glimpses of the barely visible beginnings of a movement toward the institutionalization and segregation of madpersons. That became the dominant mode of managing the mentally ill until in the last half century that trend was reversed. In the 1960s, the theoretical and clinical work of Thomas Szasz, R. D. Laing, and the anti-psychiatry movement claimed that mental illness was a "myth," or, as we now say, a social construct, one used to bring disruptive behavior under control. "The divided self," as Laing called it, was claimed to be a sane reaction to oppression in the family and the culture. This movement, of course, coincided with a period of widespread critique of the unwarranted and oppressive power of many social institutions—in the civil rights movement, the new left, the Vietnam war protests, and the feminist movement. The critique of confinement was widespread, appearing in the work of clinicians such as Laing, of theorists such as Foucault, of scholars of madness such as Andrew Scull, and in popular literature and film such as *One Flew over the Cuckoo's Nest.* While the anti-psychiatry movement itself has come in for its share of criticism, its aims have been partly achieved. Current public policy mandates the closing of institutions and the mainstreaming of the troubled-in-mind—who are now usually managed within family and community settings as they were in the early modern period.

Deinstitutionalization has been enabled by and has fueled new theories and treatments. Physicians and therapists of different stripes again take for granted the organic, biochemical, and neurological basis of mind diseases. Like their Renaissance predecessors, they increasingly view mental disorders as temporary and curable by pharmacological remedies: Prozac for depression, lithium for bipolar disorders, Thorazine for schizophrenia. But these drugs and others have side effects no less devastating and cure rates not much better than the remedies of early modern physicians: the senna suppositories, purges of primrose, antimony, and mastic, cordials of poppy, and blood-letting treatments. Patient memoirs such as Kate Millett's *Loony-Bin Trip* (1990) and Susanna Kaysen's *Girl, Interrupted* (1993) and fictional works like *One Flew over the Cuckoo's Nest* (Ken Kesey's book, 1960; Milos Forman's film, 1975) expose institutions from the inside; doctors and nurses are represented as comically demented or as frauds who madden rather than heal—like Doctor Pinch in *The Comedy of Errors* as we saw in chapter 5.

Debates over the credit, categorization, and gender-identifications of particular modes of distraction continue. Phyllis Chesler's *Women and Madness* (1972) spearheaded feminist claims that women were more likely to be diagnosed as mad and incarcerated because they were in a double bind. Female sex role stereotypes are closer to diagnosed madness than are male stereotypes, and women are more likely to be punished for deviant behavior than are men; hence they may be labeled mad if they behave in excessively feminine *or* in excessively masculine ways. Later scholars have tested Chesler's theory in particular periods and have shown that her figures claiming that women are more often institutionalized are incomplete and misleading. The sociologist Joan Busfield in *Men, Women, and Madness: Understanding Gender and Mental Disorder* (1996) qualifies Chesler's theory but does not discard it completely. She claims for the present (as I do for the early modern period) that "the most striking and most significant finding to emerge in any detailed examination of male-female differences in identified mental disorder is a distinctive patterning of diagnosed disorder by gender" (14). Certain disorders that were newly associated with women in the early modern period have consolidated and extended that identification.

While lovesickness is obviously not in the *DSM* (*Diagnostic and Statistical Manual of Mental Disorders*) and is not a pathology, it is a widespread cultural malady now overwhelmingly identified with women rather than with men, an identification whose beginnings we saw in chapter 4. Its gender coding is visible in popular self-help books such as Robin Norwood's *Women Who Love Too Much* (1985) and John Gray's *Men Are from Mars, Women Are from Venus* (1992). Its cures are various—therapy, abstinence, or, often, modern-day varieties of the coital cure—which is commonly viewed as a sign of or impetus to cure other female disorders as well. For example, in the triumphant and highly gendered case studies that extol the advantages of *Listening to Prozac* (1993) as a cure for depression, Peter Kramer reports that women patients, like Tess, gain new sexual attractiveness, "three dates a weekend" (7), and if lucky, marriage or remarriage. Men's improvement, in contrast, is signaled and secured by their achievement of increased professional success like that of Sam the architect who, on Prozac, can "complete projects in one draft" and "speak at professional meetings without notes" (x). So too, the protagonist-patient of *Girl, Interrupted* (whose "borderline personality disorder" has as one of its symptoms promiscuity or "casual sex" 148) gains release from McLean Hospital when, as she puts it: "Luckily I got a marriage proposal and they let me out" (133).

Lovesickness is a subclinical disease, hysteria is no longer a diagnostic category, and Multiple Personality Disorder, overwhelmingly diagnosed in women, may be disappearing as Ian Hacking hopes. But melancholy, completing the process of discrediting and regendering whose origins I traced in chapter 3, has become predominantly a female malady—indeed *the* female malady. Fear and sorrow, long its linked symptoms, have been split into two disorders, anxiety and depression. Just as, in Napier's practice, women suffered from stress and mopishness twice as often as men, so today these conditions are diagnosed in women two or three times as often as in men (Busfield 16). This diagnosis still has some associations with reproductive organs and the female life cycle; so we have premenstrual syndrome, postpartum depression, and menopausal (and even perimenopausal) anxiety. Mopish women now, like their early modern counterparts, are treated with friends' advice, therapists' consultations, and occasional coital cures (intercourse is, for example, a suggested remedy for premenstrual syndrome), but most commonly by medications. However, a recently viewed TV commercial offers a twenty-first-century digital cure. It begins with full screen closeup of a very sad middle-aged woman accompanied by a voice over: "Here's a fact: women suffer from anxiety and depression twice as often as men do." Then the woman's face very gradually lifts and she begins to smile as the voice over advises: "Here's another fact. You don't have to be one of those women. Visit snap.com."

There are, however, countertrends in theory and, more frequently, in imaginative writing that seek to reclaim madness in general and depression in particular as privileged sites of eloquence, knowledge, and social critique, as they are in the Shakespeare tragedies examined in chapter 2. Feminist criticism and feminist fiction of the 1960s and 1970s represented madness as a breakdown consequent on women's victimization by patriarchal gender roles, but also as a breakthrough to self-knowledge, comprehension of society's oppressions, and empowerment. This motif is present in fiction as disparate as Sue Kaufman's popular *Diary of a Mad Housewife* (1967), Sylvia Plath's *Bell Jar* (1971), Marge Piercy's utopian science fiction, *Woman on the Edge of Time* (1976), and Doris Lessing's elite and cult classics, *The Golden Notebook* (1962) and *The Four-Gated City* (1969).[1] In this last novel, the protagonist's madness and rebirth as a seer are accomplished in a basement retreat. But Sandra Gilbert and Susan Gubar's *Madwoman in the Attic* (1979) instead repositioned the madwoman in the attic, like her prototype Bertha Mason in *Jane Eyre*. In this influential book, madwomen characters are interpreted as the dark doubles of their nineteenth-century women authors, representing their suppressed "hunger, rebellion, and rage" (337, 339).

More recent memoirs of those who have returned from breakdowns eloquently rename their madness as social critique, as it is for Lear and Hamlet and, earlier, for Hieronimo, discussed in chapter 1. Kate Millett, at the conclusion of *The Loony-Bin Trip*, asks herself of the "depression" for which she refused lithium and was involuntarily institutionalized: "Wait a moment—why call this depression?—why not call it grief? You've permitted your grief, even your outrage, to be converted into a disease" (309). Susanna Kaysen in *Girl, Interrupted*, her memoir of a period of institutionalization in her teens, graphically juxtaposes the clinical records of her observed symptoms and diagnosis with the spare narrative of her own experience of interruption and confinement, figured by the "young and distracted" girl of Vermeer's painting *Girl, Interrupted at her Music* (167). These memoirs and others contest the reduction of accredited melancholy and madness to mere diagnosable diseases.

But it is not only women authors and theorists who revalidate melancholy. Currently, male melancholy is also being reclaimed once again as a prestigious heroic condition, distinct from trivialized female depressive disorders. Recent books—William Styron's *Darkness Visible* (1990), Jay Neugeboren's *Imagining Robert: My Brother, Madness, and Survival* (1997), Terrence Real's *I Don't Want to Talk about It: Overcoming the Secret Legacy of Male Depression* (1997)—attribute to men tragic melancholy, a condition once again linked to self-knowledge, social critique, and artistic expression.[2] Styron, for example, registers an objection to the name "depression": "'Melancholia' would be a far more fit and evocative word for the blacker forms of the disorder, but it was usurped by a noun with a bland tonality and lacking

---

[1] See Gayle Greene for a discussion of "Mad Housewife Fiction" and of other feminist fiction cited in this chapter.

[2] Likewise a number of popular films—*Rain Man* (1988), *Awakenings* (1990), *The Madness of King George* (1995), *Shine* (1996), *Sling Blade* (1997), *Girl, Interrupted* (2000), and *A Beautiful Mind* (2001) elicit sympathetic identification with mentally distressed (mostly) male protagonists by endowing them with unique forms of speech and validated, principled insights.

any magisterial presence" (37). His powerful memoir of what he characterizes as a "veritable howling tempest in the brain" (37) restores the anguish of the condition, defining it, as his title shows, as a descent into hell, into Milton's "darkness visible" or Dante's "dark wood" or Inferno. Real's moving book represents the struggle that he and his patients wage against depression as a tragic and heroic one, fought across generations. He compares this journey to that of Oedipus or Hamlet, or the Fisher King who brings healing after pain to the wasteland (249, 269, 281, 321, 336).

In such works our age struggles to define, as did the earlier period, the dividing line between madness and health, and to understand the journey there and back. Two powerful recent works reconnect the condition of the distracted to powerful supernatural forces whose manipulation may bring healing. In *The Ghost Road* (1995), the final novel of Pat Barker's World War I trilogy, her protagonist, psychologist and anthropologist William Rivers, struggling to treat shell-shocked, paralyzed, mind-and-brain-damaged soldiers back from the front, draws on eclectic healing practices including versions of rituals he observed while doing field work in Melanesia. He advocates, for example, painful confrontation with ghosts and their expulsion as therapy to banish his own demonic memories and those of his patients. *The Ghost Road* and the trilogy conclude with Rivers's waking vision of his mentor, the Melanesian spirit doctor Njiru, reciting the exorcism that alone can dispel the gods of destruction and despair: "O you Ngengere at the root of the sky. Go down, depart ye" (276).

Like Rivers the doctor, Kaysen the patient wonders whether current diagnoses and healing practices represent any advance and whether older conceptions of madness and cure may not still have validity. The partly parodic "Etiology," which introduces the protagonist's confinement in *Girl, Interrupted,* like the tale of Rivers, reminds us that early modern interpretations of distraction still shadow ours, and that the cures earlier sought continue to elude us. Kaysen charts the possibilities for diagnosis.

This person is (pick one):

1. On a perilous journey from which we can learn much when he or she returns;

2. Possessed by (pick one):
   a) the gods,
   b) God (that is, a prophet),
   c) some bad spirits, demons, or devils,
   d) the Devil;

3. A witch;

4. bewitched (variant of 2);

5. bad, and must be isolated and punished;

6. ill, and must be isolated and treated by (pick one):
   a) purging and leeches,
   b) removing the uterus if the person has one,
   c) electric shock to the brain,
   d) cold sheets wrapped tight around the body,
   e) Thorazine or Stelazine;

7. ill, and must spend the next seven years talking about it;

8. a victim of society's low tolerance for deviant behavior;

9. sane in an insane world;

10. on a perilous journey from which he or she may never return. (15)

Her "Etiology" precisely charts the range of conditions, diagnoses, and cures and the historical shifts in the representation and management of madness that my book traces in early modern England between 1576 and 1632.

Works Cited

Abrams, Richard. "*The Two Noble Kinsmen* as Bourgeois Drama." In *Shakespeare, Fletcher, and "The Two Noble Kinsmen*," ed. Charles H. Frey, 145–162. Columbia: University of Missouri Press, 1989.

Adelman, Janet. Introduction to *Twentieth-Century Interpretations of "King Lear*," 1–21. Englewood Cliffs, N.J.: Prentice Hall, 1978.

———. *Suffocating Mothers: Fantasies of Maternal Origin in Shakespeare's Plays, "Hamlet" to "The Tempest*." New York: Routledge, 1992.

Allderidge, Patricia. "Bedlam: Fact or Fantasy?" In *The Anatomy of Madness*, ed. W. F. Bynum, Roy Porter, and Michael Shepherd, 2:17–33. London: Tavistock, 1985.

———. *Bethlem Hospital, 1247–1997: A Pictorial Record.* Shopwyke Manor Barn, Chichester, West Sussex: Phillimore, 1997.

———. "Management and Mismanagement at Bedlam, 1547–1633." In *Health, Medicine, and Mortality in the Sixteenth Century*, ed. Charles Webster, 141–164. Cambridge: Cambridge University Press, 1979.

Andreadis, Harriette. "Sappho in Early Modern England: A Study in Sexual Reputation." In *Re-Reading Sappho: Reception and Transmission*, ed. Ellen Greene, 105–121. Berkeley: University of California Press, 1996.

Andrews, Jonathan. "Bedlam Revisited: A History of Bethlem Hospital c. 1634–1770." Ph.D. diss., London University, 1991.

———. "'Hardly a Hospital, but a Charity for Pauper Lunatics'? Therapeutics at Bethlem in the Seventeenth and Eighteenth Centuries." In *Medicine and Charity before the Welfare State*, ed. Jonathan Barry and Colin Jones, 63–81. London: Routledge, 1991.

Andrews, Jonathan, Asa Briggs, Roy Porter, Penny Tucker, and Keir Waddington. *The History of Bethlem.* London: Routledge, 1997.

Archer, Ian. *The Pursuit of Stability: Social Relations in Elizabethan London.* Cambridge: Cambridge University Press, 1991.

Aristotle, "Problem XXX, 1." In *Saturn and Melancholy: Studies in the History of Natural Philosophy, Religion, and Art*, by Raymond Klibansky, Erwin Panofsky, and Fritz Saxl, 18–29. New York: Basic Books, 1964.

———. "Problems Connected with Prudence, Intelligence, and Wisdom: Problem XXX, 1." In *The Works of Aristotle*, vol. 7, *Problemata*, trans. E. S. Forster, 1: 953a–955a. Oxford: Clarendon Press, 1927.

Ashmole Manuscripts. Bodleian Library, Oxford. Descriptions adhere to format in

W. D. Macray's *Index to the Catalogue of the Manuscripts of Elias Ashmole* (Oxford, 1866).

Astington, John H. "Malvolio and the Dark House." *Shakespeare Survey* 41 (1989): 55–62.

———. "Malvolio and the Eunuchs: Texts and Revels in *Twelfth Night.*" *Shakespeare Survey* 46 (1994): 23–34.

Babb, Lawrence. *The Elizabethan Malady: A Study of Melancholia in English Literature from 1580 to 1642.* East Lansing: Michigan State University Press, 1951.

Barber, C. L. *Creating Elizabethan Tragedy: The Theater of Marlowe and Kyd.* Ed. Richard P. Wheeler. Chicago: University of Chicago Press, 1988.

———. *Shakespeare's Festive Comedy: A Study of Dramatic Form and Its Relation to Social Custom.* Princeton: Princeton University Press, 1959.

Barber, C. L., with Richard P. Wheeler. *The Whole Journey: Shakespeare's Power of Development.* Berkeley: University of California Press, 1986.

Barker, Pat. *The Ghost Road.* New York: Dutton, 1995.

Barnet, Sylvan, gen. ed. *The Complete Signet Classic Shakespeare.* New York: Harcourt Brace Jovanovich, 1972.

Beecher, Donald A., and Massimo Ciavolella. Introduction to *A Treatise on Lovesickness,* by Jacques Ferrand, 3–165. Syracuse: Syracuse University Press, 1990.

Beier, A. L. "Foucault *Redux*? The Roles of Humanism, Protestantism, and an Urban Elite in Creating the London Bridewell, 1500–1560." In *Crime, Gender, and Sexuality in Criminal Prosecutions,* ed. Louis A. Knafla, *Criminal Justice History,* 17:33–60. London: Greenwood Press, 2002.

———. *Masterless Men: The Vagrancy Problem in England, 1560–1640.* London: Methuen, 1985.

Beier, Lucinda. *Sufferers and Healers: The Experience of Illness in Seventeenth-Century England.* London: Routledge, 1987.

Belle, Deborah, and Noreen Goldman. "Patterns of Diagnosis Received by Men and Women." In *The Mental Health of Women,* ed. Marcia Guttenberg, Susan Salasin, and Deborah Belle, 21–30. New York: Academic Press, 1980.

Belsey, Catherine. *The Subject of Tragedy: Identity and Difference in Renaissance Drama.* London: Methuen, 1985.

Bentley, Eric. "Farce." *The Life of the Drama.* New York: Atheneum, 1967.

Berger, Harry, Jr. *The Allegorical Temper: Vision and Reality in Book II of Spenser's Faerie Queene.* New Haven: Yale University Press, 1957.

Bernheimer, Charles, and Claire Kahane, eds. *In Dora's Case: Freud-Hysteria-Feminism.* New York: Columbia University Press, 1985.

Bertram, Paul. *Shakespeare and "The Two Noble Kinsmen."* New Brunswick: Rutgers University Press, 1965.

Bevington, David, ed. *The Spanish Tragedy,* by Thomas Kyd. Manchester: Manchester University Press, 1996 (Revels Student edition).

Bishop, John. *Beautifull Blossomes, gathered by John Bishop.* London: Henrie Cockyn, 1577.

Bliss, Lee. "Pastiche, Burlesque, Tragicomedy." In *The Cambridge Companion to English Renaissance Drama,* ed. A. R. Braunmuller and Michael Hattaway, 237–261. Cambridge: Cambridge University Press, 1990.

Boaistuau, Pierre. *Theatrum Mundi, the Theatre or Rule of the World, Wherein may be sene the course of everye mans life, as touching miseries and felicity.* Trans. J. Alday. London: J. Wyght, 1581.

Boas, Frederick, ed. *The Works of Thomas Kyd*. Oxford: Oxford University Press, 1901.

Bowers, Fredson Thayer. *Elizabethan Revenge Tragedy, 1587–1642*. Gloucester, Mass.: Peter Smith, 1959.

Bradbrook, Muriel C. *The Growth and Structure of Elizabethan Comedy*. London: Chatto and Windus, 1955.

——. *Themes and Conventions of Elizabethan Tragedy*. 2d ed. Cambridge: Cambridge University Press, 1980.

Bradley, A. C. *Shakespearean Tragedy*. Greenwich, Conn.: Fawcett, n.d.

Bradwell, Stephen. "Mary Glover's Late Woeful Case, Together with Her Joyfull Deliverance" (1603). In *Witchcraft and Hysteria in Elizabethan London: Edward Jorden and the Mary Glover Case*, ed. Michael MacDonald, 1–150. London: Routledge, 1991.

Braithwait, Richard. *The English Gentlewoman*. London, 1631; enlarged edition, 1641.

Brand, C. P. *Torquato Tasso: A Study of the Poet and of His Contribution to English Literature*. Cambridge: Cambridge University Press, 1965.

Braunmuller, A. R., and Michael Hattaway, eds. *The Cambridge Companion to English Renaissance Drama*. Cambridge: Cambridge University Press, 1990.

Bray, Alan. *Homosexuality in Renaissance England*. 2d ed. New York: Columbia University Press, 1995.

Briggs, Robin. *Witches and Neighbors: The Social and Cultural Context of European Witchcraft*. New York: Viking/Penguin, 1996.

Bright, Timothy. *A Treatise of Melancholie*. London: Thomas Vautrollier, 1586. Facsimile reprint, New York: Columbia University Press, 1940.

Bristol, Michael D. "*The Two Noble Kinsmen*: Shakespeare and the Problem of Authority." In *Shakespeare, Fletcher, and "The Two Noble Kinsmen*," ed. Charles H. Frey, 78–92. Columbia: University of Missouri Press, 1989.

Broude, Roland. "Time, Truth, and Right in *The Spanish Tragedy*." *Studies in Philology* 68 (1971): 130–145.

Bruster, Douglas. "The Jailer's Daughter and the Politics of Madwomen's Language." *Shakespeare Quarterly* 46 (1995): 277–300.

Bullough, Geoffrey, ed. *Narrative and Dramatic Sources of Shakespeare*. 8 vols. New York: Columbia University Press, 1966–1975.

Burton, Robert. *The Anatomy of Melancholy* (1632 edition). Ed. Thomas C. Faulkner, Nicolas K. Kiessling, and Rhonda L. Blair. 3 vols. Oxford: Clarendon Press, 1989–1994.

——. *The Anatomy of Melancholy*. Ed. Floyd Dell and Paul Jordan-Smith. Kila, Mont.: Kessinger, 1991. Reprint of New York: George H. Doran, ca. 1927.

Busfield, Joan. *Men, Women, and Madness: Understanding Gender and Mental Disorder*. New York: New York University Press, 1996.

Butler, Judith. *Gender Trouble: Feminism and the Subversion of Identity*. New York: Routledge, 1990.

Bylebyl, Jerome J. "The School of Padua: Humanistic Medicine in the Sixteenth Century." In *Health, Medicine, and Mortality in the Sixteenth Century*, ed. Charles Webster, 335–370. Cambridge: Cambridge University Press, 1979.

Cacicedo, Alberto. "'A Formal Man Again': Physiological Humours in *The Comedy of Errors*." *The Upstart Crow* 11 (1991): 24–38.

Cahill, Edward. "The Problem of Malvolio." *College English* 23, no. 2 (1996): 62–82.

Cairncross, Andrew S., ed. *The First Part of Hieronimo* and *The Spanish Tragedy,* by Thomas Kyd. Lincoln: University of Nebraska Press, 1967.

Callaghan, Dympna. "'And All Is Semblative a Woman's Part': Body Politics and *Twelfth Night.*" *Textual Practice* 7, no. 3 (1993): 428–452.

——, ed. *A Feminist Companion to Shakespeare.* London: Blackwell, 2000.

Carroll, William C. "'The Base Shall Top Th' Legitimate': The Bedlam Beggar and the Role of Edgar in *King Lear.*" *Shakespeare Quarterly* 38 (1987): 426–441.

——. *Fat King, Lean Beggar: Representations of Poverty in the Age of Shakespeare.* Ithaca: Cornell University Press, 1996.

——. *The Metamorphoses of Shakespearean Comedy.* Princeton, Princeton University Press, 1985.

Cavell, Stanley. "The Avoidance of Love: A Reading of *King Lear.*" In Cavell, *Disowning Knowledge in Six Plays of Shakespeare,* 58–144. Cambridge: Cambridge University Press, 1987.

Chambers, E. K. *William Shakespeare: A Study of Facts and Problems,* vol. 2. Oxford: Oxford University Press, 1951.

Chesler, Phyllis. *Women and Madness.* New York: Doubleday, 1972. Reissued, New York: Harcourt Brace Jovanovich, 1989.

Clarke, Basil. *Mental Disorder in Earlier England: Exploratory Studies.* Cardiff: University of Wales Press, 1975.

Clemen, Wolfgang. *English Tragedy before Shakespeare: The Development of Dramatic Speech.* Trans. T. S. Dorsch. London: Methuen, 1961.

Coddin, Karin S. "'Suche Strange Desygns': Madness, Subjectivity, and Treason in *Hamlet* and Elizabethan Culture." *Renaissance Drama* 20 (1989): 51–75.

——. "'Unreal Mockery': Unreason and the Problem of Spectacle in *Macbeth.*" *English Literary History* 56 (1989): 485–501.

Cox, John D., and David Scott Kastan, eds. *A New History of Early English Drama.* New York: Columbia University Press, 1997.

Crawford, Charles. *A Concordance to the Works of Thomas Kyd.* In Series, *Materialienzur Kunde des alteren Englischen Dramas.* Louvain: A. Uystpruyst, 1906–1910.

Crewe, Jonathan V. "God or the Good Physician: The Rational Playwright in *The Comedy of Errors.*" In *The Forms of Power and the Power of Forms in the Renaissance,* ed. Stephen Greenblatt, 203–223. Norman: University of Oklahoma Press, 1982.

——. "In the Field of Dreams: Transvestism in *Twelfth Night* and *The Crying Game.*" *Representations* 50 (1995): 101–121.

Daalder, Joost, ed. *The Changeling,* by Thomas Middleton and William Rowley. London: Norton, 1990.

——. "Madness in Parts 1 and 2 of *The Honest Whore:* A Case for Close Reading." *AUMLA: Journal of the Australasian Universities Language and Literature Association* 86 (1996): 63–79.

Debus, Allen G., ed. *Medicine in Seventeenth-Century England.* Berkeley: University of California Press, 1974.

DeJean, Joan. *Fictions of Sappho: 1546–1937.* Chicago: University of Chicago Press, 1989.

Dekker, Thomas, with Thomas Middleton. *The Honest Whore Part I. The Honest Whore Part II.* In *The Dramatic Works of Thomas Dekker,* vol. 2, ed. Fredson Bowers. Cambridge: Cambridge University Press, 1955.

Dekker, Thomas, with John Webster. *Northward Ho.* In *The Dramatic Works of Thomas Dekker,* vol. 2, ed. Fredson Bowers. Cambridge University Press, 1955.

Derrida, Jacques. "Cogito and the History of Madness." In Derrida, *Writing and Difference,* trans. Alan Bass, 31–63. London: Routledge, 1978.

Descartes, René. *Descartes: Selected Philosophical Writings.* Trans. John Cottingham, Robert Stoothoff, and Dugald Murdoch. Cambridge: Cambridge University Press, 1988.

——. *Meditations on First Philosophy* (1641). Bilingual edition, ed. and trans. George Heffernan. Notre Dame, Ind.: University of Notre Dame Press, 1990.

Dictionary of National Biography (DNB). Ed. Sidney Lee. London: Smith, Elder, 1897.

Digangi, Mario. *The Homeorotics of Early Modern Drama.* Cambridge: Cambridge University Press, 1997.

Dixon, Laurinda S. *Perilous Chastity: Women and Illness in Pre-Enlightenment Art and Medicine.* Ithaca: Cornell University Press, 1995.

Dollimore, Jonathan. *Radical Tragedy: Religion, Ideology, and Power in the Drama of Shakespeare and His Contemporaries.* Brighton: Harvester Press, 1984.

——. "Shakespeare, Cultural Materialism, Feminism, and Marxist Humanism." *New Literary History* 21 (1990): 471–491.

Donno, Elizabeth Story, ed. *Twelfth Night Or What You Will.* Cambridge: Cambridge University Press, 1985.

Doob, Penelope. *Nebuchadnezzar's Children: Conventions of Madness in Middle English Literature.* New Haven: Yale University Press, 1974.

Drayton, Michael. *The Works of Michael Drayton.* Ed. J. William Hebel. Vol. 3. Oxford: Blackwell, 1931–1941.

Duden, Barbara. *The Woman beneath the Skin: A Doctor's Patients in Eighteenth-Century Germany.* Cambridge: Harvard University Press, 1991.

Du Laurens, André. *A discourse of the preservation of the sight: of melancholike diseases.* Trans. R. Surphlet. London: F. Kingston for R. Jacson, 1599. Shakespeare Association Facsimile no. 15, ed. S. V. Larkey and Humphrey Milford. Oxford: Oxford University Press, 1938.

Duncan, Douglas. "*Gammer Gurton's Needle* and the Concept of Humanist Parody." *Studies in English Literature* 27 (1987): 177–196.

Edwards, Philip. "On the Design of 'The Two Noble Kinsmen.'"*Review of English Literature* 5 (1964): 89–105.

——, ed. *The Spanish Tragedy.* Harvard: Harvard University Press, 1959 (Revels edition).

Enterline, Lynn. *The Tears of Narcissus: Melancholia and Masculinity in Early Modern Writing.* Stanford: Stanford University Press, 1995.

Erickson, Peter. "The Order of the Garter, the Cult of Elizabeth, and Class-Gender Tension in *The Merry Wives of Windsor.*" In *Shakespeare Reproduced: The Text in History and Ideology,* ed. Jean E. Howard and Marion F. O'Connor, 116–142. London: Methuen, 1987.

Evans, Martha Noel. *Fits and Starts: A Genealogy of Hysteria in Modern France.* Ithaca: Cornell University Press, 1991.

Feder, Lillian. *Madness in Literature.* Princeton: Princeton University Press, 1980.

Felman, Shoshana. *Writing and Madness: Literature, Philosophy, Psychoanalysis.* Trans. Martha Noel Evans and the author, with the assistance of Brian Massumi. Ithaca: Cornell University Press, 1985.

Ferrand, Jacques. *A Treatise on Lovesickness* (1623). Trans. and ed. Donald Beecher and Massimo Ciavolella. Syracuse: Syracuse University Press, 1990.

Fessler, A. "The Management of Lunacy in Seventeenth Century England. An Investigation of Quarter-sessions Records." *Proceedings of the Royal Society of Medicine* 49 (1956): 901–907.

Fletcher, John. *The Pilgrim*. In *The Works of Beaumont and Fletcher*, vol. 5, ed. A. R. Waller, 153–229. New York: Octagon Books, 1969.

Foakes, R. A., ed. *The Comedy of Errors*, by William Shakespeare. London: Methuen, 1962 (Arden edition).

——. "Playhouses and Players." In *The Cambridge Companion to English Renaissance Drama*, ed. A. R. Braunmuller and Michael Hattaway, 1–52. Cambridge: Cambridge University Press, 1990.

Foley, Stephen. "Falstaff in Love and Other Stories from Tudor England." *Exemplaria* 1, no. 2 (1989): 226–246.

Foucault, Michel. *Histoire de la folie à l'âge classique: Folie et déraison* 2d ed. Paris: Plon, 1972 (1st ed. 1961).

——. *Madness and Civilization: A History of Insanity in the Age of Reason*. Trans. Richard Howard. New York: Random House, 1973.

——. "My Body, This Paper, This Fire." Appendix to the 2d edition of *Histoire de la folie*, trans. Geoff Bennington in *Oxford Literary Review* 4, no. 1 (Autumn 1979): 9–29.

——. "Truth and Power." In *Michel Foucault: Power, Truth, Strategy*, ed. Meaghan Morris and Paul Patton, 29–48. Sydney: Feral, 1979.

Fraser, Russell, and Normal Rabkin, eds. *Drama of the English Renaissance*. 2 vols. New York: Macmillan, 1976.

Freedman, Barbara. "Egeon's Debt: Self-Division and Self-Redemption in *The Comedy of Errors*." *English Literary Renaissance* 10 (1980): 360–383.

——. "Errors in Comedy: A Psychoanalytic Theory of Farce." In *Shakespearean Comedy*, ed. Maurice Charney, 233–243. New York: New York Literary Forum, 1980.

——. "Falstaff's Punishment: Buffoonery as Defensive Posture in *The Merry Wives of Windsor*." *Shakespeare Studies* 14 (1981): 163–174.

——. *Staging the Gaze: Postmodernism, Psychoanalysis, and Shakespearean Comedy*. Ithaca: Cornell University Press, 1991.

Freeman, Arthur. *Thomas Kyd: Facts and Problems*. Oxford: Clarendon Press, 1967.

Freud, Sigmund. "The Ego and the Id." 1923. *Standard Edition* 19: 12–66.

——. "Melancholia." (Draft G) 1895? *Standard Edition* 1: 200–206.

——. "Mourning and Melancholia." 1917 [1915]. *Standard Edition* 14: 237–258.

——. *The Standard Edition of the Complete Psychological Works of Sigmund Freud*. 24 vols. Trans. James Strachey et al., ed. James Strachey. London: Hogarth, 1974. Reprint, 1986.

Frey, Charles H., ed. *Shakespeare, Fletcher, and "The Two Noble Kinsmen."* Columbia: University of Missouri Press, 1989.

Frye, Northrup. "The Argument of Comedy." In *English Institute Essays 1948*, ed. D. A. Robertson, 58–73. New York: Columbia University Press, 1949.

Garzoni, Tomasso. *The hospitall of incurable fooles: erected in English as neer the first Italian modell and platforme* . . . Trans. E. Blout. London: Edm. Bollifant for Edward Blout, 1600.

Gibbons, Brian. *Jacobean City Comedy*. 2d ed. London: Methuen, 1980.

Gilbert, Sandra, and Susan Gubar. *The Madwoman in the Attic*. New Haven: Yale University Press, 1979.

Gilman, Sander L. *Seeing the Insane*. New York: John Wiley & Sons, 1985.

Goldberg, Jonathan. *Sodometries: Renaissance Texts, Modern Sexualities*. Stanford: Stanford University Press, 1992.

Goldman, Noreen, and Renée Ravid. "Community Surveys: Sex Differences in Mental Illness." In *The Mental Health of Women*, ed. Marcia Guttenberg, Susan Salasin, and Deborah Belle, 31–55. New York: Academic Press, 1980.

Gordon, Colin. "Rewriting the History of Misreading." In *Rewriting the History of Madness: Studies in Foucault's "Histoire de la folie*,*"* ed. Arthur Still and Irving Velody, 167–184. London: Routledge, 1992.

Grady, Hugh. "On the Need for a Differentiated Theory of (Early) Modern Subjects." In *Philosophical Shakespeares*, ed. John J. Joughin, 34–50. London: Routledge, 2000.

Gras, Henk K. "Direct Evidence and Audience Response to *Twelfth Night:* The Case of John Manningham of the Middle Temple." *Shakespeare Studies* 23 (1993):109–154.

Gray, John. *Men Are from Mars, Women Are from Venus: A Practical Guide for Improving Communication and Getting What You Want in Your Relationships*. New York: HarperCollins, 1992.

Green, Susan. "'A Mad Woman? We Are Made, Boys!' The Jailer's Daughter in *The Two Noble Kinsmen*." In *Shakespeare, Fletcher, and "The Two Noble Kinsmen*,*"* ed. Charles H. Frey, 121–132. Columbia: University of Missouri Press, 1989.

Green, William. *Shakespeare's "Merry Wives of Windsor."* Princeton: Princeton University Press, 1962.

Greenblatt, Stephen. *Shakespearean Negotiations: The Circulation of Social Energy in Renaissance England*. Berkeley: University of California Press, 1988.

Greene, Gayle. *Changing the Story: Feminist Fiction and the Tradition*. Bloomington: Indiana University Press, 1991.

Greg, W. W., with F. S. Boas, ed. *The Spanish Tragedy*, by Thomas Kyd. Malone Society reprint, 1925.

Gregerson, Linda. *The Reformation of the Subject: Spenser, Milton, and the English Protestant Epic*. Cambridge: Cambridge University Press, 1995.

Gulstad, William Olaf. "The Forms of Things Unknown: The Impact of Reginald Scot's Sceptical Treatise, *The Discoverie of Witchcraft*, on *A Midsummer Night's Dream, King Lear*, and *The Tempest*." Ph.D. diss., University of Illinois at Urbana-Champaign, 1994.

Gurr, Andrew. *Playgoing in Shakespeare's London*. Cambridge: Cambridge University Press, 1987.

——. *The Shakespearean Playing Companies*. Oxford, Oxford University Press: 1996.

——. *The Shakespearean Stage, 1574–1642*. 2d ed. Cambridge: Cambridge University Press, 1990.

Hacking, Ian. *Mad Travelers: Reflections on the Reality of Transient Mental Illnesses*. Charlottesville: University Press of Virginia, 1998.

——. *Rewriting the Soul: Multiple Personality and the Sciences of Memory*. Princeton: Princeton University Press, 1995.

Hall, John. "Select Observations on English Bodies." Facsimile of 2d ed., J.D. for Benjamin Shirley, 1679. Reprinted in Harriet Joseph, *Shakespeare's Son-in-Law: John Hall, Man and Physician,* 111–319. Hamden, Conn.: Archon, 1964.

Hallett, Charles A., and Elaine S. Hallett. *The Revenger's Madness: A Study of Revenge Tragedy Motifs.* Lincoln: University of Nebraska Press, 1980.

Harsnett, Samuel. *A Declaration of Egregious Popish Impostures.* London: James Roberts, 1603.

Hattaway, Michael. *Elizabethan Popular Theater.* London: Routledge, 1982.

Hattori, Natsu. "'The Pleasure of Your Bedlam': The Theatre of Madness in the Renaissance." *History of Psychiatry* 6 (1995): 283–308.

Hawkins, Sherman. "The Two Worlds of Shakespearean Comedy." *Shakespeare Studies* 3 (1967): 62–80.

Hedrick, Donald K. "'Be Rough with Me': The Collaborative Arenas of *The Two Noble Kinsmen.*" In *Shakespeare, Fletcher, and "The Two Noble Kinsmen,"* ed. Charles H. Frey, 45–77. Columbia: University of Missouri Press, 1989.

Heilman, Robert B. *This Great Stage: Image and Structure in "King Lear."* Baton Rouge, La., 1948; Seattle: University of Washington Press, 1963.

Hill, Eugene D. "Senecan and Vergilian Perspectives in *The Spanish Tragedy.*" *English Literary Renaissance* 15 (1985): 143–65.

Hillman, David, and Carla Mazzio, eds. *The Body in Parts: Fantasies of Corporality in Early Modern Europe.* New York: Routledge, 1997.

Hinely, Jan Lawson. "Comic Scapegoats and the Falstaff of *The Merry Wives of Windsor.*" *Shakespeare Studies* 15 (1982): 37–54.

Holmes, Clive. "Popular Culture? Witches, Magistrates, and Divines in Early Modern England." In *Understanding Popular Culture: Europe from the Middle Ages to the Nineteenth Century,* ed. Steven L. Kaplan, 85–112. Berlin: Mouton, 1984.

Howard, Jean E. *The Stage and Social Struggle.* London: Routledge, 1993.

Howells, John G., and N. Livia Osborn. "The Incidence of Emotional Disorder in a Seventeenth-Century Medical Practice." *Medical History* 14 (1970): 192–198.

Hunter, G. K., ed. *Antonio's Revenge,* by John Marston. Regents Renaissance Drama Series. Lincoln: University of Nebraska Press, 1965.

Hunter, Richard, and Ida Macalpine. *Three Hundred Years of Psychiatry, 1535–1860.* Hartsdale, N.Y.: Carlisle, 1982.

Ingleby, C. M., L. Toulmin Smith, and F. J. Furnivall, eds. *The Shakespeare Allusion Book: A Collection of Allusions to Shakespeare from 1591 to 1700,* vol. 2. London: Oxford University Press, 1932.

Irigaray, Luce. *Speculum of the Other Woman.* Trans. Gillian C. Gill. Ithaca: Cornell University Press, 1985.

——. *This Sex Which Is Not One.* Trans. Catherine Porter with Carolyn Burke. Ithaca: Cornell University Press, 1985.

Jackson, Ken. "Bedlam, *The Changeling, The Pilgrim,* and the Protestant Critique of Catholic Good Works." *Philological Quarterly* 74 (1995) 337–393.

——. "'I Know Not / Where I Did Lodge Last Night?': *King Lear* and the Search for Bethlem (Bedlam) Hospital." *English Literary Renaissance* 30 (2000): 213–240.

Jackson, Stanley. *Melancholia and Depression from Hippocratic Times to Modern Times.* New Haven: Yale University Press, 1986.

Jacquart, Danielle, and Claude Thomasset. *Sexuality and Medicine in the Middle Ages.* Trans. Matthew Adamson. Princeton: Princeton University Press, 1988.

Jenkins, Harold, ed. *Hamlet.* London: Methuen, 1982 (Arden edition).

Jonson, Ben. *Bartholomew Fair.* Ed. G. R. Hibbard. New York: Norton, 1977.

———. "Epicoene." In *Drama of the English Renaissance,* vol. 2, ed. Russell Fraser and Norman Rabkin, 102–41. New York: Macmillan, 1976.

Jordan, W. K. *Philanthropy in England, 1480–1660: A Study of the Changing Pattern of English Social Aspirations.* London: George Allen and Unwin, 1959.

Jorden, Edward. *A Briefe Discourse of a Disease Called the Suffocation of the Mother.* London, 1603. Facsimile reprint, London: Theatrum Orbis Terrarum, 1971.

———. *Brief Discourse.* Reprinted in *Witchcraft and Hysteria in Elizabeth London: Edward Jorden and the Mary Glover Case,* ed. Michael MacDonald, n.p. London: Routledge, 1991.

Jorgensen, Paul A. *Lear's Self-Discovery.* Berkeley: University of California Press, 1967.

Joseph, Harriet. *Shakespeare's Son-in-Law: John Hall, Man and Physician.* Hampton, Conn.: Archon Books, 1964.

Kahn, Coppelia. "The Absent Mother in *King Lear.*" In *Rewriting the Renaissance: The Discourses of Sexual Difference in Early Modern Europe,* ed. Margaret W. Ferguson, Maureen Quilligan, and Nancy J. Vickers, 33–49. Chicago: University of Chicago Press, 1986.

Kaufman, Sue. *Diary of a Mad Housewife.* New York: Bantam, 1970.

Kaysen, Susanna. *Girl, Interrupted.* New York: Vintage, 1994.

Kegl, Rosemary. *The Rhetoric of Concealment: Figuring Gender and Class in Renaissance Literature.* Ithaca: Cornell University Press, 1994.

Kelly, Joan. *Women, History, and Theory: The Essays of Joan Kelly.* Chicago: University of Chicago Press, 1984.

Kinney, Arthur F. "Shakespeare's *Comedy of Errors* and the Nature of Kinds." In *The Comedy of Errors: Critical Essays,* ed. Robert S. Miola, 155–181. New York: Garland, 1997.

Klein, Joan. "'Angels and Ministers of Grace': *Hamlet,* IV, v–vii." *Allegorica* 1, no. 2 (1976): 156–176.

Kleinman, Arthur. *Patients and Healers in the Context of Culture: An Exploration of the Borderland between Anthropology, Medicine, and Psychiatry.* Berkeley: University of California Press, 1980.

Klibansky, Raymond, Erwin Panofsky, and Fritz Saxl. *Saturn and Melancholy: Studies in the History of Natural Philosophy, Religion, and Art.* New York: Basic Books, 1964.

Knutson, Roslyn. "Influence of the Repertory System on the Revival and Revision of *The Spanish Tragedy* and *Dr. Faustus.*" *English Literary Renaissance* 18 (1988): 257–274.

———. "The Repertory." In *A New History of Early English Drama,* ed. John D. Cox and David Scott Kastan, 461–480. New York: Columbia University Press, 1997.

Kott, Jan. "The Gender of Rosalind." *New Theatre Quarterly* 7, no. 26 (1991): 113–125.

———. *Shakespeare Our Contemporary.* Garden City, N.Y.: Anchor/Doubleday, 1966.

Kramer, Peter D. *Listening to Prozac.* New York: Penguin Books, 1994.

Kristeva, Julia. *Black Sun: Depression and Melancholia.* Trans. Leon S. Roudiez. New York: Columbia University Press, 1989.

Kyd, Thomas. *The Spanish Tragedy.* Ed. J. R. Mulryne. New York: Alerton, 1989.

Laing, R. D. *The Divided Self: An Existential Study in Sanity and Madness.* London: Penguin, 1960.

Lanier, Douglas. "'Stigmatical in Making': The Material Character of *The Comedy of Errors.*" In *The Comedy of Errors: Critical Essays,* ed. Robert S. Miola, 299–334. New York: Garland, 1997.

Laqueur, Thomas W. "Masturbation, Credit, and the Novel during the Long Eighteenth Century." *Qui Parle* 8, no. 2 (Spring/Summer 1995): 1–19.

Leggatt, Alexander. *Citizen Comedy in the Age of Shakespeare.* Toronto: University of Toronto Press, 1973.

——. "Shakespeare's Comedy of Love: *The Comedy of Errors.*" In *The Comedy of Errors: Critical Essays,* ed. Robert S. Miola, 135–153. New York: Garland, 1997.

——. "Madness in *Hamlet, King Lear,* and Early Modern England." In *Critical Essays on King Lear,* ed. Jay Halio, 122–138. New York: G. K. Hall, 1996.

Lemnius, Levinus. *The Touchstone of Complexions.* Trans. T. Newton. London: T. Marsh, 1576.

Lessing, Doris. *The Four-Gated City.* New York: Bantam Books, 1970.

——. *The Golden Notebook.* New York: Ballantine Books, 1968.

Levenson, Jill. "Comedy." In *The Cambridge Companion to English Renaissance Drama,* ed. A. R. Braunmuller and Michael Hattaway, 263–300. Cambridge: Cambridge University Press, 1990.

Lothian, J. M., and T. W. Craik, eds. *Twelfth Night,* by William Shakespeare. London: Methuen, 1972 (Arden edition).

Lyons, Bridget Gellert. *Voices of Melancholy: Studies in Literary Treatments of Melancholy in Renaissance England.* London: Routledge, 1971.

MacDonald, Michael. "The Inner Side of Wisdom: Suicide in Early Modern England." *Psychological Medicine* 7 (1977): 565–582.

——. *Mystical Bedlam: Madness, Anxiety, and Healing in Seventeenth-Century England.* Cambridge: Cambridge University Press, 1981.

——. "Ophelia's Maimed Rites." *Shakespeare Quarterly* 37 (1986): 309–317.

——. "The Secularization of Suicide in England, 1660–1800." *Past and Present* 111 (1986): 50–100.

MacDonald, Michael, and Terence R. Murphy. *Sleepless Souls: Suicide in Early Modern England.* Oxford: Clarendon Press, 1991.

MacDonald, Michael, ed. *Witchcraft and Hysteria in Elizabethan London: Edward Jorden and the Mary Glover Case.* London: Routledge, 1991.

Macfarlane, Alan. *Witchcraft in Tudor and Stuart England: A Regional and Comparative Study.* London: Routledge, 1970.

Mack, Maynard. *King Lear in Our Time.* Berkeley: University of California Press, 1965.

Maclean, Ian. *The Renaissance Notion of Woman.* Cambridge: Cambridge University Press, 1980.

Maguire, Laurie. "The Girls from Ephesus." In *The Comedy of Errors: Critical Essays,* ed. Robert S. Miola, 355–391. New York: Garland, 1997.

Malcolmson, Cristina. "'As Tame as the Ladies': Politics and Gender in *The Changeling.*" *English Literary Renaissance* 20, no. 2 (1990): 320–339.

——. "'What You Will': Social Mobility and Gender in *Twelfth Night.*" In *The Matter of Difference: Materialist Feminist Criticism of Shakespeare,* ed. Valerie Wayne, 29–57. Ithaca: Cornell University Press, 1991.

Manningham, John. *The Diary of John Manningham of the Middle Temple, 1602–1603.* Ed. Robert Parker Sorlien. Hanover, N.H.: University Press of New England, 1976.

Marcus, Leah S. *Unediting the Renaissance: Shakespeare, Marlowe, Milton.* London: Routledge, 1996.

Mazzio, Carla. "Staging the Vernacular: Language and Nation in Thomas Kyd's *The Spanish Tragedy.*" *Studies in English Literature* 38 (1988): 207–232.

McDonald, Russ. "Fear of Farce." In *'Bad' Shakespeare: Revaluations of the Shakespeare Canon,* ed. Maurice Charney, 77–90. Rutherford, N.J.: Fairleigh Dickinson University Press, 1988.

Meige, Henry. "Les Médecins de Jan Steen." *Janus* (1900): 187–190.

Micale, Mark S. *Approaching Hysteria: Disease and Its Interpretations.* Princeton: Princeton University Press, 1995.

——. "Hysteria and Its Historiography: The Future Perspective." *History of Psychiatry* 1 (1990): 33–124.

——. "Hysteria and Its Historiography: A Review of Past and Present Writings (II)." *History of Science* 27, no. 78 (1989): 317–51.

Micale, Mark S., and Roy Porter, eds. *Discovering the History of Psychiatry.* Oxford: Oxford University Press, 1994.

Middleton, Thomas, and William Rowley. *The Changeling.* Ed. Joost Daalder. London: Norton, 1990.

Midelfort, H. C. Erik. *A History of Madness in Sixteenth-Century Germany.* Stanford: Stanford University Press, 1999.

——. "Madness and Civilization in Early Modern Europe: A Reappraisal of Michel Foucault." In *After the Reformation: Essays in Honor of J. H. Hexter,* ed. Barbara C. Malament, 247–266. Philadelphia: University of Pennsylvania Press, 1980.

——. "Reading and Believing: On the Reappraisal of Michel Foucault." In *Rewriting the History of Madness: Studies in Foucault's "Histoire de la folie,"* ed. Arthur Still and Irving Velody, 105–109. London: Routledge, 1992.

Mildmay, Lady Grace. *With Faith and Physic: The Life of a Tudor Gentlewoman: Lady Grace Mildmay, 1552–1620.* Ed. Linda Pollock. London: Collins and Brown, 1993.

Miller, Nancy K. "Emphasis Added: Plots and Plausibilities in Women's Fiction." In *Feminist Criticism: Essays on Women, Literature, Theory,* ed. Elaine Showalter, 339–360. New York: Pantheon, 1985.

Millett, Kate. *The Loony-Bin Trip.* New York: Simon and Schuster, 1990.

Miola, Robert S. *Shakespeare and Classical Comedy: The Influence of Plautus and Terence.* Oxford: Clarendon, 1994.

——, ed. *The Comedy of Errors: Critical Essays.* New York: Garland, 1997.

Montrose, Louis A. "'The Place of a Brother' in *As You Like It*: Social Process and Comic Form." *Shakespeare Quarterly* 32 (1981): 28–54.

——. "Professing the Renaissance: The Poetics and Politics of Culture." In *The New Historicism,* ed. H. Aram Veeser, 15–36. London: Routledge, 1989.

——. *The Purpose of Playing: Shakespeare and the Cultural Politics of the Elizabethan Theatre.* Chicago: University of Chicago Press, 1996.

More, Sir Thomas. "Apology." *The Complete Works of St. Thomas More,* vol. 9, ed. J. B. Trapp, 118. New Haven: Yale University Press, 1979.

——. "The Last Things." In *The Complete Works of St. Thomas More,* vol. 1, ed. Anthony S. G. Edwards, Katharine G. Rodgers, and Clarence H. Miller, 125–182. New Haven: Yale University Press, 1979.

Muir, Kenneth, ed. *Macbeth*. London: Methuen, 1951 (Arden edition).

——. "Samuel Harsnett and *King Lear*." *Review of English Studies* 2 (1951): 11–21.

Mullaney, Steven. *The Place of the Stage: License, Play, and Power in Renaissance England*. Chicago: University of Chicago Press, 1988.

Mulryne, J. R. "Nationality and Language in Thomas Kyd's 'The Spanish Tragedy'". In *Langues et Nations au temps de la Renaissance*, ed. M. T. Jones-Davies, 87–105. Paris: Klincksieck, 1991.

——, ed. *The Spanish Tragedy*, by Thomas Kyd. New York: Norton, 1989.

Neaman, Judith S. *Suggestion of the Devil: Insanity in the Middle Ages and the Twentieth Century*. New York: Octagon Books, 1978.

Neely, Carol Thomas. *Broken Nuptials in Shakespeare's Plays*. New Haven: Yale University Press, 1985; Urbana: University of Illinois Press, 1993.

——. "Constructing Female Sexuality in the Renaissance: Stratford, London, Windsor, Vienna." In *Feminism and Psychoanalysis*, ed. Richard Feldstein and Judith Roof, 209–229. Ithaca: Cornell University Press, 1990.

——. "Did Madness Have a Renaissance?" *Renaissance Quarterly* 44 (Winter 1991): 776–791.

——. "'Documents in Madness': Reading Madness and Gender in Shakespeare's Tragedies and Early Modern Culture." *Shakespeare Quarterly* 42 (1991): 315–338.

——. Review of *Melancholy, Genius, and Utopia in the Renaissance*, by Winfried Schleiner. *Shakespeare Quarterly* 44 (1991): 369–71.

——. "Shakespeare's Women: Historical Facts and Dramatic Representations." In *Shakespeare's Personality*, ed. Norman Holland, Sidney Homan, and Bernard Paris, 116–134. Berkeley: University of California Press, 1989.

——. "Women/Utopia/Fetish: Disavowal and Satisfied Desire in Margaret Cavendish's *New Blazing World* and Gloria Anzaldua's *Borderlands/La Frontera*." In *Heterotopia: Postmodern Utopia and the Body Politic*, ed. Tobin Siebers, 58–95. Ann Arbor: University of Michigan Press, 1994.

Neugeboren, Jay. *Imagining Robert: My Brother, Madness, and Survival: A Memoir*. New York: William Morrow, 1997.

Norwood, Robin. *Women Who Love Too Much: When You Keep Wishing and Hoping He'll Change*. New York: Simon & Schuster, 1985.

Nungezer, E. *A Dictionary of Actors and of Other Persons Associated with the Public Representation of Plays before 1642*. New Haven: Yale University Press, 1929.

O'Donoghue, E. G. *The Story of Bethlehem Hospital*. New York: Dutton, 1915.

Oliver, H. J., ed. *The Merry Wives of Windsor*, by William Shakespeare. London: Methuen, 1971 (Arden edition).

Osborne, Laurie E. *The Trick of Singularity: "Twelfth Night" and the Performance Editions*. Iowa City: University of Iowa Press, 1996.

Palmer, Alan. *Princes of Wales*. London: Weidenfeld and Nicolson, 1979.

Parten, Anne. "Falstaff's Horns: Masculine Inadequacy and Feminine Mirth in *The Merry Wives of Windsor*." *Studies in Philology* 82, no. 2 (1985): 184–199.

Paster, Gail Kern. *The Body Embarrassed: Drama and the Disciplines of Shame in Early Modern England*. Ithaca: Cornell University Press, 1993.

——. "Nervous Tension: Networks of Blood and Spirit in the Early Modern Body." In *The Body in Parts: Fantasies of Corporality in Early Modern Europe*, ed. David Hillman and Carla Mazzio, 107–125. New York: Routledge, 1997.

Pelling, Margaret. "Healing the Sick Poor: Social Policy and Disability in Norwich, 1550–1640." *Medical History* 29 (1985): 115–137.

Pelling, Margaret, and Charles Webster. "Medical Practitioners." In *Health, Medicine, and Mortality in the Sixteenth Century,* ed. Charles Webster, 165–236. Cambridge: Cambridge University Press, 1979.

Pequigney, Joseph. "The Two Antonios and Same-Sex Love in *Twelfth Night* and *The Merchant of Venice.*" *English Literary Renaissance* 22 (1992): 201–221.

Piercy, Marge. *Woman on the Edge of Time.* New York: Fawcett Crest, 1976.

Plath, Sylvia. *The Bell Jar.* New York: Bantam Books, 1972.

Plautus. *The Menaechmi.* Trans. William Warner. London: Tho. Creede, 1595. In *Narrative and Dramatic Sources of Shakespeare,* vol. 1, ed. Geoffrey Bullough, 12–39. New York: Columbia University Press, 1966.

Pollock, Linda, ed. *With Faith and Physic: The Life of a Tudor Gentlewoman: Lady Grace Mildmay, 1552–1620.* London: Collins and Brown, 1993.

Porter, Roy. *London: A Social History.* Cambridge: Harvard University Press, 1995.

——. *Mind-Forg'd Manacles: A History of Madness in England from the Restoration to the Regency.* Cambridge: Harvard University Press, 1987.

——, ed. *Patients and Practitioners: Lay Perceptions of Medicine in Pre-Industrial Society.* Cambridge: Cambridge University Press, 1985.

Potter, Lois. "Topicality or Politics? *The Two Noble Kinsmen,* 1613–1614." In *The Politics of Tragicomedy: Shakespeare and After,* ed. Gordon McMullan and Jonathan Hope, 77–91. London: Routledge, 1992.

——, ed. *The Two Noble Kinsmen,* by John Fletcher and William Shakespeare. Surrey: Thomas Nelson and Sons, 1997 (Arden edition).

Prynne, William. *Histrio-Mastix.* London, 1633.

Randall, Dale B. J. "Some New Perspectives on the Spanish Setting of *The Changeling* and Its Source." *Medieval and Renaissance Drama in England* 3 (1986): 189–216.

Rasmussen, Mark David, ed. *Renaissance Literature and Its Formal Engagements.* New York: Palgrave, 2002.

Rawcliffe, Carole. "The Hospitals of Later Medieval London." *Medical History* 28 (1984): 1–21.

Rawlins, Thomas. *The Rebellion: A Tragedy.* London: Printed by I. Okes for Daniell Frere, 1640.

Real, Terrence. *I Don't Want to Talk about It: Overcoming the Secret Legacy of Male Depression.* New York: Scribner, 1997.

Reed, Robert Rentoul. *Bedlam on the Jacobean Stage.* Cambridge: Harvard University Press, 1952.

Ringler, William A. *The Poems of Sir Philip Sidney.* Oxford: Clarendon Press, 1962.

Roberts, Jeanne Addison. "Crises of Male Self-Definition in *The Two Noble Kinsmen.*" In *Shakespeare, Fletcher, and "The Two Noble Kinsmen,"* ed. Charles H. Frey, 133–144. Columbia: University of Missouri Press, 1989.

——. *Shakespeare's English Comedy: "The Merry Wives of Windsor" in Context.* Lincoln: University of Nebraska Press, 1979.

Robinson, J. W. "The Art and Meaning of *Gammer Gurton's Needle.*" *Renaissance Drama* n.s. 14 (1983): 45–77.

Rogers, Thomas. *A philosophical discourse entitled, The Anatomie of the Minde.* London: I.C. for Andrew Maunsell, 1576.

Ronk, Martha. "Viola's (Lack of) Patience." *Centennial Review* 37, no. 2 (1993): 384–399.

Rouse, W. H. D. *The Menaechmi: The Original of Shakespeare's "Comedy of Er-*

rors": *The Latin Text Together with the Elizabethan Translation.* New York: Duffield, 1912.

Rowe, N., ed. *The Works of William Shakespeare . . . Revis'd and Corrected.* 1709.

Rushton, Peter. "Lunatics and Idiots: Mental Disability, the Community, and the Poor Law in North-East England, 1600–1800." *Medical History* 32 (1988): 34–50.

S., Mr. *Gammer Gurton's Needle.* In *Three Sixteenth-Century Comedies,* ed. Charles Walters Whitworth, 1–87. New York: Norton, 1984.

Salinger, Leo. *Shakespeare and the Traditions of Comedy.* Cambridge: Cambridge University Press, 1974.

Salkeld, Duncan. *Madness and Drama in the Age of Shakespeare.* Manchester: Manchester University Press, 1993.

Sawday, Jonathan. *The Body Emblazoned: Dissection and the Human Body in Renaissance Culture.* London: Routledge, 1995.

Sawyer, Ronald. "Patients, Healers, and Disease in the Southeast Midlands, 1597–1634." Ph.D. diss., University of Wisconsin-Madison, 1986.

Schama, Simon. *The Embarrassment of Riches: An Interpretation of Dutch Culture in the Golden Age.* New York: Knopf, 1987.

Schiesari, Juliana. *The Gendering of Melancholia: Feminism, Psychoanalysis, and the Symbolics of Loss in Renaissance Literature.* Ithaca: Cornell University Press, 1992.

Schleiner, Winfried. *Melancholy, Genius, and Utopia in the Renaissance.* Wiesbaden: Otto Harrassowitz, 1991.

Schoenfeldt, Michael C. *Bodies and Selves in Early Modern England: Physiology and Inwardness in Spenser, Shakespeare, Herbert, and Milton.* Cambridge: Cambridge University Press, 1999.

Scot, Reginald. *The Discoverie of Witchcraft.* (1584). Reprint, Carbondale: Southern Illinois University Press, 1964.

Scull, Andrew. *Social Order/Mental Disorder: Anglo-American Psychiatry in Historical Perspective.* Berkeley: University of California Press, 1989.

Sedgwick, Eve Kosofsky. *Epistomology of the Closet.* Berkeley: University of California Press, 1990.

Seng, Peter. *The Vocal Songs in the Plays of Shakespeare.* Cambridge: Harvard University Press, 1967.

Shakespeare, William. *The Comedy of Errors.* Ed. R. A. Foakes. London: Routledge, 1968 (Arden edition).

——. *The Complete Signet Classic Shakespeare.* Ed. Sylvan Barnet. New York: Harcourt Brace Jovanovich, 1972.

——. *The Merry Wives of Windsor.* Ed. H. J. Oliver. London: Methuen, 1971 (Arden edition).

——. *Twelfth Night.* Ed. J. M. Lothian and T. W. Craik. London: Methuen, 1972 (Arden edition).

Shannon, Laurie J. "Emilia's Argument: Friendship and 'Human Title' in *The Two Noble Kinsmen.*" *English Literary History* 64 (1997): 657–682.

Shapiro, James. "'Tragedies Naturally Performed': Kyd's Representation of Violence: *The Spanish Tragedy* (c. 1587)." In *Staging the Renaissance: Interpretations of Elizabethan and Jacobean Drama,* ed. David Scott Kastan and Peter Stallybrass, 99–113. New York: Routledge, 1991.

Shepherd, Michael, Brian Cooper, Alexander Brown, and Graham Kalton. *Psychiatric Illnesses in General Practice.* London: Oxford University Press, 1966.

Shershow, Scott C. *Puppets and "Popular" Culture*. Ithaca: Cornell University Press, 1995.

Shewring, Margaret. "*The Two Noble Kinsmen* Revived: Chivalric Romance and Modern Performance Images." In *Le Roman de Chevalerie au Temps de la Renaissance*, ed. Marie Therese Jones-Davies, 107–130. Paris: Touzot, 1987.

Showalter, Elaine. *The Female Malady: Women, Madness, and English Culture, 1830–1980*. New York: Penguin, 1987.

——. "Representing Ophelia: Women, Madness, and the Responsibilities of Feminist Criticism." In *Shakespeare and the Question of Theory*, ed. Patricia Parker and Geoffrey Hartman, 77–94. London: Methuen, 1985.

Sicherman, Barbara. "The Uses of a Diagnosis: Doctors, Patients, and Neurasthenia." *Journal of the History of Medicine and Allied Sciences* 32 (1977): 33–54.

Sidney, Sir Philip. *An Apology for Poetry*. Ed. Forrest G. Robinson. Indianapolis: Bobbs-Merrill, 1970.

Siemon, James R. "Sporting Kyd." *English Literary Renaissance* 24 (1994): 553–582.

Sinfield, Alan. *Faultlines: Cultural Materialism and the Politics of Dissident Reading*. Berkeley: University of California Press, 1992.

Sirasi, Nancy G. *Medieval and Early Renaissance Medicine: An Introduction to Knowledge and Practice*. Chicago: University of Chicago Press, 1990.

Sixth Report of the Royal Commissioners on Historical Manuscripts, Part I. Report and Appendix. London: Eyre and Spottiswoode, 1989.

Slack, Paul. "Mirrors of Health and Treasures of Poor Men: The Uses of the Vernacular Medical Literature of Tudor England." In *Health, Medicine, and Mortality in the Sixteenth Century*, ed. Charles Webster, 105–136. Cambridge: Cambridge University Press, 1969.

Smith, Bruce. *Homosexual Desire in Shakespeare's England: A Cultural Poetics*. Chicago: University of Chicago Press, 1991.

Smith, J. H, L. D. Pizer, and E. K. Kaufman. "*Hamlet, Antonio's Revenge*, and the *Ur-Hamlet*." *Shakespeare Quarterly* 9 (1958): 493–498.

Sorlien, Robert Parker, ed. *The Diary of John Manningham of the Middle Temple, 1602–1603*. Hanover, N.H.: University Press of New England, 1976.

Spenser, Edmund. *The Faerie Queene*. Ed. Thomas P. Roche. Harmondsworth: Penguin, 1978.

Sprenger, James, and Heinrich Kramer. *Malleus Maleficarum* or *The Witch Hammer* (ca. 1486). Trans. Montague Summers, 1928. Reprint, New York: Benjamin Blom, 1970.

Sprengnether, Madelon. *The Spectral Mother: Freud, Feminism, and Psychoanalysis*. Ithaca: Cornell University Press, 1990.

Stallybrass, Peter. "*Macbeth* and Witchcraft." In *Focus on Macbeth*, ed. John Russell Brown, 189–209. London: Routledge, 1982.

Stechow, Wolfgang. "'The Love of Antiochus with Faire Stratonica' in Art." *Art Bulletin* (December 1945): 221–237.

Still, Arthur, and Irving Velody, eds. *Rewriting the History of Madness: Studies in Foucault's "Histoire de la folie."* London: Routledge, 1992.

Stow, John. *A Survey of London* (1603). Ed. Charles L. Kingsford. 2 vols. Oxford: Clarendon Press, 1908.

Strong, Roy. *Henry, Prince of Wales and England's Lost Renaissance*. London: Thames and Hudson, 1986.

Styron, William. *Darkness Visible: A Memoir of Madness*. New York: Vintage, 1992.

Sutton, Peter G. "Jan Steen: Comedy and Admonition." *Bulletin of the Philadelphia Museum of Art* (special double issue) 78, nos. 337–338 (Winter 1982/Spring 1983): 1–64.

Sutton, Peter G., et al. *Masters of Seventeenth-Century Dutch Genre Painting.* Philadelphia: Philadelphia Museum of Art, 1984.

Suzuki, Akihito. "Lunacy in Seventeenth- and Eighteenth-Century England: Analysis of Quarter-Sessions Records, Part I." *History of Psychiatry* 2 (1991): 437–456.

———. "Lunacy in Seventeenth- and Eighteenth-Century England: Analysis of Quarter-Sessions Records, Part II." *History of Psychiatry* 3 (1992): 29–44.

Szasz, Thomas. *The Myth of Mental Illness: Foundations of a Theory of Personal Conduct.* New York: Hoeber-Harper, 1964.

Thomas, Keith. *Religion and the Decline of Magic.* New York: Scribners, 1971.

Thomson, Patricia, ed. *The Changeling,* by Thomas Middleton and William Rowley. London: A. & C. Black, 1990.

Tilley, Morris Palmer. *A Dictionary of Proverbs in England in the Sixteenth and Seventeenth Centuries.* Ann Arbor: University of Michigan Press, 1950.

Tomes, Nancy. "Feminist Histories of Psychiatry." In *Discovering the History of Psychiatry,* ed. Mark S. Micale and Roy Porter, 348–383. Oxford: Oxford University Press, 1994.

———. "Historical Perspectives on Women and Mental Illness." In *Women, Health, and Medicine in America: A Historical Handbook,* ed. Rima D. Apple, 143–171. New York: Garland, 1990.

Traub, Valerie. *Desire and Anxiety: Circulations of Sexuality in Shakespearean Drama.* London: Routledge, 1992.

———. "Desire and the Differences It Makes." In *The Matter of Difference: Materialist Feminist Criticism of Shakespeare,* ed. Valerie Wayne, 81–114. Ithaca: Cornell University Press, 1991.

———. "The (In)Significance of 'Lesbian' Desire in Early Modern England." In *Queering the Renaissance,* ed. Jonathan Goldberg, 62–83. Durham: Duke University Press, 1994.

Twyning, John. *London Dispossessed: Literature and Social Space in Early Modern London.* London: Macmillan, 1998.

Underdown, David. *Revel, Riot, and Rebellion: Popular Politics and Culture in England, 1603–1660.* Oxford: Clarendon Press, 1985.

———. "The Taming of the Scold: The Enforcement of Patriarchal Authority in Early Modern England." In *Order and Disorder in Early Modern England,* ed. Anthony Fletcher and John Stevenson, 116–136. Cambridge: Cambridge University Press, 1985.

Valadez, Frances. "Anatomical Studies at Oxford and Cambridge." In *Medicine in Seventeenth-Century England,* ed. Allen G. Debus, 393–420. Berkeley: University of California Press, 1974.

Vaughan, William. *Approved Directions for Health, both naturall and artificiall.* London: T.S. for Roger Jackson, 1612.

Veith, Ilza. *Hysteria: The History of a Disease.* Chicago: University of Chicago Press, 1965.

Wack, Mary Frances. *Lovesickness in the Middle Ages: The Viaticum and Its Commentaries.* Philadelphia: University of Pennsylvania Press, 1990.

Walker, D. P. *Unclean Spirits: Possession and Exorcism in France and England in the*

Late Sixteenth and Early Seventeenth Centuries. Philadelphia: University of Pennsylvania Press, 1981.

Walkingham, Thomas. *The optick glasse of humors.* London: J. Windet f. M. Clarke, 1607.

Wall, Wendy. "'Household Stuff': The Sexual Politics of Domesticity and the Advent of English Comedy." *English Literary History* 65 (1998): 1–45.

Walworth, Alan. "Displacing Desires in Early Modern Drama." Ph.D. diss., University of Illinois at Urbana-Champaign, 1997.

——. "'To Laugh with Open Throate': Mad Lovers, Theatrical Cures, and Gendered Bodies in the Jacobean Drama." In *Enacting Gender on the Renaissance Stage,* ed. Viviana Comensoli and Anne Russell, 53–72. Urbana: University of Illinois Press, 1998.

Warren, Roger, and Stanley Wells, eds. *Twelfth Night, or What You Will.* Oxford, Clarendon Press, 1994.

Wear, Andrew. "Explorations in Renaissance Writings on the Practice of Medicine." In *The Medical Renaissance of the Sixteenth Century,* ed. Andrew Wear, R. K. French, and I. M. Lonie, 118–145. Cambridge: Cambridge University Press, 1985.

——. "Medicine in Early Modern Europe, 1500–1700." In *The Western Medical Tradition, 800 B.C. to A.D. 1800,* ed. Lawrence I. Conrad et al., 215–361. Cambridge: Cambridge University Press, 1995.

Webster, Charles, ed. *Health, Medicine, and Mortality in the Sixteenth Century.* Cambridge: Cambridge University Press, 1979.

Webster, John. *The Duchess of Malfi.* Ed. Elizabeth M. Brennan. London: A. & C. Black, 1987.

Weimann, Robert. "Bifold Authority in Shakespeare's Theatre." *Shakespeare Quarterly* 39 (1988): 401–417.

——. *Shakespeare and the Popular Tradition in the Theater: Studies in the Social Dimension of Dramatic Form and Function.* Ed. Robert Schwartz. Baltimore: Johns Hopkins University Press, 1978.

Weller, Barry. "*The Two Noble Kinsmen,* the Friendship Tradition, and the Flight from Eros." In *Shakespeare, Fletcher, and "The Two Noble Kinsmen,"* ed. Charles H. Frey, 93–108. Columbia: University of Missouri Press, 1989.

Westermann, Mariët. *The Amusements of Jan Steen: Comic Painting in the Seventeenth Century.* Zwolle: Waanders, 1997.

Whigham, Frank. *Seizures of the Will in Early Modern Drama.* Cambridge: Cambridge University Press, 1996.

Whitworth, Charles W., Jr., ed. *Three Sixteenth-Century Comedies.* New York: Norton, 1984 (New Mermaid edition).

Wickham, Glynne. "*The Two Noble Kinsmen* or *A Midsummer Night's Dream,* Part II?" In *The Elizabethan Theatre* 7 (1977), ed. G. R. Hibbard, 167–196. Hamden, Conn.: Archon Books, 1980.

Williams, Katherine E. "Hysteria in Seventeenth-Century Case Records and Unpublished Manuscripts." *History of Psychiatry* 1 (1990): 383–401.

Williams, Raymond. *Marxism and Literature.* Oxford: Oxford University Press, 1977.

Woodbridge, Linda. *Women and the English Renaissance: Literature and the Nature of Womankind, 1540–1620.* Urbana: University of Illinois Press, 1984.

Youngson, Robert, and Ian Scott. *Medical Blunders.* London: Robinson, 1996.

INDEX

Note: Italic page numbers refer to illustrations.